THE MAKING OF THE SOVIET SYSTEM

·THE·
MAKING
OF THE
SOVIET
SYSTEM

ESSAYS IN THE SOCIAL HISTORY
OF INTERWAR RUSSIA

Moshe Lewin

Methuen

First published in Great Britain in 1985 by

Methuen & Co. Ltd
11 New Fetter Lane, London EC4P 4EE

BRITISH LIBRARY CATALOGUING IN PUBLICATION DATA

Lewin, Moshe
   The making of the Soviet system : essays in
   the social history of interwar Russia.

   1. Soviet Union—History—1917–1936
   I. Title
   947.084   DK266

ISBN 0-416-40820-6
ISBN 0-416-40830-3 Pbk
(University Paperback 895)

Printed in the United States of America

Grateful acknowledgment is made to the following for permission to reprint previously published material:

René Gallissot: "Leninism and Bolshevism: The Test of History and Power" by Moshe Lewin, originally published as "Le Léninisme et le bolchévisme à l'épreuve de l'histoire et du pouvoir" in *Les Aventures du marxisme*, edited by Réne Gallissot (Paris: Syros, 1984). Reprinted by permission of René Gallissot. This essay is a corrected version of a paper presented at a colloquium on the occasion of Marx's centenary, held in Paris, May 1983, under the auspices of the Ministries of Research and Culture.

The Harvester Press Ltd., and Indiana University Press: "Grappling with Stalinism" by Moshe Lewin, from *A History of Marxism*, vol. 3, edited by E. J. Hobsbawm, 1985. Reprinted by permission of The Harvester Press Ltd. This essay will also appear in E. J. Hobsbawm, editor, *The History of Marxism*, vol. 3, forthcoming from Indiana University Press.

Indiana University Press: "Society, State, and Ideology During the First Five-Year-Plan" by Moshe Lewin, from *Cultural Revolution in Russia, 1928–1931*, edited by Sheila Fitzpatrick, 1978. Reprinted by permission of Indiana University Press.

Macmillan Ltd.: " 'Taking Grain': Soviet Policies of Agricultural Procurements Before the War" by Moshe Lewin, from *Essays in Honour of E. H. Carr*, edited by C. Abramsky, 1974. Reprinted by permission of Macmillan Ltd.

Methuen & Co.: "Rural Society in Twentieth-Century Russia: An Introduction" by Moshe Lewin, *Social History* 9, no. 2, 1984. Reprinted by permission of Methuen & Co.

Oxford University Press: "The Kolkhoz and the Russian Muzhik" by Moshe Lewin, from *Peasants in History: Essays in Honour of Daniel Thorner*, edited by E. J. Hobsbawm, W. Kula, Ashok Mitra, K. N. Raj, and Ignacy Sachs, 1980. Reprinted by permission of Oxford University Press.

Soviet Studies: "The Immediate Background of Soviet Collectivization" by Moshe Lewin, *Soviet Studies* 17, no. 2, 1965; and "Who Was the Soviet Kulak?" by Moshe Lewin, *Soviet Studies* 18, no. 2, 1966. Reprinted by permission of *Soviet Studies*.

"Customary Law and Rural Society in the Postreform Era" was published in *Russian Review* 44, no. 1, January 1985. An earlier version was presented at the National Seminar on Twentieth-Century Russian Society, Colloquium on Rural Society, held in Philadelphia, January 1982.

"Social Relations Inside Industry During the Prewar Five-Year Plans" was originally published in *L'Industrialisation de l'URSS dans les années trente*, edited by Charles Bettelheim (Paris: Ecole des Hautes Etudes en Sciences Sociales, 1982), the proceedings of a round-table conference held in Paris December 1981.

"The Social Background of Stalinism" was originally published in *Stalinism: Essays in Historical Interpretation*, edited by Robert C. Tucker (New York: W. W. Norton & Co., Inc., 1977).

CONTENTS

vii

THE
MAKING
OF THE
SOVIET
SYSTEM

INTRODUCTION:
SOCIAL CRISES
AND POLITICAL
STRUCTURES
IN THE USSR

A selection of articles and of some lectures must be an occasion for doubts and worries for most authors. After all, a big subject is certainly an entity, multifaceted and pluridimensional, clear-cut here and shrouded in secrecy and mystery there, changing and immutable at the same time, whereas articles cannot be but fragments, probes, and approaches, limited by definition and stronger on asking questions than offering answers. Once the decision is taken to go ahead with republishing, however, leaving to the reader the decision whether the pieces do or do not add up meaningfully, the author still has to clarify to himself and to others whether there are any unifying threads or central ideas that inspire his inquiries.

This is indeed so in this case. In addition to being a store of ideas for future studies, these essays have one central feature in common: they are by a social historian of twentieth-century Russia, especially of the Soviet period, a historian who tries to practice and to promote the study of Russian/Soviet society, especially during the period in question.* This circum-

---

* We use the terms "Russia" and "Russian" to cover equally the prerevolutionary and postrevolutionary periods. Beginning with the 1920s we often use "USSR" and "Soviet" as well. The use of "Russia" for the postrevolutionary period reflects the fact that most of our material is from and about ethnic Russians; other nations and republics are very important, both separately and, in particular, as an agglomerate, but that is an immense subject in its own right that demands a knowledge of their languages and culture, as well as specialized researches. Our use of the term "Russia" should not therefore be taken as a rejection of the phenomenon called the USSR.

stance implies more than one problem, but the main, for the time being, can be summarized quite simply: the study of Russian society in our century is still an underdeveloped, even barely developed, field, a fact that for some practitioners of other aspects of Russian studies is not only unknown but sometimes even irrelevant. Their characteristic reaction: "What difference will this kind of study make?" One suspects a widespread sense that there is nothing much to be added to what is already firmly understood and can be expressed in a word or sentence.

The author does not want to say that the dimension he is interested in is the only one still unconsidered. A social system demands the efforts of all scholarly and many other professions, and there is plenty to do for all of them. The emphasis is on "plenty to do"—because it is obvious that the mood of "What difference will this kind of study make?" is deeply erroneous. The Soviet social system and its political regime are far from being sufficiently well known or understood. Facile assessments abound, but too many errors are being committed, too many assessments were and are shallow, not just for the good of scholarship but also for the good of politics and for the well-being of our little planet.

The plea here, of course, is for scholarship, not for any specific politics. But politics has contributed to different clichés getting hold of Western minds and producing damaging impediments to the study of Russia. Let us hint at some of the impediments that make students shun in-depth and innovative studies of the Soviet Union at a time when squads of talented people are urgently needed to take up a growing mountain of tasks in this field.

Competition with the United States, cold wars, and armament races have produced a powerful need to supply propaganda adequate for these kinds of contests. This propaganda is busily emitting images of the Soviet Union that do not inspire people to plunge into the depths of history, complex theoretical inquiries, or sophisticated cultural treatises. Rather it produces a deep-seated hostility, disdain, and an emotional need for bad news, horror stories, or just disparaging anecdotes which show the evil ones for what they are and allow the good ones to rest cozily on their goodness. This the media can deliver easily and effectively if they so desire. They can, if they wish, underplay massacres in some places, or treat them soberly, or blow up out of all proportion an excerpt of a speech, anodyne in itself, as almost the biggest menace ever.

Add to this the complicated phenomenon that the existence of "the other"—as long as such is the image—can serve as screen and as excuse for purely internal events with little direct relevance to a Russia, nice or naughty. The events of the Chinese "cultural revolution" looked, at the beginning, like something concerning Russia, but soon it became clear that this was purely internal to China. The anti-Russianism sweeping Paris these days is another example. It helps create persistent fears that Soviet tanks are prepared to reach the English Channel any day now. In fact, though, such phobias and fears have more to do with mutations inside the Parisian intellectual class that concern mostly themselves. That studies of Russia do not fare well in an atmosphere like this is not difficult to show.

Yet another example in which the connection with Russia is, at least, more direct can be offered: different lefts in different countries consider themselves cheated by the October revolution, for it did not stand up to its promises. So many people are "offended"—and replace their previous uncritical worship with an equally uncritical and imbalanced rejection, without realizing that in both living and studying historical phenomena to do so is to cheat no one more than ourselves; it is no good to escape one trap only to fall into another by the same psychological mechanism of self-delusion.

Certain concepts parading as "strategic world interests" of the big powers constitute precisely one such trap. Such attitudes tend to center all the problems on one target and respond to all of them by one remedy—military strength. But at the same time the real problems capable of derailing the planet are accumulating elsewhere, in numerous disequilibria that cut through the planet and through the very thickets of our civilization.

So when it is Russia that happens to be that kind of target (and it does not change anything, for them or for their problems, if they too engage in the same types of exercise), Russia's internal regime and anything it is doing, inside or outside its frontiers cease to be irrelevant to international tensions—they are used to feed them. Nothing is allowed or accepted as "internal" in Russia, although it is, say, for China. Others have "international relations"; Russia has an "international behavior," obviously a bad behavior, a product of an evil psyche with evil intentions, which the other side should handle as one handles a delinquent. Thus, it is not a country like any other that operates in a complex international environment, often very hostile to it, and has its problems with it. On the contrary, it is the only factor of trouble, and nobody else can be suspected even of engaging in any kind of mischief. Obviously, as far as propaganda goes—and many other products that don't see themselves as propaganda—anything can be ascribed to Russia, any evil intention, without a need to analyze the relations of forces and the feasibility of those intentions or to apply any of the methods of proof which are sternly demanded elsewhere. Such a free-for-all in this important field is damaging to the intellectual effort that is indispensable for the field itself and for many other related ones.

Experts who deal with the Soviet Union, whatever their specific intention, find themselves often under pressure to deliver quick and incisive prognoses—"What is it they are up to?" "When they are going to change?" or "How is your study relevant to our country's needs?"—the last being quite crucial sometimes for getting funded. The friendlier question, from practical people with quite good intentions—to do business with the

Russians, for instance—"What makes them tick?" Soviet experts are all too often approached with naivetés like that, behind which looms large a rather widespread conception—quite an "impediment" in itself—that simple answers do exist because the issue itself is basically very simple. And why was all this money wasted for studies without the secret having been discovered thus far?

There is astonishment sometimes among people who are highly competent and master complex realities in other spheres of life when they are told that "what makes the Russians tick" is not some simple mechanism located in the Politburo, but the country's history, traditions, culture, economy, social structure, international environment. Also leadership —in that order, at the end of those big components, important but a part of a larger institutional setting, in interplay with groups, classes, and traditions, through battles, compromises, and even—yes!—different ideological approaches.

Even in academic circles, where important works and achievements of scholarship can be proudly listed, the "politicization" of this particular field has a twofold impact: in the pressure on the profession to explain Russia to the politician and, sometimes, to his taste; and, in a very different sense, in the pressure of the Russian system itself, by its own deep "statism," which draws attention predominantly to the tools of power—state, leadership, ideology.

Nothing is intrinsically wrong with treating these aspects other than the fact that this one-sided concentration on political power has left "society" and its history, the broad popular classes, even the ruling groups —bureaucracy in general, elites—as well as the broader institutional complex, longer-term historical continuities, and larger civilizational aspects and mechanisms of change without due attention. If we return, then, to "what makes them tick?" in real life, the intellectual effort suddenly looks much more exacting and exciting. Any clichés and moody vacillations should be relegated to strictly private pursuits.

The "central approach" characterizing the texts selected for this book is hopefully a promising avenue in the efforts to interpret and to define another unifying thread of this book—"Stalinism." Stalinism is one phase of a chain of phases or "models" through which the Soviet political system has passed. As will be argued, the system has appeared in several versions, with more than some trifle differentiating between them, although all belong to the same authoritarian framework. Stalinism is one phase—a particularly virulent one, perhaps even "pathological," which developed and then passed away almost at the same time as its founder. The broader framework remained, however, a more complex and more durable breed.

To understand Stalinism as well as the whole chain of forms through which the Soviet system has passed since its inception, a historian, quite naturally, wants to introduce into the analysis as much of the past as is necessary. As Fernand Braudel stated, a revolution, French or Russian, is never really a break in the country's civilization.[1] What went on not only before 1937, or before 1929, but well before 1917 has to be understood and put to work, a difficult task, no doubt, and one that needs the collaboration of numerous historians, from different disciplines.* But the message is clear: Lenin, Trotsky, Stalin, and the entire Politburo all acted inside a social and cultural milieu, undergoing violent jolts within the framework of disintegrating or reemerging structures. They did not just discuss with each other, inherit from each other, or kill each other off. The picture is much more complex and often perplexing, and the question of who and what begot whom and when is a very intricate one. Moreover, what interests us cannot be properly understood if we stop with 1953, with Stalin's last gasp. What continued after him for thirty more years is crucial to a proper analysis.

Not that we intend to neglect the state, ideology, leaders, or personalities here. The titles and content of several of our chapters testify faithfully to their real intentions. But instead of proceeding from the all-too-prevalent idea that in state-dominated regimes (Soviet-style or others) everything is "politics" and "domination" whereas society is just being controlled, censored, or muted, no more than an appendix to the bureaucracy, and "atomized" at that, these studies focus on a society in the different stages of its development. Only at times, in fact, did Russian society approach a state of "atomization," but it was always a factor, a mighty shaper and definer of the march of events, and especially of long term trends in the social and political system. Without these aspects the story is not really told, nor is it understood. The last essay, "Grappling with Stalinism," illustrates the necessary approach, although in a still tentative way and without sufficient attention to pre-1917 developments. Nonetheless, many problems are raised for further study and discussion.

Basile Kerblay's recent pioneering book,[2] relevant to all the preoccupations presented here, treats the polity as one very important factor, no doubt powerful and often effective but evolving in a constant interplay with historical factors—classes, groups, traditions—that shape and frustrate the state and its leadership. Kerblay studies mainly the contemporary scene, but the same applies throughout history and even more so in the Soviet period.

The problem is not just people's rights to organize freely, to publish, argue, and contribute to the political process publicly with their own ideas. The Russian historical milieu, even if strongly and traditionally authoritarian, often exhibited powerful rifts between the political and the

---

* A group of American historians meets every year in a colloquium under the auspices of a "National Seminar on the History of Russian Society in the Twentieth Century," so the author is not at all lonely in this field. This is not to implicate members of the seminar in his own opinions, but we do share a common interest in the social history of Russia.

social spheres (popular uprisings, clandestine movements, religious dissent, cultural trends that penetrated even the upper layers of society and state). But we do not need spectacular events to illustrate our thesis. Simpler processes of everyday life from the Soviet period—"simpler" in the sense of not concerning any open turbulence or even open political criticism—can be shown to create at times insuperable obstacles to state action. We observe it when workers engage in massive turnover in search of better employment conditions, when officials are sluggish in supplying data to their superiors or are impolite and inefficient in dealing with the public, when peasants employ their zeal in their private plots and do not overexert themselves on the fields of the kolkhoz, when intellectuals develop trends, moods, and ideologies, and when youths follow fads and fashions, from life projects to career preferences, that are a far cry from what the official world would like to see. The list of such examples could go on and on. The party and the ruling strata are not immune to the corrosion by influences and cultures that the country, a huge historical laboratory, keeps creating in conjunction with its old statist tradition or, on the contrary, in tune with the numerous other traditions which shaped the minds of people and sprang out of them, high up or low down, in a constant and irrepressible interplay.

Such is the historical product called Russia, and there is no other. Such an emphasis on factors other than the organized state—or the less precise, more ideal and abstract "statehood"—create a suspicion of wanting to "depoliticize" a system where statism is officially the salt of things and is seen to be just that by many observers. But the suspicion is unwarranted. The bearers of statehood, whether administrators or ideologues, are political creatures, but they are also social beings and social groups. The aim, therefore, is to view these aspects together to reveal a more intricate picture of the state as having a history itself that is not all made by itself and not entirely to its own taste—a history, in fact, where directions and parameters are fixed by a maze of players, intentions, and givens, material and spiritual, that were often initiated far back in time and come back to haunt the unsuspecting heirs at a moment when they believe they are engaged in changing the world. The same applies to the party and to ideology which in our framework is also being treated as a product no less than a maker and gets partly shorn of the pretenses made for it by some dogmatists.* Marxism-Leninism should be treated as responding to structural changes in the country's internal and international development, changing its functions and formulae, appearances and essences, just like any other product of the social world.

The essays here are thus guided by such and similar intentions, but they are still modest steps on this road, often tentative, and in any

---

* During the centenary of Lenin's birth, in 1970, General Secretary Leonid Brezhnev ended his speech with the characteristic slogan: "Long live for the ages [sic] Marxism-Leninism!" This is probably much more than Lenin had hoped for.

case far from any claim to constituting a "theory." But a theory is not mandatory here; just careful observation and reading of facts is sufficient to discover that those important figures on our political scene—the Bolsheviks—appear in one light when all we are interested in is the power game (how they outsmarted, outwitted, or silenced their opponents), which has to be told and often was, and in another quite different light, when we also ask questions about the broader canvas on which they should be placed. From this perspective their successful power play becomes marred by a picture that is first rather bittersweet and then, outright tragic. Here was a bunch of daring and successful revolutionaries who triumphantly boarded a train—let us use a fable for the sake of more figurative illustration—after taking it by storm, even built many new cars and a locomotive, and then, confidently, began to drive it from Station Promise to Station Hope. But as the train moved it became clear to growing numbers of the erstwhile founders that the train was moving, inexorably, somewhere else, in some unwanted direction, but could not be stopped, nor could anyone get off. We can give many of the Bolsheviks credit for having tried, opposition after opposition, to correct the course of their train, but nothing seemed to work.

This fable is actually inspired by Lenin's complaint: "I doubt very much whether the Communists are the ones who are leading. I believe rather that they are the ones who are being led."[3] Such a statement is the best illustration of the fact that successful historical actors, imbued with their self-importance as history's dictators, may find themselves traveling "somewhere else." In fact, in this case they are almost all going to perish, individually and as a movement, as their actions unveiled their potential. But those actions in themselves and on their own terms will not explain the outcome. Again, it is the broader social and cultural canvas that has to be studied for assessing why "the train" traveled to an unknown destination, a destination which, for about a generation, was to earn the name "Stalinism."

We will apply to this system the same approach and try to discover what it can add and whether it explains something we did not understand before. But first we will have to construct a concept of this system's "antecedent," the historical fabric from which the next stage was constructed. Such an approach complicates the task of assessing the role of personality in the process—Stalin's in this case—which can be crucial in many ways, even in a frame of reference that puts such high stakes on longer-term cumulative and impersonal trends. Our tendency is, incidentally, to see in Stalinism not a direct outgrowth of bolshevism but rather an autonomous and parallel phenomenon and, at the same time, its gravedigger. Stalinism was a system in its own right because it reformulated quite radically the aims and strategies of the original founders to form something new. Particular attention in studying this new system will be paid to the effects of the social transformation that occurred in the early 1930s and that served as background or cause for the evolving political forms of the time and of the stages to come.

The underlying *idée fixe* in this outline of intent is the "larger canvas." As yet not enough has been done to present meaningfully a broader concept of, let us say, "a civilization," as Braudel would have us do. This would mean taking stock of the relevant traits produced by the centuries of Russia's labors, as continued or reflected by the twentieth century and its renditions and transformations, and drawing from them the indispensable picture into which the whole modern process and its actors should be placed. The state, the party, the leaders, Stalinism, and the rest will then appear less fixed and unchangeable than is sometimes imagined, more flexible, constrained, and internally ambiguous, begetting alternative forms and models within them. What will emerge is not a flow in one direction under one and the same baton but metamorphoses, crises, development, and transformation—nothing either immutable or unilinear.

We are engaging the reader in an apparently contradictory exercise. We are insisting, and continue to insist, on the importance of the social and economic effects of recent and current events because they certainly are responsible for a *new* phenomenon—the Soviet system. And assessing this system and its novelty is our main task. On the other hand, we keep inviting the interested student to take a deep breath and plunge into the Russian past, suggesting that roots of more recent events may be hidden there and, more pertinently, still exercising an influence. But the contradiction is only apparent, not real. The "youthfulness" of the Soviet system must be remembered, it being only some sixty-seven years old, but we will miss its specifics if we detach it from its historical antecedents and background. Without this framework it will remain an enigma; with such a framework it will be placed where it belongs—into a complex web spun by the past from which it emerged. Only on this condition will the real originality of its traits appear.

It is worth noting, immediately, that those sixty-seven years can be easily divided into two separate periods, which are notable for the great difference in the intensity and character of events occurring during each of them. The post-Stalin period strikes the observer—and rightly so—for its gradualism, peacefulness, slowdown, and even elements of stagnation—almost a period of placidity, without great upheavals or sharp turns. As if signs of aging could be clearly discerned in this historical newcomer. On the other hand, these signs may point to the coming of age of a model that had reached maturity and was readying itself for new transformations; whatever the answer, the problem is on the agenda.

But the impression of placidity may also be simply the result of a contrast with the previous chunk of Soviet history, since 1917 (Why not begin this count from 1904, the outbreak of the Russo-Japanese War?), which is of a very different tonality indeed. "Catastrophic," "seismic," could be the terms when talking about those years of tremors: from the Russo-Japanese War, the revolution of 1905, one world war, another two revolutions (two stages of one?) in 1917, a shattering civil war (1918–20), which also contained international participation, occupations, and a war with Poland, and next, after a short breathing space (1922–28), the collectivization of agriculture, hectic industrialization, a cascade of crises created by that collectivization and industrialization, bloody purges, and the whole topped by another world war. That, of course, was not placid. Those years saw hecatombs, famines, demographic hemorrhages, "times on the cross" for Russia and the whole Soviet society—and at the same time tremendous economic, social, and political changes, the making of a system unlike anything else known until then, a spectacular social rise for millions and the downfall, demise, death, or the denial of a chance to be born for other millions. Although this very last category of the unborn concerns only hypothetical demographic calculations, not real victims, nonetheless they point to quite a high price for society to pay.

In the light of our preceding arguments, we feel almost instinctively that the intensity of the drama must have been due to contradictions and pressures that played themselves out in such violent ways because they had accumulated for centuries, internally and not without a significant contribution from the international environment. The same hunches might suggest that in the later, more "regular" chunk of development other and different aspects of the past—cultural, political, and psychological—must have come to the fore and gone on to play their role, in conjunction, of course, with more recent metamorphoses.

But how far back do we have to go to unravel those contradictions and the tradition which we assume must have been at the heart of both the "times of trouble" and the times of stability that came almost unexpectedly after the ravages of World War II? What in this past was of durable impact, in the social landscape, the cultural heritage, the institutional setting?

There is little on prerevolutionary Russia in our articles; the work of other thinkers and historians must be used and new things written. But this introduction has had to raise the problem because university training, in most cases, has allowed too strong a divide between the Soviet and pre-Soviet periods in the curricula and departmental structures and thus does not prepare students to handle this kind of task. Most would agree that the 1861 "Great Reform"—the abolition of serfdom in Russia—may be taken as a departing point for understanding what eventually led to 1917. Several historians have said this, among them G. T. Robinson, in a book first published in 1932.[4] It is here that we can discover a particular axis in Russian history around which much of its problems kept revolving. Let us call it the "rural nexus."

▪ THE RURAL NEXUS

Already before the Great Reform two rural classes had formed this "nexus," which defined and underwrote, so to speak, the whole social and political edifice: the peasantry, then still enserfed, at one pole, and the serf-owning nobility and the gentry at the other. The abolition of serfdom created an opening for many changes, especially an important economic development that brought to Russia a small but dynamic capitalist sector, more urbanization, new social strata. Nevertheless the nexus, although juridically transformed, remained. The new developments did not go far enough to break it, and it continued to underpin, socially and politically, the tsarist system and contributed to its inability to change and modernize quickly enough.

This formulation is obviously simplified—the intrusion of the new factors, often impressively dynamic, must be fully accounted for—but as long as the components of the old power base continued their grip on the polity, especially in the court and the upper layers of the bureaucracy, the waves of industrialization and other modern phenomena kept creating mechanisms that perpetuated rather than destroyed, roadblocks and anachronisms. Among these were the court, an industrial labor force kept on in conditions of economic and juridical backwardness even in big enterprises, a bureaucracy that despite some modernizing sectors maintained sloth and ineptitude at the bottom of the pyramid, and too many backward-looking conceptions and practices at the top. And, of course, a primitive peasantry locked in an implacable conflict with the gentry over land.

The two revolutions and the civil war, 1917–20, broke the nexus, in the sense of eliminating one pole of it and replacing it by something else— an innovation of great consequence that allowed for a very new polity to emerge. But it still left the other pole of the equation, the peasantry. The tsar was gone, replaced by Lenin and the Bolsheviks, and the nobility and gentry were evicted—but the *muzhik* remained, a powerful "remnant" of the old nexus, albeit deeply transformed and facing a different political environment which he himself had been instrumental in bringing about.

The peasantry, therefore, is by no means an arbitrary departure point in a social historian's or any other perspective. The peasants, although part of the historically commanding nexus, were not in any way a governing class. Rather they formed the class at the very bottom of the social scale, the fodder of the Russian state, its soldiers and its plowmen, its reservoir of manpower and of direct and indirect taxes, centuries away from the glitter of the capitals, often famished, and mostly illiterate. They paid for it all. Although they certainly were not aware of it, they nevertheless had an impact on the country's character and polity in ways that are not always self-evident. First, being both the pillar and the menace, hence a basis that could at any moment turn into a volcano, a class of this scale in a country in which agriculture was still the main producer of the national income must have exerted a fascination over the minds of rulers and revolutionaries alike. And indeed, that it was is actually a well-known fact. At the same time the peasantry, and the lowly figure of the "dark" *muzhik,* sometimes appeared to thinkers as the downtrodden dwarf, sometimes as the popular giant responsible in many ways for the national destiny and culture.

Leaving aside hyperbolic expressions, which Russian national thinking produced in abundance, the scholar is often surprised by the difficulty and complexity involved in comprehending a class supposedly simple and primitive by definition. To be understood the peasantry has to be seen as a social system with its own specific culture, heavily pressed on by cities, markets, railroads, the state, and wars to change and to adapt—and yet surviving in its village shell and traditional forms and institutions despite all the inroads of the twentieth century. Well into the 1920s, and even after, the peasantry remained identifiable by its outlook, ways of life, language, culture, and beliefs and by its age-old store of wisdom expressed in an incredible treasure trove of proverbs. In brief, it was a world in its own right, not really from our own time. Peasants were much more capable than city dwellers of surviving disasters of all kinds and of rebuilding their villages and way of life from scratch, over and over again, whoever the invader or whatever the calamity.

The articles in this volume deal with the subjects of popular religion and rural perceptions of justice and law, among others. These are very big subjects, though, and so our treatment of them is quite sketchy. But for audiences interested in things Soviet the relevance of such subjects to the understanding of the Soviet system is not always clear, and a few explanatory remarks may therefore be of use.

Given that we are dealing with a sociocultural world of considerable complexity, despite some misleading appearances of uniformity, such a world produces, unavoidably, an intense web of beliefs, religious, ethical, and political, all marked by their own minting. The peasantry is a dense social environment, reacting to every external influence like a sieve or a filter. Instruction, propaganda, fashions, images, are rarely picked up as they are. As long as the "filter" of a specific society and mentality remains substantially in place, the "intruders" will be either simply rejected or, often, although accepted, reworked, chewed up, adapted—in brief, "ruralized." This is what happened to such major external influences as Christianity, among others. Some forms of acceptance, reworking, forgetting, and rediscovering are intricate and fascinating: a good example are some products of folklore, which were initially borrowed from the upper classes who forgot them thoroughly (or even disappeared themselves in the historical vortex), the borrower reworking the material into the most authentic element of rural culture. Some time later the creation got lost by popular memory but resurfaced through the efforts of researchers and wandered over to the desks of writers, to fructify the treasures of national literature.

Such an example illustrates only one such use and itinerary through cultural spheres, but the real activity is intense and multidirectional. In fact, most formal or official songs, poems, melodies, statements, and political slogans were and are being transformed by city and country alike into a mass of parodies, pastiches, adaptations that go into creating cultures, subcultures, countercultures, as well as into ideologies that express perceptions of reality by different social groups, especially the peasants, on whom our attention is focused here, that are different from the official versions or from those of other social classes. Whoever knows Russia must know this too. A Russian who just sang the official version of a song, recited the acceptable poem, talked the official language, prayed the same prayer, and believed only in what he was told to believe must have been a rarity, especially in the countryside, which often simply talked its own language and adored its own saints.

The religious mentality of the peasantry, which we show to have differed profoundly from official Orthodoxy (not to mention the sects, which we cannot discuss in the framework of this selection), also had great political importance in the history of the country and of its culture. This influence was many-sided, and its ramifications form a very rich, often subtle subject of study. The religious manifestations of the peasantry contained many elements of ancient mythology and demonology that were grouped as "ruralized Orthodoxy" around the church, as a layer of often pagan beliefs in and around the peasant hut, as a set of animistic beliefs in the fields and forests—all in various stages of vitality or decomposition, but still present around the turn of the century and later. All such manifestations must have profoundly affected the national scene, but we will just choose a central theme relevant to the political system.

The acceptance of Orthodoxy by the peasants was crucial for the church, as well as the state, which used the church as one of its mainstays. But there was a direct way for the regime to tap the popular religiosity, namely, the *muzhik*'s belief in the tsar–little father (*tsar'-batyushka*). The importance of the peasants' mass adherence to this belief in the faraway but powerful benefactor is clear: as long as it held, tsardom held. It is interesting to us also that such a belief is both religious in character and rural in conception. It underscored, in a rural version, tsardom's official self-image as an autocracy of divine sanction and implied also the tsar's role as head of the church. At the same time, there was between this belief and the structure of rural life a certain affinity, in the sense that the tsar–little father, very patriarchal in an obvious way, seems at the same time to have been (or emerged as) a magnified figure of what rural life imprinted on the minds of the villagers: a father and chief of an expanded family-clan, a *khozyain* (owner and chief) of the farm magnified and projected, equally as *khozyain*, onto the whole Russian land. As long as this *khozyain*-to-*khozyain* affinity lasted (despite the intrigues of grand officials and courtiers who obscured all too often this linkage, as peasants believed to be the case), the tsar could dispose of the bayonet. But such a faith could not just be taken for granted. It could easily wear thin, as events in the past proved, when peasants turned against their tsar and his landlords in some dramatic reversals of loyalty. Thus, in the seventeenth century, many peasants turned against the church and the tsar, the very authority of the Christian-Orthodox symbolism, by declaring the tsar to be the Antichrist. Such was the case of the Old Believers and other sects then and later. Other cases of peasants denying legitimacy to the state include a string of frightful rebellions, the most famous and worrying of them led by the Cossack Pugachev in the 1770s. So-called *pugachevshchina* (Pugachevism) haunted every tsar thereafter and probably also the leaders of Soviet Russia, as a classic example of peasant wrath. In this and similar peasant uprisings a somewhat different symbolism was used than that of Antichrist; here the tsar was declared to have been "a false tsar" who had killed the real one and enthroned himself under false pretenses. The leader of such an uprising would declare himself the genuine tsar, the son who in fact had managed to hide from the impostor's assassins.

Still, for or against, the battle was about and around a tsar. Not so anymore in the 1905 revolution. Here the government learned the hard way, through police reports about hundreds of manor houses pillaged or burned down, that the peasantry on whose religiosity and conservatism the government counted to support autocracy had suddenly turned radical and blasphemous.

The tsar's procrastinations in proclaiming land reforms (and finishing what had been left undone in 1861) were at the root of this popular disillusionment. But it is tempting to speculate that additional factors might have been at work, helping to undermine the powerful symbolism of the tsar image. After the emancipation, demographic and socioeconomic factors accelerated the trend of splitting big rural families into smaller, "nuclear" units, a process known as the "nuclearization" of the family. But this brought about a serious weakening of old-style rural patriarchalism and hence also a diminished reliance on the magnified patriarchal figure of the top *khozyain*. It also meant that a certain laicization of peasant political conceptions was setting in.

But those are speculations. What is not is the very real complex of concepts of justice—real in its political consequences despite having been utopian in essence. (This issue is discussed in more detail in Chapter 3.) The different principles of justice that the rural distributive commune bred in peasants' minds culminated in a vague utopia of a state-wide rural commune. But there was nothing vague in the underlying principle of the redistributions: land belonging to no one should be taken away from the gentry and given to the peasants. There is no need to strain one's imagination in order to realize that this was the mighty bludgeon that broke the foundation on which tsardom rested.

The direct and indirect impact of rural religiosity (or for that matter, of religious beliefs in society at large) on Soviet politics and culture is not easy to show convincingly, although some broad phenomena are well known and their religious origin obvious. A culture so deeply imbued with different creeds, inherited from ages of cultural experiences and preserved in different stages of integrity or decomposition (sometimes even re-composition) until the most recent times, must have colored the feelings and thoughts of people reacting to the tremendous changes that occurred around and to them. We have already mentioned that nothing escapes the work of a cultural filter as long as the filter is more or less intact. A mentality still strongly addicted to the trappings of magic, a Manichaean view of the real and the imaginary worlds—Christ and the saints versus the Devil and his countless hosts of lesser spirits—coupled with remnants of older cults, must also have an impact in many still unexplored ways on the polity itself, however secular and committed to rationalism. At times of crisis and tremendous tensions, the rational is under strain, too, and neither modernizing states nor modern individuals are that immune to the less rational springs of power and of political stratagems, if they are available. Even if the problem, as conceived by the state, is simply to counter backward influences and superstitions, the idea of combatting a cult by some countercult is already an example of a real impact of the very object to be exorcised.

In fact, the term "cult" is a good example in our case. Students of Russia noted a long time ago that the Orthodox church in general, but especially in popular minds, was more centered on the terms of worship than on other aspects of religion, such as theology or mysticism,[5] and that phenomena in Soviet politics such as the creation of a Lenin mausoleum are of the same or similar cultural and emotional origin. Whether this was just a political usage based on what was known to suit popular mentality or whether leaders responded to their own inner emotions or to those of their subordinate political cadres is immaterial in this context.

The same reasoning applies to the transfer of the Lenin cult, in much more dramatic circumstances and even more ritualistic fashion, onto the person of Stalin. Here the idea of offering the masses a quasi-religious symbol aimed at tapping the religious minds for its legitimizing effect seems quite obviously deliberate. Reviving the dethroned myth of the tsar and putting it at the service of a regime in the middle of a most complex and emotionally exacting effort was quite "un-Bolshevik"—but so was the character of Stalin's dictatorship. A suspicious and shrewd ruler like Stalin, a calculating tactician especially keen to prove that he alone was capable of outsmarting the *muzhik,* was perfectly capable of trying to avert the appearance of explosive ideas, such as the Antichrist, in opposition to him and his state, or to divert them, in some form or other, against his real or presumed enemies.

On this plane may lie the premises of the phenomenon we call the demonization of politics in the 1930s which served as ideology for the bloody purges. The idea for this term comes from reading works on the persecution of witches and heretics by courts of the Inquisition. Norman Cohn has talked about "demonisation [by the church, that is] of the heretics,"[6] but under Stalin it was not a question of attacking heretics but of a more eerie act of political witchcraft—making believe that they existed, extensively, when, in fact, there were none. This was therefore a strategy of "demonization" of political life, for its own sake, as a tool of ruling and maybe as a way of appeasing some inner demons that haunted the ruler's soul. That there was here also an expectation to arouse—for whatever the objectives of this operation—a deep echo in minds trained in and by beliefs in witches, demons, and the "evil force" (*nechistaya sila*) is not an entirely idle speculation.

But this matter is best left to the expert hands of a biographer. General ideas about tapping forms of religious-autocratic traditions for sustaining an emerging new autocracy or exploring relations between religious beliefs and the political culture of the masses and of the state, however, certainly deserve much more than the modest, previously unpublished lecture on popular religion included in this volume. Let us remind the reader again that in the 1920s the rural sects were expanding vigorously at the expense of the official Orthodox church—and here there was yet another reservoir of creeds and beliefs, outlets for popular imagination and philosophy, much less known to most observers of Russia but also influential in many ways.

The subject of the impact of the *muzhik* on the history and mentality of Russia is almost inexhaustible. We will open just one more, albeit crucial, chapter in the destiny of Russia and of the USSR after the revolution in ways that have not yet been sufficiently elucidated.

The civil war caused a partial but very damaging deurbanization of the country and the loss, in general, of much of what had been achieved by Russia's efforts to modernize after the emancipation. The civil war was thus a very deep setback for the country, and it expressed itself in a particular way in what happened to the peasantry. This class—the bulk of the population—trained for centuries to endure poverty and adversity, survived the wars, famine, and epidemics in better shape than others and turned out to be the main force, in its capacity as sole food producer, in helping to return the nation to some normalcy. But, unintentionally, it "ruralized" the country to a larger degree than before, not only by its numbers and fertility but also by the fact that other classes, especially the intellectual ones, came out of the ordeal considerably depleted.

But there was another deeper sense in which the peasantry contributed

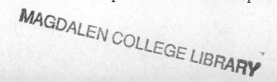

to setting back the clock of the country's development. It destroyed the capitalist and market-oriented sectors of agriculture, curtailed the better producers, restored what the Stolypin reforms tried to change, and in particular, revived a traditional rural institution—the repartitional commune. By so doing, peasants thickened their rural shell and came out of the civil war more deeply ensconced in their old *muzhik* mold, which justifies our use of the term "archaization."

As stated above, one pole of the rural nexus of tsarist Russia was thereby broken, but the *muzhik* dimension, now more *muzhik* than ever, appeared even stronger in a country enfeebled by the civil war. And the new regime, whose leaders worried about the inadequate level of the country's development, which could frustrate their socialist aspirations, found themselves saddled with a much more primitive social and economic system than the one Russia had had in 1914—and more vulnerable and exposed than ever to the older and more archaic values of old Russia.

This was obviously going to create quite a constraint on the new rulers. The task of wrenching rural Russia out of the shell into which it had hid from the ravages of earlier calamities and of pushing it up into the twentieth century would be very tough from now on. Nor will the problem look essentially better after the relative quiescence of the NEP period. To a large extent, all will again turn around the peasants. They will soon be asked or forced to accomplish a leap from the wooden hut to the giant factory and modern airport, from the proverbial bast shoes (*lapti*) to modern overalls. But more had to be changed than just *lapti*. It was to be a battle for ridding Russia of its peasantry and of the whole rural nexus altogether. Not a small matter at all—although it has probably been resolved by now in essence—at a price, of course.* At least, there is no possibility anymore of calling the peasantry a "codefiner" of the regime, as it was in the 1920s (see Chapter 8, "Leninism and Bolshevism"). During the coming era of industrialization, peasants were the biggest source of human material for building the industrial society. They were not asked what to do or how to do it. Dragged into the industrial process, however, they still, in devious ways, notably by selling hard their rural shell, contributed to the cultural climate of the 1930s and to whatever else this climate, in turn, brought about.

▪ INDUSTRIALIZATION AND INTERNATIONAL MIRRORS

Industrialization, even in the mother country of the industrial revolution, was never an easy matter. It was costly in human suffering, difficult to endure, had enormous social and political repercussions, and was—as today's

---

* Dependence on the peasantry as a key historical factor is certainly over, but agriculture is still a problem, albeit different in character today.

developing countries know so well—a must. But it was also devilishly difficult to accomplish. As a historian of industrialization in the West, David Landes, put it, "Change is demonic . . . and the victims of the Industrial Revolution were numbered in the hundreds of thousands or even millions."[7] If this is true of the West, the dimensions of the suffering, havoc, and casualities visited upon Russia during the accelerated industrialization of the 1930s were staggering, although even here one is tempted to insert, for good measure, what Landes went on to say: "(On the other hand many of these men would have been worse off without industrialization)."

This is a major and difficult debate. For the time being, it is more fruitful for us to consider some of the main facts, events, and trends. Then later we can enter into interpretations and assessments.

Acquiring an industrial economy for backward Russia was a dream of Lenin's (we remember his "Give us only a 100,000 tractors"), and it was, historically speaking, the only way to justify a socialist revolution in Russia. And not less importantly before or against his archenemies among the Russian Marxists—the Mensheviks—who haunted him with their "You shouldn't have done that." In fact, the whole Bolshevik party was committed to this task, but the major debates that tore the party apart in the 1920s turned around one problem: How can we do this? The weight of underdevelopment, even after seven years of so-called restoration, was getting even heavier. What we have termed the "archaization" caused by the civil war was not really mended during those peaceful NEP years. The peasantry was still socially and economically the same stratum as it had been before. Industry recovered its prewar gross output (although not yet in some key heavy industry branches). This recovery, however, was achieved with the old prerevolutionary equipment, which was quite worn out and produced an industrial base that was too narrow to offer the country military safety and some modicum of modernity. Some still kept talking about gradualism and "peasant-oriented strategies," but even yesterday's moderates, like Bukharin, understood by 1928 that dramatic means were necessary. But whoever knew the history of Russia realized that strong waves of industrialization were producing crises. The industrialization wave of the 1890s certainly had something to do with the 1905 revolution; another impressive surge before 1914 contributed to the growing unrest that was visible already before the war and culminated in the events of 1917. Accelerated industrialization portended trouble. The anti-Stalinist Bukharin made clear in 1928 to the highly astonished, even incredulous Kamenev that Stalin was "ready to put down peasant uprisings in blood"—which meant that Stalin knew what was in store, although he himself probably did not anticipate the full impact of the coming crisis on the shape of the system. But Bukharin did. It was he who used, in the Central Committee, the strong and provocative term "Leviathan state," which was going to result from the system of "military-feudal exploitation of the peasantry" that Stalin and his supporters were employing in order to industrialize.[8] There could not have been a more accurate prophecy.

An accelerated and successful industrialization in a country with, moreover, a great-power potential easily becomes a phenomenon and a contest of great international repercussion. It was the industrial revolution that gave Great Britain the most powerful empire ever. The industrialization of Germany was not merely an internal affair either. It was a challenge to Great Britain and to France and a steppingstone to two world wars. The United States took over its leading position as a superpower thanks to its industrial development, and the industrial drive of Russia and of Japan, each in its own way and manner, posed new challenges to the United States.

In fact, the very difficulty of the task of industrializing any country is actually a result of powerful pressures that more developed predecessors exercise on the newcomers. It is the predecessors, objectively, who define the task, the intensity of the effort, and the span of the leap to be accomplished by the developing pretender, who has to acquire and to develop the complex and costly technologies that the former created and mastered. The option of going, at least at the beginning, for some older, cheaper, and simpler gear does not seem to exist in the real world. It is, in a nutshell, the dilemma of a transition straight to the jet and the computer or continued underdevelopment and decay. Such seems to be the verdict.

The Soviet "great leap forward" during the prewar five-year plans had a great international echo that was magnified by the contrast to the deep crisis that afflicted the West during those same years. It is a good illustration of the effects and distortions given to internal events by the international environment. It is also well known that Lenin's key argument for taking power in October 1917 was the approaching revolution in Germany, in which he firmly believed at that time. And some sixty years later, the interrelation is even more direct and more intricate than then: the hectic economic development of the West and of Japan during the 1960s (as against the slowing down in Soviet growth at the same time) helped reformers in the Soviet Union to convince their government to engage in important economic reforms. By 1973 the Western drive seemed to have petered out and something like zero growth seemed to loom ahead—and now the opponents of reform in the Soviet Union gained an upper hand. Today the pendulum may be swinging again toward reform.

These are fascinating facts of contemporary history. The West, as model, competitor, and sometimes bogey, played a great role in Russia's economic and intellectual, as well as political development. Their relations were and remain tortured, probably reflecting a more universal pattern: those coming up had problems with the more developed precursors, and the relations in these cases were always convoluted. There is ample space here for inferiority-superiority complexes, distorted images, and mythologies.

The relations between today's superpowers are replete with correlations and aberrations, realism and pugilism. For Russia, the United States was and remains a model and standard for measuring and assessing its own economic performance, the state of its science, the structure of its economy. In their literature the more developed economy serves openly as a natural mirror. The United States, too, is astonishingly sensitive to Russia's successes (minimizing them is a favorite pastime of many amateurs) and failures (another favorite, for amateurs of magnification) and an occasion for sometimes even hysterical reactions. Examples abound.

Russia indulged for quite a time in the mythology of a perennial "general crisis of capitalism" and seemed riveted to watching and waiting for the anticipated, although constantly postponed, hour when the whole thing would go bust. But a learning process has gone on in the Soviet Union, and clearly, this parody of historical analysis has been replaced by a more sober, realistic acceptance of the success and might of the capitalist West. Unfortunately, an equally sober view of the Soviet Union does not prevail as yet in the West.

The United States seems to hesitate still between a perception of Russia crumbling or on the brink of collapse (yet somehow very dangerous and menacing) and Russia advancing, dynamic, and changing. The former conception also still rejects the idea that Stalinism has gone and has been replaced by something different which has to be treated differently. On the other hand, those who see Russia as a going concern, worth dealing with and settling differences with, realize that the system today shows evidence of enough strength and potential for further development and that signs of malaise in different spheres of life should not be mistaken for some final chapter.

This last point returns us to historical reflections. Development, economic, cultural, and social, is always also political—in different, not always predictable directions. It was so in the Soviet case, where, according to our view, one can observe since 1917 a succession of different political forms inside a broad framework, which makes the Stalinist phase only one in a chain of patterns of power, in both the party and the larger political system.

▪ STAGES AND FACES OF A MONOPARTY SYSTEM

The ascension of Stalin to the supreme position in the party first, and to the very unique position of autocrat next, demanded time and transitional stages. The background for it is to be seen in the transformations that the party and the whole authoritarian polity were undergoing, as the revolutionary changes of 1917, the civil war, the NEP, and the industrialization drive—each with their special effects and consequences—kept transforming the social landscape, exercising pressures and exacting their price. Thus, an idea that the governing mechanism through those years remained identical because it was a self-declared monoparty system will have to be revised. The differences among the various authoritarian arrangements, despite the monopoly of party and ideology, can be considerable and meaningful —witness the contemporary scene, which exhibits a string of so-called Soviet-inspired regimes, from Yugoslavia to China, as well as different forms and stages through which each country was moving.

Obviously, an in-depth study of such a complex problem is necessary. These essays only begin to explore it. In view of our special interest in understanding Stalinism, the possibility of seeing clearer by putting this form in some perspective, as one out of the potential models now displayed, warrants at least a brief sketch.

At the outset, before the takeover of 1917, we were dealing with a party organization composed of a network of clandestine committees inside Russia, more or less firmly directed from abroad, but enjoying, naturally, considerable latitude in action. This is a form that comes nearest to the tightly knit avant-garde party of "professional revolutionaries," as Lenin's *What Is to Be Done?* written in 1902, seemed to have anticipated. But even this text did not intimate any mechanical authoritarianism in internal arrangements, despite the insistence on discipline and unity of action. Conferences and congresses, debates and platforms, continued to be part and parcel of the Bolshevik as much as the Menshevik faction, and were considered normal party procedure.

It might have been more than just a nostalgic exaggeration when Aleksandra Kollontai, a leader of the Workers' Opposition within the Bolshevik party, claimed in 1921 that before the revolution, even in clandestinity, the policies of the party were debated first by the rank and file (her term is *nizy*, those at the bottom) and then by the leadership (*verkhi*, the higher-ups).[9] She deplored the reversal of this practice, which occurred during the civil war, and it is plausible that she did not just idealize, only three or four years after the revolution, the realities that everyone concerned must still have remembered very vividly.

Moreover, this party was not conceived for the purpose of taking power, or even for installing a socialist system. Lenin, together with the whole Russian Social Democratic party, believed then in Plekhanov's two-stage theory: the revolution in the offing was going to produce a "bourgeois-democratic" system, and Lenin's faction, with its professional revolutionaries, discipline, and unity of action, was to lead the masses to an assault against tsarism, not to take power. And this is important. Such an attitude, despite Lenin's well-known elitist assumptions (among them, that only the party could introduce socialist consciousness into the minds of the workers), led to an orientation on the masses. On the other hand, when seeking power, and especially when exercising it, the tendency is to produce an orientation on elites, cadres, and administrations.

It is true that, after the experience of the 1905 revolution, Lenin made changes in his strategic formula, but this did not yet entail a basic change in the party's two-stage approach—otherwise it would not be clear at all why the party was so surprised when Lenin changed his tack yet again, in his "April Theses" in 1917, by declaring that the bourgeois-democratic stage had already been attained and would soon be over. In the meantime, though, the Bolshevik party, a rather small party of political cadres working clandestinely, became a legal, democratic, mass party, strongly led by outstanding leaders, relying on an influential second-echelon leadership well-connected with its rank and file and its following in the factories and barracks. It was a remarkable and very active party on all these steps of the ladder, exhibiting vitality and an ability to debate politics.

The documents concerning this period show convincingly that factions —left, right, and several in between—were not only active but were also accepted as the party's *modus operandi*, including by Lenin.[10] The decision concerning the taking of power was reached only after a long and serious internal political battle. Almost all the top leaders of the party admired Lenin and accepted his leadership. However, they did not hesitate to take up cudgels against him over small and even major questions of policies and strategies. Lenin had to get what he wanted through the normal procedures of party institutions: by gaining the majority of votes. He had to accept defeat, or threaten to resign, if majorities did not support him.

This same atmosphere was still intact, at least at the top of the hierarchy, even during the dramatic period of civil war, when the party was submitted to a war emergency regimen—and quite a number of important changes began to show in the style and ways of the party's functioning. Still, its central apparatus began to be seriously built up only in mid-1919, and the party's real apparatus of power under Lenin was the Sovnarkom (Council of Commissars) and the local soviets. However, the latter were shattered by the civil war, and more and more worries and direct responsibilities kept falling into the lap of the emerging party secretariats.

The fact is that by 1921 the overwhelming majority of the party members—before the first big purge of the membership and notwithstanding its results (about one-third of the members, some 180,000 persons, were expelled in 1921)—was composed of adherents who had joined during the civil war. Their main if not their only experience in party and Soviet politics had therefore been during a period of vicious war and of particularly highhanded and coercive methods of solving problems. They did not have the culture, general or political, which most of the old guard shared, and what they brought into the ranks was of necessity a new and different political culture characterized by strong militaristic overtones and, quite naturally, by deep authoritarianism. Thus they would carry the so-called "war communism" spirit into their peacetime jobs, and one could doubt whether the short NEP interlude and the new arrivals into the ranks during the NEP would help to extirpate or transform this kind of attitude. The later recruits, in fact, as will be seen in a moment, did not have the strength to do this.

Soon after the initiation of the NEP, a recruitment drive brought hundreds of thousands of new members into the party, members who were often illiterate workers. The strengthening of the secretariat machinery, so often deplored both then and later by party oppositions, was actually the counterpart of the change in the party's social composition that was to continue, on a growing scale, over the next years. The influx of new recruits from below and the countervailing, ever tightening grip of the *apparaty* (political organs) were burning the candle at both ends. In other words, this process contributed to a deep transformation of the party in both style and substance.

So, first an ill-defined but characteristic committee network; next a democratic party in opposition; soon a ruling party at the head of a truncated state and war camp; and then, on the way to changing its skin again. For the time being, some of the old and new creatures went on coexisting in one tenuously related shell: the old guard, mostly in top jobs, continued for a time its traditions, its Marxist reasoning, the semblance, at least, of its pre- and postrevolutionary style, discussions, and ethos. But the atmosphere around them was changing quickly, with a rank and file that could not understand their discussions and listened rather to orders of officials who themselves cared little for theory or stories about the revolutionary past, the dictatorship of the proletariat, and internationalism. They understood dictatorship *tout court*—and nationalism better.

By now a situation had been reached such that the membership's principal function was not really politics, or even ideology, anymore, this being too difficult for the new members to grasp. Their function became taking and executing orders given on all levels of the new administrative scaffolding by party secretaries; or at best, for party jobholders, supervising the governmental and administrative bodies that the party was building, presiding over, staffing, and indoctrinating. In so doing, the administrative rather than political character of this machine-building machine penetrated ever deeper into the party and kept strangling the old guard, the Bolshevik party or whatever still remained of it. The party inside the party was not going to survive much longer. Meanwhile, the process took some time. During the civil war, and at the beginning of the NEP, the party's constituted bodies—congresses, conferences, the Central Committee, control commissions—still functioned. Oppositions, though forbidden by Lenin's decision to ban factions, still continued their uphill struggles (in which almost all of the old guard were engaged at one time or another). Until Lenin's death in 1924, the constituted bodies were important. By the end of 1929, however, the administrative structure, although operating under the same names, was essentially different.

After 1929, the party was led by different people and presided over by a person with a different style: Stalin. He was the leader of a group of Stalinists—people who put him at the helm and helped destroy other factions. It was a kind of political oligarchy in the party, composed of men like Kirov, Ordzhonikidze, Kaganovich, Voroshilov, Kuibyshev, and Molotov—the list is much longer and includes important lesser figures, most of them pals and collaborators of Stalin's during the civil war. They were an iron guard of energetic, hard-driving, authoritarian men of action who saw in Stalin the indispensable shrewd realist, tough and (so it looked) simple, accessible and modest. They were sufficiently attuned to the new, post–civil war realities of the party and the difficult conditions of a primitive country, not to be too squeamish about his tough and unorthodox way of bossing everybody around.

As long as these people constituted a ruling group, there was a distinct and new stage in the internal party transformation, but not yet a change in the broader social system, and not yet Stalinism. With the NEP still on, the political system was characterized by a relatively relaxed authoritarianism. Vigilant but not massively terroristic, it was a system of informal "social contracts" with the peasantry, with experts (educated in tsarist Russia and rarely party members or Marxists), and other squads of intelligentsia who enjoyed a reasonable degree of tolerance, despite some ups and downs, and with trade unions still quite attuned to the interests of workers.

The big industrialization push after the end of 1928, especially after 1929, was going to bring these arrangements toppling down by introducing a deep restructuring of the whole social system and causing yet another change in the way the party was to be led. We can say here, briefly, in anticipation of later explanations, that the group we are calling Stalinists, the engineers of the "big drive" of the early 1930s, was discovering that they were driving too hard and too much. A consensus developed among them for a new relaxation of policy and of conditions inside the party. But when pushing for a change of line they were also discovering that they were no longer co-rulers; their chief had managed to get on top of them, achieving, contrary to all expectations, the position of autocrat. Soon, he would not broach any censorship, any claim to joint rule on an equal footing with him, not even the slightest hint that they were instrumental in his own ascension to the top.

In a couple of years, most of the Stalinists would also perish. A new stage would be attained. By now the new administrative organization that superseded the original bolshevism, was also destroyed. Its established bodies ceased functioning, being convened at times only if the top leader so wished, and doing only what the leader dictated they decide and do. He also, at will, decimated such bodies by bloody purges and eliminated any leader, including the family of collaborators who were not personally persecuted, whenever he wished. This meant that not just the concept of leadership, previously a strong trait in bolshevism, was going to disappear, but that the whole party was losing its power to the one man who was personally controlling the tools of coercion and ruled as he chose, through selected organs or personalities, either inside or outside the party.*

That was autocracy, and this was Stalinism proper, in full blossom, a form of leadership and polity differing substantially from anything that went on before, even during the civil war, and depending on a kind of mass hypnosis which held sway over the country and especially over the cadres, making many of them believe that everything in the state did actually depend on one man, to the extent that they thought that everything would collapse without him. The relative ease with which things settled into a different routine after Stalin's death proved that this kind of hypnosis can be easily dispelled, but it also helps us discover how, inside the system of a capricious and murderous autocracy, antibodies kept appearing that formed the adumbration of another model still to come.

▪ LA DÉMESURE AS POLICY

The way the NEP system veered into the next stage, changing the social and political setting in a very short time and exhibiting virulent and finally pathological forms, cannot be understood without considering the lightning-quick industrialization, so frenetic that it earned a well-deserved appraisal by a knowledgeable scholar as "bacchanalian."[11] It was initiated and executed by a powerful state that considered itself to be weak: the bulk of its inhabitants were considered a petit bourgeois ocean ready to join hands with foreign powers that were expected, sooner or later, to attack the USSR. Political potentials like that, ascribed to the petite bourgeoisie, were, in addition, amenable to either a rational analysis— they were certainly not entirely unfounded—but also, in times of internal crisis and of exacerbated anxieties and phobias, to irrational, mythical uses and abuses.

---

* The obvious fact that during this period the party lost power in all but name is what makes it so difficult for the current Soviet leadership to acknowledge the facts. They would probably have fewer problems with acknowledging the atrocities, as was already happening under Khrushchev.

At this juncture it could be mentioned that Lenin's act of forbidding factions in March 1921—which was, it seems, unanimously accepted then by the Central Committee—should not be taken as the sinister root of Stalinism, as is sometimes done. The quotations from Lenin were anyway very selective, according to the circumstances and the needs of the battling factions, and it is possible to envisage the same outcome (Stalinism) even if Lenin had not imposed this interdiction. Those who want to restore freedom of debate and even factions can find enough in Lenin to support this, too.

The way this acceleration was launched and executed, its unprecedented burst of feverish activities, expenditures, and unavoidable sacrifice, produced a state of real fever in the country, but particularly in the leading spheres. Warlike mobilizations, utmost impatience with the most natural sluggishness or inability to execute, and a growing scale of coercion resulted. A kind of permanent crisis set in as the whole drive was imbalanced by definition, by the extreme character of its priorities, given to accumulation over consumption, heavy industries over light industries, industry in general over agriculture, and bureaucratic-controlling activities over any other social initiative or autonomous action. The first result, very clearly visible toward the end of the first five-year plan, was an unbelievable mess which required time and effort, and much coercion again, to clean up and to restart the economic system.[12]

This kind of handling and mishandling of the economy, destructuring and restructuring the whole system, and the concomitant movements of human tides to and from the cities, construction sites, and camps serve as background to the political developments that concern us here. The specific phenomenon, baffling because of the difficulty in explaining it, is best rendered by the French term *démesure*. It was gigantism, immoderation, refusal of realism, and it was so strongly adhered to that only very tangible damages could moderate it or activate corrective policies. The only explanation for this frenzy, which lasted for a generation in different forms, is that the show was run by a purely political will, refusing any direct countervailing mechanisms or brakes.

The sense that there "were no brakes" was, in the final analysis, an illusion. This illusion, and others, confounded men and institutions in those years of politics on the loose. Our penchant for the social background and factors which shaped or influenced policy bring us to the conclusion that here were the effects—waiting to be corrected by further developments—of all those accumulated deficiencies and imbalances in the social system that did not possess enough autonomous driving forces in the first place to accomplish the modernization of the country.

This was also the case in other Central and Eastern European countries where, despite important starts and advances, the industrial revolution that began in the late nineteenth century was not really finished, did not restructure the economy, and did not lead to the appropriate social changes even by 1939.[13] In Russia, obviously, the same occurred, and in an even more pronounced form, as 75 percent of the work force or more was stuck in the unproductive agricultural sector. Even worse, by the end of 1921 important sources of economic activity—notably the big and medium-sized entrepreneurs—were evicted from the social scene. Lenin became aware, even before he found himself in power, of the insufficiencies of Russian capitalism, but he still realized that the country badly needed those forces. He therefore tried to placate the entrepreneurs and elicit cooperation from them by launching his idea of "state capitalism" a few months after the revolution. But it was not going to work, and one more indispensable prerequisite for successful economic development was knocked off. Yet another would get damaged later, at the very beginning of the big drive.

In the West, industrial revolutions were preceded or accompanied, in most cases, by important advances, even revolutions in their own right, in agricultural production. Hence, food was no problem and no brake on development. In the Soviet case, although endowed with a plethora of peasants, the weak agriculture, mightily shaken by the violent collectivization of the peasants, actually worsened its performance, so that the big industrial surge had to be pursued in conditions of food shortages, in certain years even hunger. The search for miracle cures to solve the problem of food and to lessen the system's dependence on the peasants ended up by intensifying all aspects of the "permanent crisis."

These are therefore the links of an interlocking cause-and-effect chain: insufficiency of autonomous social foci to help accomplish the restructuring of society on a required scale leads to an ever growing state interference, and finally to a full-scale state takeover. The initiative launched boldly and massively by the state caused a social crisis, a temporary but powerful shakeup and disorientation of social structures (groups, classes) — hence an even deeper engagement and monopoly of initiative and action by bureaucracies and by the overcentralized apex of power. Thus, the apex itself became the source of *démesure*. The element of ideology also can be introduced at this juncture as it further illustrates the functioning of our "chain" as well as the interplay of the real and the mythical in a high fever system.

The reality of a poorly developed Russia during the NEP was such that a very large-scale developmental project that was going to be, as we know by hindsight, compressed in time as well could not have been accomplished by anyone or anything but the state. No normal functioning of a market mechanism, as it happened elsewhere, was adequate for such feats. On these grounds alone, an essentially administrative approach and system, at least for a considerable time, was bound to emerge anyway, whatever the ideology. But ideology here, as reinterpreted according to the needs of the day, got an additional handle on the process. Since the economy was no longer run by or for capitalists, it was therefore easily presented and sincerely believed, ipso facto, to have been socialist. The inadequacy of the market as the main mechanism in this situation was, under these conditions, easily interpreted as reinforcing the socialist character of the endeavor. This encouraged the leadership to reject the market and its categories altogether and to reinforce further the ideological purity, or appearance of purity, of the revolutionary process.

Obviously, the mobilizing effect of such perceptions or appearances was important. The cadres could believe that they were not just industrializing the country but building a system free of exploitation, a system of a higher, more humane quality altogether. Rejecting the category "commodity," which appears to convert human relations into a movement of things, and rejecting the degrading "cash nexus," they gave priority to products, whose real role was to satisfy human needs through their "use value," not to create monetary profit. The rational organization of the economy and of human relations—in tune with the broader vistas of a socialist humanism—demanded planning that could avoid the trappings of impersonal mediating mechanisms, with their ability to subordinate and even enslave human beings, and that instead could achieve mastery of men over nature and over things by direct and rational intervention of the social will.

This seems to have been their purpose, a purpose that justified sacrifices and excesses. Other tenets of the same Marxist ideology raised questions about the realism of those objectives and the reality of their socialist character, however. The Bolsheviks did not inherit a society or economy thoroughly transformed by capitalism. Quite the contrary, they succeeded precisely because no such transformation had yet occurred. Soviet Russia was engaging not in postcapitalist development but in recasting a still essentially noncapitalist social system into a noncapitalist but new and entirely different mold. Reflections like this logically belong in our conclusion, but we raise them here because the rejection of capitalism and especially of market categories, whatever the ideological interpretation of this tack, placed a special seal on the type of planning and the character of the industrial system, as well as on numerous further developments.

The planning process was based on "material balances," on quantitative counts of materials rather than on value and prices as basic accounting units. Cost, in the whole process, was also shuffled aside for a time—obvious testimony to the "extensive" rather than "intensive" character of the effort. To do as much as possible as soon as possible is no prescription for quality. The target was a quantitative indicator derived by the concept of val-planning, based on adding a percentage to output of the previous period as a way of fixing targets for the next year. Because a quantity never indicates all the essential aspects of economic life or all the desirable targets, other quantitative targets were added, an unavoidably contradictory practice, disorienting for the economic agents and quite oblivious to unquantifiable aspects of the national economy such as the organization of production, human relations, or broader aspects such as deeper motivations created by culture or the overall structure of the economy. Here better theory or education was more important for the overall performance of the economy than quantitative targets for labor productivity or output which were doled out to the factories from above year after year.

The consequences of such planning were numerous. First, it created a cumbersome system of supplies that was never able to operate smoothly. Second, it generated an elaborate set of stratagems for evasion and self-defense among managers, who wanted to fulfill the plan and earn their bonuses, notably overemployment, hiding the real potential of their enterprise, and storing resources secretly as a reserve and defense against excessive targets. Third, it was unavoidably a source of illegal markets.

Despite obvious inefficiencies, this basically administered economy and the administrative process itself developed a powerful constituency interested in perpetuating it: the state and central economic bureaucracies. All those physical units of measurement, simplistic targets, and planning-as-battle with its inevitable ultimatums gave the bureaucracy enormous power and a misleading facility for control. At the same time, it bestowed a prestigious ideological imprimatur to rule over and shuffle around, almost at will, enormous masses of labor—a deeply corrupting influence on holders of such powers, as outlined above. Bureaucratization is generally the great companion to industrialization in modern times, but in the Soviet case there was an even greater ubiquity, depth, and breadth to this phenomenon. It acquired a special dimension, which explains why we keep returning in this introduction to the notion of a Soviet leviathan.

But let us dwell for yet another moment on this economic process, in which administrative principles, so paradoxically, outweighed economic ones. This left to the post-Stalinist leadership a whole legacy of low productivity that was not easy to eradicate. Quasi-sclerotic phenomena made their appearance in the economy, expressing themselves in a falling productivity of capital and especially in a recalcitrance within the producing apparatus to introduce new technologies and innovative methods and patterns. The slowing down of the economy, which was probably unavoidable to some extent, was further enhanced by all those fits of excessive speed in the initial stages and recently brought some observers to the conclusion that the Soviet economic system was no longer capable of impressive performance.

These problems are beyond the scope of our book, but a word of caution is in order. By pessimistic standards such as these the Soviet economy should not be even where it is today. Political will can be a source of technological progress—there are enough examples of it elsewhere. In addition, though, the existing economy and social system of the USSR is in itself a new resource that was not available in the 1920s and 1930s. The millions of educated and professionally skilled citizens represent a potential for improvement and reform, albeit a new potential which has not yet played its full role. In this light, low productivity, even inefficiency, points to a vast scope for improvement, perhaps even for another important leap forward.

▪ MANPOWER AND MANAGEMENT— FROM THE SPADE TO THE BLAST FURNACE

Back to the 1930s, and to the crucial factor in the industrialization of those days: the rejection of the market, even as an auxiliary mechanism,

in the beginning stages. The sociologist Anthony Giddens takes this fact
as his theoretical point of departure for declaring the Soviet system to be
"state socialist."[14] By refusing to assign to the market mechanism the role
of motor of development, the system does not work for the creation,
sustenance, and benefit of a class of private owners of the means of production. Furthermore, the administered economy produces a class stratification that is different from other models, even those which also displayed
large dosages of statism in their economic systems in the twentieth century.
Thus, the whole of Central and Eastern Europe in the 1920s and 1930s,
Italy and Germany, the United States under Roosevelt, and especially
Japan saw the state play a central role in the economy. However, in these
cases the state was administering (or interfering in) a market economy.
The Soviet system was running its productive capacities or administering
them directly as a kind of political or state-owned economy. The activa-
tion of the system was performed by the state; state agencies served as
collective entrepreneurs and did not yield their positions easily to continual
pressures from the lower rungs of the bureaucracy, from different managerial groups, and from enterprises and their personnel for greater autonomy and for more say in policy formation.

In such a system the true elite is the political one, or perhaps the
politico-economic one. There are other elites too that gain in importance
over time: the technicians, scientists, artists, and various experts. However, these all gravitate around the power elite,* which is, at the same time,
the central or local leadership of a bureaucracy. A concept of nonbureau-
cratic political leadership had not yet reemerged in the Soviet Union.

Before going on to other social effects of accelerated industrialization,
we should mention another aspect not yet considered here. It is clear
that acceleration of economic development and of some other historical
processes is possible, ours being a case in point. But it is also clear that
only a sufficiently long period can show what was really accelerated.
Important aspects and dimensions of social life do not ripen at will, and
pushing too hard may just be destructive or produce sham results. Illusions
of change will not hide for too long the persistence of values and practices
from the past or the creation of structures and attitudes that were utterly
unintended. Running while standing still is the trick not only of a good
mime.

As we keep underlining the preponderance of "politics" in the Soviet
industrial revolution, we can point to another paradox in this respect.
Political leadership took the initiative in developing and running the
economy, pressured economic agents from above, and forced its will on
them. But here there was also a remarkable backlash from the economy:
the state leadership and the party, the political heart of the system, be-

* In contrast to the United States, for example, where business leaders seem to be more
powerful and more self-confident than the rather diffuse political elite, which has to
be connected to business—otherwise it cannot accomplish much.

came engulfed in the ever growing economic task and underwent a deep process of "economization." The point is worth some elaboration.

The party cells, to begin from below, most of which were operating in the economic sphere anyway, now became brokers in the service of their branch of the economy, sometimes even of just one enterprise. The same applied to higher rungs of the administration, mostly composed of party people, who were undergoing similar processes of "depoliticization," their professional activities becoming their only task, their main and only "politics." The biggest and most powerful parts of the state apparatus and of the party secretariat became the economic ministries (still called commissariats then) and the economy-oriented party departments. The burden of controlling the managerial bureaucracies was now devouring the political leadership. The economy was declared to be the most important "front," to use the martial terminology of the times. It became unacceptable to the leading rungs of the *apparaty* for anyone or anything to remain indifferent to this central historical task or not contribute an appropriate share to it. Hence the tendency to control and to mobilize institutions and activities in all walks of life and sectors of the state in order to harness them to the building of the country. In this way the country's cultural, artistic, and other activities were "economized." Everyone, from writers to judges and procurators, had to contribute to the battle for the productivity of labor, the quality of industrial products, or the building of dams.

In these circumstances, one more manifestation of the penchant for the hyperbolic showed its fruits: the secret police was also pushed, or pushed itself, to become a "builder of the country," in competition with other economic ministries. An interest in finding as many new "enemies of the people" as possible was triggered, to a large extent, by this "constructive" urge of the secret police to populate forced labor camps.

As economics continued to subjugate politics and impose its methods on it, politics kept "economizing" the whole culture and dominating the social fabric, which was in full effervescence at that time. The party ceased, and very definitively, to be an outlet for political activities for its members. It became transfixed by economics, turning into an organism for administrating and exhorting the population to fulfill and overfulfill the plans.*

Our essays, particularly in the last section, examine in considerable detail the social aspects of the five-year plan era. In this introductory essay we

---

* This concerned the highest echelons of the party in the 1930s. Today the economy continues to loom large, but a powerful political sector in the leadership and in the bureaucracy has been reconstituted and deals with internal and especially international politics. It is worth mentioning that the KGB does not run the camp system any more, and it is therefore no longer an economic commissariat disposing of a massive labor force. It is the Ministry of Justice that runs the camps.

will only touch on a few central themes developed there. It is worth noting at the outset the remarkable resilience of society, especially of its rural elements, to the devastating effects of war, famine, and demographic hemorrhages. The rural population managed to overcome large losses of population thanks to high fertility rates and the ability to survive in primitive living conditions. They would continue to be severely tested in this respect by World War II.

The peasantry was also the main contributor to the hectic growth of the cities and to the growing numbers of all classes of the expanding industrial society. The effect of this contribution is not easy to assess because more than just numbers are involved. But for the moment let us anticipate the findings from our essay, notably Chapter 9, showing that in those years almost the whole nation was shaken up by changes, more or less sudden, often violent, so as to make everybody switch his position in society, even if he didn't move from his locality at all. The last point is mostly pertinent to the peasants, for whom collectivization, even when it did not drive them from their villages, was felt to be an ordeal which produced mostly disappointing changes in their social position. For those 17 million peasants who settled in cities between 1928 and 1935, not to mention the further millions who joined them during the last prewar years, the change was important, although the social landscape of that period was not only occupied by those who came and settled but also marked by those who, numbering in the millions, kept coming and going, leaving and "turning over."

Looking beyond the big migrations and peregrinations, the objective social process consisted in restructuring the class and professional profile of the population to make it respond to the needs of a modern economy. An impressive social mobility, often upward, was a key feature here, as in any other case of industrialization. Another was the spectacular speed of the process, which we have already emphasized. This mobility, with its great hopes and tremendous tensions, was also coupled with a social crisis of many facets and manifestations which deeply marked the whole period, its flavor and its character.

Many peasants became workers, acquired a skill, or went to study, and many workers achieved better paying positions, including those in administration and in the political arena, or learned to be technicians or scientists. Had this been the only story, this picture of social ascension would have certainly deserved paeans to a Promethean myth come true. The official Soviet version would have preferred us to content ourselves with this aspect of things and would even allow, for good measure, a few additional words on the "great sacrifices" and "certain difficulties" encountered on this road.

There is no way the effects of restructuring—namely, upward mobility —can be disregarded. But historians deal with the whole of industrialization and its impact on the fate of millions in cultural, social, and political realms as well as the economic one. The 1930s was an era of great mobility, but for too many the direction was down, not up. Whole classes were created or grew, while others disappeared. Cadres were educated and promoted in massive numbers, while other masses of cadres were destroyed. Professional training was impressive, but the majority of the working class were still working with their bare hands. These were the *chernorabochie*, physical laborers without professional skills, often still illiterate and technically primitive. Acceding to a "position" of a *chernorabochii* and living in overcrowded barracks (not to mention *zemlyanki*, simple holes dug in the soil and covered with makeshift roofs) could not have looked like "upward" mobility to peasants who had previously had a farm of their own, however poor.

Nor can one overlook the massive waves of repression that filled the concentration camps with unknown millions of inmates. A phenomenon too large to disregard, it marred considerably the happy picture of social promotion.

But even for hereditary proletarians and other workers who stayed in the factories and progressed there professionally the advancement was by no means simple. Social position is relative. To climb a ladder when people on other ladders are climbing higher and faster may seem like standing still, or even regressing. In Chapter 10 we show the quickly growing social pyramid, within the working class and also around and above it, a stratified network of hierarchies, technical and administrative, which state policies promoted, accelerated, and solidified as a matter of deliberate strategy. Workers could not but become aware of the steepness of this about-face when they compared it with earlier stages of the new regime and even to the NEP. What was happening now was a real status revolution, which was producing and encouraging a powerful and often rude class of bosses who very soon would not only dictate their will inside the factory but become important in the party, too. This is why professional promotion, while enormously important for millions of people, was for many others, especially workers, tainted by a relative loss of status. For some others, again, it indicated a power structure which was getting too oppressive not to impair the sense of emancipation that upward mobility should have brought.

This might have been the reason why many workers, seeing their *nachal'stvo* (bosses) engulfed, wave after wave, by the purges of the later 1930s, believed that they really must have been "enemies of the people," guilty of endless acts of treason. More facts are necessary, however, to write competently about this aspect of workers' mentality.

Let us stay on the factory floor for another moment to raise a little-known chapter of labor history that we do not deal with in this volume. It is, on the whole, a chunk of Soviet social history still largely unwritten. Here we offer just a brief suggestion on this.

The social pyramids just alluded to and the status revolution were important social trends that created permanent fixtures. The style and some of the methods of policy that were used to bring about and to solidify stratification, as well as to justify it ideologically, were time-bound and pertained to the essence of "Stalinism." But the substance of these trends was inherent to the industrial society and to the authoritarian polity that was taking shape through a period of paroxysms, to preside over the new social and economic base. The policies used to achieve the required model for the industrial system were based on the well-known slogan, launched by Stalin in 1931, that condemned *uravnilovka* (egalitarianism) in remuneration as "antisocialist." In other words, the previous policies and revolutionary ethos were entirely rejected. Already during the NEP there had been considerable pressure in this direction, but Bolshevik and popular egalitarian ideologies had served as a brake. Stalin's dismissal of these ideologies resulted in a larger spread in the range of wages and salaries and a period of searching for the best methods of stimulation and motivation through a system of bonuses and privileges. This policy was also an important component of a strategy to stem the tides of disorder and flux, to tighten up the industrial system, and to get credible performances out of it.

The 1930s, more than before or after, experimented hectically with stimulation schemes to unite the right piece rates and additional bonuses with the appropriate work norms and a reasonable wage. But in this area as in others, flux was the norm. The leadership tried system after system, almost permanently reforming the pay methods, as the stimulating effect of earlier measures continued to erode. Nevertheless, the indispensable and eagerly sought stability in this sensitive domain constantly evaded them.

Many of their difficulties resulted from lack of experience, from too gross an interference "from above," from the absence of well-trained production engineers, and from the relative youth of the managers. But the main source of their many problems stemmed from the effects of "combined development," a term used by Trotsky to characterize a general attribute of a stage of development when the very primitive still mingles with and fetters the very new and advanced.[15] The other factor—excessive centralization of power and of decision making—was itself one of the consequences of that same "law." Seen from above, it looked even logical to try to solidify a chaotic situation by imposing some uniformity so as to contain the centripetal forces of localism and self-seeking. Yet imposing a single system of pay on diverse industries located in different regions and operating different technologies was often dysfunctional, especially in view of the phenomenon of commingling of different social matrices that ran across most branches and factories during the five-year plan era.

To understand these aspects better one would need a good labor history, but this is not yet available. A study of the industrial experience in other countries—Great Britain, the United States, Japan, among others[16]— shows quite a prolonged process during which organization, technology, management, and labor went through complicated phases in different combinations and systems. Industrialization would begin from, say, the putting-out system and then develop into a manufacturing system where initial artisanal methods inherited from the guilds would slowly get transformed by the growing division of labor but would still hang on for decades, in the form, notably, of subcontracting, the main way of organizing labor in the factories that replaced manufactures everywhere. The subcontractor was the real organizer of labor: he hired, organized, and paid them, whereas the factory owner might not even have known how the shop floor was operating. This system of subcontracting had to be overcome for a modern management system to emerge (the first steps on this road—accounting and personnel departments) and for modern corporations to take shape. Thus, the subcontractor either had to be eliminated and replaced by shop floor superintendents and foremen (the United States) or incorporated into the factory management as its lowest rung on the ladder (Japan).

At this juncture, bureaucratization entered the industrial world on a grand scale and penetrated the shop floor from below, through the imposition of the foremen, and from above, by the development of a managerial hierarchy, in which the foreman became the lowest link. The picture gets even more complicated with the development of the trade unions, changing technologies, and new methods of organizing systems of machines and of labor. Once the industrial system eliminated the main vestiges of preindustrial systems, it became ripe, from the turn of the century on, and especially during the 1920s and 1930s, for the big waves of "rationalization." Notably in Germany, with its emphasis on scientific management, its introduction of assembly lines, electricity and electric motors, and its huge international cartels, science played an increasing role in most of industrial activity.[17]

All of these developments in other countries highlight an important phenomenon in the Russian experience, for which we used Trotsky's term above. Russian and Soviet economists and planners studied the above-mentioned trends abroad and knew something, sometimes quite a lot, about them. Organizers and technicians visited many industrial countries in the 1920s, among them Germany and the United States, but this knowledge was purely theoretical and of no immediate use in the social avalanche that happened with the beginning of the first five-year plan. Forms, stages, phases, technologies, and systems that took decades if not centuries to develop and mature elsewhere clashed and tumbled over each other in Russia, interpenetrating, or simply coexisting, in the most checkered social mosaic.

The forms we talked about in connection with other countries existed and coexisted also in Russia. When thousands of new factories were

built despite a grave, even desperate shortage of qualified labor, technicians, and organizers, reinforcements had to be rushed from one region
to another and from abroad to support the new enterprises and the older
ones in the process of renovation. Unavoidably they brought with them
their different methods, habits, and traditions to the already confused industrial scene, with its own motley crowds. People from the old Ural industries, with their antiquated artel-type system (similar to subcontracting)
mingled with personnel from Leningrad's metallurgical plants previously
trained by foreign superintendents and managers. Highly qualified workers
operated amid a mass of simple physical laborers who had never touched
a machine in their lives. Assembly lines coexisted quite unhappily with
artisanal and semiartisanal brigades, and quantities of supermodern
machines were seen, rusting in the snow in the courtyards of numerous
factories because there were as yet no specialists capable of installing and
running them. Some factories, like the one run by the aircraft designer
Yakovlev, were shining, quiet, and clean, staffed by competent people in
white overalls who expertly read complicated technical drawings. In most
plants, however, as the boss of heavy industry, Ordzhonikidze, constantly
deplored, impassable filth (*neprolaznaya gryaz'*) was the rule. The chief
engineer of the famous metallurgical plant in Magnitogorsk, in a report
presented in 1939, pointed to the key phenomenon that interests us here
when he deplored the cohabitation of very modern technology and
methods with what he called "grandpas," preindustrial antiquities.[18]

There is no doubt that similar phenomena permeated not only industry but almost every sphere of activity: schools and universities, officialdom, and, we maintain, politics. Tsarist ways and traditions from
different "pasts" hobnobbed with German-inspired "rationalization,"
French methods of administration, American Fordism, and the very old,
rural, rhythm-setting work cry, *vzyali!* As masses of rurals learned—or refused to learn—to use a spittoon and to read, the highly talented Tupolev
designed excellent airplanes, some of the best of the day, in a *sharashka*—
a prison where he was kept, together with his entire construction bureau,
under the supervision of the political police.

Backwardness in itself is not the only problem here. But the mass of
preindustrial or newly literate people streaming into a bewildering new
organizational structure with complex modern machinery produced a
mass of backward reactions at all levels of society, both in and outside of
factories, including specialist baiting, breaking or sabotaging of machines,
hooliganism, and increased criminality, but also equally primitive counter-
reactions from management and from the political system itself. Waves
of coercive measures were one such manifestation of a general, obviously
transitory, but powerful state of "accentuated backwardness" in all areas
of life, harking back to some of the deepest recesses of a national
tradition.

In this context one further example from this period deserves mentioning: Stakhanovism. The production record broken by a miner from the Donbass region, A. Stakhanov, and the use the regime and Stalin tried to put it to, expressed the attitudes of at least some leaders looking for a breakthrough, even for miracle cures in the battle for productivity. Only heroic deeds and larger than life figures seemed to them capable of overcoming the sluggishness of workers and bureaucratic routine. Stalin made it clear that he expected this movement of heroes to serve as a whip against the administrations and to force them at the same time to produce more of such record-breaking, folklore-inspired giants.

Administrations "sabotaged" the whole thing as best they could and often paid the price. For the abler among them it must have been a very awkward way of combatting backwardness. Emphasis on the spectacular was the opposite of what a successful industrial system needed, namely, systematic work, steady rhythms, and good coordination of efforts among large cooperative communities. The orientation on supermen had a disorganizing effect, not least of all because of the resentment it produced among workers who were not up to the exploits of the few and begrudged the privileges showered upon the chosen in times of scarcity.

The whole campaign looked like an appeal to the tradition of a rural people whose work educated them to produce the extraordinary but rather short bursts of activity needed at agricultural peak time, followed by prolonged slowdowns. It may well be that industrial chiefs, like Ordzhonikidze the commissar of heavy industry, favored the idea initially but then turned against it as he realized that Stakhanovism, Stalin-style, was disorganizing the factories and discouraging the managers. Ordzhonikidze openly attacked the ideas of record breaking as a model for industrial life and defended the administrators from Stalin's accusations. His suicide (if that is what it was), preceded and followed by a carnage of managers and technicians, nevertheless did not prevent the idea of Stakhanovism from disappearing at the same time, in all but the name.

▪ A "CULTURAL REVOLUTION"?

We are now advancing a step in perceiving the results of social restructuring that the industrialization drive brought about. The cultural changes that took place as part and parcel of the process were very significant for the social climate, but to elucidate these changes requires some figures.

To begin with, during the years 1924–39 the percentage of the population employed by the state, i.e., workers and officials and their families, grew from 14.8 percent to 50.2 percent. This includes rural people working on state farms; however, the share of the classical peasantry in the employed population dwindled very significantly. At the same time (1922–40) the city-dwelling population rose from 16 percent to 33 percent, growth achieved by an influx of peasants to the cities (as well as by the promotion of previously rural settlements to the status of cities) to the tune of 80 percent of this total for the years 1928–38, as calculated by the eminent demographer Urlanis.[19] The absolute numbers of workers and officials rose from 11.4 million in 1928 to 33.9 million in 1940. Only peasants could have supplied the bulk of such an increase. This increase is all-important for understanding the thesis of the ruralization of the cities that our essays deal with and that is corroborated by three serious Soviet authors, although in guarded terms, when they allude to the havoc that ruralization caused by stating that "the passage from the rural to the urban ways of cultural life did not happen instantaneously."[20] But this is precisely why average figures concerning the cultural levels of those city populations are not surprising. "Even in 1939," these scholars note, "78 percent of city dwellers, aged ten or over, had only elementary schooling or none at all."[21] But they go on to clarify what they meant by people not acquiring city ways "instantaneously": the cultural level of workers in large cities, as measured by time-budget studies, showed that in European Russia the time workers dedicated weekly to "culture" was falling. Reading newspapers fell from 2.3 hours in 1923/24 to 1.8 hours in 1939. Time devoted to reading books and periodicals fell from 2.1 to 1.0 hours a week.[22] Not surprisingly, as shown by other sources, the consumption of vodka was going up—and for this not only "ruralization" but the falling standard of living should bear much of the blame.

Figures concerning schools and schooling effort are, on the other hand, very impressive and promising, especially for the country's longer-term prospects. All types of schools totaled 106,000 in 1914/15 but 199,000 in 1940/41. These schools contained 8 million pupils in 1914/15 and the impressive figure of 35.5 million before the war. There were 105 universities in tsarist Russia and 817 establishments of higher education in 1940, with students in them increasing from 127,000 in 1914 to 811,000 in 1940. Between 1928 and 1939 these establishments produced 700,000 alumni and 1.5 million technicians with a secondary education.[23] Are we witnessing here the oft-discussed phenomenon of "cultural revolution"? The figures point to a large-scale effort at producing an intelligentsia. But the term "intelligentsia" was used improperly in the propaganda of the 1930s and later, in order to inflate the cultural achievements of the regime, and Soviet sociologists, in the 1960s, quite properly deflated those claims. Even so, the education of experts is not the only criterion for a cultural revolution. The change in the levels of education and culture of a broader sector of the population is equally if not more significant. But already our first indication that most city dwellers had only an elementary education or none at all has warned us to avoid inflated terms.

The average figures for education received by industrial workers rose from 3.2 years spent in school at the beginnnig of the plan to 4.2 by 1940

—a change not to trifle with, especially since improvements in this field were constantly depressed by new arrivals from the countryside into the factories. Still, hardly a revolution.

More revealing is the growing number of teachers because they carried a great promise for the future. The same applied also to the improving qualification and education of the future cadres that were coming out of academic establishments. It may be useful to explore the level of education, if not the fullness of cultural achievement, of the educators and of the cadres in other sectors in order to get a better insight into the overall level they attained, and into the problem at hand.

The numbers of the cadres engaged in cultural-educational activities (kul'tprosvet), mostly teachers, reached an impressive figure of 1,791,000 in 1939. There were only 231,000 teachers in 1914, growing to 1,238,000 in 1940, which is quite a leap. Of these, 16 percent had higher education, but a solid 68 percent had secondary; thus, only 15 percent of all kul'tprosvet had an entirely inadequate education, reflecting good progress. But these educational achievements were not matched by any of the other important educated strata. Out of a medical personnel a million strong, only 11.2 percent had higher education—received mainly from quite narrowly specialized medical vuzy—whereas 68 percent of this literally vital service had only primary education or less. Another important service, crucial to the quality of life—trade employees—could not be expected to offer much quality: 83 percent of its 1,180,200 members had only primary education; 0.3 percent had higher. A very rude and crude mass indeed, from which the population suffered endless miseries and still does to a large extent today.

The next batch of figures[24] should give us a good cultural and professional vantage on the state of the whole professional and technological class as it emerged from industrialization. And from the purges. This technostructure—engineers and technicians—1,951,400 strong, included only 15.9 percent highly educated professionals—clearly an insufficient number for the needs of an expanding industrial establishment; 37 percent had no or only primary education—again, a very poor showing. Thus, people with secondary education and no professional education at all—the so-called praktiki—were numerous, and in some branches they even predominated.

The great mass of officials called, somewhat pretentiously, "workers in planning and accounting"—there were 3 million of them—can be best assessed by the following figures: half of them had no professional education whatsoever, and barely a primary one. Only 2.2 percent had higher education—the level one expects when talking about "planning." Clearly, officials were too numerous by far and poorly trained as well, clogging factories and other offices and notorious for their bad performance.

Now we shall take a closer look at the scaffolding of power, the crucial group called leaders (rukovoditeli) in all spheres of activity: those who gave orders to subordinates. Out of 2 million in this category, only 6.7

percent had higher education; only 30.3 percent had secondary; and a huge 63 percent had only primary education. Obviously, leadership in the largest sense, which included, of course, the party cadres, were very inadequately trained. If they were less dependent now, by 1940, on former "bourgeois" types, they continued to lag seriously even behind the new, still poorly trained, Soviet technostructure.[25]

This is how things looked even after the arrival of the numerous alumni of institutions of higher education (often still quite rickety themselves in those years), who obviously could not undo the ravages of the purges— although we do not know the educational levels or the numbers of those purged.

As the same three Soviet authors put it, again guardedly, but eloquently: "The cultural revolution of the 1920s–1930s was only beginning to bear its fruits."[26] The educational effort undertaken before the war, remarkable as it was, had not yet transformed the population into an adequately educated one—a task impossible to achieve in a few years. Even the leaders (they in particular) were products of a revolution but not of a cultural one. The population and the cadres had reached some halfway point, as a result of the policies and the industrial effort pursued by the regime—and it was enough to wage and win a war but not enough to avoid its terrible, excessive cost. Instead of the term "cultural revolution," it is more appropriate to use something else—"acculturation," perhaps—to express the reality of a still poorly educated population coming out from deep illiteracy, producing a growing mass of trained people who formed nevertheless, only a quasi-intelligentsia at best. "Halfway point," "acculturation," "quasi-intelligentsia"—these terms render better than others do the stage reached by 1941, not just in the sphere of culture, but broadly, in the realm of social and political relations. Further changes and advances which took place after World War II would make the term "cultural revolution" more adequate.

▪ CONCLUSION: AUTOCRACY AS DISEQUILIBRIUM INCARNATE

The general approach we have taken in this introductory essay and in the other chapters is to inquire into the main traits of the social structure, to ask what disappeared and what was bequeathed to the next stage. It is not indifferent, from this point of view, that the 1861 reforms and later attempts to improve things remained unsuccessful and that capitalism and industrial development in tsarist Russia were not able to restructure and modernize. Thus, a knot of tensions and contradictions was created that caused the system to burst asunder in 1917, bequeathing to the next system many unresolved problems which would occupy it for quite some time.

For our purposes, as stated in Chapter 12, a three-tiered explanatory construct is needed: problems inherited from the prerevolutionary society and polity were compounded by the severe setbacks of the civil war, and then by the "permanent crisis" of industrialization, which aimed to tackle once and for all the hurdles of the first two stages. The whole period, not even long enough to become "real" history, presents a succession of unsuccessful or only partly successful attempts at crisis handling during which old political forms kept disappearing and new ones evolving. Tsarist Russia was certainly a political system of its own kind, and when it collapsed in 1917 it was up to the social structure, so to speak, to show its mettle and to restore a statehood. So 1917 looks to us like a stage deliberately set to offer the social forces in attendance a chance to show what they could do. One after the other they occupied the stage, performed, and got booted off. Then a new breed came up, rather unexpectedly, the Bolsheviks, and the real, final contest began. During the civil war the forces of old Russia—its elites, officers, and officials—claiming to possess the unique experience and right to leadership, proved, to the contrary, that the fall of tsarism was no accident. They were not capable anymore of restoring the links to the population, and without such links there was no return to power for them.

Other nonauthoritarian groups and movements interested in democratic arrangements—Mensheviks, liberals, and especially the Social Revolutionaries—also had their chance: in the provisional government, in the leadership of the soviets, and finally in their own Samara Republic, which they founded in the summer of 1918 in defiance of the Bolsheviks. Their inability to defend and thus to justify their victory in the elections to the Constituent Assembly was flagrant: they could not field an army and depended mainly on foreign troops (primarily Czechs) and on White officers, whose main ambition was to destroy them.

Next followed a re-creation of a state system under the Bolsheviks, which we consider to have been, again, of a kind to itself. In the industrialization upheaval and restructuring, another type of state emerged which was an innovation on a large scale. The continuing use of symbols such as "Bolshevik," "October revolution," and "Marxism-Leninism" should not obscure the deep transformation which both the ruling party and its ideology underwent. Thus bolshevism, too, did its number and was engulfed—not just those wretched Mensheviks...

The Bolsheviks won the civil war and created a style and type of statehood because they were capable of uniting and leading popular Russia, including the new force created but not yet transformed by capitalism and not co-opted by tsarism: the working class. A new elite was quickly produced, from popular extraction primarily—from the lower-middle classes and intelligentsia (*raznochintsy* is an apt Russian term for the latter), from workers and growing numbers of peasants, with a meaningful although unwilling admixture from the lower ranks of tsarist officialdom, the lower army ranks, but also a specific group of higher ones, namely, the *shtabisty* (officers of the army headquarters). This was a new and potent configuration of forces, good for waging battles and mobilizing people—and presided over by a new type of leadership: the party, a school of and for organizers, a smithy for cadres.

Although the new power structure knew how to tap the bitterness and energies of popular Russia against the old regime, as state builders they were themselves aware of the contradictions between themselves and the same popular Russia, parts of which were not their real constituency. An unavoidable process occurred: the party and other institutions were flooded, even taken over, by the surge of candidates from below, who saw the revolution and the new regime as one to serve and to use, even if they had hesitated earlier in lending it support. Naturally, this mass was itself still a carrier of old Russian backwardness, uncouth and illiterate. This would create an ongoing problem for the party: who, what kind of leaders, attitudes, style, and methods, would be able to lead or mold this popular but "old" society and membership into a new one and reconstruct a mighty and stable statehood? The questions who, how, and how quickly opened up a renewed contest and battle in the party that raged against the background of crises from the old heritage and contributed to sharp new contradictions.

But we must remember (and I will say more about this in Chapter 12) that the civil war caused a phenomenon of "archaization" of the socio-economic system, through the interplay of a variety of factors in the social structure, the social composition of the party, the low level of culture and of schooling, and especially through the transformations that occurred among the peasantry. The authoritarian impulses in the party and state administrations from above would be met by those emanating from below, from the peasantry in particular but also from the lower classes in the cities, still deeply ensconced in patriarchalism in their social and family life and ready to respect a strong state or a strong, even if heavy-handed, *khozyain* outside their realm. These phenomena would cause great changes in the decades ahead, well into our own day. This is what we mean by "the old heritage" and its potentials.

It was finally during the industrialization drive that Lenin's hope to give Russia's new worker- and peasant-oriented state its missing modern economic base came true. The Menshevik *memento mori* certainly haunted him: they claimed that one cannot skip stages, and that he, Lenin, should not have taken power in a country not ready for socialism. Lenin tried to polemicize: what if, he said in substance, we with power in our hands move on to acquire the missing prerequisites? Why couldn't the order be reversed?[27]

It could, of course, as events proved. But when the new state, aware that the existing social basis would not maintain Russia as a power for too long, launched a restructuring effort, it was to be an all-out state effort, by state agencies, *lifting up* Russia's masses, quite forcefully, to the industrial age. In these conditions the emerging new society—still very crumbly during this transition, as we show—entered a mold fixed for it by an expanding statism, not an expanding realm of social autonomy and cultural and political freedom.

In this process the statism in question was itself using or yielding to much backward fare. Launching the cult of Stalin, for example, testified to the presence in the leadership of a hard-nosed breed who had chosen Stalin as their symbol and their chief. It was an adaptation of a very Russian statecraft, ready to use older ideological garb but also to get rid of its constraining and especially nonstatist (or antistatist), socialist features. The readiness not to bother about cost, not being too squeamish about means, the ability to press hard on institutions and people—this was the style and the temperament of those Stalinists, for whom most old guard Bolsheviks were by now too European and too "liberal." Off came the big industrialization drive, the powerful breaking of what still remained from the old rural nexus, producing a chain of crises, a "quicksand society" at a "halfway point" with its "quasi-intelligentsia" strata. The change was a display of a mighty social feat of *démesure*, and the state that initiated and presided over it found itself menaced by forces of its own making. It therefore kept hardening its posture into a growing disciplinarianism and terrorism, which created a climate propitious for veering into autocracy.

But what finds itself "halfway" may aim at moving on and settling down after the violent social change, which produced instability and flux but also the need to get over it. The leadership strata and state administrations, society at large, craved for stability, a slowing down, a normalizing of the situation. The striving for "normalcy" in times of crisis and social change was certainly a major factor, especially among the new officialdom and technical intelligentsia. They mounted increasing pressure on the state leadership to establish an orderly, predictable, and lawful system, to tame arbitrariness, and to listen to experts.

It is clear that parts of the top leadership responded to this craving for normalcy and wanted it themselves. But for some others, especially Stalin, this looked like a plot.

There was probably no plot of any kind. There might not even have been any "Kirov faction" which some authors hypothesized about. But there is enough proof that there existed something more than a faction: a widespread mood in the country, in the new intelligentsia, among the popular masses, and in the bureaucracy, to stop "excesses" and establish a more regular mode of governing. Kirov, the popular party chief of Leningrad, was certainly one of those who shared this need. Hence, the 1933–34 interlude, with the tempos of growth lowered, light industries given a renewed priority, the return to some prominence of the old oppositionists, and renewed hopes for more freedoms for the creative intelligentsia.

In the wake of such moods Stalin, and some around him, were turning violently antibureaucratic. This was the direction from which he sensed a growing opposition against his way of ruling. Soon, after 1934 and Kirov's assassination, would come the "enemies of the people" orgy and the bloody purges that epitomized the blossoming of Stalinist autocracy, the period of "high Stalinism." But there were no enemies around, no agents of foreign intelligence agencies. It was the administrative party and its leaders, the Stalinists, who were caught up in the industrialization crisis and were now losing their power and lives. There also was a new and growing social structure and bureaucracy, products of the same revolution and of a reality that was here to stay, whatever the havoc wreaked on them by the purges.

Thus, the same period that saw the making of "Stalinism" also saw the emergence, timid at first, of a second authoritarian model in the Soviet state: bureaucratic in its attitudes, but not based intrinsically on coercion; oligarchic but opposed to capricious autocracy. This "version" was Stalin's real enemy; there was no other. It is this "enemy" who would take over and considerably reshape the system after Stalin's death. By then, the industrial revolution would be finished, social reconstruction would have reached a threshold after which new problems would begin to emerge and to produce new pressures. This stage is before our eyes, for any observers of Russia to scrutinize.

In the 1930s, after the deep political revolution of 1917, came the stage of an industrial revolution—and there the legitimate use of the term "revolution" ended. Industrial changes produced a remarkable acculturation, but also a real "cultural counterrevolution"—an adequate term for the obscurantism, the destruction of whole fields of cultural creativity and scholarly branches and of many of their creators, and the related phenomenon of a political counterrevolution. Stalinism expressed the inability of the system during times of transition and crisis to adapt to the changes of its own making or to control the uses and tools of coercion. As coercion ran out of control, it turned into sheer arbitrariness. The only institution that was now allowed stability was composed of one man—hence the term of "autocracy." But because of the mainly coercive and "hypnotic" pillars of this type of rule, this Soviet autocracy never felt secure. Stalinism was therefore disequilibrium incarnate. It was quickly becoming an anachronism even for the freshly hatched, still unconsolidated Soviet industrial society, which would settle for more orderly political forms after the autocrat's death.

·1·

THE
RURAL WAYS:
MORES
AND MAGIC

1

RURAL SOCIETY IN TWENTIETH-CENTURY RUSSIA

A Preliminary Sketch

We are dealing here, in substance, with some twenty-five years of Russian rural history, ca. 1905–30, and it would be appropriate to keep in mind some main features of this period as our background as well as the main trends that influenced events. One can say that it was a period unusually rich in drama, tremors, and spectaculars. It contained one "local war" (the Russo-Japanese, 1904–5), a world war, and a civil war. It was enough to shatter a world just on this account; but the period also contained two—perhaps three—revolutions (1905; February 1917; October 1917), a prolonged economic slump early in the century, an impressive industrial upsurge before World War I, a devastating social and economic cataclysm in 1917–21, a very peculiar economic formation known as NEP, with its slow but obvious recovery, but on a foundation so different from what preceded it, and it all culminated in yet another upheaval beginning in 1928. That only ten years ahead lay yet another world war is not without its importance—although already outside our purview.

Next, we can point to equally important and remarkable phenomena and events that took place in the midst of peasant society and that were related or sometimes independent of all these tremors that we have just sketched out as "background." There were many changes and developments occurring in rural life that began earlier, and they cannot be handled in this framework. Despite a longstanding conviction concerning the conservatism and immobility of the Russian peasants, there was plenty

49

that was moving and undergoing transformation, sometimes at a very slow pace indeed, sometimes in leaps. But these changes went in different directions. Sometimes they contributed to a better integration of the peasantry into a market economy and a modernizing society; sometimes trends in rural life ran in opposite directions—into stagnation, or collision with the cities, retreating into its own shell, sometimes even into something new and rather unanticipated.

The period we are dealing with exhibited all those versions. In other words, the peasantry was pushed back and forth, so to say, into and out of the molds they were normally expected to move in. Long-term trends of economic development, as well as social and cultural trends, were at work that led into one seemingly predictable course, but they were coupled with the powerful impact of mighty jolts and thrusts that introduced quite unpredictable changes of the peasantry's historical itinerary. Take, for example, the Stolypin reform of the pre–World War I years. Here was a very bold feat of social engineering "from above"—quite risky, but by any account based on trends already at work in peasant society for some time and launching the rural world onto the path of capitalist development, involving social and economic stratification and destruction of ancient institutions and customs. Next came the agrarian revolution of 1917–21, which thrust the rurals back again. And next, with the dust of those events not yet really settled, the collectivization produced yet another jolt, a very violent one at that, onto a new and very different path indeed. The earlier NEP period, although itself a very sudden turn, was nevertheless a turn to gradual and socially peaceful changes, an intermezzo between storms with plenty of character of its own, impacted partly by sequels of the agrarian revolution that were being either assimilated or overcome, and partly by sequels of another momentous upturn of a political character we have yet to mention—the Bolshevik revolution.

Let us dwell a little on a period and upheaval that is particularly intriguing to me—namely, the agrarian revolution of 1917–21. Intriguing because I feel that it had a deeper impact on the peasantry and on the fate of the Soviet regime than is usually realized.

This revolution annulled all that the Stolypin reform had done and more: most separated homesteads (Stolypin's famous *khutory*) were reintegrated back into the villages, except for regions where they had already constituted a widespread way of life for some decades. The whole budding capitalist- (or market-)oriented agriculture on the southern and western outskirts of the empire was severely curtailed if not entirely throttled. The rural community—the famous *obshchina*, Stolypin's main target and already under heavy pressure—was resurrected, and with a vengeance, as it became the predominant form of rural life all over Russia, except for those western regions where it was very weak or nonexistent in the first place. And it served as a main tool for a process of social "equalization" (*poravnenie*), a considerable shrinking of the poles of social differentiation composed of the kulaks at the top and the poor peasants at the bottom of the ladder. Through land redistribution and the weakening of the market orientation of the peasants, the peasantry came quite near to an ideal kingdom of the middle ground of the *serednyaki*.

What it all meant was that the peasants came out of their redistributive frenzy—and frenzy is the right term here—looking more *muzhik*, as it were, than ever before, more sui generis, more family consumption–oriented, less "farmers" than ever since the emancipation. If the peasants on those *khutora* or other better-off peasants could legitimately be dubbed "small-scale producers" or "petite bourgeoisie," how should one classify the parcellary-communautary peasantry at the end of the civil war? The term "capitalist" is simply spurious here, and it will remain a real nonsense even in later years when some stratification scissors had reopened. But even the term "petite bourgeoisie" is here inadequate at that time because to earn such a classification this stratum, not unlike the city artisans, should, at least to a large extent, produce for the market. If a presumed "petite bourgeoisie" produces no merchandise or sells an insignificant fraction of its produce—the bulk going for internal family and farm consumption—why insist on its "bourgeois" quality?

I tend to think that in this period the peasantry lived in an entirely different social setting—without capitalists, without any important merchantry, without the gentry, without as yet a strong supervisory administration of the type that supervised the state peasantry before 1861, or the *zemskii nachal'nik* and the lower officialdom that did the same from the 1880s onward. Also, without the powerful kulaks but with a strong, reinvigorated (for a time) commune. So, what to make of this? There is clearly here a change in the socioeconomic essence of the peasantry as a class or as a formation, elusive conceptually but obviously there, much less stratified than before, more archaic without doubt, setting the historic clock back in many ways as if readying itself either for a new developmental leap forward or for the introduction of some new bondage; it certainly was not a state of affairs that could last very long.

Be that as it may, it is the contention here that this restructuring of the peasantry lay at the root of some of the later developments of the Soviet system, which would have preferred and hoped for a different kind of peasantry, more amenable to its influence. But here was really a quite unusual situation: a huge peasantry *accentuating* suddenly, reinforcing its *specificity* rather than diluting it, as would have been more usual under the united pressure of cities, railroads, schools, markets, seasonal migrations, cultural factors, and other carriers of change. In fact, all such "dissolvents" were weakened or in crisis themselves, and they could barely fend for their own survival, leaving the peasantry free to chew up its new land and institutions and cultivate its *muzhik* quality.

Thanks to these circumstances we have a chance to observe such a peasantry as some kind of species in its purity and to dwell on some of the less studied traits of its social uniqueness.

▪ LABOR, SOCIAL PSYCHOLOGY, AND PERSONALITY

Agricultural labor and the nexus of family as a *production unit,* mainly geared to feeding itself—these three factors (labor, family, self-sufficient production unit) shaped mightily rural social life. The big cities, already in the early decades of our century, did not know much about any of these anymore. We realize that the conditions of rural life in Russia at this time and the whole of its labor process still remained at a level which prevailed at some earlier century in Western Europe, maybe at the level of French rural life sometime in the sixteenth century. It was still an existence without electricity or any other form of street lighting, agricultural machinery was still extremely scarce, even the plow was not yet the dominant tool of agricultural work, and fertilizer was mostly unknown to the peasant. The ancient three-field system, too few cattle, not even a proper chimney on the roof of most huts, all confirm the impression of an earlier stage in the history of civilization: the differences between night and day, winter and summer, are sharp; most illnesses remain mysterious and mainly fatal; a man is old at forty and death is always present, matter-of-fact, and without appeal, at most maybe amenable to some manipulation and delay through folk medicine and the help of a sorcerer.

The "biological" character of agricultural production was reflected not just in the fact that it depended on biological factors but, more ominously, in that life depended most directly on just the current crop. When the inventories were low, the survival of the family depended on the current season and a bad crop was an immediate catastrophe. This was simple and obvious; basic food was at risk, and when it was not there only a thin cushion, if any, delayed the moment of forcing the family to beg. The whole productive effort was, moreover, badly distributed because of the unpredictable and capricious switches in weather conditions and its being entirely geared to this crucial next crop. This trait is of immense socio-psychological import. Innovations, improvements, investments demand planning ahead and a readiness to take risks. But the peasant at this technological level already took enormous risks. The cost of change was extremely heavy, and the propensity to go on doing things as one's elders did was powerful. In the light of these facts the reverse was also much clearer, namely, the difficulty, sometimes insuperable, encountered by the more enterprising or the young who came up with new demands or ideas which may have had the effect of a shock for both sides.

But the power of the elders as teachers and real leaders is reinforced by yet another factor, which can be called "structural." Life in the countryside was, in the period under consideration, still almost fully regulated by the "agricultural calendar." This was not necessarily written up or printed but was at the same time—and, of course, not by accident—identical with the religious timetable for celebrating saints and festivals. One can state with some certainty that it was the religious aspect that was adapted to and superimposed onto the agricultural cycle with its seasons, type of work, and recurring peaks of activity. But this is a separate question. The fact remained that peasants knew from the elders that by mid-April summer sowings should be undertaken; May is the time for timber felling and cutting and for early fallow; at the beginning of June one should take care of late fallows; whereas in late June it was time for harvesting rye and in July for harvesting wheat. August and September were dedicated to threshing without neglecting the sowing of winter crops. The intensity of these occupations was remarkable, especially when it is realized that the list was far from finished: time had to be found for weeding (*propolka*) early in the season and for cutting hay later on. That a calendar-style guidance and some other regulating institutions were necessary is obvious.

As mentioned, the same calendar also regulated holidays, festivals, almost the whole of agricultural life, and set some guidelines for concluding business deals. These were best carried out, say, between October 14 and March 14 (*ot Pokrova do Evdokii*) or till May 6 (*do Egoriya*). It goes without saying that only the elders could advise on this whole agricultural and spiritual complex, which we have sketched out only in the bare essentials.

Not surprisingly, people in such a system think and act "seasonally," not in terms of hours or minutes, which are appropriate for a very different labor rhythm. Kipling wrote about peasants in this way: "This life is a long-drawn question mark between a crop and a crop." He was talking about the 1890s in India, but it reflects reality elsewhere, too. Working and reacting in terms of seasons does not necessarily mean being lazy, or sluggish or preferring a leisurely pace. It is all very different. The whole process during the working period, especially at peak times, was risky, precarious, and accident-prone. Long periods of leisure, inactivity, or even indolence had to be followed by outbursts of feverish activity. Capricious weather conditions and primitive technology (if any) sometimes produced the phenomenal bursts of energy and effort needed to finish cutting hay, or to deliver grain to a shelter at the sight of an approaching cloud, or to get a heavily loaded cart stuck in a muddy road out quickly. Thus a labor process which was permeated by time-consecrated routine methods also commanded intuitive, temperamental jolts, chaotic deployment of emotional, nervous, and physical energy. It is, therefore, reasonable to think that the same process that produced caution and conservatism also contributed to a preponderance of personality types which tended to be easily irritable, easy to provoke, and ready to explode, human beings who were sanguine-tempered rather than phlegmatic and cold-blooded.

In fact, the releasing of blind, powerful tempers was all too often observed in rural life and could partly be traced to the effect of bad food, but certainly belonged to an observable collective psychology of peasants. Sudden angry, massive, drunken brawls or even beastly wife beating, or, in a different vein, outbreaks of religious ecstatic manifestations, were well-known traits of rural life.

Interpretation and diagnosis is not too easy here and demands more work, but we might want to venture some thoughts on relations between such traits of personality or social psychology and some still little-known properties of rural criminality. The whole problem is certainly not easily analyzed. Certain criminologists and sociologists, when describing city brawls among workers in Russia in the 1920s (referring to people who were not professional criminals), contended that when a worker was out on a Sunday for a party he usually left his knife at home. The Sunday brawl that flared up was therefore obviously unintended and unplanned and ended mostly in a few broken limbs but few serious casualties.

But the brawl in the countryside, for instance, during one of the well-known religious feasts (*prestol'nye prazdniki*), was intended, planned, and relished in advance. Youths brought knives and weights with them to the party, and adults joined in when the "action" flared up. They always found on the spot something heavy to get hold of and use. In this situation, when violence began it was aimed at the whole body, causing atrocious mutilations and many deaths. Seen from this angle the countryside was a mass killer—the killings being carried out, on the whole, by younger or older folk who were not criminals in any way in their normal life. How do we explain this?

One criminal psychologist surmised that more must have been involved than ill-tempered personalities. Atavistic mechanisms, dimly preserved reminiscences of old, protracted, long-solved, and seemingly forgotten land feuds between villages might have kept unextinguished residues of hatred and a desire for vengeance which was ready to flare up on some occasion or other against real or apparent culprits of an almost mythical past.

In any case, a dead body did not create the same emotional stir in the countryside as it did even in small towns. Unlike the city, the countryside has a more direct approach to the facts of life and death among humans and animals, especially when the dead body is of somebody unknown. They do mourn and try to revenge their own, of course. But here, too, inside one's own family, death or the approach of death was looked and commented upon unemotionally. Without the slightest intent to hurt, a relative could tell his ill next-of-kin, "you won't be treading green grass much longer, Petrovich," this being meant as a simple statement of fact, maybe even with a touch of commiseration. If somebody was very ill, or a cripple, the advent of the obvious might not seem to have been worth fussing about too much.

▪ CRIME AND CUSTOMARY LAW IN THE VILLAGE

The understanding of rural specifics of those days may profit further from studying the reactions of rurals to crime or to what they considered to be a crime. In the cities in the 1920s more crimes were committed in total than in the enormous countryside, but the countryside saw much less theft and far more murders. Transgressors in cities went more for property; villagers, it has been suggested, more for the body. One kind of theft was important, however—horse stealing. The peasant tended to see the theft of his grain or of his horse as an attack upon himself, not as a crime as officially defined and punished according to a code which sought to reeducate rather than to take revenge. This official attitude was not well received in the villages. The peasant perceived the offense personally, to be reacted to on the spot by direct action, with fists or, if a group or the whole commune were involved, by lynching. This was especially so in the case of the theft of cattle or horses. The reasoning might go as follows: What does some judge from the city understand about *my* stolen horse?

But testimonies from an earlier period (1880s) showed that in the case of murder, on the contrary, villagers would deliver the suspect to the police without themselves "handling" the case. Not so when catching a thief *in flagrante delicto*: they would rather lynch him. The thief could then try to save himself by admitting to a fictitious murder—and he then stood some chance of being delivered to the police rather than being atrociously mutilated. Why? My source does not venture any explanation, but we might try one: the peasants sometimes made a distinction between "crime" and "sin." And they were not in the business of punishing sinful actions.

Another set of problems—for the sociologist, criminologist, and judge alike—arose in those numerous cases where "the book" defined as crimes what peasants considered to be their right or just a normal thing to do: moonshining, wife beating, cutting timber without permission from the state's or landlord's forests—the list is much longer and weightier than this. Governments, for example, often tried to limit the dividing up of farms between fathers and sons, and in such cases it was always the law that lost.

After all that has been said, it may not come as a surprise to hear that the rural world—except for the category called *khuligany* which flourished in the 1920s—did not have much of a criminal underworld, knew little of procuring and brothels, but saw and tolerated, for some time, violent group rape. In the 1920s group rape began to decline somewhat as a result of the process of continued nuclearization of the family, the appearance of divorce, and a change in attitude toward women and in the attitude of women themselves. This was to be a revolutionary process in the long run, but was still at an early stage in those years. A woman who wanted to protest against ill treatment by her husband began to learn to use the courts or just ran away from the husband—an act frowned upon by rural public opinion. A husband getting rid of his wife by simply chasing her out —not an infrequent occurrence—met with much less public disapproval.

Looking at attitudes toward crime as evidence which can be used to probe into broader problems of social psychology, ethics, and culture also helps us to raise yet another highly significant set of problems related to the specifics of rural society. We have in mind the big question of the customary law (or, less grandly, juridical customs) of the Russian peasants. This subject, so important for understanding the history of any society and its law, was handled by a number of important Russian jurists in a debate which went on in prerevolutionary Russia and was, rather recently, resumed in the Soviet Union. This debate—one of the great historical quarrels of Russian historiography—is little known, though. Students of Russia know better the discussions on the history of serfdom, or on the rural commune.*

The village will be the last theme to be mentioned here. The Russian term for it is *derevnya*, and it had its roots in the Northern forests (before it took to the Southern prairies to become *selo*), predictably the kingdom of exclusively timber-log huts, although, surprisingly, the term does not stem from *derevo* (timber). It was the living cell of rural society in Russia, but unfortunately very little has been written on it. We are still more in the stage of global, macroeconomic, cultural, and sociological studies. But unless we "crack," so to speak, the village, something very crucial for the understanding of rural society will be missing. Probably also for the understanding of Russia. It is inside the village that forces were at work— neighborhood networks, family systems, labor processes, social hierarchies and values—that maintained this huge mass of rural humanity and sustained, shaped, sometimes blocked Russia—as they do still elsewhere. It is quite interesting to note and to reason why so much study was devoted to the commune and so little to the village. But let us consider just one fact. The collectivization tempest, as is well known, eliminated or superseded the rural commune—but the *derevnya* remained. And with it, for some time longer, the peasantry.

---

* For a study of customary law see Chapter 3, which also has much to say about the rural commune. Incidentally, for the Soviet period it is better to use the term "community" rather than "commune," which has been largely used since the revolution to denote a collective farm with a full "communization" of the means of both production and consumption. No confusion is possible when tsarist Russia is discussed because there were no *kommuny* at that time. It is good to bear this in mind, as in the present book a strict distinction between these terms has not always been respected.

2

POPULAR RELIGION
IN
TWENTIETH-CENTURY
RUSSIA

Weber's monumental work on world religions was trying to find an answer to one central question: Why the West? The results of his inquiries remain controversial, but the central methodological orientation—to study religion as a joint preoccupation of history and sociology in an effort to reveal this powerful sphere of life as an indispensable explanatory factor of whole civilizations, including their economic traits—remains valid. The one difficulty is that there are few Webers nowadays, and coping with problems of social inquiry on the level of whole systems demands various forms of cooperation among many scholars as well as the ability to ask the right questions.

My own involvement in problems of religion was initially inspired not by reading great authors but by personal experience with peasants and with their societies, in practice and especially in research. It soon became clear that in order to understand Russia it would be necessary to "cope" with its peasantry and with *their* belief systems. This chapter, therefore, deals specifically with "popular religion," the one the Russian *muzhik* actually practiced. There is no need to expand here on the role of the peasantry in Russia and in early Soviet history. But it may be less apparent how crucial their role was in the Stalinist period (which interests me particularly), not just in creating problems for the state but actually in shaping it. This statement should not sound too extravagant to anyone who knows that the making of Stalinist Russia involved a large-scale, protracted social war

waged by the regime against the peasants during the so-called collectivization drive. This contest was portrayed, not without reason, as one against
a "backward" and "dark" mass. Another term used in discussions in this
part of the world was a "petit bourgeois mass," basically motivated by
rather primitive, acquisitive urges and handicapped by a very narrow cultural and political horizon.

The problem is not to dispute such terms but to find out what was
the reality, social and cultural, behind them. "Primitive," "dark," or "petit
bourgeois" may seem self-explanatory, but their use may, in fact, hinder
understanding if we do not try to explore, describe, and analyze the
mentality and culture of peasant societies in sufficient detail. Ethnographers and ethnohistorians take such things for granted, but not so other
academics and politicians. More and deeper study could help to see the
peasants not just as passive recipients of all kinds of "development" but
also as a powerful factor that can shape states (even if the role is in fact
exercised in a "passive" way).

In the course of my own studies it became clear that dwelling on the
more obvious aspects of the "state versus *muzhik*" battle—namely, the
economic, political, and ideological fronts—was indispensable but insufficient. To answer the question "Who was the *muzhik*?" more fully
and to understand his role in Russian history, this enormous social stratum
had to be approached as a sociocultural entity (or system)—more
specifically, as "a nation-class" as well as "a nation within a nation."
These terms are not self-explanatory, but they are helpful in grasping the
complex realities of a primitive society. The paradox is not just a play on
words. It points to the real problem: Why such a peasantry? What is a
class emerging directly from the fifteenth century doing in the twentieth?

Religion is a key component of the peasants' social and cultural world,
an important factor that allowed them to survive and to retain their
identity as well as to manifest enormous resilience and resistance to change
whenever "change" looked menacing. The industrial and cultural impulses
for change coming from the cities, still weak and accompanied as they
were by insatiable demands for squeezing resources from the countryside,
made change so costly to peasants that their resistance can be understood
in more sympathetic and comprehensive terms than just by alluding to
their being "ignorant" (*temnye*).

Studying peasant religion could also help with crucial problems of the
Soviet period, as we ask ourselves how the peasants related to the
kolkhoz, how they settled in the cities, to which they flocked in the
millions during the 1930s, how they responded to official ideology, and
how they found their way in the complex social and institutional universe
of the new Soviet state.

But the study of all these questions still lies ahead. The ordering of
even the preliminary data for the study of the religious sphere in rural life

alone presents the students with quite a task. There is no one modern book on religious life of the Russian peasants in our century. We have quite a literature on the Orthodox church and, to a lesser extent, on the sects that opposed this church. (The sects too, incidentally, were mostly peasant cultural manifestations, but they will be excluded from our treatment here.) Still, a correction in the title of this chapter should be made: there are peasant *religions* in Russia, not just one, but, as stated, no modern study of them. A pioneering work (by Kravchinsky, published in England) raised the problem in about 1882, and a good article by Donald Treadgold made the same complaint in 1968. Additionally, a charming work, by Pierre Pascal (1973), dealt with the question but, unfortunately, without the use of empirical material. Clearly this is a topic that will warrant special attention among scholars in the future.

▪ RURAL RELIGIONS

Russian peasants were always described as very "pious," a trait which they manifested by frequent genuflections, crossing themselves, praying, prostrating themselves, fasting, confessing, and repenting. Asked who they were, they would say: We are the Orthodox (*pravoslavnye*). They did not need to add: We are Russians. Orthodoxy was the state religion, and up to 1905, when the relevant legislation was changed, every Russian was considered Orthodox, and opting for a different religion was forbidden. Many did switch, of course, despite interdiction and persecution.

Nevertheless, the statement "We are the Orthodox" is not to be taken lightly. Some authors (Belinsky, Chekhov, Lenin) said that the Russian peasant was not really as pious as he was "superstitious." He was too practical to be truly and deeply religious. But many authors, including Dostoevsky and some of the later "god seekers," claimed the opposite: the peasant was deeply Christian. Pascal would add that they—or, more nearly, their popular Orthodoxy—actually represented Christianity par excellence, pure and undiluted, the epitome of Russian religiosity—more so than the official Orthodox creed. At the same time, the peasant was not "clerical" and not dependent on the church.

Against it, Kravchinsky would argue that the peasant was not really *pravoslavnyi* at all but rather pagan, or at best practicing a dual faith, a mixture of Christianity and paganism.[1] Such opposing views have persisted well into our times, nor are they the only difficulty.

Sociologists (Weber again) and ethnographers (Malinovskii) taught that religious beliefs and systems are products of societies and of status groups (or social classes). If they are right, then we can assume a priori that official denominations never express reality in matters so complex. We are therefore allowed to hypothesize that as long as peasants live in conditions and an environment which set them apart from other social groups in society, they will certainly develop and stick to their own way of believing. The idea that they should fully share a religious system and outlook with the higher clergy and other upper layers of city dwellers can safely be discarded. The same applies equally to, say, Catholic Poland or Italy, certainly so in past centuries and more than probably still today. In fact, all the great religions, eager as they have been to conquer popular allegiance, have had to conduct a protracted warfare against, as well as agree to compromise with the old, pre-Christian beliefs of the masses—who were predominantly peasant. In the words of Reinhard Bendix, quoting Max Weber, "Neither the prophet nor the priest can afford to reject all compromise with the traditional beliefs of the masses."[2] The same applies equally to the pre-Christian era, as well as our own, but no doubt to political systems, too.

Considering the deep-seated specific traits of their society, mentality, and culture, city-made and state-imposed Christendom (at least in Russia, in the tenth century) had somehow to be assimilated and become a *muzhik* religion—otherwise it was bound to lose out in the countryside. Historically, this was in fact the way it happened. The church adopted many of the pagan festivals, rites, and rituals and adapted them to its needs and symbols. All rural religions are deeply dependent on magic, and the church was particularly virulent in fighting this expression of heathendom. Yet at the same time the church itself introduced, although in its own form, some of the magic it so bitterly opposed. It did practice, often or occasionally, exorcism, in order to compete with popular healers and quacks; it claimed credit for miracles in order to eliminate magicians; it persecuted witches for having sold their souls to Satan—thus admitting that Satan was active in everyday life and that witchcraft existed, although we know that much of this was officially disavowed from the eighteenth century on.

Be that as it may, the coexistence of the "miracle" (by saints) and magic (by witches [*ved'my*] and sorcerers [*kolduny*]) is an important component of popular religion, in our cultural area and elsewhere, and we can see here a continuation of the historical compromise, this time in the minds and the imagination of the peasants themselves—even if the official church in our century would disagree.

This leads us to another preliminary assumption: the process of adaptation during the compromise certainly worked both ways. The church adapted herself and adopted popular customs in order to rule and to maintain its monopoly over the supernatural and the sacred as defined in its own terms. In turn, the rural world did its part from the other end. They accepted, selectively, the official new creed, but chewed up and transformed many of its elements. The peasants also preserved many components from their own old religion and carried them down through the centuries into our own time in a peculiar symbiosis with official Christendom. Thus, like much else in their life—culture, popular law, social organization—it was a popular religion very much of their own making, a religion they have practiced even into the twentieth century.

▪ THE CHRISTIANITY OF THE *MUZHIK*

The majority of Russian peasants, well into the late 1930s, were Orthodox Christians and said so. The *muzhik*, on the whole, did believe in God and, probably even more, in Christ. Although he was never polled on this question, it is safe to say that deity and Christology were enmeshed in his mind, strongly seconded by the veneration—very special to the Orthodox creed—of Mary, as a kind of supersaint. He accepted the sacraments and was a churchgoer—not for daily services, on the whole, but for the more important holidays, especially Christmas, Easter, and the Pentecost. He also fasted fervently, knew of life after death, and had some hope for salvation, although some claim that this aspect of his creed was not central to him. After all, if salvation depends on heaven, the salutary effects of a rain falling at the right time for crops to succeed could overshadow other blessings. He might have felt differently at the "supreme crisis," when facing death, but here too one expects reactions different from those of other social strata. (We have no exit polls, unfortunately, to be sure about these points.) Peasants also followed, and probably were impressed by much of the ritual and liturgy. Altogether, they had a good deal in common with the church. There are, however, "buts," and many of them.

First, the peasant (except, to some extent, the sectarian, who is not our topic here) knew nothing of dogma; he could not explain many of the church's principles, assuming he ever heard of them, and—quite pertinently when dogma is mentioned—like most, he could not read. But when there are no constraints of dogma, much more freedom is left for the imagination and all kind of deviations. The peasant shared with the church the veneration of icons. They were his Bible. He could not read, so he followed the Biblical stories as depicted on the icons assembled on the iconostasis in the church. At the same time, the icon that was displayed in his hut in the place of honor—the "red" corner above the family table—was also his physical and symbolic link to his ancestors, from whom the icon was inherited, and a shield against adversities. The role of the icon in the peasant's mind is often debated. Some say that it is just a symbol, a Christian symbol; others that it is the real person of the saint, not a symbol but a source of magical protection, pre-Christian in character.

The cults of the saints were also shared with the church. But here, too, a strongly accentuated adoption and adaptation—or, to put it plainly, ruralization—occurred. According to some researchers, many of those saints were local pagan deities appropriately "rebaptized." Perun, the god of lightning and thunder became Elijah—also "responsible" for the same forces of nature. Volos (or Welles) became Saint Vlas. Many other local idols became saints. Saint Nicholas, for example, was both a national saint and a local namesake.

Many of the numerous saints (the Orthodox church has about 300 of them), insistently and predictably were supposed to serve the special needs of a rural constituency, namely, the whole agricultural calendar. A saint patron existed for the most minute agricultural function and action: Vlas was responsible for cattle; Frol and Lavr for horses; Elijah for rain and thunder. Those were some of the national saints. Locally there were other patron saints, such as Peter Polukorn (fodder), Vasilii Kolesnik (wheeler), Irina Rassadnitsa (planter), Ermolai Zapryagal'nik (harnessman), Muchenitsa (the martyr) Paraskeva was patron of flax and yarn and was called, appropriately, a woman's saint (bab'ya svyataya). The list goes on and on.

Thus the peasant's Orthodoxy was a very special rural version of the official creed, as was the parish priest (pop), who came from the peasantry himself and, unlike the Catholic priest, was not very much respected. The wretchedness of the pop was proverbial and their drunkenness notorious. So was their greed, a direct result of their poverty and low level of education.

The peasant often despised the pop and bargained hard over the price of religious services, the main source of the priest's income. Peasants were not generous in either the sacred, or the profane spheres. The priest was often an object of superstitious fears (it could be ominous to stumble upon him in the dark when he was not on duty), but he was welcome to the huts to secure different treby (services) and sacraments as well as to participate in processions around the household, with icons and incense, to protect cattle and the fields against parasites and epidemics.

The pop, who had no fixed salary, depended entirely on his flock. He also squeezed them, if he could, and the flock defended themselves as best they could. But all this did not necessarily diminish their attachment to their faith, even though such a priest could not be powerful enough to solve all the problems befalling a peasant community. The numerous saints did their share better, but they too, probably, had limited power, and it was to be expected that a vigorous and needy social class would look for more support elsewhere to cope with those aspects of life which were out of the church's competence.

Without as yet overstepping the limits of the official faith, the peasant, Pascal suggests, had at his disposal more than just the rural church as his religious forum. His own house, his izba—the focus of his life cycle, the basis of the productive and reproductive family unit—was heavily sacralized and served as the breeding ground for an elaborate mythology. Here was placed the icon, which elevated the hut to a mini-shrine, more potent than and probably of equal status with the chasovni (road shrines) often found at country crossroads. The main ceremonies that related to birth, marriage, and death took place in the hut, and here too was located the cult (or, shall we say, numerous remnants of the cult) of the ancestors, shared, of course, with the local cemetery. This aspect of peasant beliefs was shared only partly with the official church, which celebrated memorial days (*pominki*) and otherwise remembered the dead (who, as a matter of Orthodox dogma, were all included in the church community). But the peasants went well beyond their common ground with the church: they preserved ceremonies and customs from time immemorial. Those were especially prominent in the traditional festivals, which were a real treasury of old pagan rites. Peasants left food for their dead parents after ceremonial meals, "invited" them to come and join them at their table, went to the cemeteries at Easter time to place triple kisses on ancestors' graves (*khristosovat'sya*), offered them *bliny* (ritual food), exchanged thoughts and had chats with them at their graveside. The rural funeral, a solemn ceremony permeated with ancient customs and marked by the heartbreaking laments of relatives or of professional mourners (*plakal'shchitsy*), would normally end later on in monumental feasts in the homes or at the cemeteries, with much heavy drinking for a better and fonder remembrance and to celebrate life.

We know how important the family is in the village. This key institution led all too often so precarious an existence that its survival and well-being could not do without all the support it could marshal. Ancestors, especially parents, certainly could be relied upon as benevolent spirits. And their souls were never too far away from their huts, which they too, somehow, still needed very much. Thus the extended family was actually more extended than met the eye; it included past generations and a network of relations.

This, of course, was already beyond the pale of official teachings. But this "deviation" is only the beginning. Around the *izba* much more was going on than the occasional visit of a defunct parent. In fact, there was a whole population there, in and around the hut, which no census ever counted, all belonging to the kingdom of "evil spirits" or "forces"—*nechistaya sila.*

▪ RURAL DEMONOLOGY

"The priest goes his way, the devil his own" (*pop svoe, chert svoe*), is a common peasant saying. In the countryside the two worlds—the church and the demons—coexisted, each with its own sphere and rules. The peasant, actually believing in both and dealing with both, operated in between these two complicated and opposing poles of their sociomythical system. However, there was more than a simple duality in that religious world. Not just the church versus the Devil but also the church versus the *izba*. The church provided (and accepted) the Devil, and the peasants,

of course, accepted him and his cohorts, too. But the hut—as said before—
was an independent breeding ground of its own mythology, one that co-
incides only very partially with that of the church. In this peasant mythology there are about forty names for various devils and evil and not-so-evil
spirits.

Again, not unlike the saints, these are divided into categories and
functions dictated by the realities of rural life. Thus we find, first, the
house and household spirits, who reside in the house as well as in the
barns and other farm buildings. Among them are the house spirit
(*domovik*) and his spouse (probably), the farm spirit (*dvorovik*), the
bathhouse spirit (*bannik*), and the one in the grain dryer (*ovinnik*).

Next are the spirits causing (and explaining) illnesses, like *kiki-
mora*, who causes widespread female hysteria, called *klikushestvo*, and
the spirits causing different forms of febrility (*tryasukha, likhoradka*).

Finally, there are the spirits from the fields and the natural environment. In the field you find the *poludnitsa*, a female-spirit "active" in the
fields, appearing mainly at midday (hence her name) and very vicious if
she meets anyone. There is also the "specialized" devil of the fields, the
polevik. The forests are the domain of the *lesovik*; the rivers and lakes
shelter the menacing water spirit *vodyanoi*.

On crossroads, especially in the forest, and many other places where
they can meet you alone and at night, a variety of all-purpose devils
(*cherti*) engage in various forms of mischief, misleading people, especially
drunks, of whom they are particularly fond. They also like women, and
as they can transform themselves into almost anything, they come to the
villages and visit all kind of maidens, wives of soldiers, and widows. Many
a pregnancy becomes explainable in this way, but so do ailments and
especially mental illnesses. You had better put two pieces of wood in the
form of a cross on your water receptacle and cross your mouth promptly
after a yawn—they penetrate everywhere, given the chance.

Obviously, these spirits are unseen, and yet so many peasants, somehow,
meet them. The stories of such encounters are legion, not only in folklore
but also in literature and theater, evoking awe and laughter simultaneously.
Relations between the peasants and the mythical population, especially
the *cherti*, are complicated. These devils are a joke and a menace, but this
paradox is only apparent. The peasant was reacting to something very
familiar, something he believed in, was worried about, but also knew
quite well. Devils can be communicated with, not only through spiritual-
ism but in more direct ways. The Devil can be bribed; like most of us, he
is not infallible; he can be placated, persuaded, even frightened off. There
is a whole arsenal of means—Christian and magical—for chasing him
away, and it is all available in amazing, practical detail, like recipes in a
cookbook or a medical prescription: take such and such herbs, say a certain formula three times, put the cross on your back, and so on.

It is interesting that the Devil can be outsmarted. Toward a creature so powerful and so concrete the peasant must develop a sense of combat. The *muzhik* has a self-image like everybody else. He is not learned, but he can be smart. And only he (certainly not the other classes) can outsmart the Devil (as well as representatives of those other classes, all of whom are more powerful than he).

The "evil ones" are numerous. There are swarms of them (*sonmy*). They have servants and families, tails and horns, and their behavior ranges from rather friendly to murderous, with the gamut of nuances in between.

There is also an intermediary category on which we cannot now dwell, people whom devils or sorcerers have transformed into a wolf or other creature, the Russian mythical *oboroten'*, who leads a tragic and frightening existence and is very dangerous.

There are special days in the year when devils are allowed to roam freely everywhere and are very angry. They prey on humans, snatch newborn babies (and substitute a *chertenok*) from mothers who happen to curse the baby when overtaken by pain.

The descriptions of this "population" are so concrete that the saying about the priest and the Devil becomes very clear to us, as is another version of the same saying, which uses the term "God" instead of "priest." Peasants, to my knowledge, believe in God but do not describe him. This means they don't even try to imagine him—they find enough material for their imagination elsewhere.

Considering the massive evidence of the vitality of belief in these various demons, it becomes obvious that the church never succeeded in uprooting this ancient layer of spirits or "lower demonology" (which are somehow related to ancient polytheisms) or in assimilating and thus legitimizing them. Had it tried, it would have had to condone the widespread belief in the "evil eye" (*porcha*), without which the peasant could not explain all kinds of everyday trouble. Telling him that this all resulted from his "sins" would probably be counterproductive.

▪ "OUTCAST SOULS"

The *zalozhyne*, or "outcast souls," are yet another very interesting category of mythological creatures that bring us back to the souls of the ancestors. A serious study published in 1916 by Zelenin, an ethnographer and student of religion, showed that in popular belief the dead, or rather their souls, were divided into two categories, "ancestors" and those who died prematurely of unnatural causes. The latter included children who died before they were christened, people who drowned, and suicides (a particularly reprehensible act in the rural view). The *zalozhyne* were supposedly not accepted by "mother earth," that is, they would not, if buried normally, rot away and would damage crops. They were therefore not buried in the regular way but "put away" into a crevice or swamp, or at least not in any decent burial places.

The problem with these souls was that they would become "evil." That is to say, the "evil ones" (*nechist'*) or devils would take them over to serve as their slave, or courtesan, or wife. Another term for these dead and dead souls (somehow body and soul is not clearly separated in the "evidence" peasants offer on these matters) is *mertvyaki* or *upyri*—ghastly corpses, as pernicious as vampires.

Thus far, this category sounds rather sinister. And it is. These dead have to remain in limbo, somewhere around their unpleasant graves, for as long as it is necessary to use up the balance of time between their premature death and what would have been their normal time of death. What happened next is unclear. The peasants are not certain about this, and neither is the Orthodox church, which does not accept the concept of purgatory but does accept life after death. Only some cases are mentioned of such dead that were salvaged and returned, although rarely, back to the living world. Some of these are prematurely dead children plagued by the unwitting curses of their own mothers. They haunt their families, moan, beg their mothers to save them. Something can perhaps be done, if the demon hasn't yet taken full possession of them. A particularly tragic lot, those lamenting infants.

One special and complicated subcategory of *zalozhnye* is worth singling out: women, old or young, who fall into this category of "irregularly" dead became *rusalki*, water-nymphs who live in rivers and on shores. Although they make us think of mermaids and sirens, they are actually very Slavic, and there is a lot of information about them. They are either young and extremely beautiful (mostly in the south of Russia) or old and ugly. They walk around naked, of course, have big breasts (most sources agree), and are very playful and like to dance and prance, to use tree branches for seesawing. Their beautiful, enchanting voices affect the passer almost fatally, and they like to play with men . . . by tickling them to death. They can do the same to women. When hearing their voices it is best not to respond to them. If one does stumble upon them, it is prudent to draw with one's neck cross a circle around oneself, as large as possible, and not move at all, because the angry *rusalki* will crowd around the circle and throw stones at the irritant. To move in this situation could prove fatal.

The descriptions of these creatures that were collected at the turn of our century (later they began to fade away) were so vivid that researchers hypothesized the *rusalki* to have been rather recent entries into the mythological world (and eventually denied longevity). At the same time, it was clear that the behavior of *rusalki* was like that of rural girls (who, however, did not tickle anyone to death). They were very much alive, and yet daring or lucky people who came close to them and got away with it noticed that their eyes were glazed and fixed. These beauties were *dead,* probably one of the traits of those mythological products endowed with so vivid and detailed a nonexistence.

A special, very ancient festival called *rusal'nitsa*, taking place around the Pentecost complex of holidays (*Troitsa-semik*), is dedicated to accompanying the *rusalki* back to their streams after a time-off on land. The name, incidentally, does not stem from *rusyi* (red or ginger) but from the Latin *rosalia*, the name of a Roman festival. The *rusalki* had red hair in the south but green (and green eyes) in the north of Russia. It is obvious that here was an outlet for peasant sexual fantasies, and one in which girls as well as boys were interested. That they could attract the attention of writers is also quite understandable, and Gogol can be quoted describing the enchanting creatures as the epitome of amorous temptation and feminine attraction. Some Russian ethnographers, too, writing about rural mythology, would inescapably append to their articles a verse by Pushkin in which *rusalki* are featured prominently, dangling on tree branches—their favorite pastime.

▪ MAGIC AND SORCERY

We have examined, as a competent writer put it (Maximov, 1903), the Christian (*krestnaya*) as well as the "evil" (*nechistaya*) force. There remains, however, a third source of beliefs and mythological production: the "mysterious force" (*nevedomaya sila*). This included remnants of the ancient cults based on the veneration of forces of nature (sun, water, wind, storm and the soil) that were heavily present, together with remnants of fertility cults, in the rural festivals, especially in obviously pagan ones like the *maslenitsa* (Shrovetide, end of winter, beginning of spring) or *Ivan Kupala* (summer), as well as in official Christian ones like Easter. In all of them, specialists discern amazingly well-preserved vestiges of the ancient agricultural belief systems, with their Dionysian, orgiastic, phallic elements interposed with later Christian symbols and rites.

If the family dwelling and the village are so heavily populated and surrounded by mythical, yet familiar creatures causing problems to crops, to cattle, and to humans (drought, and famine, fires, illness, especially mental illness, suicides), there is an urgent and obvious need to deal with them. Presumably, the official church and the strictly Christian component of the creed did not satisfy all the demands of rural life and imagination. With so many spirits lurking everywhere trying to block the smooth flow of seasons, tampering with rainfall, interfering with the fertility of women and the soil, remedies could be found at the same old source which begot the demons in the first place. Tilling and sowing and hard labor alone were not enough. Magic was needed, precisely in order to help the seasons flow unhindered, to assure good health to men and cattle, and for all to breed abundantly and to escape the ravages of epidemics.

The use of magic was considered by Weber and others as the trait par excellence of rural religions. We have already seen how peasants adapted many Christian symbols and rites to this purpose, especially the icon, but also candles, processions, and holy water. In addition, they had at their disposal a great choice of their own prescriptions and of the ever present divinations. All the many needs of a peasant household were taken care of by magic rites, formulas, potions, herbs, all helping to find the thief and recover the stolen goods, to assure a successful birth (including that of domestic animals), to protect the newlywed (and everyone else) from the "evil eye," to preserve the family from ominous influences that a corpse in the house awaiting funeral could create. All the stages of the cycles of nature and of life required protection.

It was unthinkable that peasants could engage in such intense magical activity without "professional" help. They had no choice but to appeal, albeit very reluctantly and fearfully, to the sorcerer or the witch (ved'ma), fearsome, mean creatures who were the heirs to the ancient magicians and shamans. Only an evil eye cast by them could explain why a cow's udder suddenly dried out, or why a young girl began to languish, and only another sorcerer could undo the mischief one of his kind had wrought.

The strength of the sorcerer was shown by his ability to operate magic, an ability one could possess only at a price. In order to acquire such powers they had to sell their souls to the Devil and thus become themselves part of the nechist' (demonic world). And the price they paid was indeed terrible: protracted and painful agony before dying (described in great detail by numerous informers); becoming zalozhnye after their death (and hence, no decent burial, with all the consequences this entailed); numerous outbursts of peasant wrath against the sorcerers (who would be crudely mobbed on such occasions; from the eighteenth century on, the church—and the state—forbade this as "an act of superstition" and hence criminally punishable).

But more often than attacking them, peasants used the sorcerer's and witch's services widely, as well as those of more benign alternatives—healers (znakhari), fortunetellers (vorozhiki), and diviners (gadalki). Networks of such practitioners, competing to some extent with the church, were widespread in the rural world, which produced religious and semireligious figures of other types, too. Out of the countryside came a plethora of wanderers (stranniki), saintly hermits and elders (startsy, who were sometimes acknowledged but often ignored by the church), and the very intriguing figure of the "God's fool" (yurodivyi), an interesting and picturesque personality of Russian national and religious life that became part of folklore, art, history, and belief. In addition, the world of the sects produced a plethora of "Jesuses" and "Marys" and all kinds of prophets and other religious leaders, all testifying to the significant fact that the religious life of the Russian peasantry was richer and more complex than is sometime realized.

▪ A MAGICO-RELIGIOUS AMALGAM?

The term "dual faith" (*dvoeverie*) may, after all, be misleading. Given the coexistence in the Russian rural religious universe of different subsystems, all equally interesting and most very ancient, one would do better to talk of a *system* of antipodes, not just "pagan versus Christian" but also "church versus the *izba*," "miracle versus (or complemented by) magic," "Orthodox versus Christian anti-Orthodox," and more. Influences from Asia, the Classical world, the Middle Ages, the modern world, old Slavonic creeds, and Manichaean and Cathar and other old heresies all converged in shaping this rural religion. The peasantry absorbed them and preserved them, chewed them up or "lost" them, sometimes only temporarily, for they always left traces in the popular cultural treasury, a living museum and a laboratory of cultural and religious synthesis and innovation. We remember the main "subsystems" described earlier: the Christian one, heavily "ruralized," as we have shown; the Orthodox and anti-Orthodox versions, some even anti-Christian; the elaborate demonology, the *nechistaya sila*, in a specific conjunction with remnants of the cult of the ancestors, as well as the subcategory of the "outcast souls" and remnants of cults of fertility and other forces of nature, all put to good use through the working of either the miracle or the less saintly forms of magic.

Even if some of these components were rudimentary and already on the wane in our century, they were present, and, whether in full force or on the wane, they contributed to the web of beliefs still in actual use. What remains unclear is whether we can talk here of "a religious system" or of coexisting, and quite different structures and disjointed elements. Do we have here basically a Christian system (Orthodox), tinged with the unavoidable dose of "superstition"? Or, perhaps, a basically pagan creed with a Christian veneer?

The first proposition has many adherents, who sometimes offer an additional argument that the Orthodox church, more than the Catholic, is a popular religion in its own right. Many factors argue in favor of this interpretation: the "communality" (*sobornost'*) of this church; the rural character of its parish clergy; the prevalence of liturgy over dogma in Orthodoxy; the preponderance (or, at least, equal standing) of the icon over written texts. Such students would ignore the rich demonology and relegate most of the non-Christian elements (we think they were more than "elements") to the realm of "superstition," a term which would evoke sharp criticisms from other scholars who would claim that, if one uses it, one had better stop studying religion at all.

Provisionally, I would abstain from claiming to make an "interpretation," of the material at hand and would group the popular religions of the Russian peasantry into three streams. First of these are the sects, who in the early 1920s had millions of adherents, are here lumped in one "stream," although they exhibited a great variety of creeds, from Protestant of several denominations to the non-Christian "Sabbatarians." Second, the Christian Orthodox church in its ruralized version could be called a popular religion in its own right, and many peasants adhered to just this approach.

The third stream, the most widespread still in the early decades of this century, is the *popular creed*, which interests us here: a unified construct, felt and practiced by the peasants as one system. Despite the seemingly conflicting polarities that analysis can discern, *chert* and *pop* (priest and the devil), church and hut, miracle and magic, the Holy Trinity and the multitude of spirits and demons were quite tightly knit in a cultural-religious synthesis expressing the age-old traditions and interests of a rural community and class. A changing but still distinct agricultural civilization (undestroyed as yet by industrial and urban development) was weaving its beliefs from a variety of often very ancient roots, deeply modified by Christianity but again remodified by peasant life and imagination.

We can thus call this religion "rural Christianity," which, not unlike rural Islam, is essentially an amalgam of Christian symbolism welded onto a bedrock of an old agricultural civilization. The fact that this civilization could withstand crises and upheavals can be attributed not to one particular institution, such as the church (although it played its role) but to various factors inherent in the social reality of the village itself, with its powerful mechanisms of conflict resolution and solidarity, neighbor and family networks, which act as very efficient socializers, and the family itself, supported by its ancestors and by its household spirits (*domovye*), all trying hard to cope with, placate, and outsmart the legions of *nechist'* swarming between the hut and the church.

Such an amalgam does create what some Russians call "the existential religion" (*bytovaya*), meaning the one which emerges from and merges with the crucial functions of everyday life and helps explain its longevity. I would add, to strengthen this last point, that peasant women, with their special role in and around the family household, were and continue to be the (sometimes sole) carrier and mainstay of this rural Christianity and ensure its vitality.

But the official church can in this context be dispensed with, and peasants can fall back on other resources when they find the church wanting or persecuted and when the churches are being closed. It is so with peasant societies in most spheres of life. When in crisis or under pressure, they can retreat into their own shell, opt out of the "larger society", ensconce themselves in their own "world" (*mir*), which has at its disposal a self-contained economy, a system of law, and a religion. This potential of the traditional peasantry is always feared by rulers and intellectuals, and with good reason. The peasants can effect a retreat from the market economy through the "naturalization" of their needs; turn away from the official world of culture, of courts and tax assessors, and back to a more primitive stage. It could indeed be a catastrophic course, both the cause and result of some social cataclysm.

In such or similar circumstances, the home shrine, the magic, and the mythology are sufficient to preserve the present religious integrity without, or against, the official church. At such times their own religion can offer what religions are supposed to offer: the spiritual resources to compensate for deficiencies of material life; solace and support in times of crisis and catastrophe when religious feelings are heightened in the effort of survival; the strength needed to cope with individual life-cycle dramas. The supernatural forces available, sacred or evil or both, will come to play their role and supply additional symbolic resources when it is necessary to fight the state or the combined forces of church and state. Russian peasants did produce, and use, powerful mythical mobilizers when engaging in a contest with the state, and this left an indelible memory in the consciousness of every ruler of Russia. The obvious example is the revolt of the "Old Believers" (seventeenth century), who challenged the state and *its* church as manifestations of the Antichrist and the emperor as the Antichrist in person.

At this point, namely as we mention a powerful religious symbol used by dissidents to mobilize believers against the emperor, the political aspects of popular religious beliefs—their eventual impact on political events and, deeper, on the political culture of the state itself—comes to mind. It is in fact a major and highly intriguing problem to which we will keep returning, especially in the last chapters of this book. But much more is in store for the adventurous researcher—and some younger ones have already begun to explore this intricate field.

3

CUSTOMARY LAW AND
RURAL SOCIETY
IN THE
POSTREFORM ERA

The answer to vexing questions concerning the juridical practices of Russian peasants—even questions of a narrowly juridical character—are to be sought first of all in social institutions and the fabric of everyday life. To be sure, juridical systems have a momentum of their own, but it remains sluggish and diffuse until the judiciary, jurists, and legal theories acquire a widely recognized autonomy. The Russian peasantry did not reach this stage before the revolution or for some time thereafter. Peasants in Russia, like their counterparts at comparable historical stages elsewhere, did have customs that could qualify as "juridical," but they did not reason abstractly or produce treatises about them and were never allowed to work out a full-fledged system and live according to its precepts. So it is in the practices of daily life, in *byt*, that we must seek an understanding of customary law (*obychnoe pravo*) or the law of the common people (*narodnoe pravo*).

For the period between the abolition of serfdom and the collectivization of agriculture, we can apply to Russia Redfield's conception of "the little community" and "the big community."[1] Paradoxically, the immense majority of the nation lived in the "little" community, while the "big" embraced the powerful minority—the ruling classes, the cities, and the state. Redfield's distinction reminds us that rural society is isolated, with its own attributes, setting it apart from the religion, economy, art, and mentality characteristic of the national state and metropolitan culture.

Moral codes and the institutions and customs used for resolving conflicts in the village were also distinctive. Hence we are justified in viewing rural society as a system, as a "nation class."

Yet pushing this point too far could lead to fallacies: either to an 'idealization" or to a global negation, even hatred (which is another way of idealizing). Both kinds of fallacy generate misconceptions of processes and factors of change that operate in rural society. Villagers were bombarded by cultural shifts, fashions, economic trends, and all kinds of pressures from the state. Many of these were forces for dissolution, but some produced powerful opposition and served to solidify the little community, which, as long as there is life in it, reacts by assimilating, distorting, or rejecting pressures from without. It is the interplay of the "little" and the "big," the degree of communication and integration between them, that decides the fate of rural society as well as of the social and political system as a whole.

▪ OBYCHNOE PRAVO—YES OR NO?

By 1861 the rural world, although potentially menacing, seemed to educated observers like a rather uniform, primitive, dark agglomerate; all that mattered then was "to emancipate," to induce appropriately controlled change. In practice this meant (1) to emancipate the peasants before they emancipated themselves; (2) to make them render redemption payments and taxes; (3) to prevent their proletarianization; and (4) to defend them from the still overwhelming power of the *pomeshchiki* (landholders), which might de facto re-enserf them. To achieve these goals it was deemed necessary to insulate peasants from other classes by a bulwark of special peasant institutions and state institutions created for them.

This was a mixed bag of intentions, and the results were mixed, too: a legal construction which segregated peasants into a separate estate of the realm (*soslovie*), blending tutelage from above with self-administration, and manifesting, within a coercive structure, an apparent respect for the specifics of the peasants' way of life.[2]

Without entering into the details of this complex system or its evolution, we can single out some more important components of the post-emancipation rural order:

1. The *nadel*, or allotment of land. Taken from the holdings of the squire (or the state, in the case of state peasants), it was at once bestowed upon and imposed upon the peasants, so as to ensure their subsistence and assure the flow of revenues to the state.
2. A system of rural self-administration, at the village and canton (volost) levels, capped, as of 1889, with an extra element of tutelage in the form of the land captains (*zemskie nachal'niki*).

3. Village society (*sel'skoe obshchestvo*), the lowest level of peasant self-administration. Sometimes the boundaries of village society corresponded to those of the commune (*obshchina*); sometimes they included several communes, or parts of communes, according to the pattern of manorial landholding that had prevailed prior to 1861.[3]

4. Special village courts, with the judges initially elected by the village assembly (*skhodka*), later selected by the land captain.[4]

5. These courts, and some higher ones, were empowered by statute or by decisions of the Senate to follow customary law (*obychnoe pravo*) or, according to some texts, simply "custom" (*obychai*). The jurisdiction of the cantonal courts (*volostnye sudy*) embraced the bulk of civil conflicts and criminal cases in rural Russia, with only murder and some other serious crimes excluded.[5]

6. Finally, an elaborate network of informal institutions—elders, neighbors, families—would arbitrate and adjudicate most of the flow of human dealings that needed such intervention: problems involving the inheritance or redistribution of land, contracts, offenses of various kinds, conflicts within and between families, and even moral transgressions.[6]

Thus, the rural world was subjected to a double system of statutory law applicable to peasants only (*krest'yanskoe pravo*) and unwritten, customary law. The government's preoccupation with the peasants' obligations to the state caused a constant increase of controls and strictures imposed on the peasants and on their institutions, until the problems created by this system of fetters engendered its erosion and, from 1905, its piecemeal dismantlement. Even in 1917, however, much of the postemancipation settlement was still in place, notably the allotment as an obligation and the *obshchestvo* as institution of self-administration serving also as a government agency charged with collecting taxes and dues and controlling the peasants' movements and land use. Before the Stolypin reforms, allotment land could not be sold unless redeemed, and even redeemed allotments could not be sold to nonpeasants. Leasing was also forbidden, although realities were often stronger, in this sphere, than the official rules. Concommitantly, peasants could not refuse allotment land, and they could not leave the village without the permission of the *obshchestvo*—and later also without the approval of the head of the household. Redemption payments and taxes that were collected according to the principle of mutual responsibility (*krugovaya poruka*), ascription, and the passport—these and other elements made up the complex of constraints that replaced bondage to the *pomeshchiki*. Under Peter the Great, peasants were *glebae adscripti*; they became *domino adscripti* under Catherine II. After the emancipation they were enmeshed in a triple harness: the *obshchestvo*, state officialdom, and the fetters associated with the patriarchal family system. Bear in mind that until 1903 peasants were the only estate of the realm that was still subject to punishment by flogging and that most rural officials, although nominally elected, were entirely dependent on and subservient to the land captain. A growing number of enactments enlarged the sphere of peasants' rights, but many traits of this special regime, including many that the peasants themselves felt as discriminatory, persisted until the revolution of 1917.

▪ DEBATES AND STUDIES, 1880–1914

Within the framework of this complicated system of limitations and controls, peasants could live according to their own customary law. What was this customary law?

The Editorial Commission drafted the reform legislation of 1861, in which respect for customary law was embedded, but the members of the commission did not know what this law was. Research in the domain was very scanty at that time. In time, the results of research would be quite impressive. For the moment, however, the legislators gave the peasants something with the intention of finding out later just what it was.

Alexandra Efimenko was the pioneer investigator of customary law.[7] Kistyakovskii and Orshanskii followed her lead. The Lyuboshchinskii Committee conducted a massive survey on the functioning of the cantonal courts. Pakhman, in turn, drew on the work of this committee in his magisterial two-volume study. Yakushkin produced four installments of a bibliographical guide to customary law, with valuable commentaries. Ethnographic expeditions, notably those sponsored by Count Tenishev's "ethnographic office," helped to expand existing knowledge. Further contributions were made by able jurists like Leont'ev, Khauke, Meiendorf, and Druzhinin, and by writers like Kachorovskii drawing on government surveys, especially by the Witte Commission's committees, with 11,000 participants, including officials, landowners, and some peasants.[8] The study of customary law had become a booming trade.

The result was a debate, indeed, one of the big controversies in Russian political and intellectual history. It was part and parcel of the larger debate over the "peasant question," but less known because of its intricate juridical and technical aspects.

Leont'ev, author of two excellent books in the field and also of a survey of the controversy itself, explained why the topic was so important. The bulk of the nation lived in two, not always compatible realms of written law and unwritten customs. Without a proper understanding of the two realms and their interaction one could do much harm.[9] Kachorovskii showed what kind of damage was or could be done when the state promulgated laws in disregard of the peasants' interests and views. The most common outcome was that peasants simply disregarded such laws (if they even knew of their existence). The laws and rules concerning division of households provided a good example: peasants kept dividing and subdividing as they saw fit, law or no law.[10]

Those among participants in the debate who recognized the importance of customary law would depict, often in eloquent, even majestic terms, an impressive structure of popular law; they emphasized its praiseworthy ethical basis. Kistyakovskii, for example, called on educated Russians to learn from the *narod* such presumed traits of its legal practice as informality, attention to details of human life and activity, and a pervading sense of basic justice.[11]

Not everyone was so carried away, but many writers held that popular law was deeply enmeshed in the fabric of peasant society and that its special institutions and customs had no equivalent among other social groups and often no counterpart in the official civil and criminal codes. Underlying the practice of popular law was a perception of a specific legal order (*pravoporyadok*) which found expression in ways the commune and the peasant household handled problems concerning land, the division of homesteads, economic and social conflicts, and relations within the family. Efimenko felt one could discern an overriding principle that guided such decisions, the principle that labor and labor alone was the source of rights to the use and enjoyment of property. Kachorovskii elaborated upon her discovery.[12] To the *pravo truda*, or right of labor, he added *pravo na trud*, or right to labor. These two principles supposedly regulated many aspects of peasants' life but also complicated their social and legal practices as well as their political views, for the two principles were complementary but also contradictory.

Many authors agreed that some kind of "labor principle" operated in peasant life and guided customary legal practices,[13] but Kachorovskii's construct was particularly interesting. The right of labor postulated that land should be in the hands of the person who tilled it, and this meant that the squire (*pomeshchik*) did not hold his land rightfully. In addition, the same principle actually guided decisions concerning the disposition of the assets of a household by inheritance, division, or separation and also concerning various kinds of tort.[14]

The right to labor was more complicated. From it followed every family's primordial right to exist and to subsist. In the village, this could mean only one thing: the right to a land allotment as the means of subsistence. Where land shortage prevailed, the right to labor reinforced the drive, generated by the right of labor, to expropriate the *pomeshchik*. It was also, however, the source of the mechanism of redistribution of land by the commune and of the persistence of the repartitional commune with its associated low-yield, three-field system.

The contradictions between the two principles flowed from the fact that the right to labor imbued the peasantry with a solidarity and a penchant for collectivism, while the right of labor, which seemed so menacingly radical to the *pomeshchiki*, imparted an individualistic, almost capitalistic spirit—or at best a narrow group-ownership mentality.[15] So if the one principle led to the stubbornly maintained utopia of a "black repartition" (a social and political vision that the Social Revolutionaries made the basis of their "socialization" program), the other nourished the trend toward the noncommunal family farmstead (*khutor*), on which the regime began to pin its hopes after 1905.

Whatever the underlying principles of popular law, a number of authors urged that it must be preserved and warned against the premature and artificial imposition of state codes. Leont'ev and others even proposed improving popular law by codifying it, as with other systems of law in the early stages of their development.

However, the opponents of those who idealized popular law had much to say.[16] They observed, for example that rural customs were often simply barbaric—lynching thieves, parading unfaithful wives naked through the village, and much worse; that the cantonal court was a shambles, its judges were illiterate, drunken, and corrupt, and its decisions derived not from peasant mores but from the clerk (*pisar'*), who simply invented "customs" according to his whims; that many peasants said (and indeed they did), *U nas obychaev netu* (We have no customs);* that, if there were any customs, they never extended beyond the limits of one village. In short, these critics charged that the admirers of the supposed system of popular justice and law were dreaming. Witte even stated that the whole structure of popular law was built by Pakhman (and borrowed from him by others) on the flimsy basis of the Lyuboshitskii Committee's investigations in the late 1860s and early 1870s and that that inquiry had blatant weaknesses.[17]

So, these critics charged, there was no such thing as customary law. Indeed, how could such a system have emerged under serfdom, where the peasants' practices hung on the squire's arbitrary will (*proizvol*)? Whatever patterns and practices emerged in the servile village—including the hallowed principle of land redistribution—were created by the state with a view to maintaining the *tyaglo* (unit of taxation) or they were imposed by the squires. And all this was now to be abolished, together with every remnant of *soslovnost'*. Peasants should participate in the general system of law, which alone is capable of securing for them a legal order and equality of rights with others. Until they did, the bulk of the nation would continue to live in plain anarchy, a primeval lawlessness where no rights could be secure, or even understood. The price was fetters on the individual, impediments to productivity, and harm to the nation.

There was enough in this line of criticism to make one gasp. But there were fissures, too. Witte showed a sign of hesitation. If, he said, some viable customs do exist, we know nothing about them; a big research effort is necessary to establish what they are. But he felt he knew in ad-

---

* It would be frivolous to take at face value the statement "We have no customs," except for times of turmoil and strife, provided one appreciates that many customs which could be classified as "juridical" cannot be nearly separated from ethical and religious views.

vance what such an effort would show. Druzhinin, for his part, charged that the "idealizers," without even noticing it, drew their conclusions solely from regions where state peasants predominated. These peasants had never been serfs, he argued, and therefore juridical customs might indeed have emerged in their midst.[18] Indeed, if state peasants had really been "free," then more than half of the rural population could and did develop at least some juridical notions of its own. And Yakushkin contended that the serfs on *obrok* (money dues, as opposed to labor on the demesne) had been allowed to live and work very much as they wished, so that they, too, could have taken on juridical customs.[19]

The eminent jurist Khauke claimed that any peasant custom is *eo ipso* particularistic—it cannot but be local—and both the idealizers and the gainsayers were barking up the wrong tree.[20]

Leont'ev, one of the advocates of popular law, was well aware of the shortcomings of the peasants' rules of conduct. According to him, the critics were right: there was no peasant customary law. But they also were dead wrong, because there was, and had to be, something else instead. Peasants did not understand fixed abstract norms, and the rules that prevailed among them could not be valid on a national scale. (To be sure, Muslims did have such a system, shared through the reiteration of hundreds of juridical sayings that their judges knew by heart). What Russian peasants did have were juridical views (*yuridicheskie vozzreniya*). These expressed the conditions of their life, they were fairly widespread, and in their basic elements of they were quite uniform. These views had to be respected, studied and codified before they died out.[21]

This formulation is persuasive. Taking it as a point of departure, we could trace these "views" to the basic village institutions. If these institutions were indeed similar in essence, or limited in their variation, then their juridical expressions, even though infinitely varying in detail from one locality to another, would be correspondingly consistent.

To come nearer to a better understanding of customary law, the basic peasant institutions have to be studied and scrutinized: first the commune (*obshchina*, as opposed to the *sel'skoe obshchestvo*), an object of heated controversy; then the peasant household (*dvor*), a topic of great complexity which mainly concerned specialists; finally, family relations within the household and practices of succession and inheritance, which present a tangle in their own right.

▪ THE RURAL COMMUNE AND *LAPTI* SOCIALISM

The reform legislation of 1861 made the commune the legal recipient of allotment land* and the representative of the peasants in matters of all kinds. The functions of the commune were correspondingly broad and

* Except in those areas where household tenure was firmly established.

various: managing the common enterprises, distributing and redistributing plowlands and meadows, resolving conflicts, building bridges, and fulfilling some welfare functions. The picture was complicated by the administrative, fiscal, and police functions imposed by the state. The commune was answerable for taxes and other obligations, under the system of mutual responsibility—an onerous burden and a stranglehold on the commune and on the freedom of its members.

But most researchers agree that the essence of the commune was redistribution of land among the households. The commune did not plow, sow, or reap; it managed the landholding system. But was the commune the owner of the land? The answer turns out to be tricky. Different property regimes prevailed for different categories of land: one for allotments, another for pasture and other common lands, a third for lands purchased by the commune, and yet another for the *usad'ba*, the household plot.[22]

Let us return to the land granted to the commune for distribution among its households. Was this land the property of the commune or of the household? The commune had no right to deprive a household of its allotment provided there were no significant arrears of taxes and dues. And if the household redeemed its allotment, it could shift from communal to household tenure (*podvornoe vladenie*). Hence many authorities held that the household was the owner of the allotment land. There were counterarguments, however. Even when the village adopted the household-tenure system, the commune did not disappear. More important, it was the commune that received the land—the household did not have any defined share of the commune's assets, as real owners would. The commune had the right to prevent the household from renouncing its allotment, and the household had no right to refuse land. It could simply surrender the allotment and leave, but then the land would remain in the hand of the commune, without compensation. And the commune as a whole could impose a shift to household tenure, if it so wished. On the basis of these considerations, some concluded that the land was the property of the commune and that the rights of the household essentially derived from membership in the commune.

Scholars contended back and forth.[23] What did the peasants say? They often said nothing, but acted *skopom* (en masse) and said that this was how peasants acted. Sometimes they could be heard to say, "*Zemlya mirskaya*" (The land is the commune's), and they stuck by the commune until economic trends and government policies undermined communes to such an extent that interests and opinions split among the peasants as they would among their betters in similar circumstances. There ensued a conflict, sometimes bitter, between the *mir* and the *khutor*, between two different social, economic and juridical systems, each of which mirrored historical trends working through rural societies everywhere.

The key function of the commune was the redistribution of land. This was done either according to the amount of labor power in the household or according to the number of mouths—*po edokam.* The decisions were made by the village assembly, an extremely interesting institution, which baffled observers. It acted amid an indescribable hullabaloo, with everyone shouting, cursing, and yelling. "A travesty!" said its detractors. Its defenders rejoined that peasants do not know of procedural niceties, but insiders understand what the shouting is about. Suddenly, the brouhaha would end, and the decision was taken. The complex job of carrying out the redistribution would now proceed with a high degree of precision.[24]

To understand how complex it all was, it is worth saying a few words about this distribution. A three-field system is based on common grazing on the stubble and on the fallow. Hence the strips cultivated by particular households could not be fenced off, because animals and people had to pass freely; hence also every household had to follow the same agricultural regimen, to sow the same crop at the same time. Plowland was allocated in narrow strips, so narrow that at times a harrow could pass along on one side only. A household would have a number of strips, often at some distance one from another. Why were these strips so scattered, so numerous, and so narrow? What was the rationale of this exiguous system? It was the imperative of scrupulous justice observed during the redistribution of land. The commune's lands differed in quality, location, shape, grade, distance from the village. Each of the three fields would be subdivided into blocks (*yarusy*) of more or less equal quality, and each block would be subdivided into "shares" (*doli*)—as many as there were "mouths" in the village. Thus the household with five "mouths" would get five such shares in each block. Suppose there were five blocks in each of the three fields; a household would get, for the sake of justice, fifteen widely dispersed strips, many of them quite narrow. In practice, there could be forty or more strips—seekers for equality measured with so small a rod that some intellectuals derisively called the result *lapti* socialism.

When demographic development caused changes in the composition of some households, the commune would arrange for periodic partial readjustments (*svalki i navalki*), taking strips from some and giving them to others, until a new general redistribution, which the law permitted only once every twelve years—that is, under the three-field system, once in four crop rotations.

This complicated system hampered agricultural progress—who would fertilize or otherwise improve his land with redistribution hanging over his head?—and perpetuated primitivism. Such at least was the prevailing opinion of agronomists. Some knowledgeable people argued that the problem was not the commune but factors like taxation, the price of land, and insufficient agronomic instruction. They could point to cases when communes introduced four-field cultivation and sowed fodder crops. Still others saw the commune as progressive as long as the three-field system was still necessary but held both had become obsolete by the turn of the century.[25]

According to answers given to this question, opinions split about the attitude to be taken toward the commune: to preserve and develop it; to destroy it; to let die naturally without administrative pressure, for the sake of social peace with the peasants. Such were the options.

After forty-five years of tenaciously upholding the commune, the government opted for its destruciton in order to undo the harm supposedly caused by this institution: constraint on able and enterprising peasants and the inculcation of disrespect for the rights of private property. The latter objection was perfectly valid. The reform of 1861 did nothing to foster attachment to private property among peasants, and postemancipation policies did little.* It was only with the Stolypin reforms that the state attempted to create a large class of peasant private farmers and tried to impart to the peasantry a respect and a desire for private ownership. Even the richer members of the *mir* had often shared the view that land is no one's property and belongs to those who till it and hence that land should be distributed equally among peasant households. This view correspond exactly to Kachorovskii's "right of labor" and "right to labor." It did not favor the selling or buying of "nobody's [God's] land" or the use of hired labor. If all this was true, then the bulk of the Russian peasantry—despite Lenin's worries that the countryside was "producing capitalism every day, every hour"—was actually rejecting capitalism, and perhaps rejecting the twentieth century as well, as long as the *pomeshchiki* still held their estates.

When Stolypin began his "revolution from above," some 70–90 percent of peasant families and peasant land (the western provinces excluded) were on communal tenure. By 1916 or 1917, 25–27 percent were rather firmly anchored in other forms of tenure, but the commune had survived.[26] Obviously, the reform came too late. Probably both scholars and government authorities misread the seeming "extinction" of many communes. When a commune did not carry out a redistribution for a long period, observers tended to see its communal spirit fading away, the right-to-labor principle dying out, and ownership being vested de facto in the heads of household. But other observers warned that such conclusions were unwarranted. Things might have been brewing, as in a volcano, inside many of the "extinguished" communes, with the richer peasants resisting a new redistribution, the poorer ones pressing for one. Although calm for a time, the commune could and often did begin suddenly to move, like a hill of ants, after one of those noisy *skhody*. And in 1917 and 1918 there was such movement on a national scale, when something like a "supercommune" suddenly came to life, straight from the old utopia.

---

* There was, to be sure, a disposition toward family farms and hereditary tenure in regions where communes were few or did not exist and even in sections of provinces where communal tenure predominated.

▪ THE HOUSEHOLD AND THE FAMILY

The household (*dvor*) was as complex as the commune and replicated many of its traits. It was a unit of production, holder (through the commune) of allotment land, vessel of ownership, and focal point of family life. Researchers noted that according to concepts traced to customary law and upheld, although hesitantly, by the Senate:

1. The assets of the household were the "common property of the family."
2. More particularly, added some specialists, this was artel-type property, not unlike the holdings of a corporation. Included were not only relatives by blood, but other workers adopted into the family, while family members who had lived elsewhere for a considerable time were excluded. Such an "artel" was based as much on the right of labor as on kinship.
3. Succession through testament was inapplicable to this type of ownership, further complicated by the fact that the household's allotment land was communal, in most cases, and subject to periodic redistribution.
4. Implements and buildings were "common," however, and certain types of property were indeed private and could be handled like any other private property.
5. The household was headed by a *bol'shak*, most usually the father, but he was not the owner of the *dvor*. He must act with the consent of the co-owners, the other adult members of family. They shared in the whole entity without any rights to specific parts, until the time of division (*razdel*), which would occur at the death of the *bol'shak*, if then.

All these conceptions were hotly debated. Many objected to definition of the household as an artel-like family association and held that it made no sense to invent democratic-sounding institutions when it was plain that the head of the household was the real boss (which he undoubtedly was) and also the real owner (which he was not). The *bol'shak* wielded extraordinary powers, as was to be expected in a deeply patriarchal system, and he was noted for his use and abuse of his right to beat his wife or any other member of the household without mercy. How then could one deny he had the rights of ownership?

These were good questions, but there were some countervailing facts. If the family boiled over in turmoil or if the *bol'shak* was particularly incompetent or idle, the commune could replace him with another member of the family. He could not bequeath the household's assets. He could, if he wished, write a will, or make his wishes known orally, but his will would apply only to his personal belongings. After his death, the household would remain in the hands of the same family under a new head—his son, his brother, or, very rarely, his widow. Alternately, the assets of the household would be divided among its members. These modalities were pure customary law, not covered by the civil code, and subject to considerable variation from place to place. In small families, the father as *bol'shak* acted to all intents and purposes like an owner, but after his death there was an artel. And instead of a division, there could be a split (*vydel*), whereby a person or a couple got a part of the household's assets and went off on their own. This could happen when the elder was still alive and with his, sometimes unenthusiastic, consent—and the whole affair was governed solely by customary law.[27]

Thus the problem of locating ownership within the household is similar to the question of ownership within the commune, for the *dvor* was part of the *obshchina* and shared some of its essence and some of its ambiguities. These ambiguities derived from the heavy external pressures upon both and the conflict within each between communal and artel-like principles, on the one hand, and tendencies toward individualism and private ownership, on the other.

▪ THE FAMILY

Introducing the family makes the picture even more exciting. Rural families were undergoing a transformation from the big complex family— almost a mini-commune in itself—through a smaller complex family (parents, children, and at least one lateral member, such as a married brother) that prevailed around the turn of the century, to the small nuclear family that prevails today. This transition brought momentous changes in rural life. Our present concern is primarily with the big and the smaller complex forms, which dominated the rural scene well into this century.

In such families, in addition to the power of the *bol'shak*, mentioned above, we must also consider the awesome power of the mother-in-law. Her power explains why rural girls, desiring marriage, also feared it. Peasant girls saw service under the redoubtable *svekrov'* (mother-in-law) as akin to slavery. This was particularly true in big families where the *svekrov'* ruled literally with an iron rod over several daughters-in-law (*nevestki*), seeing them as a menace to her position. The fight over the oven prongs (*ukhvat*) and the dough (*kvashnya*) was a real struggle for power, and the *svekrov'* was determined to keep control over the stove and the food. Her husband, on the other hand, kept a watchful eye over the purse (*koshel'*) especially when outside earnings provided income to younger sons and brothers and temptations for them to hide some of it.

This fight over *ukhvat, kvashnya,* and *koshel'* was no minor affair.[28] It created enormous tensions, cleavages, enmities, and powerful incentives for adult sons and their wives to press for separation from the household. In addition to the clashes between father and son and the *svekrov'– nevestki* power play, there also was the problem of the *bol'shak's* sexual advances on the daughters-in-law, or *snokhachestvo*.[29] All these could make the position of younger sons or brothers, and especially their wives, quite intolerable.

If we project these internal tensions onto the broader canvas of the commune, we can see internal and external contradictions joining forces to enhance the centrifugal tendencies which operated simultaneously within the commune and within its constituent families. There was a potential for conflict between the commune and the heads of household, many of whom pressed for more independence from the commune and for shifting from a communal to a household tenure system. This trend had its parallel inside the family, where *bol'shaki* sought to do away with *artel'*-type ownership and make the whole *dvor* their private property. These people were not acquainted with Roman concepts of property rights, they were responding to a combination of market pressures and demographic trends. It took the agrarian revolution of 1917–20 to stem, for a time, these centrifugal forces.

Consideration of the position of women within the household will further illuminate these intricate trends. Women, probably including the *bol'shukha* (or *svekrov'*) herself, were a kind of underclass—not a comfortable position for a member of a class which was itself the object of discrimination. The oppression of younger women was real and it was threefold: by the husband, by the *svekor* (or *bol'shak*), and by the *svekrov'*. Before marriage, girls were protected by their mothers, although child-rearing methods in the village were tough. The mother's protection often continued after the daughter's marriage, if the mother could manage it.

The shift to a nuclear family wrought important changes in this state of affairs, but these changes were still well ahead. In the meantime, some old habits were dying slowly. Within the *dvor*, women did not have the right to inherit upon the death of their father or husband, unless they were widows with children, and then only thanks to these children. Other old customs, to be sure, held some advantage for them. A woman had the right to her own *korob'*, which was composed of a dowry (prepared by herself before her marriage), her *kladka* (gifts from her fiancé and her mother), and personal earnings, to which all women had an exclusive right in most rural areas (a part of the flax and income from weaving and from other work on the side). These bits and pieces sheltered the women somewhat in time of distress, and they could bequeath the *korob'* to their daughters. We are not dealing with economically significant quantities except in one case: when a young husband managed to hide some of the money he had earned away from the village, on *otkhod* (seasonal labor). Such sums, together with the *korob'*, would feed the young couple's ambitions to leave the husband's parents and found their own household. The newly discovered ability to make money, coupled with support from his wife and exhaustion from the big family's quarrels, might induce a young man to break up the whole family artel.[30] Heads of household and state legislation tried for a long time to stem the trend toward this kind of independence, but the trend proved irrepressible.

One point from the Stolypin legislation is relevant here. With the stroke of a pen, Stolypin ended the dispute about who owned the assets of the household. The law now declared that once a household passed out of the commune, rights of ownership were solely in the hands of the *bol'shak*. This enactment was supposed to clarify the tangle of property relations that had prevailed and to inculcate a healthy devotion to the rights of private property and perhaps an ardor for its acquisition.[31] Some observers speculated that this legal revolution—the de jure expropriation of sons and brothers—could have incalculable social consequences. They probably were right.

▪ CAN HISTORY ITSELF ANSWER ITS QUESTIONS?

A resolution of the debates and problems that emerge from an examination of customary law and the social fabric in which it was embedded will require further sophisticated research. The literature is rich, and it is thick with question marks. A glance at events after 1917 may show that the same questions concerning the commune and the household were clarified by what happened during the agrarian revolution and the NEP, although this clarification often generated a host of new questions.

Was the commune a genuine *muzhik* institution, or was it essentially foisted on the peasants by the state? Was household landholding private or "common"—at least in the eyes of the peasants themselves? Was there an *obychnoe pravo*? During and after the revolution of 1917, events— let us rather say, the peasants—answered Yes quite clearly to all three questions. But this momentous agrarian revolution did more than just "answer" these questions.

First of all, the action of the peasants themselves finished most of the job that the reforms of 1861 had left undone, notably the elimination of the estates belonging to the gentry and of the gentry itself as a class. Second, the Stolypin reforms, with their considerable inroads into communal landholding and the private property enclaves they fostered, were all almost completely wiped out (except in the western regions, where there was not much communal tradition in the first place). Third, all this happened because the commune, wounded but still strong, came back with a vengeance, to serve as main tool for the great redistribution of the lands of squires and other private landowners in waves of massive, hectic redistribution. So powerful was this frenzy for redistribution that the lands of kulaks were drawn into the whirlwind; most consolidated extra-communal holdings (*khutora* and *otruba*) disappeared, and their owners returned to the fold of the commune. By the same token, the household reemerged in its pristine purity as common or artel-type ownership within the communal landholding structure. The Stolypin legislation vesting property rights in the head of household was annulled, and the Land Code of 1922 formally restored other members of the household to their previous rights.[32] Not only did the commune undergo a general resurrection, with 95 percent of all peasant land now held on communal tenure,[33] but it now became a truly free commune. For the NEP years it was free from undue administrative pressure and from the state chores which had choked it before the revolution. Taxation and other official functions went to the village soviet, freedom of movement was restored, passports abolished, and so on. In addition, the vessel of state power, the soviet, was a weak and relatively uninfluential institution in the NEP countryside; it was the commune and its assembly that managed land and many other aspects of rural life.[34]

Moreover, the great peasant utopia was realized: the "nationwide commune," with all land now the patrimony of the whole people, meaning that those who tilled the land also managed, distributed, and redistributed it according to a simple labor-cum-consumption principle. It was no utopia anymore. The dream, which the SRs had made the basis of their program, was spirited away from them in 1917 (or "nationalized," if you wish) by the same Bolsheviks who had criticized this program so severely. Land was no longer a commodity, according to the 1922 Land Code. Hired labor was allowed only in emergencies, or on state farms. The program that came to be implemented under the egis of Bolsheviks was, obviously, one of the antinationalization. According to the philosophy of the commune and widespread peasant opinion, land belonged "to nobody" and the state should play the mainly supervisory role of ensuring the good working of the "national commune" and seeing to it that every peasant got the share of land that was his due.[35]

These results—or "answers"—obviously did not correspond to the Bolsheviks' dream. Nor were they oriented toward increased production. Backward, small-scale agriculture was perpetuated under a new formula, and the new rulers had to preside over what they saw as a mean *delezhka*, or sharing out. The Bolsheviks had no choice, however; they had to bide their time.

In the 1920s, there was again a big debate dealing with all the social and juridical problems concerning the *obshchina*, the *dvor*, and the essence of the property relations and interrelations that prevailed within them. Often this debate ran parallel to earlier disputes. The Land Code gave the two institutions the most generous, unambiguous recognition—but the regime also professed neutrality toward forms of landholding and allowed freedom of choice to peasants. They could shift to *khutora* or to collectives if they wished.[36] The overwhelming majority chose the commune. The new elements in the debates concerned a different dilemma: can the antediluvian commune evolve into a socialist collective? Sukhanov, the chronicler of the revolution and a student of agrarian problems, and Dubrovskii, then a young and ardent rightist Bolshevik, both answered in the affirmative. Others said no, and it became a resounding "no" sometime in 1930.[37]

The commune vanished during the collectivization drive, although its traces would linger on to await discovery by attentive research. The other traditional rural institution, the household, did survive almost intact.[38] After years of silence, the household as an institution returned to recognition in print around 1940,[39] gained legal standing, and is still present today. However diluted by modern developments, it carries on with many of the antics that vex jurists and delight ethnographers.

·2·

COLLECT-
IVIZATION –
OR SOMETHING
ELSE?

—4—
THE IMMEDIATE
BACKGROUND OF
SOVIET
COLLECTIVIZATION

▪ THE NEP: WEAKNESSES IN PARTY POLICY

Toward the end of 1927, the New Economic Policy entered upon a period of crisis. Was this crisis necessarily its death knell, or could this particular socioeconomic structure still have been preserved and consolidated?

This question was to be the subject of much bitter debate between the majority and the right. All that need be said here is that the leader of the Stalinist majority and, no doubt, some of his closer collaborators had already lost faith in the NEP as a viable policy and were no longer concerned to rescue it; on the contrary, the only effect of their actions was to hasten its end. And so the NEP was soon to go under for good, but—and this is a point of crucial importance—*before any alternative forms or structures had taken shape, even in the minds of the leadership.* This to a great extent explains the gravity of the problems which were to face the regime from the winter of 1928 onward, and also the exceptional nature of the measures which were adopted to rescue it from its impasse.

Something should therefore be said about the problem of the NEP crisis and the "procurement crisis" which arose in the winter of 1927/28. This crisis was the result of a number of interdependent factors. The opposition on the left saw the principal cause of the trouble in the weakness of industrial growth, especially in the *delay* in implementing measures of planned industrialization, which they blamed on the majority who held the reins of power.

This was, on the whole, a fair interpretation. It explains the fact that the regime had been unable to provide the peasants with adequate technical means or with a sufficiency of low-priced goods.

However, other analysts tended rather to stress the weaknesses inherent in agriculture, the division of the land into extremely small holdings, the low cultural level of the peasants and their lack of knowledge of agronomy, etc. In this context, it had been hoped that long before the country's heavy industry was developed it would be possible, for some time at least, to maintain and develop agricultural production with the aid of "classic NEP methods." The great hope not only of Bukharin but also of Stalin and most of the leadership during the NEP period lay in the development of rural cooperation. By this means, and also by measures directly undertaken by the state to assist the farmers, it was hoped that agricultural production would continue to increase.[1]

Much was said at this time of the possibilities opened up by the provision of a basic minimum of agronomic instruction for the peasants (the "agrominimum")—selected seeds, better implements and better soil cultivation, multiple crop rotation instead of the traditional three-field rotation (trekhpolka), and other "minor improvements," including bringing about the consolidation of holdings (zemleustroistvo) which were still widely scattered and broken up into small strips. The elimination of this grave defect alone, it was felt, would make for a substantial improvement.

This was by no means an unreasonable argument either. Indeed, a body of such measures, together with the "implement and horse stations," the spread of instruction in schools and classes, and intensified training of agronomists and technicians, could not have failed to stimulate agricultural production.

Unfortunately, despite all these hopeful prognoses, after several years of undeniable progress, NEP began to show signs of foundering. Agricultural production began to mark time; livestock raising, which had even exceeded the prewar level, lost its impetus and soon began to decline, although it was already a result, in part at least, of the "emergency measures" policy.[2] The situation was particularly bad in respect of the production of food grains. For a population that had increased by 14 million and was growing by 2 to 3 percent annually, production was still below prewar level.

The situation was seriously aggravated by the well-known problem of tovarnost', a term which is not easily translated, but might be rendered as "marketings" or "off-farm." Before the war, the estates and the kulaks had produced half the total grain and provided more than 70 percent of the country's marketable grain. Now, all the grain was produced by the peasants, who, as a result of the revolution, had undergone a leveling-out process (oserednyachivanie) and now represented socially a more homogeneous group. But they consumed the grain instead of sending it to the market. The tovarnost' was barely half of what it had been prewar: 13

percent as against 26 percent of the harvest. This meant that in 1927, for example, the state collected 630 million poods as compared with 1,300 million poods marketed in 1913.[3] Furthermore, the Soviet state had no reserves, against either war or famine.

This was the root of the problem. Grain production was smaller than it had been before the war, the marketings less, and the requirements much greater.

Meanwhile, the relationship between industrial retail prices and state agricultural prices was much more unfavorable to the peasants than it had been before the war. Industrial products were dear, of poor quality, and scarce into the bargain. There was constant talk of the "famine of goods" (*tovarnyi golod*). Prices paid by the state for procurements (*zagotovki*) of grain were low and often failed to cover the cost of production.[4] Prices for livestock products and industrial crops were much more favorable. For this reason, the peasants preferred to concentrate on producing and selling the latter, while keeping their grain as a reserve for themselves and their livestock, or hanging on to it until such times as they could sell it for a higher price either to private buyers who would resell it or to other peasants whose reserves were not so good.[5]

Some of the peasants, especially the better-off ones, were in a particularly good position to act in this way because they were earning enough money on industrial crops and livestock products to pay their taxes, make their purchases, and wait for the spring, when grain prices usually went up.

In such circumstances, prices for agricultural produce on the free markets would obviously rise considerably, and the growing divergence between these prices and prices paid by the state gave the peasants no incentive to sell their grain to the government.

Thus it was that, after the *zagotovki* had been successfully carried out in October 1927, there was a drop in November, which by December had become catastrophic, and the authorities found themselves taken unawares by the "grain crisis."[6]

Could this crisis have been avoided? Too many mistakes were made, especially in relation to rural economic policy, for the answer to be in the negative. The government's economic policy (from 1925 onward) only served to aggravate the weaknesses of NEP. In particular, apart from the "structural scissors," inevitable in a backward country in process of industrialization, agricultural price policy was incoherent. This was confirmed by many sources.[7] It acted as a brake on agricultural production[8] and weakened the incentive to market grain.

Cooperation, the major propaganda theme, was making some progress, but the efforts directed to this vital sector were modest in the extreme. Indeed, the leadership, absorbed as they were in their routine problems and their internal struggles, had little time to spare for cooperation, a fact of which Kalinin was to express public disapproval. When it was felt necessary, the regime was capable of mobilizing its resources and directing an appreciable effort toward vitally important sectors. But despite the declared importance of agriculture, and of the peasants in general, despite the slogan about the "cooperative plan" (ascribed to Lenin), it cannot be denied that the regime did not deploy sufficient forces to create a worthwhile cooperative sector in the countryside.[9] Quite plainly, during the NEP years it did not consider this to be a question of primary urgency.

There was another even more surprising fact: the leadership had almost completely abandoned the state and collective sectors in the countryside. The sovkhozy at that time were chronically and notoriously poor and backward, and often in a lamentable state. The existing kolkhozy—communes, artels, TOZs (loose producers' cooperatives), and other simpler forms of collectives—despite the fact that they represented tens of thousands of families, were neglected and engaged in a desperate struggle for survival and, paradoxically, against the obstructive attitude of the authorities. In fact, during the final years of the NEP, the entire state and collective sector not only failed to develop but was occasionally in a state of decline.[10]

As for the famous "minor improvements," which had been the subject of a considerable number of decisions, they remained for the most part purely on paper.[11]

Given a more logical price policy, a better developed cooperative movement, a more adequately maintained state and collective sector, and a serious effort to provide agronomic assistance for the peasants, how can one resist the conclusion that the "grain crisis" of 1928 and many of the disastrous developments that ensued might have been avoided or at least mitigated?

At all events, the view which sees in Stalinist policy during the final stages of NEP the direct expression of an ineluctable historical necessity takes no account of the part played by the subjective errors and shortcomings of party policy and is therefore ill founded. We shall be returning to this problem in our conclusion. During the course of NEP, especially in its second phase (from 1925 onward), the leadership seemed to be relying on NEP to function "automatically," and on an increase in agricultural production among the better-off peasants resulting from the important concessions which had been made to them in 1925; the leadership gave little thought to any preparation of alternative policies or of "strategic positions" in the countryside.[12] The responsibility for this blindness must lie with Stalin, as well as with those of the future right. Their absorption with the struggle against the left cannot obscure the fact that the administration was guilty of a lack of foresight and perspicacity.

One significant example serves to illustrate the administration's lack of preparedness for the future developments which were so soon to overtake them. The decision to build a tractor factory at Stalingrad had already been taken in 1924 but was, like so many other decisions, pigeonholed, and subsequently implemented some five or six years later, in a single year, at the cost of immense sacrifices and waste, and much too late.[13] Rykov was to state in 1928 that many important measures which were then being put into effect with such haste could and should have been implemented much earlier.[14]

▪ WHAT PART DID THE FIFTEENTH PARTY CONGRESS PLAY?

The congress was held in December 1927. The leadership was already aware of the bad news from the "procurement front" but said almost nothing about it to the delegates. The congress was primarily concerned with the "liquidation ritual" of the left, despite the fact that, in practice, it had long since been vanquished. The part of the proceedings devoted to discussion of future policy was not very important. Indeed, the leadership had as yet nothing new to suggest. All that was discussed was the broad outlines which should be followed, and these were, moreover, strongly influenced by the program of the newly defeated left.

However, there is no doubt that, at least so far as intentions were concerned, the leadership was aware of the need to formulate a new policy. This was just as true of Stalin and Molotov as it was of Rykov and Bukharin. But, behind these common aspirations, a difference of emphasis was already apparent between the Stalinists and those who were soon to be known as the right wing. The declarations made by Stalin and Molotov during the congress were perceptibly more radical in tone, particularly in relation to the class line to be followed, but the resolutions adopted by the congress were full of appeals for prudence and moderation, reflecting rather the right-wing attitude.

About this time, Rykov had fairly clearly adopted an "industrializing" line. He had accepted not only the need for *perekachka* (pumping resources out of the agricultural sector into industry)[15] but also the principle of priority for heavy industry. He and Kalinin and Bukharin were prepared to limit the activities of the kulaks and to adopt more energetic measures in favor of collectivization.[16] But so far as they were concerned, the objectives were moderate ones only, and any such measures were to reflect a proper degree of prudence. They had no thought of a crash program; they already suspected some of their colleagues of wishing to ride full tilt, and it was for this reason that the resolutions before the congress bore ample witness to the need for balance and moderation. In Rykov's view, any effort at industrialization which was not conducted with due care was likely to end in widespread crisis.[17]

Thus, the *perekachka* too was to be moderate in its application, with no excesses; limitation of the activities of the kulaks was to be achieved purely by economic measures and taxation. The framework of the NEP and its methods were to be preserved, which meant that the Nepmen, middlemen and kulaks, would stay. Moreover, this was also implicit in the left-wing program. Molotov for his part had sworn that NEP would continue to exist as long as the private farmer existed.[18] But in his case a certain ambiguity was apparent about the definition of the NEP.

The difference between Stalin and Molotov, on the one hand, and Rykov and Kalinin, on the other, emerged particularly clearly over the problem of the kulaks.[19] Stalin and Molotov were distinctly more hostile toward this particular social stratum, and even spoke in terms of "liquidation." This was the basis of the rumors which circulated among senior officials about the imminent dissolution of the NEP.[20] But undoubtedly *none* of the leaders at this stage saw quite so far ahead.

During this congress the "collectivization" theme appeared somewhat more vociferous than before, but not in any big way. A last minute statement which did not figure in the initial draft prepared by the Central Committee was even added to the resolutions (before the conclusion of the congress) about "collectivization as being henceforth the Party's major task in the countryside." No such statement was made by any of the speakers at the congress. But whatever the motives behind the insertion of this clause in the resolutions, none of the trends in evidence at that time gave cause to expect anything other than a gradual process, based solely on the state's ability to provide adequate technical means. The firmer, more radical note sounded by Stalin and Molotov on the subject of collectivization was in practice the expression of a moderate aim at *strengthening the specific weight* of collectivist elements in the countryside, but nothing more than that.[21]

It was Rykov, in his closing speech, who underlined the new prospects for socialist development in the countryside as reflected in the resolutions, and Molotov was the one who declared, "No fantasies!" in this context.[22] At all events, at this particular stage neither side was concerned with anything other than broad aims. Beyond the desire for a change of policy, there were as yet no concrete programs. So far as agriculture was concerned, few practical decisions were taken. Those that were taken related mainly to the setting up of the "*Soyuz soyuzov*" for the administration of rural cooperation and of the agricultural department of the Central Committee (and at lower levels of the party pyramid).

On overall social and economic policy, few practical short-term decisions were made, As we know, it was not till a year and a half later that the five-year plan was to be adopted. Most of the delegates did not even seem to think that anything new had come out of this congress. But among the leadership there was a widespread feeling that a turning point had been reached, although none as yet knew the way ahead.[23]

• THE ROLE OF THE "GRAIN CRISIS"

The procurements crisis took the party unawares.[24] As late as October 1927, Stalin had publicly assured the country that the policy so far pursued had been successful and that everything was going well. In particular, he claimed that relations with the peasantry were excellent.[25] This could not have been a simple case of a misleading "official optimism," for such an unwise statement could not have been made if Stalin had foreseen what he would shortly be describing as the "peasants' strike."

When deliveries reached a dangerously low level and the attitude of the *muzhik* was threatening to cause famine in the towns, the Politburo headed by Stalin decided to resort to emergency measures. In the case of any threat the reactions of the leadership were automatically conditioned by their experiences in the civil war. What happened in effect was mobilization of the party's resources, the dispatch of plenipotentiaries with emergency powers and of workers' brigades, the repression and purging of authorities who were thought to be either inefficient or recalcitrant, the setting up of troikas for organizing the collection of grain, etc. The operation was military in character, as had been the case during the civil war. Similarly the "class line" was of the same inspiration: the poor peasants were promised 25 percent of the grain confiscated with their assistance from the better-off peasants. Clause 107 of the Penal Code introduced in 1926, concerning speculators, was invoked against peasants hiding grain.

However, despite the "class attitude" and the accusations made against the kulaks and the better-off peasants (at this stage little account was taken of the differences which might exist between the two categories)— Stalin officially explained events as a "strike of the kulaks"—the real root of the problem lay elsewhere. Stalin knew, and said so, in another context; Mikoyan also made a statement to this effect in the party organ: the bulk of the grain which had to be found was not in the hands of the kulaks but rather of the *serednyaki*, the middle peasants, and they had no incentive to sell so long as there was nothing much for them to buy with their money.[26] How then were they to be prevailed upon to sell, and to sell, moreover, not on the free market but to the state?

The method chosen was the most expeditious one: closing the markets, applying administrative pressure, mopping up monetary surpluses. All this could not have been aimed just at the kulaks but precisely at the great majority of the peasants. These were very serious measures; and it was undoubtedly a time of crisis, particularly around about the summer, during the second wave of emergency measures, which had been introduced after the April plenum had in fact promised to end them.

Since the crisis was an unexpected one it is obvious that this "left turn" on the part of Stalin was not a line which had been well thought out in advance but a series of steps dictated by circumstances. This is a characteristic feature of the history of the Soviet "leap forward" and of Stalin's policy during this time.

At all events, once the regime was committed to compulsory procurements and repressive measures, the effect could only be to aggravate the crisis by setting up a chain reaction which henceforth dictated policy and confirmed it in the increasingly radical lines it was to follow until the denouement in the winter of 1929/30.

But it would be wrong to look upon the great leap at the end of 1929 as having been conceived all of a piece at the very last moment. For, in a sense, the decision to undertake overall collectivization had its roots in the "grain crisis" at the beginning of 1928. Stalin's ideas on policy germinated during the testing time of this crisis, although only in essentials, for *at that stage he was concerned only with a short-term policy of moderate aims,* but by reason of the growing crisis he was constantly obliged to extend the objectives with which he had set out at the beginning of the year.

Indeed, the "grain crisis" was of crucial importance in the shaping of future events, among other reasons because Stalin derived from it a whole series of new conclusions and the elements of a new plan of campaign. During his visit to Siberia, where he had gone to urge and compel party officials to "take" the grain ruthlessly, he had felt that, in addition to the weapons of compulsion, he ought to have something to offer these officials in the way of a long-term policy and a more optimistic perspective. None of his statements in Siberia was published at the time, but we now know in what terms he spoke.[27]

It was at this juncture that he became aware of the urgent necessity for establishing "strongpoints" in the countryside, similar to those the regime had built up in the towns. So it appeared that the hitherto accepted thesis to the effect that cooperation could serve as this "strategic position" was in practice dropped. This was replaced by the discovery, which was new coming from Stalin, of kolkhozy and sovkhozy—those feeble organisms hitherto the Cinderellas of the regime.[28] It is at this point also that he expressed the thought that the Soviet regime was "walking on two unequal legs"—the socialist sector in the towns and the private sector in the villages—and that this could not go on indefinitely.[29] It can be deduced from this (and Stalin in fact admitted it explicitly the same year) that he no longer believed in the NEP as a viable policy. The more his methods intensified the crisis, the more his skepticism increased.

Toward May, his faith in the kolkhozy and sovkhozy as the sovereign remedy was further strengthened. He discovered that these organisms had a considerable marketing potential; it was suggested that this was four times greater than that of the private peasants. At this time Stalin was also greatly preoccupied with another important problem; how was the regime to ensure that kolkhozy and sovkhozy would hand their grain over to the state? Here he went straight to the heart of the matter.[30] He believed, and rightly so, that what would be impossible with the existing 25 million farms would become more practicable if they were merged into a smaller number of large farms.

Stalin's strategy, as it emerged at this stage, took the following form: there was an imperative need for a new policy, comprising a renewed effort on the industrial front and the establishment of a powerful kolkhoz–sovkhoz sector. The private sector in the countryside would remain and would in fact continue to function as an essential element in grain production, but this was no longer enough.[31] In Stalin's view, the scale of the socialist operation in the countryside would be determined by the quantitative target which he had set himself. As he saw it, matters must be so arranged that the state would be absolutely sure of having at its disposal some 250 million poods of grain (in other words, about a third of the quantity required by the end of the five-year plan). Sovkhozy, kolkhozy, and contracts signed with peasants' associations would produce this quantity, and the state would thus be able to supply the key sectors of the economy and the army and to operate on the national (and international) markets, thereby forcing the peasants to sell their surpluses to the state because of competition due to the reserves it had in hand. Stalin would have liked to achieve this objective within three to four years.[32] His colleagues were of the opinion that it would take four to five years.

The regime was, therefore, still a long way from any kind of "total collectivization," but, as we know, it was already on the road, although it was hardly aware of it at the time.

Stalin's thoughts about the situation had crystallized by the July plenum and still followed the same main lines, irrespective of the maneuvers in the internal struggle against the right wing, which, brought into the open by the "procurement crisis," was now at its height. Stalin knew, and told the Central Committee in a speech which was secret at the time, that the peasants would have to pay a "tribute" (*dan'*) for the requirements of industrialization.[33] This was Preobrazhensky's theory, but with none of the latter's scruples or reservations. Stalin realized that the workers, too, would have to be made to pay, and that this would give rise to increasing social contradictions. How, then, were things to be kept going for another four years or so, until such time as the state and collective sector would bring an improvement in the situation? Stalin had made up his mind: in the meanwhile, the regime would use emergency measures to collect the grain. He had already done this in the course of the year. He suggested it again in July and had made official policy of it by April 1929.[34] Bukharin scarcely exaggerated when he said to Kamenev: "He will have to drown the risings in blood,"[35]—but this Stalin was prepared to do.

This was in July 1928. But we should not forget that, at that stage, these were draft programs. Stalin seemed to be more preoccupied with consolidating his position and forging the weapons of domination which would henceforth become an integral part of what came to be known as Stalinism.

It was the time for creating myths which would serve to mobilize and discipline the party officials and the people, and in fact to bring them to heel. Thus we had the myth of the "foreign conspiracy," the myth of the "saboteur in foreign pay," the "kulak menace," or again the "danger from the right" and the "right-wing appeasers." We shall not, in the present context, seek to analyze these concepts, which were deliberate instruments of domination. Nor is it intended to question the existence of particular dangers, plots, or instances of sabotage. They did undeniably exist, but in their Stalinist form they outgrew their real dimensions and were transformed, as we have suggested, into convenient myths which could be used to keep a crisis-ridden country in check and to explain all its difficulties away by laying them at the door of saboteurs and deviationists.

In December 1929 there came another myth, which was to crown the mythological edifice: the myth of Stalin the infallible, the object of a cult.

Toward the end of 1928, the programs which had been conceived at the beginning of the year were finally to take shape in the express appeal to the country to accomplish a veritable leap forward. The October plenum was to launch its famous slogan, *Dognat' i peregnat'* (Overtake and pass), but at this stage all that was intended was a program of industrialization. In the rural sector, the objectives were as yet unaltered: the aim was to establish, within four or five years, a limited but demonstrably superior state and collective sector made up mainly of poor peasants and based on considerable state support.

▪ BETWEEN INTENTION AND REALIZATION

It is right to underline the fact that, in the meantime, almost a year and a half had elapsed (the whole of 1928 and up until June 1929) without any significant worthwhile measures having been taken to implement the new policy. The year 1928 was patently a year of drift. It naturally required some time to plot a new course, but this rudderless year was nonetheless a heavy price which the country had to pay for lack of foresight on the part of the leadership during the preceding period. The leaders were absorbed in the struggle with the right wing, and this no doubt kept them from acting. This too explains, in part, the "dead season" to which we have referred. But apart from a number of objective factors, simple waste of time is not the least of the weaknesses for which the leadership may be held responsible.

The only sign of energetic action to which one can point lay in the creation of some sovkhozy and giant kolkhozy on which preparatory work was done and the projects put in hand. At this period, the sovkhozy were looked upon as the most effective short-term remedy and one which, moreover, was most directly dependent on purely governmental action. Whether this particular solution did in fact afford the hoped-for improvement in the situation is another question. Again, during the years 1928 and 1929, when the leadership was feverishly searching for programs, methods, or devices which would bring about the desired transformation in the countryside, they were in turn to pin their hopes on the "contract" method (*kontraktatsiya*) or on "giant kolkhozy" and other organizations of this type, or on "tractor stations" of the kind proposed by Markevich on the Shevchenko Sovkhoz (near Odessa) or on "stations" of the cooperative type. Without going into the relative merits of these different solutions (they all had something to recommend them, except for the utopian giant kolkhozy and the even more utopian "agroindustrial combines"), we can say simply that all these collectivization methods, of which so much had been hoped, were fairly soon dropped, without sufficient time having been allowed for the necessary adjustment or experimentation, and that the regime finally directed all its energies toward the artel, partly within the framework of an MTS (machinery and tractor station) of a new type which differed both from the Shevchenko model and the cooperative "tractor columns."

It is interesting to note that, at this stage, the artels, as well as the other kolkhoz organisms—communes, TOZs, and various associations— were just as neglected as they had been in the past, and certainly more so than any other sector. In the winter and spring of 1928, thousands of poor peasants responded to the official propaganda, which had been put out along the lines of the Fifteenth Congress decisions, by rushing to join all sorts of collective associations, in the hope of bettering their lot with the help of state support. The propaganda statements had been generous with their promises.

Unfortunately, the authorities were overwhelmed by this more or less spontaneous response, small in scale though it was, and the government was unable to make proper use of this shift to the *tovarishchestva*.[36] We know that at this time Stalin was already thinking in terms of a powerful collective sector, but, for the present, the opportunity afforded by the mass movement in the spring had been missed. During 1928, little was done to encourage the movement in any serious sense. There was still little indication of any preparations for a large-scale movement. As an example it may be noted that, at this time, limited in scale though the collectivist movement was, the authorities had only one agronomist for fifty kolkhozy and sixty other associations;[37] no serious attempt had yet been made to start preparing cadres, either for the existing collectives or for those still to be formed. In other contexts, as we know, the Soviet regime was capable of preparing cadres, imperfectly perhaps but by the hundred thousand, when they felt that the need was urgent. But at this stage was it not already time for such measures to be taken? In 1929 we find Kalinin complaining that there was not one single research institute for the study of problems relating to collective agriculture, whereas there were thirty institutes engaged in the study of industrial problems.[38]

While very little was being done in practical terms to hasten constructive solutions, a fact which Stalin himself was to admit toward the end of
1928,[39] the regime was already very actively engaged in the field of class
warfare. In the towns, an offensive was launched against the private sector
—industrialists and middlemen, tradesmen and artisans—while increasing
pressure was exerted in the countryside against the better-off peasants and
special legislation was introduced to further the "struggle against the
kulaks." The value of this class strategy from the point of view of timing,
methods, and results is more than a little questionable. The offensive
launched against private enterprises, particularly against private trade,
gravely disrupted the normal commercial network, for no provision had
been made for the establishment of adequate state, or other, channels.[40]
In a country suffering from scarcity, the only result was even greater chaos.
This was all the more true since this particular struggle, carried on, among
other reasons, under the watchword of abolishing "pseudo-cooperation,"
resulted in the destruction of the handicrafts sector and of small-scale
industry, acts for which the regime bears the consequences to this day and
which contributed to a deterioration in the standard of living of the
masses.

The official offensive against the kulaks, or rather against the better-off
peasants, still affected the great mass of middle peasants (*serednyaki*),
given the specific conditions of the NEP village. Procurements under
emergency measures inevitably had adverse effects on all the peasants. One
of the first effects was a dangerous drop in sowing. In order to combat this
danger, the authorities found themselves forced to entrust the difficult
task of ensuring that the sowing was done to the state (and party) machine. Soon, the other important tasks of the agricultural year ceased to
be done "automatically," as they had been for centuries past, and fell
heavily on the shoulders of authority.

The forces which had been deployed to seize the grain, officially only
from the kulaks and the better-off peasants, struck continually at the
peasants as a whole, infuriating them and embittering relations between
the regime and the peasantry. The party leaders were well aware that the
real problem was not the kulak but the "middle peasant," and they introduced measures plainly directed against the *serednyaki*, such as the forcible
introduction of *bednyaki* (poor peasants) or workers into the village
soviets (*obednyachivanie*)[41] or the right henceforth accorded to these
soviets to annul any decisions made by the assemblies of the peasant communities if such decisions were held by them to be wrong.[42] Relations with
the peasantry worsened, and the outlook for private agriculture became
darker, both from the point of view of the peasant, who no longer knew
where it would all end, and from the point of view of the authorities, who
were now in an impasse so far as the agricultural situation was concerned
and who were more and more inclined to seek a radical way out.

In other words, what was officially a "purely anti-kulak" maneuver had in practice resulted in a breach with the middle section of the peasantry termed officially as "allied" with the regime. Kaganovich openly admitted this toward the end of the year.[43]

This, therefore, was an unfruitful year, and the lack of consistency in government policy only served to make matters worse. In particular, the offensive against "class enemies," which had been launched without any real discernment and without thought for the preparation of alternative positions, was especially harmful and further aggravated the crisis.

About the end of the year, as we have said, Stalin made a dramatic declaration to the effect that the race to *dognat' i peregnat'* must at all costs be run and that henceforth the task of "reorganizing agriculture on a new technical footing" was of paramount importance if the restoration of capitalism was to be avoided.[44]

This time he was more than ever right about the urgency of the problems to be solved, although his warning about the restoration of capitalism may perhaps have met with a certain skepticism on the part of his audience. But despite the manifest urgency of the problem, it was not until the summer of 1929 that any resolute and even moderately coherent policy on the rural front was to take shape.

• THE RIGHT WING

The differences between the right and the Stalinists may be summed up in terms of the controversy on one issue: Was industrialization and the transformation of the countryside to be carried out in the main by politico-economic methods or, on the other hand, by having recourse to "emergency measures," in other words, to compulsion? Was the regime to opt for a vast network of coercion or for another, more flexible approach?[45] In this dilemma, the future of the whole of Soviet Russia was at stake.

The right naturally inclined to the flexible approach, and its faith was based on the possibility of achieving progress "by NEP methods" and on its analysis of the crisis, which differed from that of the Stalinists. According to the right, the origin of the crisis lay in a number of errors: faulty planning, a faulty price policy, failure to implement a number of decisions relating to aid for agricultural production.[46] As opposed to this explanation, the view of the majority in the Politburo tended much more to stress objective factors, such as the smallness of peasant holdings and the prevalence of strip cultivation.

According to the right-wing analysis, the crisis could have been averted, and might still be prevented from recurring, if the authorities were prepared to retreat from their previous position by making certain concessions to the peasants (reopening the markets, better prices for the producers, aid to the private sector, and, if necessary, importing grain, etc.)[47] for, as Bukharin was to point out, it was better to import grain than to resort to emergency measures.[48] Later, when the atmosphere was somewhat calmer, consideration could be given to long-term measures.

The right recommended a return to economic and fiscal measures as the principal method of influencing the market. It said relatively little about the sovkhozy, which it looked upon purely as an emergency measure; its attitude to the kolkhozy was more favorable, but it was all for caution in this direction and favored further creation of kolkhozy only insofar as the latter were demonstrably superior to and more viable than private holdings.

Later, about April 1929, the right wing called for a two-year plan (*dvukhletka*) within the framework of the five-year plan and expressly designed to improve the condition of agriculture and overcome its backwardness.[49] The right believed that there was still hope of progress in the private sector, and they wanted to preserve the NEP, with its Nepmen, kulaks, etc. They were prepared to restrict the power and growth of the kulaks, but only through fiscal measures. The need for industrialization was by and large accepted by the right at this stage, but they were against forcing the pace to the breakneck speed that appealed to Stalin.[50] According to their spokesmen, the country had by about the end of 1928 already reached the limit of its investment potential, and consideration must now be given to building up reserves and to ensuring that the construction projects which had been undertaken bore some relation to the construction materials which were actually available. As already stated, the right also accepted the need for *perekachka*, but within limits which would still leave the peasants free to build up some reserves.

According to Bukharin, one of the reasons for the country's difficulties lay in "a certain anarchy" and in "faulty planning and faulty intersector coordination," which were continually aggravated by the unjustifiably rapid growth rates. His "Notes of an Economist" and other writings were a plea for scientific economic administration,[51] which, as we know, was hardly the strong point of Soviet industrialization, either during the first five-year plan or in more recent times.

In contrast to Stalin's thesis of the class struggle, which would intensify with the gradual progress of socialism, Bukharin's watchword was "No third revolution!" In his view the time was not yet ripe for taking communism to the countryside.[52] The alliance with the peasantry (*smychka*) must above all be continued on the basis of the cooperative movement.

The foregoing is only a brief outline of the right-wing position. Part of their ideas have come down to us from Stalinist sources and we do not have a complete record of all their proposals or discussions. But the core of their beliefs is there and cannot lightly be brushed aside. Some of their analyses (for example, overreliance on the price mechanism and fiscal measures in a country which was engaged in a tremendous bid for industrialization; too much emphasis on the potentialities of the private sector

in agriculture and not enough on the urgent need for fostering new organizational forms) were clearly mistaken. Others seem to have been completely justified, such as their objection to overly rapid growth rates, to
excessive exploitation of the peasantry, to the lack of scientific method in
the planning and implementation of the process, and to the exclusive
emphasis on coercion.

▪ THE FIVE-YEAR PLAN AND STALIN'S ATTITUDE

In conception, the social objectives of the agricultural part of the five-year
plan were not very far removed from the ideas of the right. So far as the
planners were concerned, the private sector would still be dominant, and
despite the existence of certain restrictive measures, there was no question
of anything approaching a "liquidation of the kulaks." What the plan was
aiming at, very reasonably, was the creation of a state-cum-collective sector
of restricted scope but superior quality which would act as a counterforce
to the better-off suppliers and force them, through economic competition,
to sell their surpluses.[53] It was into the private sector that the greater part
of the supplies and credits were to be channeled by way of the cooperative
movement, which was regarded by the plan as being of the very greatest
importance. The planners were relying to a very large extent on the contract system (between the cooperative organizations and peasant associations formed for this purpose).[54] An important part in the process of
cooperation, with the gradual development of simple forms of productive
cooperation, was to be played by the agrarian community (the *mir*).[55] In
the kolkhoz sector which it was proposed to set up under the plan, the
main organization would be the TOZ and not the artel,[56] and the socialization of property was to affect only arable land and certain types of equipment (mainly heavy), but very little livestock.

It should also be added that the "stations" of the Shevchenko type and
the cooperative "tractor columns," which were much discussed at this
time, were to be the means of creating a very promising relationship with
the peasantry by collectivizing the most arduous tasks, which were also
the most important ones in the grain-producing regions, but without abolishing the peasants' private property, and leaving their livestock untouched.[57]

The five-year plan had no convincing answer to the question of easing
current supply difficulties while waiting for the plan to bear fruit. At all
events, it was decided that, until the end of the five-year plan, there would
be no export of grain.[58]

No one had yet dreamed of mass collectivization as a rapid and effective
means of solving both current and long-term problems at one and the
same time. The plan was ratified by the Congress of Soviets in May 1929.
The great majority of the *party leadership* did not, either at this stage or

in the autumn, foresee what decisions were to be taken some six months later.[59] At that time, everyone was uttering warnings about overly hasty action in relation to changes of organization in the countryside. The party was convinced, as Kalinin and Rykov put it at the time,[60] that the scale of collectivization must be related and adapted to the state's actual ability to provide machines and specialists. They all sincerely believed that the entire operation would be carried out exclusively on the basis of voluntary membership.

But it was precisely at this moment, when the plan, with its relatively moderate and feasible aims for the agricultural sector, had just been launched, that Stalin arrived at quite different conclusions. At the plenum in April 1929, his lack of faith in the private agricultural sector and in the NEP finally came to the surface.[61] Just about this time another procurement campaign had been carried through in the face of enormous difficulties and had yielded *less grain than in the previous year*, despite the use of a whole body of coercive measures, which had been applied more or less throughout the country but especially in the Urals and in Siberia.

It was clear that Stalin was already planning to launch a really large-scale operation. He "informed" the Central Committee that the kulaks and other hostile forces were "preparing to undermine" the Soviet regime— a type of assertion which, as we now know, was a sign that he was either preparing to attack or to drive home his attack. Indeed, he told the Central Committee (it should be borne in mind that his speech was secret at the time) that "the days of the capitalists and the kulaks are numbered."[62] And yet the Sixteenth Party Congress, which took place just after the meeting of the Central Committee, had no thought of numbering anyone's days, at least not so far as the kulaks were concerned. The discussion about the kulaks, which was in fact very heated, was concerned not with any proposal to get rid of the kulaks but simply whether to allow them in the large kolkhozy.

Around this time there was a readily discernible divergence between the thought processes and intentions of Stalin (and possibly of one or two of his immediate lieutenants) and the opinions of the majority of the Stalinist Central Committee. So long as Stalin spoke in general terms, extreme though these might be in tone, without outlining any concrete proposals (which had scarcely taken shape at this juncture) the party and the Central Committee were not conscious of the divergence, despite the critical remarks of the right-wing leaders.

At the meeting in April 1929 Stalin explained that the backwardness of the agricultural sector was likely to create a breach between the towns and the countryside. It was a similar fear which had prompted Rykov's proposal for the agricultural *dvukhletka*. But Stalin's conclusions, unlike those of Rykov, were that agriculture must be reorganized, and quickly, in such a way as to keep pace with industrial growth rates.

The USSR has never to this day brought off such a feat, but it seems that Stalin was already beginning to take such a possibility seriously and that this strengthened his resolve, all the more so because the critical situation and dangers looming on the peasant front were daily growing worse. This is why Stalin now put the question to the government and to the countryside in the form of a clear choice: either the kulaks or the kolkhozy.[63] *Tertium non datur.*

The moment the problem was stated in this way it was inevitable that whatever policy was followed in practice must fit one or other alternative.

In fact, there was already a certain trend in this direction (in addition to the anti-Nepman activity of the previous year): a purge was started in the party and also in the state and trade union organizations. For all practical purposes, the right was already defeated. The five-year plan, which had only just been ratified, underwent a never-ending series of increases at the behest of the Politburo which, as Jasny has said, turned the plan into "a facade," which was to screen an operation that differed very widely from that envisaged in the text and in the minds of the planners. Since the essence of the operation was speed, a point which Stalin made clear at that same April meeting,[64] what counted was not planning but *the race against time*, for the leader and his immediate supporters believed that time was pressing and that the race could be won, thus bringing a speedy solution to their difficulties. This explains, in part, why the conduct of the operation assumed the proportions of an attack which gradually grew in scope until it became an all-out offensive waged simultaneously on all fronts—on many more fronts, in fact, than had ever been intended. The other part of the explanation lies in factors which the leaders themselves did not foresee.

Why was the leadership so sure that there was no time to spare? Was there imminent danger of foreign intervention? No such danger yet existed, nor did the leaders say so at the time. The threat of outside interference played an important part in the developments of which we are speaking, but only in the sense of an as yet undefined future eventuality, certainly not an immediate possibility.

The violent and impetuous character of the decisions which were taken is more readily explicable by certain internal factors. Stalin expressly stated in April[65] that he was relying on emergency measures to solve the grain crisis. He was well aware that such a policy could not last long without leading to a disastrous clash with the peasantry. This was the reason behind the attack on the Nepmen and industrial specialists in the towns and on the better-off peasants in the countryside, for care must be taken to weaken any elements which might eventually rally an outraged peasantry. The same motive underlay subsequent decisions (toward the end of 1929). Again, the anti-kulak measures, apart from their role in the campaigns for wresting grain from the peasants, were a maneuver aimed at the social encirclement of the middle peasants, designed to divide them and to block all their escape routes, leaving them only one way out.

Here one recognizes the hand of Stalin, the master tactician. In fact, his social and political "tactics" were much better than his "strategy," for the latter calls for a greater capacity for theoretical analysis, which he did not possess. At all events, could it be said in April–May 1929, when he had already made his intentions quite clear, that the practical program embodying ideas on the scale of the reforms which were to take place and the methods by which they were to be achieved had received consideration, preparation, or ratification from any organization whatsoever?

In the writer's view, Stalin at this point still did not know where his actions would lead six months later. It would seem that his aims, and those of his immediate lieutenants, were still in line with the provisions of the five-year plan, although in certain respects going beyond these. Several months were still to elapse, until the end of September, before the economic results of the year would be known, when Stalin and his Politburo would *once more revise* the existing plans, involving decisions on an unprecedentedly large scale.

▪ THE RESULTS OF THE YEAR 1928/29

The economic results of the year 1928/29 were much worse than had been expected. This was admitted by Mikoyan.[66] The better-off peasants had cut down their sowings and the authorities struggled to make good the loss by increasing the areas sown by the rest of the peasants. The results thus obtained were not encouraging.[67] Worse still, the numbers of livestock began to decline for the peasants were short of fodder and food. The towns too were short of food. Ration cards were introduced in February 1929,[68] while in the factories management was putting increasing pressure on the workers to step up production. The workers retaliated by mass defections from one factory to another and by an enormous wave of *brak* (faulty production), for which they could not of course be held entirely responsible. The rise in the price of bread grains and other agricultural products caused a rise in prices throughout the economy.[69] Speculation was rife; bread tended to disappear from the towns into regions which had none, especially those which did not produce bread grains, or into provincial towns which the government was not supplying. Living standards dropped, and all the time administrative pressure and state tyranny were growing. Grain procurements, as we know, had been very inadequate, whereas private middlemen had succeeded in buying more that year from the peasants than in previous years.[70]

Thus, the upheavals taking place in agriculture were clearly having repercussions on the national economy. In the view of the majority of the Politburo, the bad state of agriculture was entirely to blame for the crisis.

However, in addition to the part played by faulty economic policy, the great effort which was going into industrialization contributed enormously to the strain and was very largely responsible for the crisis because, as Bukharin had said, it was excessive. And yet the leadership was convinced that their only hope lay precisely in an even higher rate of industrial growth. Moreover, they were borne out in this by the fact that, to all appearances, the annual industrial plan for 1928/29, which had been officially declared to be the first year of the five-year plan, was going well. However, this was in appearance only, a point of capital importance in understanding the change in policy which took place at the end of the year.

About September, the table submitted by the market research (*konyunktura*) organs must have had a profound influence on the party leaders: quantitatively, the general rate of growth was satisfactory. The percentage increases in industrial production were impressive. Nevertheless, it could not be said that the plan was being successfully implemented. In the first place, all the so-called qualitative indices—labor productivity, costs of production, quality of products, organization of work—had shown a negative result. Evidently those indices which were directly dependent on the human factor, on such factors as enthusiasm and conscientiousness, were those in which the failure was apparent. The process of industrialization, as carried out by the Soviet authorities, entailed enormous wastage of human and material resources. This inevitably led to a fall in living standards and further strained an already critical situation. The failure of the plan to improve labor productivity and reduce costs led to an increased demand for manpower which far exceeded the provisions of the plan. The unexpected drain on the wages fund undermined the financial plan. The government had to increase taxes and the note issue.[71]

On the agricultural front the plan failed utterly. Agricultural production, including industrial crops, was on the downgrade.[72] The food processing industry also declined, and the chemical industry and agricultural machinery plans were not fulfilled. It should be recalled that the trade networks had been gravely disorganized as a result of the offensive against the private traders.

It can readily be understood that in a situation of this kind the leaders would feel that they had their backs to the wall and that the regime would be impelled to bring to bear the full coercive power of its dictatorship.

In the view of the party leaders, it was exclusively the rural sector which was to blame for the disequilibrium. This sector had recently opened a second front "against the regime," being now engaged on a "livestock offensive," in addition to the "grain offensive" which had already assumed serious proportions by the beginning of 1928.

The pace of industrialization was not thought to be excessive; on the contrary, the Politburo thought it both desirable and possible to step up rates of growth, a decision which was to be taken at the Central Committee meeting in November 1929. In this way, the authorities hoped to rescue the country from its troubles and steer it into calmer waters with the minimum of delay. In the minds of the leadership, the state of agriculture was the biggest obstacle to their aims.

In September 1929, when the leadership was already aware of the year's economic results, it seems that the small Stalinist leadership, having evaluated the situation, made up their minds: if in the course of the coming months, which were the only ones in which a state campaign could be launched in the countryside (before sowing was begun) some radical change did not take place on the rural front, the drive for industrialization would unquestionably have lost its impetus by 1931, if not sooner.[73]

It was this reasoning, at this precise moment, which dictated Stalin's change of policy at the end of 1929, particularly in view of the fact that the results of the forced collectivization which had been started in the summer seemed to give grounds for much optimism.

■ ON TO THE ATTACK

It was not until June 1929 that any significant and far-reaching attempt at implementing the new policy in the countryside became apparent, and even then the exact nature and extent of the course which was to be followed had still not assumed any definite form. The development of the new program, or rather the new course of action (for there was as yet no definite program in the accepted sense of the term) seems to have been characterized by a continual process of "sliding," as it were, toward the objectives in question, while the latter were continually being enlarged. This curious process lasted from the beginning of 1928 to the end of 1929, with a period of extreme acceleration which set in in the summer of 1929. The incessant changes which the plans for agriculture underwent will serve to illustrate this "sliding" process.[74]

The Politburo was constantly changing its directives because they had no definite system of objectives. Events, some of a negative character, and others which appeared positive and encouraging, spurred the leadership to action. Thus, from summer onward, a whole series of measures showed that the center had begun to act in earnest, and in great haste.

There was a major reorganization in rural cooperation, which was radically reshaped and given the organization of the collectives as its main task. It should be underlined that the main concern at this stage was still with the loose associations, in which the extent of socialization was less than in the artel, not to speak of communes. In order to achieve the desired result, all the means by which influence could be exerted in the countryside—machinery, implements, seeds—were concentrated in the hands of the cooperative administration. Credits for the most part were henceforth channeled to the associations, while aid to the private cultivator was substantially reduced.

The confidence that had been placed in cooperation, and in its reorganization, proved totally unfounded. The result of the hastily devised reorganization was to set up a complicated, cumbersome, and inefficient apparatus which played no useful part in collectivization. On the contrary, the real process of collectivization took place, though not for any reasons connected with cooperation itself, outside the cooperative movement, and indeed on the basis of the latter's ruin. Shortly after the reorganization, a further reorganization had to be undertaken.[75]

Meanwhile there was a revision of policy on the "contract method," for which the authorities also had high hopes. This method was soon to be transformed into a compulsory state campaign and to end in failure.[76]

Mention should be made of another disappointed hope and another false move which took place during this period of intense but confused activity: in the creation of the kolkhozy, up until the famous about-turn of March 1930, emphasis was placed on the "giant kolkhozy" and the "agroindustrial combines" as the mainstay of the operation. In the present context we cannot go into this interesting problem at any length—there is a very close parallel between this phase of Soviet "agrarian utopianism" and the move toward the people's communes in China at a later date—but here again there was complete failure in a very short space of time.[77]

In summer 1929 the Soviet press was already mentioning a new phase, that of "mass collectivization." The countryside was mobilized by thousands of agitators and activists of all sorts. The rural Communists, under the threat of disciplinary measures for the first time, were instructed to join the kolkhozy in order to set an example.[78]

The Kolkhoztsentr was granted wider powers and began to set up its network at oblast, okrug, and raion level, while another organization, Traktortsentr, was set up to administer the MTSs and to create a fairly large number of these tractor stations as quickly as possible.[79]

For the first time, the trade unions found themselves faced with an imperative demand to assist in the collectivization of the villages, an unfamiliar task for which they were in no way equipped.[80] In fact, at this period almost all the state and party organizations were called upon to collectivize and to direct the process of collectivization. In its feverish haste, the Politburo delegated responsibility to so many organizations that there was soon a veritable administrative tangle, the results of which were harmful in the extreme.

In addition, the party and the specialized services spent that year preparing, with a degree of energy and efficiency rarely to be encountered in other fields, for the procurement campaign, which in fact was to be more successful than ever before because of the unprecedented extent of the resources mobilized for the purpose. Once the procurement task had been accomplished, the enormous forces which had been concentrated in the countryside were redeployed and instructed to apply themselves to the task of collectivization. After the procurements, the bulk of these forces were available mainly as from January 1930. The actual process of organizaing the kolkhozy now began to develop in a number of interesting ways. There was marked progress. Kolkhoztsentr decided to double (between June and October) the area occupied by the "giant kolkhozy," and during this period the kolkhoz movement as a whole was doubled, increasing from 3.9 to 7.6 percent of holdings collectivized.[81] At this stage the movement consisted mainly of poor peasants who had been influenced by propaganda and attracted by the quite unrealistic promises showered on them and by the state aid which was being channeled to the kolkhoz sector. This success ought to have been consolidated before any further advance was attempted, but the effect of it was rather to encourage the leadership to step up the campaign and to exert even greater pressure.

In its initial stages this movement, although not strictly speaking a spontaneous one, was nonetheless not the result of coercion, although some elements of administrative pressure had been in evidence as far back as the beginning of 1928. According to recent statements from Soviet sources,[82] coercion began to play an increasing part from the early autumn of 1929, and one might add that, with the onset of winter, it had become the regime's main weapon.

By various methods the Politburo encouraged the local party organizations to go all out and to beat all records in the drive for collectivization. During the summer, there began to appear in the grain-producing regions *raiony* with 10 to 19 percent of households collectivized (with, already then, some administrative pressure, the extent of which is hard to determine). This appeared to suggest a way out which the center would increasingly adopt. The term *raion* (or *okrug*) *sploshnoi kollektivizatsii* then came into use, and local party officials, having been urged to promote collectivization as a state campaign, with all the characteristics usually associated with such a campaign—pressure from above to show results, rivalry between the various regions of the country, and prospects of either promotion or demotion for the individuals concerned—began trying to outdo each other.

By decision of some local party offices which were more zealous than the others, certain areas were soon proclaiming themselvss *sploshnaya*, which meant that they undertook to reach a figure of 50 percent or more of households collectivized with the minimum of delay. Such decisions were based not on an appraisal of the people's readiness and willingness to join the kolkhozy but on the party organization's determination to ensure victory.[83] And so pressure on the peasants increased, while the center was deluged with reports giving it the news it most wanted to hear. The Politburo was well aware of the methods being used but set more store by the results. Encouraged by these and motivated by other considerations which we have already outlined, the center launched an all-out effort to which no limit was set and which called simply for maximum results.

It should be noted that the falling off in numbers of livestock was becoming increasingly obvious and was regarded as an extremely dangerous development. The solution arrived at was once more the same—more collectivization, more collective herds in the kolkhozy.[84] The results of this policy are only too well known.

The more specific decisions about the "great turn" in collectivization appear to have been taken by the Politburo in the month of October, although the evidence for this assumption is still incomplete. At all events, a short time previously no such decisions had existed.

Toward the end of October, *Pravda* finally stated the problem in unequivocal terms: all the forces which had been massed for the procurements campaign, it said, must be thrown into collectivization.[85] In view of what is known about the methods employed during the procurements campaign, the order is not without significance. In fact, from this time onward the press was to be full of denunciations of the kulaks and appeals for mass collectivization. The incitement to violent methods was barely concealed, although no definite indication was given about the nature or extent of these methods or how they were to be applied. This was no accident. The leadership had now opted not for reforms but for revolution.[86]

On November 7 Stalin published his famous article on the "Great Turn," in which almost every element of his appraisal of the situation was incorrect. In particular, he stated that "the middle peasant has opted for the kolkhozy," which according to present-day Soviet sources was not at all the case. According to these same sources, Stalin was anxious to induce the forthcoming meeting of the Central Committee (the November meeting) to adopt the decisions he wanted by presenting the members of the Central Committee with a view of reality colored to suit his own aims.[87]

The November meeting accordingly complied, although with certain reservations attested by present-day sources.[88] The plenum adopted an unrealistic plan for industrial growth, called for a more rapid rate of collectivization, with a move toward "kolkhoz–sovkhoz composites"—mythical organizations which never in fact existed. At this meeting, it was decided to set up a new all-union commissariat for agriculture, to build two new tractor factories and two more for combine-harvesters, etc.[89]

Molotov, who presented the principal report on the problem of collectivization, suggested "dekulakization" without explicitly saying so (and indeed, there were instances of confused anti-kulak measures in a number of places very shortly after); he spoke disparagingly of the five-year plans for agriculture, since in his view it was "the coming months, weeks, and days which counted." He said that before long not only *okrugi*, but whole republics would be completely collectivized, and the time which he thought such an undertaking should take was exactly five months.[90]

The leadership was plainly reluctant to impose any terms or limitations on the activities of the officials. Some members of the Central Committee insisted that a commission be set up within the Politburo to direct collectivization and to see that the whole operation, particularly the process of dekulakization, was carried out in an orderly manner. We can but guess at the reasons why the the Politburo took three weeks to set up this commission, which was made up of the most experienced representatives of the oblast authorities and specialists from the central departments.

Two weeks later the commission produced a draft resolution and a detailed plan of action, but Stalin altered their proposals to give them greater urgency and wider scope, his main preoccupation apparently being to give the least possible excuse for delay and the freest possible rein to uninhibited action.[91]

The subcommittee responsible for the draft proposal on dekulakization was even dismissed and replaced by another in January 1930. Without waiting for its conclusions, Stalin on December 27 publicly gave the green light to the "liquidation of the kulaks as a class," without putting forward at the time any suggestions or directions about the manner in which this terrible operation was to be carried out.

Some weeks previously, on his fiftieth birthday, Stalin had been hailed, for the first time, as the greatest Marxist-Leninist and the greatest strategist of all time. From now on, he was the infallible leader, the object of a cult.

▪ WAS THERE ANY CHOICE?

The historian is often perplexed when faced with the question, Was there any other way out? And yet this is not a question which one can easily evade unless one is convinced that in fact no alternative existed. As for the problem at present under discussion, the following argument suggests a number of replies:

Compulsory collectivization was launched under pressure from a crisis which threatened not only the country's drive for industrialization but also the stability of the regime itself. There may be reservations about the truth of this allegation, but the fact remains that this is how the situation appeared to the effective leaders of the party at the time.

It is true that the weaknesses inherent in the structure of agriculture had a disruptive effect on the national economy, that they threatened to reduce the country to famine and served as a breeding ground for a number of adverse social elements, etc. But it is undoubtedly true that agriculture was not exclusively to blame for the crisis.

The measure of industrialization which was already going on at the time represented an enormous burden, the size of which was largely the result of the excessive rate of investment. But a particular rate or speed of growth is not exclusively dictated by the pressure of objective needs (in the case of Russia rapid industrialization as such may be accepted as an objective necessity); *they are also the result of a choice, an appraisal, a certain level of political and economic planning and administrative capacity.* Here there exists an enormous margin of error in decision making and the conduct of affairs. In this particular context, it is our view that the leaders did in fact make mistakes over a whole number of questions and that the quality of their administration was poor, and at times disastrous. In particular, the rate of industrial growth was excessive, and the decisions taken by the leaders were often quite arbitrary, since the leaders themselves had little inclination to listen to the suggestions put forward by experts or those of moderate opinions. Bukharin was right (and Trotsky agreed with him later) when he said that it was absurd to embark on a building program knowing in advance that the requisite materials would not be available.[92]

In fact, the excessive rate of growth and the lack of administrative skill in the handling of affairs were such that, in the first place, in practice the progress of industrialization during the first five-year plan was not the result of the "five-year plan" or of any other coherent plan. Such was the extent of the confusion in the administration of the five-year plan that it led, among other things, to the famous method of "priority (shock) projects" (udarnye stroiki) in which everything was sacrificed for the achievement of a handful of objectives which were judged to be of key importance. The method was a salutary one, no doubt, in the given situation, but it originated in confusion and gave rise to excessive waste. This was not planning in any sense of the term.

Secondly, the excessive growth rates which ruined the five-year plan as a planned and properly organized operation also contributed to the resultant wastage of resources. It is impossible to say just what the excess cost of the five-year plan was, but it is a fact that, in a country short of resources, what human and material resources they had were all too often recklessly squandered and consequently yielded no advantage. Economists may be able to calculate the extent of the waste in Soviet industrialization (a feature which was to remain characteristic for a long time to come), but there is one inescapable conclusion: it cannot be said that this excessive speed, the shock methods, the waste of resources, etc., were unavoidable, or that they were the only possible solution. It is therefore reasonable to assume that if industrialization had been carried out at a more moderate tempo (there are other ifs, but in the present context we shall confine ourselves to the essential ones) fewer resources would have been swallowed up in the process, the resulting social strain would have been lessened, and consequently the crisis engendered by the whole operation would have been much less severe. To pursue this line of thought a little further, one might well be justified in asking whether, if this had been the case, the results would have been any less impressive.

There is in this context one further consideration. In the constant interplay of influences between a backward agricultural sector, which acted as a brake on industrialization, and a too-rapidly growing industrial sector, which weakened agriculture, the part played by industry might have been appreciably less distorting, even without any change in the structural framework, if another group of leaders had been in command.

An analysis of the second major contributory factor in the crisis, i.e., the state of agriculture, discloses a number of ills which might have been avoided or mitigated if steps had been taken in time.

First, during the years of NEP, especially from 1925 onward, the leaders placed overmuch reliance on the ability of NEP to function "automatically" and either did not perceive or neglected a number of factors which were to cause them untold difficulties at a later stage; in this connection, the future right wing undeniably bears a great deal of the responsibility. At this stage, there was already some substance in the allegation made by the left opposition that a more serious attempt at industrialization could have been begun at a much earlier date. We previously cited as a significant example the case of the tractor factory at Stalingrad.[93] Whatever might have been the practical considerations which led to a failure to implement this project in 1924, they reflect a poverty of statesmanship.

In addition, we have referred to agricultural price policy during the NEP period, which Molotov described as a series of "colossal stupidities." If these "colossal" stupidities had been avoided, could it possibly be said that subsequent events, particularly the "grain crisis" in the winter of 1928, need not have been as severe as they in fact were?

The total neglect of the collective movement in the countryside was a blatant and unpardonable error. The same was true of the sovkhozy, which were in a notoriously backward state. We have already mentioned the views of Rykov, when he asked in 1928, Why was a major campaign on the sovkhozy not launched earlier? He had in mind a number of other measures which might have encouraged agricultural progress but which were never introduced.

The idea of a powerful state-and-collective sector, which would be limited in scope but well organized, might have played a part of the very greatest importance. Nor can it be said that the Bolsheviks were incapable of conceiving such an idea prior to 1928. And yet the fact remains that it was not until 1929 that this "discovery" was made and energetic action was taken to build up this sector. How it was done, in what conditions, and with what results is well known. Having failed to pursue a reasonable policy, the regime found itself thrown back on the disastrous alternative of mass collectivization.

Prior to 1928, and for some time after this date, there were a number of elements in the social structure of village life which could have been of the greatest importance as a starting point for promising developments in the collective and cooperative field. The institution of the *mir* itself could have been used to form one of the many variants of the producers' association (*tovarishchestvo*), as had been suggested by Gosplan in 1929. But this avenue was first neglected and then finally left unexplored.

There were abundant examples in the countryside of spontaneous cooperative movements, particularly the "simple producers' associations" (*prostiye proizvodstvenniye tovarishchestva*). We cannot discuss these at length in the present context, but they were in fact spontaneous, owing nothing to the initiative or support of the authorities. In most cases they did not even form part of the official cooperative movement (the same was true of a great many of the kolkhozy), and they were, therefore, described as "wild," or beyond the pale. But this need not have been so.[94]

The way in which the authorities handled the cooperative movement, both before and after the "grain crisis," left much to be desired. Behind the figures which recorded quantitative results one could discern a movement stifled in the grip of bureaucracy which left the mass of the peasantry no scope for genuine initiative and hence for constructive education. Lenin's dream of cooperation was in no way utopian. Furthermore, "kulak domination" of the cooperative movement was neither as real nor as unavoidable as it was made out to be in the subsequent official interpretation. The party never deployed any appreciable forces in this sector, either in terms of quantity or quality, nor did it devote much thought to the problem. This is why the future process of collectivization, curious and paradoxical though it may seem, was in fact carried out on the ruins of the cooperative movement.

Up until the end of 1929, the kolkhoz movement consisted for the most part of TOZs, a not very highly collectivized form of organization which was plainly favored by the peasants and also by the majority of the party activists concerned with this problem. The directive calling for the abolition of these organizations and the imposition of the artel, the fact of *having made one single form of organization obligatory* in a country which had a whole range of such structures, the fact that no opportunity was afforded for experimentation with other possible types of organization—all these facts add up to a policy which it is impossible to endorse with the seal of inevitability. We have no hesitation in suggesting that these were fatal errors.

Whatever the circumstances may have been which led the Stalinist group to interpret the "grain crisis" as a sign that the NEP was doomed, and which set them on the road to mass collectivization, all of their decisions and appraisals are open to criticism and to question.

It may be admitted that the "grain crisis" in the winter of 1928 called for a series of administrative measures, although this point of view was in fact disputed at the time by certain party experts as well as by the right opposition. What is open to question is the exclusive reliance on coercive measures, which consequently became increasingly violent and further aggravated the existing difficulties. If some pressure had to be exerted, it could have been accompanied by the social and economic measures proposed by the (future) right wing. Some imports of grain, a rise in the procurement prices, imports of manufactured goods—all of these might have helped to ease the nature and the extent of the pressure and might perhaps have lessened the impact of the crisis and gone some way to improving relations with the peasantry. But these measures were rejected, or worse still, they were first of all rejected and then adopted (in part) later, in fact *too late*.

The decision to collectivize the greatest possible number of peasants and to dispossess and deport the better-off peasants, which was taken toward the end of 1929 and which certain observers accept as having been inevitable, is equally open to question, at least in respect to its scope and timing. It is true that at that moment, because of the failures of the past, some of which we have already mentioned, there are strong indications that the leadership felt themselves compelled to take exceptional and very dangerous measures. But it is significant that a number of Soviet scholars nowadays express doubts not only about the speed and the excessively administrative nature of the collectivization but also about the timing of the dekulakization measures undertaken at this stage. They maintain that the mass of the peasants, and particularly the middle peasants, were as yet unprepared for collectivization on such a massive scale and therefore not ready for liquidation of the kulaks.[95] By making such a statement, they call into question the whole of the spectacular change of policy at the end of 1929.

Our present analysis is not so much concerned with the "sudden change" as with the long period which led up to it, and we have tried to focus attention on certain factors in this period which have tended to be disregarded by the policy makers, or certain errors which appear particularly blatant. The purpose is not one of speculation about other courses which history might have taken, and so this is not an essay in "if history." It is simply an attempt at isolating a fairly large number of concrete factors which together might have gone to make up a different body of measures, or in other words a different policy, although within the same institutional framework. This might in itself suffice to answer the question, Was there any alternative? Let us conclude, however, with a few general observations.

The situation in which Soviet Russia found itself was such that a vigorous campaign of industrialization became a matter of prime necessity, and this could not be achieved without "tribute" from the peasants, the workers, and in fact the entire population. As Preobrazhensky had accurately predicted, this was bound to involve a period of social strain, particularly during the initial phases of the industrial effort. In addition, it may be said that to meet with success in its efforts, the regime had to be a "tough" one, a resolute dictatorship.

This precondition does not, however, exclude the element of choice in respect to the behavior of such a regime and the policy which it pursued. Granted that "tribute" was inevitable, its size was still a matter for choice and not a fixed quantity rigidly laid down by some immutable law of history; granted that, in the given situation, some form of dictatorship was necessary, it should not be overlooked that dictatorship, like democracy, can assume many different forms. In this situation, dictatorship would seem to have been a logical necessity, but not necessarily in the autocratic, terroristic, cult-producing guise which it in fact assumed; granted the need for industrialization, the problems of "how much" and "how" were still open to choice. While it is agreed that the process of industrialization was bound to involve sweeping changes in the countryside, it is, in our view, wrong to suppose that these changes could not have been effected otherwise than by collectivization as Russia experienced it. Why the insistence on the kolkhoz as the exclusive form of collective, when village structures suggested several alternatives? Is there any reason why the time limits which the Politburo chose to set should be accorded the status of immutable historical laws? And what of the wholesale condemnation of any private sector?

Changes in the structures of rural life, necessary as they undoubtedly were, need not have followed a uniform pattern but could have been effected by the setting up of several different sectors, the nucleus of which already existed during the NEP period, and which could have been either sovkhozy, kolkhozy (of which there were several types) or other forms of cooperative or joint association with varying degrees of socialization and varying degrees of integration of private farms and private property, including (why not?) a private peasants' sector.

If we agree that the road which Soviet Russia had to travel left the regime so little room for maneuver that it had to choose between its own destruction and the path which it in fact took, then it would be logical to see in Stalin's policy the direct expression of historical necessity and to accept all the methods which were used as having been justified, with reservations only in respect of certain errors or excesses; in this case, one might logically argue that what was achieved could only have been achieved by a dictatorship of the most despotic kind, and by one individual—Stalin. This is the logical conclusion of the opinions expressed by Dr. Schlesinger.[96] His theory that the elimination first of the left wing and then of the right wing were indispensable if the regime was to survive and to succeed in its task of industrialization fits logically into this pattern.

In our view, there are certain weaknesses in this argument. As the present study has shown, there were a series of factors which could have been combined to form an alternative. Again, it is an indisputable fact that Stalin had no foreknowledge of the great "leap forward" which he was to take, or of all its consequences, and that he had no such ambitions, least of all in 1926 and 1927, when he was concerned with the liquidation of the left. Doubtless, he was already an "industrializer," as Dr. Schlesinger suggests,[97] but no more so than his associates at that time, for example Rykov (Was the intensification of the industrialization drive in 1926 embarked upon against the wishes of someone like Rykov or Bukharin?). Generalizations about an industrialized Russia, which everybody accepted at the time, are of less account than practical measures. In practical terms,

Stalin was a supporter both of industrialization and of the NEP (he was simply more cautious in his statements than an unskillful politician like Bukharin), and therefore he moved with prudence and moderation in this domain. For these reasons the theory that the left, which was enthusiastically proindustrialization and anti-kulak, had to be liquidated as an essential prerequisite for future industrialization, and by a Stalin who at that time had still so little thought of what his future policy was to be, is a rather odd theory. It may be accepted if one accepts another equally odd theory, which presents Stalin as a sort of *deus ex machina*, the only man in the party who was capable of transforming Russia into an industrial country. If this were so, then one would in fact have to accept the elimination of the left as having been necessary, not because of its "sectarian appeal" to the workers[98] (there is no reason to believe that the left was incapable of demanding sacrifices from the proletariat), but because anything that might have stood in the way of "the only man who was able to act" had to be sacrificed for the good of the cause.

As for the elimination of the right, in order to show that this too was indispensable one would have to prove, first of all, that all of their proposals were basically wrong whereas everything that Stalin proposed, and did, was basically right. This was far from being the case. The sequence of events after 1928, and the results of Stalinist policy, suggest that what the Stalinist administration particularly needed (we leave aside here the eventual need for its own abolition) was precisely the moderating influence which the right could have exerted. What was called for, therefore, in the case of the right was not elimination but at most restriction of its responsibilities within the framework of its rights as a minority. The methods which were used by the leaders of the right wing in their struggle against Stalin show that these same leaders were perfectly capable of remaining within the bounds of discipline and of refraining from carrying on their controversy before the general public, or even the party as a whole, provided they had some assurance that their views would not be rejected out of hand and that they would be given some opportunity of exerting a restraining influence.

And so events took their course. Historians and other analysts record these events and try to interpret them. But an essential precondition for analysis is the ability on the one hand to identify urgent social needs dictated by circumstances and on the other to judge the practical solutions to these problems which were the result of subjective choice on the part of the leaders. By making this distinction, we are able to appraise the actions of historical personages and to pass judgment on the quality of the leaders.

5

WHO WAS
THE SOVIET KULAK?

This essay does not attempt an answer to the question posed in the title. Many studies will be needed—and they are only beginning in the USSR itself—to provide something more satisfactory. A team of research workers, if it could be established, would be desirable. But the subject needs to be treated, even if only as an inducement to study and discussion.

The pitfalls in this field are many: the condition of the statistical data, numerous but incomplete and contradictory; lack of documents and other evidence; a confusion of ideas and concepts—all make the study of this problem hard, but all the more tempting. The sweeping overturn known as dekulakization has the feel of something grim far back in history, whereas in fact there are still plenty of witnesses, survivors, and consequences of this operation on the Soviet body social.

However, despite the importance and notoriety of dekulakization, there is as yet not a single work of reasonably acceptable scholarly standard on the kulaks. Soviet scholars are well aware of this, and new research—which already appears to be under way—may be expected from the USSR.

The underlying problem, that of differentiation within the peasantry, of which the kulak problem is a part, was already vigorously discussed in the controversy between the Populists and the Marxists about capitalism in Russia. This discussion broadened out after Stolypin's reforms, which aimed at dismantling the peasant village commune by accelerating the process of differentiation within it and by creating a stratum of "strong" peasants, efficient producers and supporters of the existing order.

The term "kulak" appears with increasing frequency in this period. However, it was at first used to indicate not the new prosperous peasants but rather a section of village extortioners, the "skinners alive," those who "eat up the commune" (*zhivodery, miroedy*), men of special rapacity whose wealth came from usury or trading rather than from agriculture. It is in this sense that in his work for the development of capitalism in Russia Lenin used the term for these familiar elements of the pre-capitalist countryside, while the prosperous peasants—who in his eyes were the channels of rural capitalism—are "peasant entrepreneurs."[1]

Having set out to study in this article the Soviet kulak in the period leading up to 1927–29, before his eradication, I shall avoid an overlong historical inquiry. It is enough to say here that notions like "rural capitalism," "kulak," and "rural capitalist" had no commonly agreed content, no more before than after the revolution. Divergences in the number of kulaks before the revolution illustrate the flexibility of the notion: they were 13.3 percent of all households according to Lenin but only 9 percent according to the Central Statistical Board (TsSU) cited by Larin.[2]

Whatever the analysis, the phenomenon concerned was before the revolution much more clearly in evidence than the one we know in the Soviet period. The kulaks before the revolution had some 80 million hectares of land; Nemchinov ascribes to them 38 percent of the country's grain output, a proportion of off-farm production (*tovarnost'*) amounting to 34 percent, and a substantial place in the off-farm wheat—50 percent of the country's total.[3] There were as many as 600,000 farms of up to and over 50 desyatins (55 hectares).[4] Such peasants, strong producers for the national and international market, are perhaps easier to define socially. But this stratum was swept away by the revolution, or rather by what happened between the period of *kombedy* and the end of the civil war, in which many of the strong Stolypin-type producers were active in the White camp.

Toward 1921, when the NEP began, the countryside had become, in appearance at least, evened out and equalized in accordance with the dreams dear to the Socialist Revolutionaries, while the number of peasants isolated in *khutora* (homesteads) and *otruba* (consolidated smallholdings) had considerably diminished owing to a spectacular resurrection of the village communes or, rather, communities (*obshchiny*).[5] What had become of the previous rich peasants, kulaks or others? How had they disappeared, and where? It is difficult to answer these questions, for lack of data. Two facts, however, are incontestable: the old big peasant farm had disappeared, but the terms "kulak" or "village bourgeois" lived in the vocabulary of the party.

Some years later, by 1925, a new differentiation was becoming visible, with its social polarities and political dangers. This differentiation had existed in bud among the "leveled" peasantry. Little was needed for differences of well-being to appear among the poverty-stricken and primitive peasantry: the deeper the general poverty, the more such differences were resented. Now, after "war communism," one feature was particularly important in stimulating social inequality in the countryside: the unequal redistribution among the peasants of cattle, animals, and implements.[6]

The peasant deprived of the wherewithal for working his plot had to move to the town or work for a more fortunate neighbor, or let part of his land, or hire a plow and horse from a neighbor. It is easy to see how such a situation carries prosperity to some and prolongs or brings poverty to others. Some reserve in grain or, especially, in money, which the old "strong ones" had been able to keep from the storms of revolution, intensified this evolution, and there were many other factors working in the same direction. But the most important factor lay in economic policy (the NEP), which by about 1925 had become a kind of "Neo–NEP" providing new concessions profitable, above all, to the prosperous peasants.

When social polarization, which had been regarded as abolished, began to make itself felt again, the party had recourse, not without hesitation among some militants, to the old terminology which had been forged in the discussions with the Populists about capitalism, and also to the old term "kulak." Economic inequality in the countryside caused a sort of reflex action in the Bolsheviks, as in other Marxists, in the direction of looking behind this inequality for a rural capitalism, for the classes proper to capitalism as such. This is how the new stratum of better-off peasants in the Soviet countryside got the appellation "kulaks" and came to be identified, in the same spirit, now with "rural bourgeoisie" and now with "village capitalists."

By this almost "spontaneous," even in a way subconscious process, the terms were carried over from one historical social structure to another, without preparatory studies or effort at clarification. Moreover, the notion of a kulak meant, in any particular period, different things among the Bolsheviks themselves.

The RSFSR commissar of agriculture, A. P. Smirnov, in a pamphlet issued in 1926, distinguished two categories of better-off peasants. One was the kulak, exploiter and "devourer of the *mir*," who possessed "not a little" land, hired *batraki* (laborers), traded, and lent money. This was a "skinner alive," whose tendency was to get his hands on everybody around him. But, said Smirnov, this type has almost disappeared from the Soviet countryside and must be vigorously combatted if it reappears. The second category, on which the commissar did not grudge his praises, was that of the farm called "strong" (*krepkoe trudovoe khozyaistvo*) based on the labor of the family and devoted essentially to agriculture.[7] This classification may be compared with that of Bukharin, who, in the same period, classified in one group "the well-off innkeeper, the village usurer, the kulak," who were distinct from the group of "strong farmer hiring some *batraki*" —this in a theoretical work which enjoyed authority at the time.[8]

We see in these notions a double departure from the concepts which were to become predominant a little later and to persist in the party until our days. The kulak here is not classed with the well-off peasant of the NEP period, and the latter is not identified with the village capitalist.

These views of Communist leaders link up with notions spread by certain observers outside the party. Bazarov, for example, identified the kulak with "the capital usurer" who precedes capitalist accumulation, while for Sukhanov the kulak was a case rather of "commercial capital."[9]

Contrary to these opinions, Larin, a renowned "anti-kulak," put all kulaks in the category of "entrepreneur" but distinguished types among them, as follows: kulak-employer, kulak-trader, kulak-speculator, kulak-usurer.[10] An official governmental decree made yet another distinction in indicating the "kulak-entrepreneur," who seemed to comprise all Larin's types, and a kulak "of peasant kind" (*krest' yanskii*), who was, presumably, devoted above all to agriculture.[11]

This by no means exhausts the profusion of terms and definitions for kulaks. Trifonov spoke of "the reactionary class of kulaks" but contradicted himself on the same page in using the term "capitalist elements."[12] *Voprosy istorii* recently spoke of a "class of rural exploiters"; in Lyashchenko the kulaks are "small-capitalist producers of merchandise," while Danilov spoke of a "primitive capitalism," but he was referring to the middle peasants—in his eyes "petit bourgeois"—whereas for him the kulak is simply a village capitalist without complications.[13] It appears that Academician Strumilin, who dealt in 1929 with peasant differentiation, did not accept, at that time at least, the current "kulak-capitalist" identifications; in his attempt to calculate the range of social strata among the peasantry he referred to "well-off peasants," and the term "kulak," as another author pointed out, "escaped" from his classification.[14]

The indefiniteness in terminology covered lack of clarity as to concepts and ignorance of the facts. It is again Strumlin who says frankly: "Even the fundamental question of criteria for distinguishing a kulak from a *serednyak* and a *serednyak* from a *bednyak* has not yet found an authoritative solution."[15]

Another party specialist on agrarian problems, Milyutin, declared at the Fifteenth Party Congress: "What is a kulak? Hitherto, at bottom, no clear, exact definition has been given of a kulak in respect of this differentiation which is actually taking place."[16]

We add to these contemporary statements a recent one by one of the best Soviet specialists in agrarian history: "In works concerning the class struggle in the countryside, we cannot consistently find a scientific characterization of the social forces in the countryside and of their disposition."[17]

It is significant to read today, after the "liquidation as a class" of a large section of the peasantry, that there were no precise criteria for singling it out. The question is more complicated by the fact that, in the rural conditions of the NEP, the agencies which had to determine particular categories "on the ground" for purposes of taxation or dispossession were often in difficulties despite the fact that they were provided with some more or less definite theoretical criteria. An investigator expressed this well in a discussion at the Communist Academy in 1928. He who knows the countryside, he claimed, "knows full well that one cannot reach the kulak directly, one can't get hold of him, one can't establish by direct methods that he is in fact a capitalist."[18]

The statistical services and research institutes have made many attempts to delimit the social strata in the countryside. I have described elsewhere a series of such attempts and the methods employed.[19] We must here limit ourselves to data on the kulaks, leaving aside the more general problem of the differentiation of all peasant groups.

The most developed criterion inherited from the zemstvo statisticians was that of sown area. It is on this criterion that Larin, for example, established his first classifications for the prerevolutionary period and immediately after the revolution in defining as kulaks those sowing more than eight desyatins. The Central Statistical Board (TsSU) continued for a long time to use the same criterion, until it was denounced by the Commissariat of Inspection (RKI). This indicator was attacked on all sides as unacceptable. A large peasant family often possessed more land than a real rural entrepreneur. Indicators based on the number of horses and cows, readily used by various agencies, were no more effective for measuring the scale of an eventual rural capitalism.

Since this was what was sought so persistently, the simplest way was to go chiefly by the amount of hired labor. But everybody knew that one was thus likely, in the Russia of the NEP, not to discover very much. Hired labor was often camouflaged in the countryside in various ways, such as adoption or "help" from a parent; often the hiring agreement was simply not declared; but, on top of all this, employment for wages was relatively little practiced in the Soviet countryside.

This is why some investigators, Kritsman of the Communist Academy at their head, saw the principal indicator of rural capitalism and its field of essential activity in the hiring out of means of labor (implements, machines, draft animals). But this method was violently attacked, notably by Sukhanov, the chronicler of the revolution, and by a party member, Dubrovsky, who even thought it necessary to use the columns of *Pravda* to protest against Kritsman's procedure.[20]

For Sukhanov, there is no capitalism other than that of the big farm employing and exploiting *batraki*. The hiring out of implements and work animals was no more than "commercial capital" and was, moreover, too ephemeral to be used as an indicator; it sufficed for the peasant in question to obtain a state loan at the cooperative to acquire the plow and horse which he lacked, or to rent them from a state "station," for the exploiting function of the hiring to be ended. This is, therefore, according to Sukhanov, nothing more than a simple "antagonistic relation" (such as exists between sellers and buyers), not to be confused with a *class* relation.

According to Dubrovsky, hiring out means of production could be a valid indicator on condition that this is done by a kulak already classified as such on other grounds (exploitation of hired workers), since the hiring out of implements and work animals was so widely practiced by all the peasants that one risked—in considering these implements as capital and the borrowers as exploited proletarians—seeing an extraordinary amount of capitalism in the poverty-stricken Russian countryside.

Nemchinov tried to resolve the difficulty by proposing to use the value of the means of production which a farm possessed. The man with more than 1,600 rubles' worth of means of labor was to be considered a kulak.[21] Lyashchenko found that by this index 3.24 percent were "small capitalists." But other investigators found no lack of arguments on which to reject this index as a basic one.

The only procedure left to the investigators and statisticians was to delimit the best-off section of the peasantry by a statistical series which combined a variety of indicators constructed in accordance with the concepts of the authors concerned, by procedures that were often ingenious and in any case laborious.

But events pressed, and the politicians did not want to await the discovery of the most perfect analytical devices. In 1929 the "individual tax" was introduced: this was to hit the kulaks only. The financial authorities first of all, then others a little later, were requested to decide the matter in the form of decrees, so that officials on the spot would know what to do.

Here we approach the first part of an answer to the question: Who was the kulak? It is, in the first place, he who is declared to be such by the authorities.

Narkomfin, the People's Commissariat of Finance, was, probably, the first to exert official authority, and it was this body which instigated the commission convened by Sovnarkom, the Council of People's Commissars, in May 1927 to consider the incidence of taxes on the population.[22] It was this commission, composed of Larin and Kritsman (Communist Academy), Strumilin (Gosplan), and Pashkovsky (TsSU), which, for the first time, fixed "the methodology for the definition of social structure in the USSR." As for the kulak problem, the commission was content to evaluate the number of households which hired workers for a period (*srokovye*, from fifty days per annum) and to leave to another commission the task of discerning within this number "the group of kulaks." It was Nemchinov, Dubrovsky, and Larin who "picked out" (*otobrali*) the kulaks.[23] Those were recognized as kulaks—"along expert lines," as

Dubrovsky said thirty-five years later—of whom it could be considered that "even a single one" (!) of the following indicators appertained:

1. the hiring of two *srokovye batraki*, even if one of the two was employed for less than half a year;
2. ownership of at least three draft animals (four in Kazakhstan);
3. sown area of more than 10 (12, 14, 16 according to region) desyatins;
4. ownership of a processing enterprise even with only one hired worker, or no hired worker if there was a hired worker in another section of the farm;
5. ownership of a trading establishment, even without hired help;
6. ownership (private, or in a narrow association) of a complex and costly agricultural machine (tractor, threshing machine) or of a considerable quantity of good quality implements.

This was "the kulak" of whom this commission found 3.9 percent of the peasantry to consist. We recall that Strumilin, himself a member of the commission, did not accept its conclusions as "having authority." Nevertheless it was this decision which came to be the model for subsequent regulations.

Narkomfin, in its instruction for taxing kulaks,[24] adopted part of these criteria but added usury, purchase and sale, and hiring out means of production. But the "agricultural" indices—number of animals and sown area —were to be dropped. In March 1929 Sovnarkom ratified the instruction of Narkomfin, adding some details.[25]

This legislation was soon crowned by a key piece from Sovnarkom entitled "Indices of Kulak Farms in which the Labor Code Is to Be Applied." Sovnarkom put forward the following criteria (of which one was sufficient) to designate a kulak:

1. hiring of permanent workers for agricultural work or artisan industry;
2. ownership of an "industrial enterprise" such as a flour mill, dairy, establishment or equipment for husking, for wool carding or combing, for making starch or potato flour, for drying fruit or vegetables, and so forth—but only if provided with an engine or a windmill or waterwheel;
3. the hiring out, permanently or seasonally, of complex agricultural machines driven by an engine;
4. the hiring out, permanently or seasonally, of equipped premises for dwelling or business purposes;
5. the presence of members in the family who are engaged in commerce or usury or who have other sources of income not derived from labor. This category includes ministers of cults.[26]

One of these criteria is enough for a family to be classified as kulak. The law does not say how many workers one had to employ to be a kulak; it was clear that one was enough. Some of the indicators are disturbingly vague, especially "commerce," "usury," and above all the clause "other sources not derived from labor." The size of these "industrial enterprises" or "handicraft workshops" should also be noted: it was enough for them to employ one or two wage earners for their owners to be classfied as "class enemies" of the regime.

We have dwelt on these decrees, especially on the last, because they give an exact idea of what the authorities understood as "rural capitalism." Furthermore, it was this last decree which served as the basic document for orienting the men in local charge of dekulakization. It was also the basis of immense abuses. Already for the "individual tax" on the kulaks—an operation almost idyllic compared with dekulakization—the press had noted cases of kulak taxation imposed on sellers of sunflower seed or bottles of milk at a railway station ("commerce"?),[27] or on people who let a room of their house ("other source not derived from labor"?). Later, in the chaotic assault atmosphere of the dekulakization, under the pressure of unbridled propaganda against the class enemies, what restrictive value could there be in a document vague enough to permit the inclusion of almost any peasant in the fateful list, especially if he enjoyed some relative prosperity?

In effect, the policy of dekulakization attacked and practically destroyed the better-off part of the peasantry covered by the general term *zazhitoch- nye*. In a calmer period a research worker (Gaister) allowed himself to conclude that this term "has no class content," i.e. that a *zazhitochnyi* was nothing more than a *serednyak* a little better off than the others. But the official statements, especially when the tension was rising, kept using, without distinguishing them, the two terms "the kulak" and "the *zazhitoch- nyi*" together, as a single characterization, to designate the enemy.

This kind of identification puts into question any claim of the party to the seriousness of its analysis in terms of class. The deliberate invention of the term *podkulachnik*, signifying anybody opposing collectivization, irrespective of his social status, is a still more indicative example of the fact that these terms were used as political means, irrespective of possible Marxist sociological analyses.

Professor Carr has justly observed that, since a certain point in NEP, "it was no longer true that the class analysis determined policy. Policy determined what form of class analysis was appropriate to the given situation."[28]

Now that we know which categories of peasants were included among the kulaks, a second question arises: What was the economic potential of this section and the weight of an average representative? No precise answer is possible because of the state of the statistics and, above all, of the criteria described above. Already the problem of their number is visibly worrying research workers.

The number of kulaks was assessed differently in the inquiries undertaken by the various state agencies and research bodies. They should have been 3.9 percent of 20 million households, according to the Sovnarkom commission in 1927; 4.2 percent, said Narkomzem somewhat later, but Stalin in the same period (1928) settled it: 5 percent![29] We do not know where he got this figure from, for Gosplan at the beginning of 1929 spoke of 3.9 percent, while Danilov, for the end of NEP, cited even 3.2 percent.[30] The difference between Danilov's and Stalin's assessment is more than a third, a difference of some 400,000 households, at least 2.5 million souls.

The Sovnarkom, already cited, estimated the kulak population at 4.9 million souls in 782,000 households, but Molotov, two years later, threw out a figure of 1.2–1.3 million households. At the same time a subcommission of the Politburo, entrusted in December 1929 with dekulakization, estimated the number of souls in kulak families at 5–6 million.[31]

Thus, it is officially against 1.2–1.3 million households that the dekulakization attack was made, without counting all the still more numerous zazhitochnye and the number that cannot be calculated of podkulachniki.

Let us look at this 1.2–1.3 million households, which should correspond to one of the indicators in the May 1929 decree.

What area did they sow? Here we have the same profusion of estimates, of which we shall note only a few: 15 million hectares in 1928, according to one source: 11 percent of the national sown area (Strumilin) or only 6 percent (Gaister) or 13 percent (Konyukhov); 9.4 desyatins on the average per farm (Lyashchenko) with only 0.8 percent of the farms exceeding 18 desyatins, of which about 12 would be under crops. Recalling that the Sovnarkom classed as kulak farms those with from 10 (12, 14, 16 according to the region) desyatins, we can establish the order of size of the indicator wanted.[32] The kulaks hired additional land, but several sources concur in that they thereby added, at the most, 20 percent to their sown area.

As far as livestock and draft animals are concerned, only a small minority of households would have had more than three or four cows and two or three horses (except for regions of nomads with their herds).

The kulaks' power was relatively considerable because they held a fairly important part of the means of production and above all of the more up-to-date agricultural machinery. The concentration of the means of production in the hands of the richest was most pronounced in Siberia, the Urals, and the North Caucasus, regions where there was a more marked differentiation than elsewhere. According to one estimate for the North Caucasus, 5.9 percent of households owned 30 percent of all the means of production of the region. In the Ukraine the kulaks held 18.7 percent (20 percent according to another source). In the country as a whole they were in possession of 16.1 percent of all the means of agricultural production (or 20 percent) and in particular of 21.7 percent of all agricultural machinery in 1927, the last year in which the kulak class as a whole was still growing. The same source estimates the proportion of the rural population with more than 1,600 rubles' worth of means of production per household as 3.2 percent of all households and puts the average per farm at some 2,623.3 rubles.[33]

According to Nemchinov, they gathered 13 percent of the country's harvest, or according to Gaister, 8 percent, or according to Trifonov, as much as 15 percent; that is to say, taking Nemchinov's figure, 617 million poods (10 million tons). The proportion of each household's production which was marketed was estimated by Nemchinov as 20 percent and the aggregate share of commercial grain in the country also at 20 percent, so the kulaks would have sold (in 1926) some 126 million poods (against 660 million before the war). Nemchinov's famous table served as a basis for Stalin's appraisal of events "on the grain front."[34] Taking a figure of 800,000 kulaks for this year, an average kulak farm would have harvested some 750 poods (12 tons) and sold 150, which shows a fairly low level of kulak production and income.

Let us take some figures relating to kulak incomes. In 1927 Molotov said that according to the calculations of the fiscal authorities, a peasant employing workers (*srokovye*) averaged 166 rubles of taxable income. Two years later Strumilin calculated their income at 400 rubles, five times more than the income of a *bednyak*, but the kulak paid twenty times more tax. Another source estimates that the kulaks secured 10 percent of all the money income of the peasants.[35] Kritsman told the Communist Academy that a skilled worker sometimes earns more than a minor kulak.[36] But did not these "minor kulaks" constitute the majority of the whole stratum?

In 1928/29, when the attack on the well-to-do peasants was stepped up, Narkomfin, now less indulgent than in previous years, claimed that 890,000 households enjoyed an income in excess of 700 rubles a year. Trifonov provides yet another figure: that the kulaks would have had "a net accumulation" of 150 million rubles a year.[37] We do not know among how many households this sum should be divided—whether Molotov's 1.3 million or Narkomfin's 890,000. Let us divide by 1 million. We shall then have a net accumulation of 150 rubles per household of six to seven persons per year and per "exploiter." Such a sum, if it is exact, would not be negligible in Soviet rural conditions. But we should also take good care here not to use terms appropriate only to a much larger economic scale.

A problem which was surrounded in mystery was that of the stocks of grain which the kulaks were supposed to have accumulated. In the course of the forced procurements during the "grain crisis" at the beginning of 1928, Stalin urged onward the militants of Siberia, demanding that they seize the kulaks' reserves, which he estimated as fabulous. We do not know who provided his calculations. At the Fifteenth Party Congress Sokol'nikov estimated that the stocks of the whole of the peasantry in 1928 approached 1 billion poods, enough to feed the country for three months. This is a very modest figure, which another source further reduces by 100 million poods.[38] The left opposition platform, inclined at this period to exaggerate the kulak danger, ascribed to the kulaks some 400–500 poods of stocks per family. This is far removed from the figures of Gaister, who estimated that in 1927 in the regions of greatest differentiation the proportion of total stocks of the peasants in the Urals was 18.4 percent held by 9.3 percent of households, and in the Ukraine and the North Caucasus up to 12.8 percent held by more than 5 percent of households in each of these regions.[39] If we take 10 percent for the whole country as the portion of the stocks held by kulaks, this would give only 100 poods per kulak household, compared with the opposition's figure of 400–500 poods. Even if we double the 100 poods, 200 poods (3.5 tons) of stocks per household is still a very modest amount. We must keep in mind that a peasant household had to have a necessary reserve to feed its members and animals till the next harvest. It had also, if conditions permitted, to hold an emergency reserve in case of famine. Only the amount of grain over and above these quanti- ties, which were essential for the normal functioning of a village household, should have been considered as commercial reserves indicating economic strength and capacity for accumulation. In the light of our calculations, we are inclined to agree with Bukharin, who in his "Notes of an Economist" (*Pravda*, September 30, 1928), when he was still a member of the Polit- buro, wrote that the legends about the peasants' stocks had proved baseless. Besides, whatever these reserves might have been, they had considerably diminished during the course of the forced collections in 1928 and 1929.

We must now review the three factors which served—and which still serve—for different authors as "direct social indicators" enabling us to observe the formation of a distinct kulak class. These factors are the renting of land, the hiring out of the means of labor, and the employment of workers. Besides this, authors do not agree as to whether all these three indicators are included in the category of "direct social indicators." For certain authors, only the employment of workers would be valid; for others (Yakovtsevsky) the employment of workers and the renting of land; for still others the employment of workers and the hiring out of means of labor or, above all, this last index (Kritsman) or all three (Danilov).[40]

To begin with, it must be established that the letting of land for farming was not a very widespread phenomenon during the period of the NEP. The Commissariat of Inspection, which usually raised the TsSU figures to cover possible illegal deals, estimated for 1926 that 17.4 percent of farms had recourse to renting land and that the total area of rented farmland was around 11 million hectares—whereas by the 1890s the peasants were already renting five times that amount, 50 million desyatins.[41] Yakovtsevsky claims that the principal lessees were the kulaks, but his own figures contra- dict this allegation: it was the middle peasant who had most of this land, 7.8 million hectares out of 11.2 million, and a further part was held by the *bednyaki*. Danilov, then, would be right in saying that "the *serednyaki* have begun to play a role of the first order as tenants of land."[42] But these two modern authors are in agreement that the renting of land "was intermingled in kulak farms with the exploitation of manpower and was of an entrepreneurial (*predprinimatel'skii*) character."[43]

This allegation requires examination. The figures indicate, firstly, that less than half the kulaks rented additional land.[44] They took some 18.7 percent of all rented land, according to one source, which would have given them 20 percent more land than their share. Another source gives specifically 7.5 hectares of extra land per kulak lessee. But, in contrast to the authors quoted above, Lyashchenko maintained that in the regions where there was most renting there was little employment of workers and vice versa. Yakovtsevsky's and Danilov's argument is rebutted most strongly of all by a Siberian investigator, Kas'yan, in the course of a discussion in the Academy of Sciences in 1961.[45]

There still remains one category, those sowing large areas, which must be examined separately. According to Danilov, those who sowed 16–25 hectares rented half of their land. Those who sowed more than 25 hectares rented an average of 19.3 hectares per farm. The former, according to Danilov, had to employ paid workers.[46] Unfortunately the author does not give us his estimate of how many of these peasants sowing large areas there were, and how many *batraki* they could employ. It seems that this was only a small minority of the kulaks themselves. On the other hand a large peasant family could well manage a substantial area without recourse to paid workers except at peak times. Can one distinguish between such a family and a kulak household?

The hiring out of means of labor was a more widespread phenomenon than the renting of land since a great many poor peasants—35 percent of all peasants according to the official estimate were *bednyaki*—as well as a good number of so-called weak peasants (*malomoshchnye*) did not have plows, agricultural machinery, or horses for cultivating their land. Some 40 percent of the peasants hired means of labor and some 16 percent or 20 percent of the peasants provided them with this service.[47]

The *bednyaki* hired principally simple tools and draft animals but not machines. It was the kulaks themselves and some of the *serednyaki* who hired more sophisticated tools and agricultural machinery. Numerous *serednyaki*, perhaps a quarter of the total, hired out the means of labor. It is clear that they were the most important section of those who hired out. The cost of this to the borrower must have been fairly high: the hire of a simple piece of equipment (plow, mower, or sowing machine) could cost 19–20 percent of the harvest from the land worked with it. If the equipment was hired with a horse, the return demanded could be as much as 52 percent of the harvest, which is a high degree of *zhivoderstvo* ("skinning alive"). The *serednyak* or kulak hirer could also demand payment in money or in labor service. However, the author from whom we have taken these data maintains—contrary to Danilov—that both hiring of the means of labor and wage earning "were not decisive and did not occur widely" in the Soviet countryside.[48] This is in spite of his data showing that 45 percent of kulaks as well as numerous other peasants hired out means of labor.[49] The fact that the author minimizes the role of this hiring may perhaps be explained by his awareness that most frequently the function in question was merely a service between neighbors practiced a little by everybody and was very rarely a stable activity with the aim of gain. To interpret it as a major or simply an important sign of capitalism would deprive the very notion of capitalism of all meaning. This is the sense of the passage from Dubrovsky quoted above.

We come now to wage earning, which should serve as the principal test for an analysis of class and for the identification of rural capitalism. But the key to the problem is not yet found, not even in the indicator of wage earning, for this indicator is in no better case than the previous ones. The employment of wage earners inside villages and by peasant farms was, firstly, not widespread; secondly, insofar as it was practiced, it was practiced by all classes, even by certain *bednyaki* who *employed* wage earners and kulaks who *took employment*; and thirdly, it was not widespread even among the kulaks.

According to a calculation made for 1927, more than half of the *bednyaki* and a third of the *serednyaki* provided manpower. This was mostly short periods of employment of day workers in times of peak activity and was thus a supplementary rather than a permanent means of livelihood. It was the agricultural workers, the *batraki*, who took employment for a fixed period, for at least fifty days a year.

There was never any suitable census of the different categories of wage earning, and the figures vary no less—if not more—than for the other phenomena which we are studying. There are said to have been 2,310,900 *srokovye* in 1928, but of this number only 1,492,200 are said to have been employed by private peasants.[50] Certain authors rush to assert that these were employed above all by the kulaks, but the available figures are not so categorical. One would have to add to the quoted figures an estimate for 2 million day workers who took employment sporadically. For about the same period the number of farms which employed regular wage earners is estimated by one source at 1.4 million. If we also count the temporary employment of day workers, the proportion of farms which had recourse to wage earners is estimated at 18 percent in 1927 and 20.1 percent in 1929.[51]

An interesting table published by Danilov[52] shows that the total number of days of paid work was distributed as follows:

21.1%, *bednyaki*, employed 5.7% of the total
26.3%, "weak" peasants, employed 11.9% of the total
30.8%, *serednyaki*, employed 30.5% of the total
13.6%, well-to-do *serednyaki*, employed 31% of the total
 3.2%, kulaks, employed 20.9% of the total

Apart from adding one more example of a distribution of social classes, the striking fact demonstrated here is that they all hire workers but that the principal employer is the *serednyak* and not the kulak. Kas'yan asserted to the Academy of Sciences in 1961[53] that it was the *serednyak* who employed the largest number of wage earners and that it was he principally who hired out the means of labor and let land. Other authors add that the *serednyak* was also a principal producer and seller of grain and the chief owner of livestock and means of production.[54] These conclusions are banal to someone who knew the village—and the economy—of the NEP period. But they are of great importance for our subject because, when reached today by certain Soviet investigators, they indicate a latent re-evaluation of the whole kulak problem.

All things considered, how widespread was the employment of workers by the kulaks? Firstly, one important point is established: only half the kulaks had recourse to the employment of *batraki*,[55] about half of these employing one single *batrak* and the other half more than one.[56] To this must be added a certain number of day workers, which is difficult to estimate—but this does not substantially change the general picture: the employment of workers was not very widespread; the average kulak employer cultivated his farm mainly with the help of members of his own family, employing wage earners only to make up the balance, and half the kulaks did without wage earners altogether.

This brief survey shows that the size of the kulaks' farms was modest, whatever their economic power in relation to the other categories of peasants may have been. This is not to deny in any way the existence of differentiation among the peasantry or the importance of this phenomenon in the life of the village and the country. Of course differentiation existed, although to a considerably lesser degree than before the revolution. Nor is it to deny the influence and the social role of the well-to-do peasants—as will be seen further on—provided that this influence and this role are not exaggerated, as is often done from a desire to justify past policy at all costs. What we are rejecting is certain claims about the social character of the category called kulaks and above all the thesis that they were a distinct and, in addition, capitalist class.

Certain investigators qualified these claims with important reservations as, for example, Kritsman, who declared: "We are dealing with a capitalism which is not only not very widespread but is also extremely fragmented,"[57] and which exists only in an "embryonic" state. But these reservations as well as a series of "diminutives" such as "petty-capitalist" or "semi-capitalist" used by certain authors do not weaken our objections.

The kulak, better off than the other peasants, sold only 20 percent of his grain. Even if this official figure is an underestimate, the kulak still lives, like the other peasants, to a great extent in a relatively closed natural economy; his farm is not highly specialized and is based mainly on the labor of his own family. Supposing that some of them, under favorable circumstances not necessarily then in existence, would be able to strengthen their position and raise themselves to the rank of entrepreneurs, to farmers of the American type, use of the term "embryo" of the future farmer, of the future capitalist, is still not justified because it leads the search for reality astray and prevents the investigator from grasping the real situation.

The kulak was not sufficiently separated from the better-off section as a whole, estimated at 10 percent or 15 percent of all the peasants, to constitute a separate class. On the contrary he is notable for the fact that he unquestionably belongs socially to the peasantry as a whole. Certain elements, baptized "entrepreneurs," owning "enterprises" of the type described in the Sovnarkom decree, could not have amounted to more than 0.9 percent of households or been large enough in most cases to affect the social nature of the farm.[58] The kulaks who were classed by Narkomfin as *krest'yanskie* were the majority. The term used by the Polish sociologist Gałęski, "enlarged family production," would be the most appropriate here.

We must, however, draw attention to another category equally called "kulak" in the official terminology but which seemed to have crossed the quantitative border level and to constitute a different group. A few sources, notably Larin, speak of the existence of farmers who were important in a different way.[59] These were true entrepreneurs employing several permanent workers and a score of day workers. The population called them "new *pomeshchiki.*" There is also mention of considerable areas of land which they hired, mainly from the state, and of a substantial number of animals, etc. These entrepreneurs were most active in certain special branches such as tobacco and market garden crops near large towns.

How widely could such a phenomenon have occurred? There are no figures or special studies on this. They were, however, rare cases which depended on local corruption rather than a widespread phenomenon. Whatever the number and character of these enterpreneurs may have been, "our" kulak, the million households which we have examined, does not belong to the category of "new *pomeshchiki,*" and the use of the same term "kulak" in both cases is inadmissible. The mass of peasants who were called kulak and subjected to dekulakization, with all that this involved, *comprised the owning pole of the peasant social scale,* of which one can legitimately speak in Russia of the NEP period, the opposite pole being the *bednyaki* and *batraki.* A certain part of the latter were employed by the kulaks but above all by the middle peasants. In different circumstances this differentiation could have taken different forms, notably the ultimate appearance among the kulaks of a capitalist farmer class. This did not ocur in Soviet rural society, so the kulak should be analyzed as a peasant. The hurry to see at all costs in the peasantry the equivalent, more or less formed, as if overnight, of the owning classes in a capitalist society falsified theoretical analysis and had grave consequences for political developments.

The social position of the kulak in the Soviet village is not merely one of exploitation of his neighbors. He certainly played an important and positive role there, as was confirmed by Kalinin, who was unquestionably acquainted with rural life. He explained that the political influence of the kulak, despite his rather insignificant growth, stemmed from the fact that he "fulfilled certain positive functions in the peasant economy."[60] The poor peasant, according to Kalinin, knows that the government does nothing but promise help, while "Tikhon Ivanovich will help him out at a time of difficulty" with a loan of money, seed, a plow, or a horse. He also knew that if the kulak killed a cow, the *bednyak* would be able to get a pound of meat out of it. This attitude on the part of the poor peasant, Kalinin noted, existed despite his knowledge that "Tikhon Ivanovich" would have to be paid handsomely for his services later.

This important point shows the one-sided nature of the official allegations about the hatred of the kulak by the peasant masses. Manifestations of hatred by the *batraki* or other peasants are supposed to have occurred here and there, but in general the life of the village during the NEP period did not at all proceed under the sign of a social struggle against the kulak. If even many *bednyaki* reasoned in the way Kalinin describes, the *serednyak* himself not only did not hate the kulak but respected him as a good farmer (*khozyain*) who often served as his model. The covetousness or jealousy which could be combined with this did not arouse widespread social hatred. The *serednyak*, on the contrary, despite official propaganda, disdained his poor neighbors for he was inclined to attribute their poverty to idleness.

That there were sporadic explosions of hatred on the part of poor peasants hard-pressed by a neighbor, kulak or otherwise, a recurrent rural phenomenon, cannot be denied. Sometimes recollections of the civil war came into play, notably in the North Caucasus and the Ukraine, when the *batrak* or the *bednyak* had rallied to the "Reds" and the kulak fought on the side of the "Whites." But these facts already belonged to history. The kulak was no longer as widespread and was often no longer the same person, and the old *bednyak* could well have changed his place on the village social ladder too and become a *serednyak* and, who knows, especially if he were a member of the party, perhaps even better off than that. In short, in the village of the NEP period no important anti-kulak action would have been produced for a long time without the most direct intervention by the authorities.

The study of the kulak's political attitude, insofar as valid sources can be consulted, shows that no longer, or not yet, did he see himself as detached from the mass of *khozyaeva* of his village. We can draw on

Angarov's study based on material accumulated at the Communist Academy.[61] The author asserts that "the kulak has taken into consideration his lack of organization and now . . . he is trying to attack as an organized political force." This amounts to an admission that the kulaks did not constitute an organized force before 1929. As for the attack "as a political force," this expression seems to be just a formal concession to the political requirements of the time, for the author himself takes the trouble to correct this judgment by saying that things did not have to be viewed mainly as "the attack on the part of the kulaks" for "the kulak only attacks in certain places but in general it is he who is attacked."[62]

This last statement corresponds more closely to the political reality on the eve of collectivization. The kulak was strongly pressed during the grain collections. Attacked on all sides as an enemy of the regime, he sensed that it was planned to eliminate him from the village. This drove him to defend himself, but his defense, however ferocious it could be, shows clearly a lack of even slightly developed political consciousness.[63] During their utterances and conversations before collectivization "they" had neither the capacity nor the desire to formulate political slogans appropriate to themselves. They do not set up watchwords against the towns, and nothing is heard from them of "the peasant alliance," nor of general opposition to the workers. At best the kulaks' aims scarcely extend beyond the limits of their *raion*, and they show no trace of either a political program or an organization of their own. For, according to Angarov, "the kulak is preoccupied above all with his village business."[64] which amounts to saying that he does not see himself as a member of a separate social or political class and that he has no specific political vision. This verdict is confirmed by Syrtsov, the future head of the government of the RSFSR, who reported to the party conference "a certain crystallization, a growth of consciousness of themselves as a class, among the kulaks." This growth of consciousness, he claimed, had been produced "recently." The kulak nevertheless does not distinguish himself from the mass of the peasants but waits patiently until the authorities in power move against the interests of the middle peasantry.[65]

This explanation also confirms that the class consciousness of the richer peasants is only beginning to show itself, while the fact that the kulak is not distinguished from the mass, presented as if a deliberate tactical move, was rather a straightforward statement of fact. When attacked as though they were an entity, which they were not, these elements tried to dissolve in the mass. They were nothing without the bulk of the *serednyaki*, and without being defended by this mass they had no means of their own to defense or action other than individual acts of desperation. On the basis of his experience in Siberia, where the social tension caused by the forced collections was particularly acute, Syrtsov informs us that the kulak was beginning to want to leave the existing Soviet framework but "he lacked capacity for adequate organization,

organization on a national scale, had no legal fund of terms which could have legitimized his movements as a movement on the union scale, and he did not have at his disposal personalities with authority on whom he could have relied in this affair."[66]

In other words, even when forced to become a class and to act accordingly, the kulak was not capable of it. As the assault of the authorities in power against the kulak was confirmed and broadened, his principal weapon was the diffusion of reports discrediting the kolkhozy.[67] With his back to the wall, and frightened by the dismal prospects facing him, he sought to escape the blows by flight to the towns, to other villages, or even into the kolkhozy if he was admitted. Finally, certain individuals driven to despair and hatred countered with individual attacks of terror: attacks with rifle or hatchet, or more simply with stick or fist. But this only sealed their fate. This last desperate form of defense had evidently not occurred during the NEP years but only on the eve of collectvization. The authorities had then put the kulaks in a situation from which there was no escape, and it was this which generated these outbursts of hatred. They became more and more frequent during the course of the forced collectivization and dekulakization, but they did not reach a scale of any importance among such hunted men as the kulaks were.* A violently anti-kulak article which appeared in Bol'shevik in October 1929 admits that the kulaks' tactics consisted rather in presenting themselves as citizens loyal to Soviet power, which is why they saw no sense in taking a rifle and shooting.[68]

The party's attitude toward the kulak, and the question of the fate which was to be reserved for him in the course of the transformations which were being prepared, is characterized by hesitations which reflect an uncertainty and lack of clarity about the real social character of the kulaks. To be sure, everybody was in principle hostile to the most well-to-do section of the peasantry, but even during the crisis years of 1928 and 1929—until the end of the autumn of 1929—nobody dreamed of expropriating them. It was commonly admitted in the party that a "dekulakization" made no sense, at least not according to some.[69]

Kalinin, from the official party platform, ridiculed those who wanted to "strip" (razdet') them, which would be too easy and scarcely constructive. In his view the kulaks had to be combatted by effective economic competition from the state and cooperative organizations.[70]

---

* Official documents attach great importance to the terrorist activities of the kulaks, but the figures published are only partial, for certain periods or certain regions, never the full picture. It is not clearly stated what sort of terrorist activity is meant, whether assassination, woundings, or simply beatings. Besides, village brawls, so widespread in the countryside, are often termed terrorist acts if one of those implicated is suspected of being a kulak. The true extent of this terrorism still remains to be established.

During this period kulaks still continued to participate officially in the cooperative movement, although without the right to be included in the management committees. They were also admitted, at least up to the autumn of 1929, to kolkhozy: this by a series of explicit authorizations granted by the party committees of several large regions and even by a decision of the Central Committee taken in relation to the problems of the North Caucasus. The famous Shevchenko sovkhoz saw no objection to making contracts with kulaks to till their land—albeit with certain restrictions—which was in conformity with current pratice more or less everywhere.[71]

During 1929 the problem discussed widely in the press and rather bitterly at the Sixteenth Party Congress in April was that of the admission of kulaks to the large kolkhozy. In the press, Karpinsky above all denounced as anti-Leninists the radicals who opposed such admission of kulaks to the large kolkhoz organizations.* At the Sixteenth Congress this position was defended by Kalinin, a member of the Politburo, who ridiculed the platform of the "revolutionaries" like Shatskin and Lominadze who demanded the exclusion of kulaks from the kolkhozy and some form or other of separate installation of these kulaks on land outside the kolkhoz lands. It is significant that the conference was not able to settle this disagreement, nor was the special commission composed of first-rank figures (Stalin, Molotov, Kalinin, Ordzhonikidze, Syrtsov) which had been appointed by the conference to draw up a line of policy in this field. It was finally decided to leave the question to the Politburo.[72]

The latter made its decision some six months later: "liquidation of the kulaks as a class." Even during the dramatic days of December 1929, when dekulakization had in practice already begun, another commission appointed by the Politburo to consider methods of collectivization proposed that the great majority of expropriated kulaks be admitted to kolkhozy.[73] But the working group which made these proposals was to be dismissed and another commission called in January 1930 to decree the progress of dekulakization.

We see that right up to the last moment when radical measures were decided the party was in the process of proposing one of two solutions: either to admit kulaks to the large kolkhozy or to forbid this and rent to the kulaks land on the borders of the collectivized villages. No authoritative voice advocated more radical measures. The first proposal, in a sense the more moderate one, would have led in practice to the disappearance of this specific stratum insofar, of course, as the kulaks would agree to belong: the anti-kulak proposal led paradoxically to the continued existence of this stratum. Such a situation did not excessively alarm the anti-kulaks at the

---

* In the Central Black Earth Region, Middle and Lower Volga, North Caucasus, and the Ukraine their number fell by 381,100 to 256,800.

time. Did not the five-year plan too envisage not only the existence of kulaks at the end of the five-year period but even the growth of their numbers and their income?[74]

It can be seen that the Bolshevik party, insofar as its advice was asked, did not dream of extremist measures against the kulaks, not even on the eve of the application of such measures. The how and why of such a volte-face is not part of our subject. What interests us is the fact that the party, both its theoreticians and most of its militants, hesitated and did not propose going very far because the social nature of the kulak, his "class character," which was so persistently underlined officially, seemed to them neither clear nor certain. Will there be one day a kind of self-criticism on this subject and a "rehabilitation" of the dekulakized?

While the destiny of the kulaks was still not foreseen by anybody, the realities of the fight for grain conducted highhandedly by the government against the peasants, persecutions of possessors of grain, and anti-kulak propaganda during the collections, resulted—according to numerous sources —in the contraction of this stratum and its economic weakening. Frightened at the prospect of being hounded to the borders of the villages, maltreated by the grain collectors with their demands, the kulaks began to reduce their activity, to dream of finding refuge somewhere, and some even rushed to the kolkhozy, handing over their property in the same way as the others in order to find shelter.[75] During the years 1927–29 numerous kulak farms were considerably weakened. Their stocks began to disappear, they reduced their sowings by some 40 percent if not more, their livestock decreased, and they dismissed many *batraki*, creating unemployment among them.[76] In 1927, in eight grain-producing regions, those who sowed more than 17 hectares provided more than a quarter of the marketed grain of these regions, while in 1929 they only provided 14 percent. It may be surmised that they often stopped renting land—in the Ukraine their renting diminished by 63 percent—and there was considerable talk[77] of their "self-dekulakization," of "the reduction of their farms," of their "transformation into *serednyaki*" (*oserednyachivanie*).[78]

We observe here a process of weakening and reduction in the number of kulaks,* under the impact of legislative and administrative measures. Against this we must take into consideration, as a competent Soviet investigator points out,[79] that their sales of livestock and implements brought them considerable sums, but his chief conclusion is that these

---

* At this period collective farms were in general very small, sometimes with little more than a dozen families. The authorities were now envisaging the organization of very large ones, around the state stations and cooperative columns of machines and tractors, in accordance with the example given by the Shevchenko sovkhoz. Contracts signed between the large tractor stations and whole villages were to give rise to these large collective farms. Subsequent developments did not go in this direction.

processes of reduction, as well as the behavior of the kulak, have not been investigated and are consequently little known.

We emphasize the data concerning the reduction of kulaks because these facts, firstly, contradict the allegations of the strengthening, tenacity, and general danger of the kulaks and, secondly, show clearly that when all is said and done it took little to bring the kulak socially and economically to the situation of a middle peasant. It was enough for him to sell his agricultural machine or dismiss his *batrak* or close his "enterprise" (his barley husker, for example) for there to be nothing left of the kulak as defined by the law.

Was this so easy and simple to pass "from one class to another"? How would this peasant without his *batrak* or without his threshing machine be treated from then on? As *serednyak* or as exkulak? Would his attitude to the policy of forced collectivization change from the moment when, according to the indicators, he was no longer a kulak? These questions are of a more political nature and cannot be treated within the framework of this study.

6

"TAKING GRAIN": SOVIET POLICIES OF AGRICULTURAL PROCUREMENTS BEFORE THE WAR

During the so-called era of the five-year plans in the Soviet Union, and indeed during the whole of Stalin's rule, grain (and the ways of securing it) played a crucial role in the Soviet system. It was a strategic raw material indispensable to the process of running the state and of industrializing it. The term "strategic," with its military connotations, is quite appropriate here; the grain, as leaders would constantly remind their subordinate administrations, "would not come by itself" and had therefore to be literally extracted. Such extraction of grain from peasants could not proceed as a normal economic activity. In order to succeed, so the leaders felt, a state of mobilization had to be declared for the duration of the campaign, with party cells and specially created shock administrations mightily seconded by the state's punitive organs.

Not surprisingly, as the whole operation assumed the character of a quasi-military requisitioning, it contributed toward shaping the Soviet economy as a *"sui generis* war economy."[1] *Zagotovki*—the Russian term for procurement of agricultural produce which we shall be using here— was probably a linchpin of this war economy, as the single activity which required more large-scale mass coercion than any other state activity in those years. Year after year, the *zagotovki* campaign was a difficult affair taking up the energies of many agencies, including the Politburo itself, which supervised closely all the stages of the campaign and constantly intervened in it. For a good quarter of a century, extracting grain from the peasants amounted to a permanent state of warfare against them and was understood as such by both sides. For the peasants, *zagotovki* became a symbol of arbitrariness and injustice, and they employed all possible means of passive resistance and even sabotage against the squeeze. The state responded by devising countermeasures to outmaneuver every subterfuge and to close every escape valve which could be used by peasants—not to mention the crudest punishments whenever these were deemed necessary.

A campaign of this scope and character, naturally enough, became the central activity of the state in the countryside and molded the state's relationship with the peasants. It became the essence of party policies in the countryside, to which all the rest was subordinated. In this way, Soviet agriculture, the kolkhoz system, and in many aspects, the character of the whole polity were shaped by this peculiar and simple procedure of "taking grain."*

It is therefore worth our while to sketch out, briefly, the main stages of the *zagotovki*, its methods and its features. As grain procurement was the crux of the matter, we shall devote most of our attention to it; the extraction of other farm products, like meat and milk, although important, can be dealt with only cursorily, for the methods applied in this sphere were borrowed from the grain front.†

▪ TOWARD A NEW PATTERN, 1928–30

During the NEP period, from roughly 1924, when the tax-in-kind was replaced by a simple tax-in-cash, and up to 1928, the state resorted to grain procurements through its commercial agencies and government-controlled, cooperative organizations. But this was then, essentially, a commercial operation, consisting of buying grain from peasants at a market price. To be sure, some gradual changes were introduced during those years which favored the state agencies and discriminated against the private dealers, such as denying to the latter credit by banks or putting obstacles in the way of their shipment arrangements. From 1925, govern-

---

* The Soviet term is, in fact, *vzyat' khleb* (taking bread), and party leaders would say, triumphantly, that this year "we took" such and such a quantity of grain. The term expressed the reality of the procedure.

† The procurement campaigns would begin almost simultaneously with the harvest and last well into the spring of the next calendar year. But the entire action was included in the "economic year," say 1928/29 (beginning on October 1, 1928, and ending on September 30, 1929). Thus, "the 1928/29 procurement campaign" means procurement of grain from the harvest which grew in the (calendar) year 1928. From January 1, 1931, the "economic year" was abolished, and planning and other economic activities were subsequently to be conducted in the framework of calendar years. Hence the procurement campaign of, say, 1933 means the campaign based on the harvest grown in 1933. It would, in the post-NEP years, be virtually finished by the end of the same year.

mental price limits were introduced, which the state's agents were not supposed to overstep. But the private dealers were not eliminated, there was no state monopoly in grain, and sales to the state were not made compulsory. Furthermore, the numerous state and cooperative agencies engaged in those purchases conducted their businesses with peasants exactly as any market operator would do it; they competed among themselves, disregarded the price limits, bid up prices and collaborated with the skillful private traders either by buying grain from them or by using them as their purchasing subagents. One should also be reminded that toward the end of the NEP state purchases managed to concentrate some 12–14 percent of the gross harvest and some 56–57 percent of the marketable grain that the peasants were willing to part with. These figures will become more meaningful to the reader as we proceed.[2] But this Nepmen's near idyll ended abruptly in the winter and spring of 1927/28, when such methods of procuring grain stumbled and ushered in the "grain procurement crisis," as peasants preferred to sell better-priced animal products and technical crops rather than relatively underpriced grain, which could be put to better use in stock breeding, for personal consumption, or for building up reserves.

The government, alarmed by the dwindling procurements and the prospect of being starved out of power by the peasants' self-interested behavior, resorted to so-called extraordinary measures, consisting of confiscating grain, though still paying a near-market price for it and even raising it quite considerably during the next campaign.[3] Such measures were presented as temporary and, at the beginning, sincerely so. In fact, normal market procurement practices were never afterward restored, and the "extraordinary" soon became ordinary practice, although not without dramatic upheavals.[4]

1928/29 was still a transition year in the history of the *zagotovki* campaigns. Private merchants were hard pressed and driven out of the markets, but many were still functioning and, obviously, preferred by the peasants, as they were willing to pay them much more than the state. The numerous governmental agencies still kept competing with each other and, on the whole, coped badly with their task. The extraordinary measures, which were, as promised, eased at the beginning of the campaign, were soon restored, but the overall result was nevertheless, weaker than in 1927/28, itself an emergency year: only 10.7 million tons of grain were collected, against 11 million in the earlier campaign, (but in this later total, the share of food grain as against forage was significantly higher).

Such facts definitively swung the government into a complete reshaping of its relations with the peasantry. The first five-year plan, with its ambitious targets and insatiable pressures for ever more investment resources, had just been launched and was becoming a huge national effort on an unprecedented scale. The countryside, if not properly controlled and mastered, could wreck the whole effort: such was clearly the conclusion drawn by some of the key leaders from the "grain crisis" and the continuing difficulties thereafter. The two campaigns conducted by emergency methods in 1927/28 and 1928/29 gave the necessary experience, and preparations were made to meet the next challenge during 1929/30 on entirely new lines. The two major far-reaching innovations introduced in the autumn of 1929 were the launching of the collectivization drive, and the abolition, de facto, of the whole NEP framework. The single clearly discernible factor which triggered off these two interconnected changes was the transformation of the *zagotovki* into a compulsory state duty and, particularly, the set of means employed in imposing this new policy on the peasants. Critics of the government charged its policies contemptuously with having "slid into forced collectivization on the wave of forced *zagotovki*"—and this was a substantially correct statement.[5] We shall show later the relevance of the methods of squeezing grain to the ways of forcing peasants into kolkhozy and of running the kolkhoz system. But let us first outline the main stages through which the whole system passed before it evolved into a stable pattern.

The 1929/30 campaign should concern us, to begin with, because it exhibited many of the features of the framework which was to emerge in a definitive form by the end of 1933. The agencies which previously competed with each other were now unified, considerably streamlined, and organized into a powerful apparatus led from the center by specially designed bodies.[6] Instead of the numerous central, republic, and local organizations, only a few were now allowed to operate, to ensure unity of policy, command, and control of the entire campaign.

On the eve of the following year a method of contracts (*kontraktatsiya*) had been introduced into the grain exchange sphere which was borrowed from the areas of technical crops. This method consisted of signing up individual peasants, whole peasant communities, or kolkhozy before the sowing campaign on contracts for the supply of grain to the state. It was intended to be a bilateral agreement, freely signed, with obligations on both sides, as a deal with reciprocal advantages. The government was supposed to advance money, to supply goods and means of production, and to help with grain loans when necessary. The peasant would agree to deliver a certain, not clearly specified, minimum amount of grain, and enjoy special bonuses for sales of grain above those minimums. Initially, neither the signing up nor the parting with surpluses above those stipulated by the contracts was compulsory.

The government pinned great hopes on this method—and it stuck to this practice until the end of 1932. It was meant to be a powerful new tool for planning agricultural production which would introduce predictability to the thorny delivery process and ensure stability and security in the country's food supplies.

The idea was no doubt interesting, and it was many years later successfully applied by the Polish government after they abolished the kolkhozy in 1957. But in the Soviet case this idea was killed before it came to be seriously tested and operated. The trouble was that already, in the autumn of 1929, signing up became compulsory, and the prices paid to producers—compulsory too—were by now beginning to lag seriously behind the market. Furthermore, the government began evading its contractual obligations. Advance payments were soon to be abolished, and promises of supplies were not kept. Obviously, in these conditions both sides lost interest in the contracts, although, as mentioned, the government stuck to the procedure and made it an obligation to sign, especially for the kolkhozy. But whatever the content of such a contract, the actual quantities of grain to be delivered were by now fixed by planned delivery quotas prepared by the government and handed down by local officials to every village. Kolkhozy became aware by now, as a special decree of April 1930 brought home to them, that they would have to deliver from one-quarter to one-third of their crop in grain-producing areas, and one-eighth in the other areas. Furthermore, the delivery was to be accompanied by a vociferous campaign enjoining kolkhozy and also private farmers to give up not just these or other legally prescribed quantities but "all surpluses," with the notion of "surplus" becoming dangerously extendable, much at the discretion of local authorities.

For the well-to-do and the kulaks a special procedure was devised: they were not allowed to sign contracts, but had fixed (*tverdye*) quotas imposed on them independently of their sowings and output. By this token thanks to the extendability of categories like "kulaks," and especially "well-to-do" (*zazhitochnye*), many peasants were stripped in this campaign—and in the two previous ones—of all grain reserves they might have accumulated during past years.[7] For the stronger producers of the Soviet countryside the loss of reserves meant the beginning of the end for them as farmers. In fact, as the *zagotovki* were proceeding in the autumn and winter of 1929/30, they eventually grew into a full-fledged "dekulakization" of the well-to-do, whereas millions of the other peasants were forcibly driven into kolkhozy.

Unfortunately for the newly established kolkhozy, they were themselves handicapped at their birth by the same *zagotovki*, partly because of the tough delivery quotas and partly because of the extremely chaotic way in which these quotas were distributed. The method of central plans descending from above as an imperative command, split into local quotas by intermediary echelons of the administration, and finally worked out into detailed assignments to kolkhozy, villages, and private farmers by the *raion* and the *selsovet*, had all the unavoidable features of "mechanical" planning which have characterized all Soviet planning ever since. In the case of agriculture, with its infinite diversity of local conditions, such a method was particularly pernicious. Targets coming from above were accompanied by a powerful pressure on lower echelons to meet those targets "at any price"—an expression quite current in administrative orders, and coupled with a reminder of the appropriate paragraphs of the Criminal Code in store for the laggards. Such pressures did not leave much leeway to local officials to adapt the final quotas to the conditions and possibilities of kolkhozy and the other farmers. A mechanical distribution of quotas resulted, mindful only that the sum total demanded from above be secured, although many experts were calling for a more sensible approach.[8]

For delivery quotas to be an economic proposition, or at least not to wreck the producing unit, such quotas had to be calculated on the basis of a carefully composed grain and fodder balance (*khlebofurazhnyi balans*), which would consider in detail the needs and possibilities of exery kolkhoz separately, and of whole *raiony*. Such balances by their very character could not be anything but a basically local affair, with data coming from below and made dependent on the estimates of the producers themselves, to a large measure. Producers would obviously be able to use such balances in order to defend their own interests—and this was the reason which determined the government's attitude to the whole problem. It soon came out very strongly against all those who wanted balances to serve as the basis for *zagotovki* assessments, presenting such demands as a subterfuge for defending the peasants and for sabotaging the interests of the state.[9]

As the "mechanical" assessment gained the upper hand during the 1929/30 campaign, its damaging influence on the economics of the kolkhozy became apparent immediately; and in later years, as we shall see, the sapping of production capabilities of the countryside resulting from this way of doing things was to acquire catastrophic proportions. But one instance of such a sapping effect can be quoted now, as observers were already pointing to it in 1930: with the reserves of the well-to-do entirely wiped out by "extraordinary measures" and the delivery quotas becoming tougher, the *zagotovki* soon enfeebled, and later dried out almost entirely, the quantities of grain which used to circulate in the intervillage and interdistrict grain markets.[10] Such intervillage commerce played an important role in helping out in case of a local crop deficiency or in some plans for modest improvements on the farm, but the deep inroad into this resource by voracious *zagotovki* contributed toward rendering the countryside extremely vulnerable to the slightest climatic setback.[11]

The government seemed rewarded and pleased by the result of the *zagotovki*: toward the end of 1929, earlier than in any other campaign, the plan was met and an unprecedented 16 million tons gathered. But at the same time the bread supply in the cities had to be rationed, and during 1930 rationing was to spread to all foodstuffs. The government had only just begun building up some state reserves of grain, but much more than before was now needed for the growing cities, technical plant growers, and the non-grain-producing areas, and the government was also keen to resume substantial exports of agricultural produce to obtain foreign currency for purchasing machinery. But as at the same time collectivization was being forced on reluctant peasants, a new calamity befell the country, a quite predictable result of the policies of the government in the winter and spring of 1930: as peasants saw their horses and cows herded into the collectivized stockades against their wish, they preferred to slaughter their animals and sell or eat them before they themselves joined the kolkhoz. The blow caused by this process to the national economy was even worse than the damage inflicted on Soviet stock breeding by the German invasion eleven years later. Such slaughtering was to go on for some time, but even when it stopped, the numbers of draft animals and cattle still continued to dwindle as the result of inadequate care and bad husbandry. A trend toward recovery in this branch, which became discernible from 1935 onward, would not be sufficient to make good the losses before the war.

In 1930, in any case, which interests us here, the slaughter of cattle produced at first a transitory abundance of meat, soon to be replaced by an acute shortage of animal products aggravating the already tense food situation.

The authorities tried feverishly to stop the damage by temporarily discontinuing the collectivization drive at the end of the spring and by letting people leave kolkhozy; the kolkhozy that survived were now allowed to let their members keep a family cow and a small private plot— two measures which were previously refused by the leadership. Another step taken consisted of transforming the *zagotovki* of animal products, which were up to now a market operation, into a compulsory operation on the pattern of grain.[12]

Thus, when the time came to prepare for the next campaign, in 1930/31, i.e., the one to be conducted basically after the harvest in the second half of 1930, the authorities resolved that it was to be based on two pillars: firstly, the campaign would be centered on an exact delivery plan prepared beforehand and reaching every village well before the harvest; secondly, the compaign would have an emergency character and the entire party would be mobilized for that task as its central activity during the *zagotovki* season.[13]

The commissar for internal and foreign trade, A. Mikoyan, was the chief planner of the operation. Once the central targets were approved— or imposed—by the Politburo, his office had to prepare targets for the big national regions, whereas the commissariats's local organs (in republics and oblasts) would break the general figures down into more differentiated norms (so many quintals per hectare per crop) for their appropriate areas. On the basis of such norms, specially constituted committees in the *raiispolkomy* finished the planning and assignment job by computing the amounts of grain to be imposed on every kolkhoz and (with the help of the *selsovety*) on every private farmer. The same committee was also charged with the arduous task of assessing the prospects for the future crop in their district, which had, of course, to be dealt with before the quotas were distributed.

As already mentioned, according to existing decrees the amounts to be taken from kolkhozy had to fluctuate within the limits of one-quarter to one-third of their crops (one-eighth in the non-grain-producing areas) —a very high toll indeed, but in fact not the final word yet, as the propaganda was hammering into the kolkhozy that any pood of grain sold to anybody other than the state amounted to helping class enemies and to criminal antistate action. This meant that the official limits were not to be taken too seriously as guidelines, but that "all surplus" was the real target. But this was no longer any guide. It was never defined and almost undefinable. Therefore the laborious planning by Mikoyan's agencies, their norms and quotas, were only lower limits—as was made perfectly clear by Mikoyan's (and the party's) own propaganda and actions against sales of any grain on the markets.

During the new 1930/31 campaign the badly battered kulaks were to be taxed, as previously, with firm quantities of grain, and the other noncollectivized peasants—still a majority of the rural population at that time—were legally bound to deliver prescribed norms of grain per hectare of their sowings, but not less than the amounts per hectare which the kolkhozy would have to supply.[14]

Both kolkhozy and private farmers were promised bonuses in industrial goods for either accurate deliveries or overfulfillment of quotas, but such promises were all too often broken. The supply of goods to the countryside was extremely badly organized, and in any case the quantity of goods assigned to rural areas fell toward the end of 1930, compared with previous years.[15] But whatever the quantities of industrial goods, they were now firmly welded to the zagotovki campaign: those who were promised goods would not necessarily be supplied, but those who failed to deliver their quotas would be punished by refusal of indispensable merchandise.

The crop that grew in 1930 was a gift from heaven. All the disorders and excesses of the spring notwithstanding, it came to the excellent figure of 83.5 million tons, the biggest crop since 1913 (by certain estimates even bigger than in 1913). It was in anticipation of such a bounty that the zagotovki plans were drawn aiming at new records in grain collecting. The amount actually gathered from the 1930 crop was a record indeed: 22.1 million tons, compared with 16 million the previous year.

Such a crop and such procurements should have helped in mitigating the food shortages and in normalizing supplies. Paradoxically, this was not to be the case. On the contrary, a further aggravation of the country's situation was in store. One reason for this was that the crop figure was exaggerated, and the real crop, though still respectable, was nevertheless much lower: 77.1 million tons according to one source.[16] This would mean that the *zagotovki* in fact mopped up about 30 percent of the crop, against some 14 percent in 1928 (see above). Other reasons for the ensuing aggravation will be given later.

The reaction of the peasants to this type of campaign was predictable: it became current practice for them to use any possible device, subterfuge, or escape hatch to ease this burden, in fact to sabotage it wherever possible. Every ounce of peasant shrewdness was put into practice, including hiding data on real sowings, harvests, and grain actually threshed; premeditated poor harvesting or threshing so that they could return later for a second go and use the returns for themselves; pilfering and hiding any grain they could put their hands on. Somewhat later, during the hungry years of 1931/34, many would go out into the fields and cut off spikes before the harvests—the "hairdressers" (*parikmakhery*), as the press called them.[17]

It very soon became clear to the authorities that there was no difference between the still uncollectivized peasants and the *kolkhozniki* insofar as trying to defend their bread was concerned. Kolkhoz members would call—and the press would predictably dub them "kulak slogans"—for using the grain "first for ourselves." Many peasants would hide grain in holes, and kolkhoz administrations all too often connived in such practices. And, the sum of irony, the allegedly proletarian sovkhozy, "The people in leather jackets" as Mikoyan euphorically characterized them, who went out into the steppes and built the new grain factories, soon began to display a behavior common to other producers.

So, despite the good harvest, the campaign in the autumn of 1930 proceeded with great difficulties. The Ukraine, for example, was so stubborn that it even at some stage put the entire plan in jeopardy. The harassed local authorities and *zagotovki* agents preferred to concentrate on the more easily controllable kolkhozy and weakened their attention toward the private peasants. These could thus sell certain amounts on the black market and make money, whereas the strictly supervised *kolkhozniki* came out of the whole affair considerably worse off than the nonaffiliated. This was in itself not a small ideological setback because it made the kolkhoz even more unpalatable and discouraged potential new entrants.

To put things right, to make "the economic superiority of the kolkhoz" over the private farmers convincing and to save the *zagotovki*, the authorities redoubled their energy: a special mobilization of workers and party officials to be sent to the countryside was decreed; a deluge of heavy fines was hurled on the recalcitrant peasants and taxes and delivery quotas were increased to punish them; mass searches for hidden grain were conducted; finally, to crown the operation, mass arrests were conducted and numerous court cases brought against the dodgers of the grain quotas.[18]

It goes without saying that the battle was joined by the leadership in terms of warfare against class enemies, with the well-to-do peasants (by now dekulakized, deported, or in any case impoverished) serving as the main villains. The trouble with these slogans was that the opposition to *zagotovki* was a general and genuine mass affair. By implication, "kulak" came to mean just any peasant who tried to evade the *zagotovki*. This fact was unintentionally acknowledged by the party, as its propagandists began to circulate additional epithets like *podkulachniki* (kulak hirelings) or the still more unspecified *kulatskie podpevaly* (kulak choirboys)—terms that relinquished any claim to a sociological content but had a clear polit- ical intention: to attack any disobedient peasant or official.*

So, the *zagotovki* of 1930/31 became growingly violent and, as in the previous year, developed into a new wave of deportations and the re- newal of the temporarily dormant (since the spring of 1930) pressure on more peasants to join kolkhozy. This sequence became by now an estab- lished pattern: a *zagotovki* campaign in the autumn, with governmental reprisals growing as peasants offered stubborn resistance; then a new wave of mass arrests and deportations, as a shock treatment to prepare the next stage; finally, in the last stage, inducing new millions of peasants to join kolkhozy.

The same pattern was to be repeated on a grand scale during the next two years, and on a lesser scale and with modifications in the ensuing years. Obviously, still more shattering blows had to be delivered to the peasants before a somewhat more regular kolkhoz system emerged, pointing to a certain degree, at least, of acceptance by peasants of the kolkhoz and of the *zagotoviki* as an unavoidable reality. Events during the following two to three years amounted to precisely such an "educa- tion" of the peasants, to make them accept the new order.

■ ZAGOTOVKI AND FAMINE, 1931–33

Although some of the events of the ensuing years will look like a simple repetition of the pattern just alluded to, in fact, as they constantly gained in breadth and in gloom, they finally reached proportions of a major national catastrophe.

The *zagotovki* seemed to proceed smoothly at the beginning of the 1931 campaign, but toward the end of the summer, grain suddenly "stopped" flowing in. Immediately, 50,000 emissaries were sent from the cities to help the local officials. As crops in the eastern regions (the Urals and Siberia) were poor, the government, however reluctantly, had to re- duce the quotas for these regions, but pressed harder on the others to secure the overall target. The Ukraine and other areas had their initial targets raised, so that the Ukraine, though its crop was mediocre, was finally forced to give up more grain than in the bountiful previous year. Once more, no grain came from the peasants spontaneously. As peasants

* See Chapter 5.

kept resisting and numerous local administrations claimed that the targets were too big, the central authorities reacted by more of the same: demotion of local administrations; dispersal of the whole kolkhozy; mass arrests; and numerous expulsions from the party.[19] The government knew that the peasants would not become more cooperative, especially because it did not intend to, or could not, keep its own promises. The anticipated plan of supplies to rural areas was fulfilled only by half, and the goods shortage in the countryside became an additional strong disincentive for peasants to part with their grain. In fact, many rural areas, as an authoritative source put it, "became entirely stripped of manufactured goods."[20] It was a reflection of an overall economic crisis which the country was plunged into; the inadequacy and ineptitude of the state's trade networks was a further aggravating factor. These networks, created hastily to replace the destroyed private and cooperative circuits of the NEP period, could barely cope with their tasks.

The familiar feature of the previous campaign—the inability to distribute the quotas to fit real possibilities of districts and kolkhozy—became by now a real scourge for the countryside. Some kolkhozy and villages were overtaxed, and nothing more could be taken from them, whatever the repressions. As a way out, the numerous professional and voluntary "plenipotentiaries" (*upolnomochennye*—a familiar figure of the emergency methods of those years), backed by repressive legislation and GPU squads, returned with renewed demands to those who had already fulfilled their quotas. Such reimposition was a breach of promise and of legality which matched the worst of what the "kulak propaganda" was anticipating, and as these practices went on, the countryside was squeezed dry, especially the numerous regions in which the crop that year was very poor. Kolkhozy suffered probably more than other farmers. Many of the kolkhozy saw all their fodder taken away, and much of their seed as well, and the authorities kept coming back, sometimes three or four times, and demanding ever more, of extra (*vstrechnye*) plans.[21] No wonder that the passive resistance grew into serious political trouble in the Ukraine, the North Caucasus, and Kazakhstan,[22] where "anti-Soviet demonstrations" were reported—a term meaning different forms of rioting, protesting, and attacking officials.

Nevertheless, the planned quantities of grain were forthcoming—and they were bigger than in the previous campaigns—but by now the central authorities had become worried about the effects of the orgy of violence to which peasants were submitted. A kind of cooling-off operation was begun, announcing a drive against excesses and the illegal treatment of peasants which was committed—so the center claimed—in breach of the government's "line." Such temporary halts on the overzealous local executors of central policies were not new. They probably resulted from some internal pressure and criticisms of the policies in the upper leadership and amounted to putting the blame on local officials for their "illegal" repressions. There was in fact hardly any problem in locating the real culprit: it would suffice to read the central press and numerous decrees of those days, with their shrill appeals to get the grain and to suppress any "kulak" talk, or the attacks against the criminal "reductionist tendencies" (*skidochnye nastroeniya*, demands to reduce the unfeasible quotas), to find out. But suddenly, when the bulk of the expected grain was already in the governmental granaries, the leadership became liberal and interested in legality. On this occasion the Ukrainian Central Committee thought fit to disclose that many local administrations were engaged in something amounting to "kulak-inspired provocative abuses" against the peasants.[23]

The same Ukrainian CC was somewhat later to admit that the chaotic onslaughts of the *zagotoviteli* (procurement officials) during the 1931 campaign caused difficulties in sowings in the autumn and following spring, which implied that people had no seeds or no energy to sow. In a fit of honesty, this CC declared that the "excesses" of the *zagotovki* caused a complete disorganization of the numerous kolkhozy. We can easily gather that these badly mauled and harassed organizations could not cope with such a routine peasant activity as sowing.

But more was looming behind it all. A great and growing trouble had by now emerged in the Ukraine and other grain-producing areas (elsewhere too, as we learn from modern sources): the ugly specter of famine made its appearance. The Ukrainian CC spoke of numerous regions, especially Vinnitsa and Kiev, in which "many kolkhozy found themselves faced with a critical food situation"—an expression used as a euphemism for famine by this Central Committee and later by modern Soviet writers for the same purpose. The emerging picture was distressing: famine began to spread in grain-producing areas, although their crop, however poor, was not catastrophic and would not normally produce such calamity. The government (Ukrainian in this case) blamed local officials for being blind to the signs of growing trouble until it was too late,[24] and the reader will by now be aware of the reason for the scapegoat operation "against excesses" undertaken from Moscow after the *zagotovki* campaign was basically over. Moscow would not admit any responsibility for the disaster.

But it was impossible for the government to claim that only local leaders were blindfolded so soon after the vicious campaign against some of the same local leaders who were clamoring against excessive *zagotovki* and warning about impending difficulties. Mikoyan certainly anticipated no problems at all when, at the end of 1931, he fixed for the next campaign the fabulous target of 29.5 million tons; but later, when the situation in the countryside toward the beginning of the 1932 campaign became increasingly alarming,[25] he would have to lower his target for grain to 18 million tons and to half that for livestock products.

But these reductions occurred later. In the meantime the preparations for squeezing what Mikoyan initially planned were as stringent as ever. The Ukrainian CC which had recently fulminated against "abuses," was now again on the battle lines fulminating against the eventual "enemies" who were preparing to sabotage the coming campaign by pretending that the targets were too big. The Ukrainians were thus inviting the unavoidable new wave of "excesses" (*peregiby*) and imitating thereby the familiar maneuver of the Moscow Politburo, which consisted in alternating damaging pressures with accusations against lower officialdom for the damages done.[26]

As the new campaign was being deployed, the local agencies were still suffering from a relative torpor resulting from the very recent punishments meted out to some of them for those excesses, and it took some time to spur their energies into a new wave of the same—especially as many local officials were aware of the desperate situation of the peasants, with many of them already hungry and with prospects for the new harvest at best quite poor. In addition to unfavorable climatic conditions, the work badly done by the disoriented and demoralized kolkhozy could not promise anything better.

Peasants, whether members of kolkhozy or still on their own, after having endured the difficult winter and spring of 1931/32 and well aware of the gloomy prospects ahead, were desperately preparing to use every technique in order to retain some of their grain.

All these factors conduced to a very sluggish start of the 1932 *zagotovki*. As the new crop began to be threshed, *kolkhozniki* tried to divide among themselves as much of the fresh grain as possible, with the connivance, or under the direct leadership, of their managements. Grain was used to feed the peasants working in the fields, to create all kinds of seed and reserve funds, to advance payments on the *trudodni* earned by the members—all actions which were supposed to be taken only after the state had taken its share. Not before, as was made clear by a circular of the Commissariat of Justice, which equated "consumption of foodstuffs and forage over and above the established norms" and "consumption of grain and forage above the plans established by authoritative organs" with "pillage and dilapidation of national property."

Naturally, this campaign in the by now desperately hungry countryside moved more slowly and worse than during the corresponding autumn of 1931. But the Politburo would not relax its vigilance. A new offensive was launched—and first of all a terroristic wave against agencies and local authorities still too reluctant to reengage in excesses. Thanks to powerful "stimulants," new records of antipeasant repression were to be beaten.[27] The local authorities had no other way out than to return the pressure downward. Formerly attacked for their ruthlessness, they now saw themselves attacked for "rotten liberalism" toward the laggards, especially in the three principal granaries, the Ukraine, the North Caucasus, and the Lower Volga (responsible for some 60 percent of all *zagotovki*). Officials understood well the meaning of the calls addressed to them to engage in a "truly Bolshevik struggle for grain," to "wield blows" against the squandering of grain (this aimed at the above-mentioned unauthorized distributions to fieldworkers and kolkhoz funds), and finally, to get the grain "at any price" (*vo chto by to ni stalo*)—another of those rather vague directives with a clear meaning, but still easy to be disowned by the leadership when necessary.

Spurred by a flood of orders and pressures, the local agencies now veered sharply from their alleged "rotten liberalism" into another batch of "sharp measures of repression," as our source put it.[28] Although the physical limits of an exhausted countryside and poor crops forced the government to lower its demands in many regions (the Ukraine and the North Caucasus had their quotas lowered consecutively four times[29]), it still needed a big battle to take the rest. The Ukraine, the North Caucasus, the two Volga regions, and other grain-producing areas, according to archives quoted by a modern author, "dropped out of the organized influence of the Party and government,"[30] and the government responded by transforming these areas into a vast arena of an unprecedented repressive operation. Stalin, who took over personal command and shaped these policies, called for "a smashing blow" to be dealt to *kolkhozniki*, because "whole squads of them," as he saw it, "turned against the Soviet state."[31] A special Central Committee meeting was held in January 1933 to endorse some of the old and to adopt new, severe measures to keep the countryside under control.

Some of the actions taken before and after this plenum can be mentioned here. An unspecified but large number of peasants were arrested, and often, especially in the Kuban District (North Caucasus), were deprived of most of their belongings and deported to the North. Mass arrests, purges, and dismissals struck many party members for having been engaged in "defending kulaks" and in "antistate sabotage of the *zagotovki*." In many places the squads of *zagotoviteli* went berserk (with an unmistakable blessing from above: Kaganovich, Molotov, and other top leaders were on the spot) and stripped the recalcitrant villages of any grain they could lay their hands on. This included grain the peasants had legitimately earned and been paid for their *trudodni*.[32] This was an obvious sentence to death by starvation, although an unknown number of actual shootings also probably took place.

As these events were unfolding, the grain-producing areas were by now, in the winter and spring of 1932/33, in the throes of a terrible famine. The Soviet government never officially acknowledged this fact, though the general formula used by the Ukrainian CC ("the critical food situation in many kolkhozy") was the nearest to the mark. But publications in the post-Stalin period, especially belles-lettres, said much more, though without giving estimates of the scope of the disaster.[33]

Many factors contributed to the famine. The vagaries of climate and crops were this time not the central cause. The crops in 1931 and 1932, although poor, were not catastrophic. Collectivization, which played havoc with agricultural production, was even more of a factor. The slaughter of stock dealt a shattering blow to Soviet agriculture, and the remedy the government attempted by allowing *kolkhozniki* to have a private plot and a family cow came too late to avoid the damage. As to the surviving herds, the newly founded and hastily organized kolkhozy did not know how to cope with them—and the hemorrhage continued for quite a time.

But the squeeze operated on the rural economy by the *zagotovki* was probably the main factor; 32 percent from the 1931 crop (and an even higher percentage from kolkhozy) was a bloodletting. And this was a national average. In some regions—the Kiev District, for example—no more than one-fifth of the crop was left to the *kolkhozniki*.[34] Facing the dwindling cattle and the disappearing grain, the newly organized kolkhozy, caught in the *zagotovki* clutches, lacked both experience and interest in doing a proper job for ensuring the next crop.

Moreover, as if the cup was not yet full enough, the government, fascinated by its heavy industry targets and mindless of minimal precautions, embarked upon an ambitious grain exportation policy. During the NEP only relatively modest amounts were exported, but in 1930 a massive 4.8 million tons, and the next year another huge 5.2 million tons, were shipped abroad. This turned out to be folly. In the spring of 1932 the situation in the countryside was so bad that the government even had to import some grain, although it was only a trickle which could not do much to alleviate the situation. Prestige was probably the reason why more was not imported to help out the starving.

Economists can easily estimate how much this 10 million tons of exported grain in two years helped industrialization, as against the losses in human lives and the economic potential of agriculture.[35] In any case these exports were soon stopped, and the unsoundness of this policy acknowledged in deeds if not in words.

▪ "HARD LINE," "SOFT LINE"? 1933–34

Against this background of tenuous battles for grain in a famine-stricken countryside (its repercussions were still being felt and seen well into 1934), the government embarked upon a considerable overhauling of its procurement policies and machinery, to meet the campaign of autumn 1933 in strength and to introduce some stability into the shattered rural economy. The essential ingredients of the new strategy were as follows: firstly, at the end of 1932, a new centralized administration was created, the Committee for Procurements (Komzag) under the auspices of the interministerial coordinating body for labor and defense (STO). But the centralized might bestowed upon this body was further underlined by attaching it, somewhat later, directly to the Council of Commissars (Sovnarkom). At all administrative levels of the country special bodies (local *komzagi*) were created, down to every *raion*. Kuibyshev, former head of Gosplan, was put at the head of Komzag, soon to be replaced by M. A. Chernov.[36]

The main idea behind such a body was to secure unity of command and structure and to give it enough power both to cope with the formidable *zagotovki* function and to make its agents independent from local pressures and dedicated only to their own administration. The practice of creating such special bodies, endowed with emergency powers, to impose the state's will down to the remotest village and to make its agents, hopefully, immune to the all-dissolving mass and local influences, now became a standard way of the "Bolshevik style of organization." The civil war is the quite obvious source of inspiration for such methods.

Secondly, yet another special shock administration was organized and sent to the *raiony* to serve as political departments in the machinery and tractor stations. Reporting only to its own hierarchy directed from the center, this administration was given superiority over the regular local party and soviet bodies and, significantly, included, in every station, a special GPU deputy (himself rather independent from the rest as he had his own command line), and 23,000 experienced cadres, with longstanding party affiliation and administrative, often military, careers behind them, were selected to staff these bodies (*politodely*), which were made responsible for managing the kolkhozy, the rural economy, and much else besides.[37]

Thirdly, through a set of enactments, principles for grain deliveries were formulated and presented as a new and long-term policy; the chief part of this legislation was the government and party decree of January 19, 1933.[38]

This law was a result of the tacit recognition by the government—soon made explicit in the press commentaries—that the existing practice of target distribution and grain levying was faulty. It was chaotic in the extreme, and it fettered agricultural production. As delivery plans were in fact unpredictable and capriciously changing, it introduced instability into kolkhozy and lack of security as to their future incomes and production possibilities. But its own incomes, which interested the government above all, were also unstable and unpredictable, as experience had shown, and could not be secured without enormous efforts.

The innovation consisted in declaring that the *zagotovki* become a compulsory state tax. Compulsory they were, as we already know, but now, as a tax, they were supposed to become a regular and predictable norm, although it was to be a harsh norm, high and independent of the size of crops—as the decree made clear. Also it was not liable to changes, other than by the central government; the local governments were forbidden under penal responsibility—so the law firmly promised—from changing the plans and engaging in those fatal repeated reimpositions which the peasants hated and the economy could not bear.

At present, the government intended to create conditions for enhancing the interest of peasants in promoting kolkhoz production by solemnly promising that the kolkhozy would know several years in advance what amounts of grain per hectare they would have to supply and that the surpluses above the quotas would be entirely at the disposal of the kolkhozy, either for internal use or for sales on the kolkhoz market.

Such markets had already been legalized in the summer of 1932— probably the gloomiest year of the five-year plan crisis—in an effort to improve the country's desperate food situation as well as to provide some incentives to the *kolkhozniki*. Both the kolkhozy and their individual members were allowed to sell their surpluses on these markets at prices freely formed through supply and demand interplay. This was a retreat into some pale version of the NEP, and at first did not improve much; on the contrary, as this move raised hopes among peasants and some officials that compulsory deliveries would be abolished, the current state procurements suffered additional setbacks. But the error was soon to be corrected; any kolkhoz trade had to stop as soon as *zagotovki* began, and markets would be allowed to reopen, by special decree, only in those districts that fulfilled their quotas. Otherwise the culprits were promised to be pursued as speculators. The 1933 decree on *zagotovki* as a compulsory tax now put a special stress on the right to trade on kolkhoz markets any surpluses remaining after the deliveries. At least some in the government seemed to be sincerely interested in discontinuing the devastating reimpositions and introducing some certainly both to the state's incomes and to the production process. In such a way the kolkhoz system would be offered minimal conditions for doing its job.

We shall see later whether such hopes were to materialize. For the moment, we should draw attention to one element, at least, in the whole strategy, which was undermining at the outset the promised predictability of the state's obligations. The new legislative package made it obligatory for the kolkhozy to pay the MTSs (machinery and tractor stations) in kind for their services. Hitherto the MTSs were paid a fixed price in money per hectare for their plowing or harvesting. The payment being independent from the results of their work (from the crops and yields), the MTSs—as the Commissar for Agriculture Yakovlev bitterly complained—were interested in inflating in their reports the acreage dealt with by their machines, but they were indifferent as to whether they were sowing or harvesting grain or weeds.[39] The new law ordered the payment to be called henceforth *naturplata* (payment-in-kind, to distinguish it from the tax-in-kind, the *postavki*).

Consequently, all the talk about fixity of payments applied only to the part of deliveries called *postavki*, but the newly introduced category—

the *naturplata*—was to be paid as a percentage of the crop, and thus only relatively fixed. The actual amount would become known only after the whole crop was gathered. The decrees on *naturplaty* were formulated in a harsh antipeasant tone. They granted the MTSs a decisive role in assessing the actual amounts of kolkhoz dues and the right to collect it from the kolkhozy "without demur" (*bezogovorochno*).[40]

At the beginning of 1933, when these decrees were promulgated, it might not have occurred to many what was involved in the *naturplaty*. But the MTSs were increasingly relied upon by the government as the key organ for securing the advancement of agricultural production and for controlling agriculture. The important special administration (*politotdely*) created to provide teeth for this MTS as the new strategic lever has already been mentioned. The MTS, the sole state agency actually present on the fields of the kolkhozy, seemed well adapted to become also a major collector of *zagotovki*. In fact, in a few years' time, the *naturplaty* were going to become the main part in the state's overall grain collections,[41] but this part, as we know, was not a fixed figure, but a *pro rata*. The actual amount of grain to be supplied by kolkhozy became once more, by this bias, uncertain, quite contrary to the letter of the legislation which introduced this system.

This uncertainty was further deepened by a quite extraordinary device introduced formally in the same year of the great overhaul: the state took over full control and the last word over the assessment not only of the prospects of yields and crops but also of the final figures. One more special administration was created for this purpose, centrally run, like all of them, and with the same pattern of local agencies made dependent on their special line from the center. Some friction is reported to have taken place between the commissar for agriculture and the Sovnarkom; the former wanted to give the kolkhozy themselves a say in assessing what their actual crops were, but the latter rejected this approach.[42] The final assessment of the figure, which was crucial for fixing the delivery quotas, especially of the payments to the MTSs, was firmly lodged in the government's hands, to the exclusion of the producers themselves.[43] It is not difficult to imagine how this method would influence the government's share in the real agricultural output.

Besides the assessment of the crop, the other key figure for the calculation of the delivery dues was the sowing acreage. The new decrees now legalized what had already been established practice for some time: the sowings were to be done according to governmental targets sent in from above to every village and made, like much else, compulsory and not open to reductions. Such reductions were explicitly forbidden[44] (although, one would guess, not increases of targets). The *zagotovki* dues would thus be calculated on the basis of the planted sowing targets, and peasants, or kolkhozy, would later have no end of trouble if they did not actually sow the prescribed acreage and crop.

In such a way, the main criteria for computing its imposition became wide open to the government's wishful thinking. Once the targets were fixed, however, the problem of getting the grain from the peasants needed an additional lever: control over the threshing process. A decree therefore prescribed firmly (with appropriate penal clauses quoted in the text of the decree to warn transgressors) that 90 percent of the proceeds of threshing had to go to the *zagotovki* and only 10 percent distributed to peasants as advances for their labor, as long as the quotas were not fully met. It was clear that a fierce opposition was to be expected from the peasants against such a practice at a time when they themselves badly needed grain at a labor-intensive peak of the season, and when the reserves of food from the previous harvest would be all too often long exhausted. To ensure that the sensitive threshing operation suited the needs of *zagotovki*, the decree made it compulsory on kolkhozy to sell to the MTSs all their bigger threshing machines; if they had to do the job with smaller ones, the work had to be done on special grounds organized and supervised by the MTSs.[45] In this way, the keys to the operation were transferred to the MTS, and another opening through which grain might have escaped the government was hopefully closed.

From the middle of 1933 and until Kirov's death in December 1934, a relative lull seemed to have set in in many fields of Soviet policy. A set of more liberal measures could be discerned, beginning with more moderate targets of industrial growth and a promise of more attention to consumer needs during the next five-year plan. Eventually, the cruder methods of mass repression, shootings, and deportations were considerably curtailed. Behind the scenes, in the top leadership, pressures were exerted for a change of course and the adoption of different strategies in running the country. Stalin's policies might have been questioned and his removal contemplated among certain leaders. Observers link all these pressures and doubts to the emergence of a Kirov faction or trend—although the existence of such a trend, however plausible, has never yet been convincingly proved.[46]

This problem cannot be dealt with here comprehensively, but for our central topic—the *zagotovki*—some proof can be given to substantiate the existence of pressures for rethinking agricultural policies. As the rural economy, now largely collectivized, continued to be a costly and largely disappointing affair, one would expect a tendency to arise to do something in order to make agriculture move. This could hardly be achieved without trying to improve the relations of the state with the mass of bitter, frustrated, and hostile peasants. The press spoke freely about the fact that peasants distrusted any promise or pledge given by the government; and one can surmise, as we just have, that stronger feelings than mere distrust must have been widespread.

It was in fact a public speech by Kirov, although not, to my knowledge, in published speeches by any other leading figure, that a strong hint could be found of disappointment with the results of the current policies. In this speech, after having paid the ritual homage to the "sacredness" of the *zagotovki*, Kirov objected to what was in fact, to use his own term, "a squeeze" (*vykolachivanie*)—a term which very aptly characterized the whole procedure. Kirov by now knew very well, and said so, that such *vykolachivanie* was fraught with the danger of jeopardizing the development of agriculture and of putting a brake "on the further development of the kolkhozy and sovkhozy."[47] More research is needed in order to discover what actual policy changes were proposed by Kirov or others, but the central thesis on which to base the changes, and a justification for such changes, is unmistakably present in this speech.

According to many sources, in the lower echelons of officialdom too a certain amount of opposition was present, in different forms, against the terroristic line toward agriculture and especially against the same *vykolachivanie* which Kirov criticized. To be sure, the traditional hard-liners kept pressing for the harsh treatment of peasants, and the official legislation, as we shall see, followed suit, showing that these still had the upper hand. The fighting slogan of hard-liners was the term "sabotage"— and evidently appeals for treating recalcitrant peasants as saboteurs were tantamount to applying terror against them. Thus, for example, the militant journal of Komzag presented the situation in the following terms: "Day in, day out, the central press keeps bringing a multitude of facts pointing to the existence, all too often, of an organized opposition to the deliveries of grain."[48] The press material which this source had in mind consisted of numerous reports about peasants and managements of kolkhozy hiding grain, falsifying reports on sowings, preparing padded grain and fodder balances, and a host of other subterfuges. From the severe pen of the general prosecutor came appeals to the courts and other agencies to deal properly with such actions.

But the same journal and other sources allow one to infer that this time the peasants enjoyed a measure of support from sections of local state administrations, and the accusations of sabotage were directed against such people not less than against peasants. Many local officials seemed to be rather stubborn in demanding the lowering of the delivery quotas. Hard-liners would castigate such behavior as "reductionist tendencies," "orientations on reduction" (of delivery quotas), although the translation of the Russian *skidochnye nastroeniya* does not render the flavor of this coinage. That these "orientations" were seen in the most sinister light by the hard-liners can be gathered from their accusations that such officials tend to "put the interests of the kolkhozy above the interests of the state"—a charge which in the prevailing conditions was in fact easily reformulated as sabotage.[49]

All this was a serious affair in the eyes of the leadership. The "reductionist" tendencies were strongly attacked during the July 1934 plenum of the Central Committee by leaders like Vareikis, Kossior, and Postyshev,[50] although no source openly shows any top leader attempting to protect such moods of lower officials. In fact, even during those days of a relative relaxation of terror, many officials paid with their jobs or party cards, and sometimes were prosecuted in court, for their leniency toward peasants. Quite numerous among them were directors of sovkhozy, of MTSs, and secretaries of *raion* party committees, for what clearly was either a defense of kolkhozy from impossible exactions or a fight to defend the economic viability of their own outfits.[51]

It is of particular significance that many officials of the political departments of the MTSs, this crack unit of administrators sent at the beginning of 1933 to install obedience and order in the countryside, engaged themselves in such activities. They criticized unrealistic plans, often defended kolkhozy managements from accusations of embezzlement, and refused to endorse criminal prosecutions against them.[52] One modern writer frankly takes their side: these people, he states, well knew that the crop data were exaggerated and therefore that delivery quotas based on such data were unjustified.[53]

In conclusion, however scarce the data, it becomes clear that what the hard-liners from Komzag called "organized sabotage of the *zagotovki*," as we have quoted above, was quite a serious affair; many local administrations, including the political departments, were reaching conclusions about the state of agriculture and the lines to follow which differed substantially from the prevailing tendency in Moscow. The irritated reaction of the Politburo proves this point. The political departments were now found guilty of "having become identified (*sroslis'*) with local people" and thus of having outlived their usefulness for Moscow. At the end of 1934 the departments were dissolved.[54]

Notwithstanding pressures from below and the debate and hesitations in the center, some of the legislation pertaining to *zagotovki* and policies in the countryside shows a persistent tendency to go on with the type of *vykolachivanie* policy which Kirov would have liked to mitigate. Against one concession to peasants—the arrears of deliveries for 1933 were canceled and repayments of seed loans spread over three years[55]—several new measures were announced, surpassing in their antipeasant fierceness many of the previous enactments. First, the *kolkhozniki* who grew some grain on their plots saw their norms of delivery raised to the level hitherto applied only to private peasants—10 percent more than kolkhozy were paying in zones not served by MTSs.[56] This meant that a treatment reserved only to an openly discriminated category was now extended to all *kolkhozniki*. The same tendency is apparent in yet another decision, according to which obligatory deliveries of meat, milk, and eggs by private peasants and *kolkhozniki* alike would not depend on their economic situation: they should supply these products even if they had no livestock of their own.[57] At a time when the numbers of cattle were declining and millions of peasant families had no stock, it seemed particularly sinister to impose on them deliveries of animal foodstuffs. Or was it intended as an incentive to spur peasants to acquire stock? If it was meant to provide such an incentive, the government soon reached the conclusion that it had better help peasants to acquire private cows. Poverty was a sufficient incentive for a peasant family to want a cow, but they had no means to get it. "Cowlessness" was a disaster, and Molotov promised solemnly that in just two years the problem would be solved,[58] although it eventually took more than two years to endow all *kolkhozniki* with this vital support.

The link between *zagotovki* and the collectivization drive, the pressures, that is, applied to peasants to join kolkhozy with *zagotovki* quotas as a whip, can be illustrated by events which took place in the second half of 1934, pertaining to the remaining 5 million peasant families which had managed to stay outside the collectives. It was still a considerable mass— some 20 percent of all peasant households—but their share in the country's agricultural production was already very small. This was not, as officially claimed, a result of the "superiority of the kolkhozy." It was rather the oppressive delivery quotas, special taxation, and other vexatious measures that made their lives unbearable and served both as a boost to join kolkhozy and to ensure such "superiority" of kolkhozy.

In 1931 the delivery quotas of these smallholders were made bigger than those paid by kolkhozy. They were assessed according to sowing plans which were imposed on them, and dues were exacted from them often without regard as to whether they had actually sown that much, or indeed whether they had sown anything at all. Their sowings incidentally could be—and often were—just taken away from them, their horses subject to mobilizations for the benefit of kolkhozy, and cases were reported of whole families mobilized to work for kolkhozy, although such treatment was on some occasions condemned by the leadership as having been a "deviation from the party line."[59]

Somehow, during 1933—and despite continuing harassment—the mass of the unenrolled peasants were given a sort of respite; local officials, who were hard pressed to show results in collections, preferred to concentrate on kolkhozy, as it was an easier job to get considerable amounts from them rather than to chase after the numerous, evasive smallholders. Some of those officials obviously thought that in any case there was not much left that could be taken from the small fry. Therefore, although delivery quotas were demanded from them, there was less repression applied to them during this period, and especially not much pressure to join kolkhozy.

The officials were right in this sense. There was enough trouble in running the kolkhozy as they stood, and many kolkhoz members and managers did not see much interest in accepting new people, who in any case would dispose of their horse or cow before joining, if they still had any left. It may even be that some local authorities explicitly forbade the acceptance of such people.

But sometime during the summer of 1934 the Central Committee found this situation wrong and stepped in forcefully. The existence of 5 million "speculators" was found undesirable. The July plenum therefore launched a new campaign to complete collectivization by enrolling the remaining millions of families. There was no more talk this time of dekulakizations or violent repression in order to achieve their aim. As Stalin advised a gathering of secretaries in July 1934, the method should consist of "strengthening the taxation press"; what he meant by this can be gathered from the measures taken by the government to make this "press" work. In October an extraordinary levy in cash was decreed on the private peasants—and the decree did not even bother to explain why this had to be done.[60] Another decree, enacted soon after the plenum, was in fact even harsher: the delivery quotas for the smallholders, which stood at 10 percent above the quotas for kolkhozy (not in MTSs), were now raised to 50 percent. All the allowances which had previously existed for sowing above the plans were abolished, and a special new law was added to allow for confiscation of all but a few specified personal belongings for failure by smallholders to meet the quotas.[61]

Such monetary and grain taxation went beyond the solvency of the smallholders. The government was going "for the kill." Only two ways were left (for those who could not go to the cities): either to join the kolkhoz or to become salaried laborers in sovkhozy, if these were around. By signing up with a sovkhoz the peasant would become exempt from zagotovki. The role of the zagotovki as a whip for driving peasants to kolkhozy is thereby once more illustrated.

Before closing this section, it would be illuminating to listen to a frank explanation by a leader of why this renewal of the collectivization drive took place. It was offered, once more, by Kirov, in one of his speeches. Kolkhozy, he explained, were often very weak producers, and their standards of living lagged behind the nonenrolled peasants. The kolkhozniki— and the others—saw no advantage in the kolkhoz; they were worse off in the kolkhoz than the private peasants who could still find some escape valves (some sales on the black markets, for example) which were not open to the kolkhoznik. Therefore, Kirov concluded, the coexistence of the kolkhozy with private smallholders had become an anomaly which had to be ended.[62]

Not much additional comment seems necessary. Here was a frank and bitter admission that kolkhozy could not stand competition and comparison even with the pauperized smallholders of those days.

■ *ZAGOTOVKI* UP, OUTPUT DOWN, 1928–41

We should now have a look at the output figures of Soviet agriculture during the five-year plans, between roughly 1928 and 1941, to be better able to assess some of the results of procurement policies (and of collectivization for that matter). It was officially admitted prior to 1958 that during the first five-year plan agricultural production suffered, but this was presented as an unavoidable cost involved in the complex undertaking of creating a radically new organization of agriculture. The slump could not but be transitory, and, it was claimed, after 1932 things were cheerfully improving.

But a statistical handbook published in 1959 showed that reality was very different and the situation in the prewar countryside much gloomier than even the figures computed by Naum Jasny were implying. In the same 1959 a Soviet expert gave the first detailed account of the crop-assessing practices after 1932.[63] This is quite a complex story, describing different methods of doing the job, including notions like "the optimum barn-yield" which was practiced first, some intermediate way coming next, and finally, from 1939 on, the strictly speaking "biological crop" or "standing crop" (*na kornyu*). In any case, the results of these assessments were not published, and the crop statistics in physical units became during the second five-year plan a state secret. Only the figure for the bountiful 1937 crop was made known.[64]

A special administration which we have already referred to—the Central Commission for Assessing Yields and Crops (TsGK)—was entrusted with the job and, characteristically, was not interested in discovering the amounts of grain which were actually reaching the peasants' barns. It preferred to compute one or another of the variants of "biological yields," meaning the estimate of the "standing crops" before the harvest, without discounting realistically figures for losses which took place before the grain reached the barn. But the norms of delivery were based on such hypothetical assessments and the peasants found themselves taxed, to a great degree, on nonexisting income because the inflated assessment base had been higher than the actual yield by some 30 percent. This was one of the basic reasons for the "reductionist tendencies" referred to above among some local administrators, who tried to defend the peasants from this peculiar governmental form of cheating.

As in the case of taxing the products of nonexistent cows, overtaxing through the device of "biological crops" might have had behind it some strategy aimed at making the peasants improve the quality of their work and reducing the losses in grain occurring during and after the harvest. Such losses were staggering, and the leaders became acutely aware of it in the middle of 1934. Kirov in particular seemed deeply disappointed by this state of affairs. He quoted estimates showing 40 percent of the crops in important agriculutral areas being lost because of poor husbandry, and he could not but brood regretfully over the big improvement in the situation which could be achieved if only such losses could be reduced.[65] This topic was certainly among those being debated at the top leadership level, as some would tend to explain the losses as resulting from government policies, but the hard-liners, notably Stalin and Molotov, would prefer to explain things in terms of "kulak propaganda" or "petit bourgeois mentality" and to see the losses as grain actually wasted by the peasant. It was up to the peasants—so this position seemed to imply—to stop this nonsense; the method of teaching them the right way, advocated by these leaders, was to be implacable on *zagotovki* targets.

Mentality obviously counted for something, but this should include the mentality of leaders, too. The *zagotovki* as "incentive" did not seem to work. The figures emerging after Stalin's death show a picture of declining agricultural output not only during the years 1928–32 but also up to 1937. Some improvements in subsequent prewar years could not make

TABLE 6.1

GRAIN CROPS AND GOVERNMENT GRAIN PROCUREMENTS, 1928–40

Year	Crop (all grain) (million tons)	Procurements (million tons)	Share of procurements in total crop (%)	Share of procurements in crops of kolkhozy (%)
1928	73.3	10.7	14.7	—
1929	71.7	16.8	22.4	55.7
1930	77.1	22.1	26.5	27.5
1931	69.4	22.8	32.9	37.8
1932	69.8	19.0	26.9	27.5
1933	68.4	23.6	34.1	35.5
1934	67.6	26.9	38.1	35.3
1935	62.4	28.3	37.8	39.1
1936	—	—	—	—
1937	87.0	31.9	—	—
1938	67.0	—	—	—
1939	67.3	32.1*	—	—
1940	95.6†	36.6†	38.0	—

* The average per year for the whole period of 1938–40.
† This figure probably includes the grain from the territories incorporated after September 17, 1939. Therefore to be comparable to the previous figures it should be diminished, but the point is not clear to me.

Sources: Y. A. Moshkov, *Zernovaya problema v gody pervoi pyatiletki* (Moscow, 1966), p. 225, and his contribution to *Istoriya sovetskogo krest'yanstva i kolkhoznogo stroitel'stva v SSSR* (Moscow, 1963), p. 270; I. E. Zelenin, in *Istoriya SSSR*, no. 5 (1964), p. 18; M. A. Vyltsan. *Ukreplenie material'no-tekhnicheskoi bazy v gody vtoroi pyatiletki* (Moscow, 1959); I. A. Gladkov, ed., *Sotsialisticheskoe narodnoe khozyaistvo SSSR, 1933–1940* (Moscow, 1963).

TABLE 6.2

GRAIN PRODUCTION AND PROCUREMENTS IN TSARIST RUSSIA
AND DURING THE FIVE-YEAR PLANS IN THE USSR
(annual averages, in million tons)

Years	Crop	Yield (quintals per hectare)	Procurements
1909–13	72.5	6.9	—
1928–32	73.6	7.5	18.1
1933–37	72.9	7.1	27.5
1938–40	77.9	7.7	32.1

Sources: *Narodnoe khozyaistvo SSSR v 1958 godu*, p. 352. For the pre-five-year plan period, according to one source the yearly crop for 1924–8 was 69.3 million tons, which is not small. Another author quotes for 1925–9 a yearly crop of 73 million, with a yield per hectare of 7.9 quintals. See M. A. Vyltsan, "Sovetskaya derevnya," in *Ukreplenie material'no-tekhnicheskoi bazy v gody vtoroi pyatilatki* (Moscow, 1963), p. 41; and V. P. Danilov, *Sozdanie material'no-tekhnicheskikh predposylok kollektivizatsii sel'skogo khozyaistva v SSSR* (Moscow, 1957), pp. 94–95.

good the damage and significantly improve on the figures in the precollectivization or prerevolutionary years. Tables 6.1–4 will illustrate our point. As we do not dispose of definitive and authoritative data on the whole period, our data are compiled from different Soviet sources without checking or recalculating them; the figures are therefore not entirely consistent, especially the percentages which refer to crops differently estimated by the sources, and they have to be seen as an illustration rather than as any definitive computation. Annual figures for subsequent years in Table 6.1

TABLE 6.3

INDEX OF ANIMAL PRODUCE, 1928–40
(1913 = 100)

Year	Animal Produce
1928	137
1929	129
1930	100
1931	93
1932	75
1933	65
1934	72
1935	86
1936	96
1937	109
1938	120
1939	108
1940	114

Source: *Narodnoe khozyaistvo SSSR v 1958 godu*, p. 350.

TABLE 6.4

PRODUCTION OF FOODSTUFFS (OF ANIMAL ORIGIN), 1913, 1928, AND 1940

Year	Meat and lard (live weight, million tons)	Including Procurements (million tons)	Milk (million tons)	Eggs ('000 million pieces)	Wool ('000 tons)
1913	5.0	1.8	29.4	11.9	192
1928	4.9	1.6	31.1	10.8	182
1940	4.7	1.7	33.6	12.2	161
In kolkhozy alone*	0.9	0.2	5.6	0.5	78

* This means production of the collective farms but not including the output of the family plots of the kolkoz members.

Source: I. A. Gladkov, ed., *Sotsialisticheskoe narodnoe khozyaistvo SSSR, 1933–1940* (Moscow, 1963), p. 360.

were not available to me, except for 1937, with its not too probable crop of 97.4 million tons and 31.8 million tons of collections; we shall therefore use the available official annual averages to complete the picture (see Table 6.2).

If subjected to closer scrutiny, some of these figures too would be doubted, for example, the yields in tsarist Russia. In any case, for the general picture to be clearer, some additional figures would be useful,[66] especially for animal produce.

These figures are sufficiently eloquent, though, even if they do still embellish the situation somewhat. Value estimates are in this case less reliable than data in physical units, which are given in Table 6.4 for some selected, but important, items of animal produce.

It is worth repeating that stock breeding did begin to recover slowly from 1935 onward[67] but this could not yet improve the situation much prior to 1940. The 1913 level was not reached by then either in numbers of heads or in production of foodstuffs from animals. Characteristically, the role of kolkhozy in this sensitive field remained insignificant. The bulk of animal foodstuffs was produced by the *kolkhozniki* on their private plots and from their privately owned stock.

Thus, the general picture of agricultural production, both grain and animal husbandry, showed first an absolute decline, with a slight improvement during the three prewar years but without any serious breakthrough: output of animal foodstuffs was lower than before the revolution, and the grain output was not substantially higher than in the NEP or before the revolution; it was gathered from a much larger sown area and had to support a bigger population. The one branch which did produce substantially more were the technical crops.[68]

But as grain crops fell or stagnated, one column in Tables 6.1 and 6.2

displays a pronounced upward trend: the *zagotovki*. Whatever the state of the branch, whether its output kept falling or improved somewhat, the size and share of *zagotovki* in the gross output almost reached the 40 percent mark—an extremely heavy toll to be taken from the small crops and low yields of those years. It will be noticed that all the improvement of 1938–40 was swallowed up by the increase of *zagotovki*. The device of "biological crop" estimates helped to achieve such a result, as this high percentage of the *zagotovki* share in the grain outputs became evident only after the crop statistics were appropriately deflated. *Vykolachivanie* was indeed doing what Kirov felt it would: strangling agriculture as a branch (and peasants as a class, which is another matter to be considered). For the bulk of the Russian peasant population, grain was not just a product such as most industrial outputs are. It played here a unique manifold role: besides being the output of the farm, it also constituted its means of production (seeds), its raw material (forage), its circulating capital in part, as well as the subsistence means and wage fund of the producers. Grain was thus—and still often is—a complex life-stuff for the branch and not just food for the cities or means of getting foreign currency. The government seemed not to be interested in this sort of consideration. NEP peasants, who, as we know, produced not less on the whole than the kolkhozy some three five-year plans later, did not market more than 22 percent of their grain output. They needed, in very rough figures, some 12 percent for seeds, 25–30 percent for their livestock, up to 30 percent for feeding themselves, and the rest for reserves and sales. By taking 30–40 percent from poor, sometimes falling, crops, the whole production cycle was heavily damaged. The still extremely feeble kolkhozy were given an unmanageable task. They were given no chance to prosper. This will become more evident when another major aspect of the *zagotovki* policy is examined—the prices paid to producers.

On the whole, this pricing problem is simple: prices paid to producers for their deliveries remained at practically the same level between 1928 and 1953.[69] But not so the cost of living and of producing. Some rises were given in 1935, but this did not alter the overall picture much. These prices were inadequate and, as a Soviet writer put it, soon became no more than "symbolic."[70] It is not easy to explore this problem fully. Price indices were not published, probably not even computed, in the 1930s, and the costs of production in kolkhozy were never studied at all during those years. But cost estimates did exist for sovkhozy, and prices paid to them for grain were probably the same as those paid to kolkhozy. Some of these data can give us an inkling of the problem.

According to a competent Soviet author using archival sources, the cost of producing a quintal of grain in sovkhozy in the period 1933–38 was 27 rubles on average (with a maximum of 33.9 rubles in 1934 and a minimum of 17.7 rubles in the abundant year 1937). But the producer's prices were of the following order (for 1935, after a small increment): rye, 6–6.2 rubles a quintal; wheat 9.1–10.4 rubles; oats, 4.9–5.5 rubles. Not surprisingly, the sovkhozy were showing huge cumulative deficits, especially when it is considered that up to 80 percent of their grain was taken away from them without regard to their internal needs. The state subsidies to which they were entitled as state enterprises were not sufficient to cover such deficits.[71]

For kolkhozy, we can quote one Soviet estimate for a later year, 1953, which sums up the economic policies in the countryside during twenty-five years. With producer prices remaining on the same level during the whole period and the value of the ruble having dwindled tenfold, the story is told. In 1953 the prices paid to producers (for nine basic grains and animal products) covered producer's costs no more than to the extent of two-fifths. Grain prices covered only 19 percent of their cost, and no more than one-fourth of the cost of animal products was met.[72]

Such a picture of devastating exploitation would at least have the merit of simplicity. But producer's prices evolved into a more complicated pattern than just the simple price for the delivery (postavki), and it is worth sketching out some of this pattern because of its economic implications. Two additional price categories have to be mentioned: the purchases (zakupki); and the "decentralized procurements," each with its own set of prices.

Zakupki were introduced in 1933. The peasants were told that after their deliveries to the state and to the MTS, they would be asked to sell to the government, additionally, a certain amount of grain for a higher price than normal zagotovki, and with the additional incentive of the scarce industrial goods to be supplied to sellers. The relevant decree promised that the kolkhozy would be entirely free to decide whether they chose to sell.

This was said in January 1934; but the promise was broken in another decree, signed by Molotov and Stalin on August 31 of the same year, which made the whole "selling," in fact, a compulsory affair.[73] The decree prescribed that the distribution of grain to kolkhozniki for the trudodni they earned would not begin before more grain was offered in the form of zakupki. Consequently, the "purchases" tended to be organized as the regular zagotovki: quotas, distributed and handed down to every village, pressure exerted on peasants to comply, and all the rest of it.

This was another instance of breaking promises. With such zakupki, on top of payments to the MTS, the solemn intention of the 1933 reorganization, to give the countryside some sense of stability and predictability with regard to procurements, had vanished. As the share of such "purchases" and MTS payments kept growing in subsequent years, the fixed and predictable part of it—the state tax (postavki)—became a small share of the whole. Once more, the total of deliveries in all their forms became an unpredictable shifting quantity, bringing back to the kolkhozy much of the insecurity of the first five-year plan, which had made the planning and managing of their farms a more than tricky endeavor.

The peasants well knew that the *zakupki* would not be what the state promised. They listened to speeches of Politburo members castigating kolkhozy for refusing to "sell," they heard and read enough of the familiar tunes about "kulak choirboys" and understood very well that *zakupki* would become just another additional tax. "A new tax" was in fact their own term for these *zakupki*.[74]

"Decentralized *zagotovki*" became an additional channel for acquiring extra animal products and vegetables for the cities. They were introduced in 1932 and allowed factories, city cooperatives, and other institutions to go shopping in the countryside for animal products, potatoes, and vegetables after the basic deliveries to the state had been made. A special network was created of "convention bureaus" at all administrative levels to fix prices for this trade and to regulate it. Not more than three agencies were to have licenses to operate in any administrative region (*raion*) to avoid competition, although this was to be no more than a pious wish. Such agents would purchase the products from kolkhozy or preferably sign long-term contracts with them, for sales which were to be paid at high "conventional" prices and additionally rewarded by help offered to kolkhozy by these agencies in acquiring production means and other industrial goods.

Space does not allow us to deal in detail with this interesting "decentralized *zagotovki*." They soon became permeated, like everything else, with elements of compulsion—kolkhozy were too vulnerable to pressures from local authorities, deprived of rights and defenseless as they were— but such pressures were much less prominent than in the case of *zakupki*. The central government did not meddle with it too much, and the whole operation soon became a predominantly chaotic market affair. Swarms of agents from cities descended upon *raiony* which had something to offer; they bribed officials to get the trading licenses—a whole black market for such licenses developed in "good" *raiony*—and engaged in quite lucrative deals with kolkhozy, based on barter and spinoffs to local officials.

This activity did add something to the diet of industrial workers and officials, but not less, probably, to channels of speculation on black markets. The cost of these agencies and of their bargains was huge. In 1934 a total of 859 million rubles' worth, of potatoes and vegetables mainly, was purchased, but the cost of the agencies included in this total oscillated between 29 and 55.8 percent. The anticipated norm of operational costs should have been only 14 percent.[75]

We can now sum up the phenomenon of multiple prices which developed, contrary to initial intentions or anticipations, in the wake of the *zagotovki* policy. As we know, a certain rather "symbolic" price was offered for the basic *postavki*, the part of overall *zagotovki* which was officially presented as a compulsory state tax. For the second category, the *naturplaty*, nothing was paid to peasants. These were considered as payments in kind to the MTS for its work; it looked like a kind of sharecropping system with not much say for the sharecropper in fixing the rates, as was the case in most such systems.

The next category—*zakupki*—were paid 20–25 percent more than the basic *postavki* rates; this was the case in 1933/34, with some rises during the following years which did not take this price, in any case, substantially any further from the basic rate. Some bonuses could be paid for *zakupki*, and industrial goods were made available to complying kolkhozy, although goods never materialized in promised quantities, as they were either not available at all, or not supplied to the countryside, or embezzled—facts which the press abundantly illustrated.[76]

The next price category emerged in the kolkhoz markets, where kolkhozy and *kolkhozniki* could trade their surpluses after having received permission to do so. Here the prices might have been as much at 13.2 times higher than those in private commerce in 1928 (for five basic agricultural products), and it was by selling a small share of their production on kolkhoz markets that peasants made about 60 percent of their whole monetary income.[77]

The prices for grain reaching the illegal black markets were even higher than on the kolkhoz markets, as speculators took very considerable risks to operate their trade; but they existed and seemed irremovable, although the scope of this trade cannot be gauged.

For animal foodstuffs a four-tier price system evolved: the official *zagotovki* price; the "conventional" price for decentralized *zagotovki*, some three to four times higher than the official price; the kolkhoz market price; and the black market.

Thus some compensation would accrue to the producers, heavily underpaid for the bulk of their output, through the practice of higher prices on *zakupki*, kolkhoz market prices, and some black market sales; but these could not make up the losses made on the bulk of the output. These compensations did not change the general picture of a branch of the national economy allowed to cover only a fraction of its costs.

The underpayment and the multiple-tier pricing had a profound effect on the kolkhozy. Not enough study has been done to analyze the impact of such pricing, but one phenomenon can be pointed to, following one rather angry statement by a modern Soviet writer. According to him, the fact that a kolkhoz was paid different prices for different lots of the same product played havoc with the kolkhoz economy. The poor and inefficient kolkhozy—these were, no doubt, the majority—did not have much to offer over and above the quantities levied as compulsory state quotas. Such kolkhozy were particularly hard hit, and their poverty was thereby perpetuated. Some of the better or luckier kolkhozy who did happen to have grain above the compulsory quotas could be rewarded by getting additional income for *zakupki,* and bonuses for grain over the *zakupki* minimum, then more income from sales on kolkhoz markets and eventually even more on black markets. They could in this way make quite a lot of money and even become rich. The existing price system, complained the author, wrecked the poor and enriched the rich, and this situation was "worse than capitalist anarchy."[78]

■ SOME CONSEQUENCES

The facts and figures as they emerge from this scrutiny point to a twofold conclusion: the Soviet state was successful in organizing a large-scale squeeze of agricultural output from the peasantry, but failed as a manager and organizer of successful large-scale agricultural production. It was, in fact, the very successful facet of the operation which was accountable for the failure of some other vital facets. To base the economic activity of a whole branch, and of a social class, on "taking" without rewarding would be inconceivable without the application of mass coercion on a permanent basis. But tools and energies needed for such a compulsory process were different from and contradictory to tools and energies which were necessary for promoting kolkhozy as successful producers and a viable socioeconomic structure.

Incidentally, the extraordinary display of mass coercion, without which this type of *zagotovki* would not work, contributed heavily to the hardening of Stalin's Russia into a bureaucratic police state. Violence applied to millions of peasants year after year was a training ground for institutions and methods which could later be applied to other groups. With the treatment of peasants in the first five-year plan as background, the gloomiest years of the subsequent purges of cadres, however bloody, look like a reedition on a smaller scale.

All the sources agree that the state made the *zagotovki* quite explicitly its central activity in the countryside. The leadership made no secret of it and kept hammering into the heads of peasants and officials that the *zagotovki* were the principal, most important campaign in the life of the whole state, not just of the countryside. It is enough to leaf through *Pravda* between September and November of, say, 1934, to discover that during these months even industry is somehow in the shadow. Kirov in the same year put it bluntly: the *zagotovki* "are the concentrated expression of the totality of our policy in the countryside, the kolkhoz, the sovkhoz and the smallholders." Another leader, Vareikis, saw in this activity the main way of educating the peasants; Chernov would add that *zagotovki* were helping the *kolkhozniki* in overcoming the limitations of their petit bourgeois psychology. The delivery, another text explained euphorically, is the supreme test of the socialist essence of the kolkhozy.[79] Even religious overtones were used to instill into the peasant a sense of the sanctity of the delivery: *zagotovki* became the "supreme commandment" for the kolkhoz.

For the peasants, all this meant that the grain was no longer his but the state's. And the same attitude applied to the whole kolkhoz. The peasants learned this lesson after a display of terror and an "education" which heavily concentrated, among other methods, on administering starvation as a way of teaching.

The peasants yielded to superior force, but never really accepted the rule that the state's interests were more important than their own. As long as they could, the peasants behaved according to different rules, such as "no bread, no work," or "a pound of labor for a pound of bread." And one big lesson which they learned especially was best expressed as follows: don't trust the state; they don't care for peasants.

In the prevailing conditions, there could be no such thing as the shedding by peasants of their "petit bourgeois psychology." Quite the opposite was true. As the peasants learned that the state did not consider their interests important, the obvious lesson for them, borne out by a mass of facts, was to take care, as far as possible, of their own interests. The emergence of a collectivist psychology was hardly possible here—unless as a defensive group or class posture. Squeezing peasants to the core bred apathy among them and forced the state to look for ways to overcome this apathy by instilling some stimuli and incentives into them, so they would become interested in doing something for their kolkhozy. The irony was that all such incentives were catering to the very petit bourgeois mentality and self-interest which the state was allegedly out to eradicate. Such measures as reestablishing the right to keep a private cow, to have a private plot, to trade on kolkhoz markets, special prices and bonuses, were medicines for curing ailments which the *zagotovki* were hard at work to inflict.

Applied simultaneously, such treatments were self-defeating. They contributed to the creation of a peculiar hybrid system with deeply seated, built-in disincentives and fetters. As the authorities were poised for the squeeze and the peasants for the defense of their livelihood, production could not become the main worry of either the one side or the other. The state wanted the quick organization of threshing with 90 percent of its proceedings going straight to its elevators; and if at the same time much of the yield remained unharvested, or not properly put in stacks and liable to get wet and rotten, it did not interest the officials very much. It would be up to the factor who was the last to be paid to carry the brunt. There is no lack of material for documenting such a state of affairs.

The peasants knew it. They therefore responded by doing the minimum on collective fields as their way of perceiving realities. Facing such a mass expression of what became popular wisdom, the state was forced to take direct responsibility over a growing range of agricultural activities for which the NEP peasants used to care themselves: plowing, sowing, weeding, harvesting became a state activity, to be planned and regulated by quotas and indicators. It led to a new interference in every aspect of kolkhoz life, in minute detail. When to begin to sow, where and what to sow, how to work, and how to remunerate, how to take care of horses—all was handed down from above, and different officials sent in to ensure the execution of the detailed plans.

The situation verged on the ridiculous. It was the normal peasant stuff and needed their zeal to be done properly. But as long as the *zagotovki* were the state's central worry, it led to warfare with the peasants instead of winning them over. As the peasants responded, in fact, by a protracted *grève de zèle*, the estrangement on both sides exhibited a tendency toward self-perpetuation. The state, deeply distrusting the peasants, took over ever more responsibilities for the agricultural cycles with which it was unable to cope; the peasants learned new ways of evasion and looked to their private plots and cows.

The system which grew out of such interaction was an agriculture in which peasants saw their main means of production taken away from them, the threshing taken over, estimates of crops made over their heads, planning of their sowings dictated from above. Furthermore, no autonomy of any consequence was allowed to the kolkhozy and no important sphere of their work left without interference. The formally proclaimed democratic organization of kolkhozy had no meaning, as their management was imposed on kolkhozy, and any chairman who engaged in defending his outfit would be demoted and replaced by another nominee. The state wanted the internal administrations to be watchdogs of the *zagotovki*, not representatives of the producers. This accounted for a constant turnover among kolkhozy chairmen, who all too often had no chance to accumulate enough experience in running a complicated enterprise.

For the kolkhoz to become an efficient producer it needed conditions in which to acquire a personality of its own, a sense of pride and belonging. It needed dedicated leaders to preside over the kolkhozy and to help these leaders to acquire enough experience and authority in the eyes of fellow *kolkhozniki*. But government policies were hard at work against the emergence of this type of solidarity in kolkhozy. Through constant interference and petty tyrannies by its local officials, through the unpredictability of its exactions and the whole essence of its agricultural policies, the state kept, in fact, disorganizing the kolkhozy. Without a minimum of rights, independence, and esprit de corps, the kolkhoz was condemned to stagnation.

Peasants, of course, could not escape their own condition. They had to feed themselves, but the small plot in which they invested a disproportionate amount of their labor and energies was too small to supply the family with bread and enough forage. It was a physical impossibility to live without participating in the kolkhoz works, not to consider the legal constraints to participate. Once in the kolkhoz field, the minimum of *trudodni* were imposed, norms and some labor discipline were demanded, supervision and pressures by management and party officials, and on occasions security organs, too, helped to keep things going. There was no other way than to accommodate to the conditions, to earn *trudodni*, and to sell something in the kolkhoz markets in order to make ends meet. It was the cruder incentive of elementary needs which made the system tick, rather than stimuli of a higher order. Because income on the kolkhoz field was only an unpredictable residual after many other claimants had been satisfied, much dedicated labor was wasted on the tiny plot because it actually gave some secure food minimum, and much sluggishness and indifference was deployed in the modern, large-scale sector equipped with machinery, but a low-yielding and insecure remunerator. In this way the peasants continued to perpetuate themselves as a separate peasant class, but they were not allowed to be either efficient smallholders or dedicated cooperators.

Neither was the peasant a citizen, even in the Soviet sense. Compared with the NEP period, the social status of the peasants deteriorated. Under the NEP the peasants, however poor, had some reason for self-esteem. The majority of them felt they were independent producers and saw themselves as *khozyaeva* in their own right, a class which had recently emancipated itself from the degrading conditions of serfdom.

But during the next period they were transformed into a mass deprived of rights, surrounded by discriminatory practices and limitations, and submitted to an entirely new regime. The passport system and restrictions inside kolkhozy deprived them of much of their freedom of movement. They were subjected to compulsory state corvées, like road building and timber cutting, which did not apply to city dwellers. They had no representation of their own, no right to organize themselves for the defense of their interests. Peasants paid special higher prices for the means of production and for some consumer goods. They were submitted to a labor system which reminded them all too often of the conditions from which the revolution seemed to have redeemed them for ever. Peasants in Stalin's times were indeed legally bound to their place of work, submitted to a special legal regimen, and—through the kolkhoz—to a form of collective responsibility with regard to state duties. They were transformed, not unlike as in pre-emancipation times, into an estate placed at the very bottom of the social ladder.

Some twenty years after Stalin's death many changes have occurred, and numerous discriminatory traits of the special regime have gone. Peasants in the Soviet Union today are paid for their labor and allowed to make profits; they have salaries and pensions and produce much more and better than twenty years ago. But these are very recent developments. Soviet agriculture has not yet managed to effect a real technological revolution similar to the one which took place some time ago in other developed countries. Agriculture is still rather primitive and a great problem; and there is no doubt that the consequences of the first quarter of a century of kolkhoz history still weigh heavily and are far from having been definitively overcome.

7

THE KOLKHOZ
AND THE
RUSSIAN *MUZHIK*

The story of the private family plots farmed by members of the kolkhozy is, on the face of it, the story of a simple rural pastime or hobby, at best a means to vary the diet and earn some pocket money on the city market by selling a few eggs or potatoes.* What else would one expect from a sown area amounting to less than 4 percent of the total and distributed to the peasant families in small allotments of a maximum of half a hectare?

However, a closer look at these privately farmed plots shows that they are much more than a hobby. In fact, we are facing here one of the anomalies and paradoxes of Soviet social and economic life, rich in unexpected contradictions, and the consequences of these extend far beyond the apparently insignificant scale suggested by the figures on sown area.

The official views seem, at first approach, to minimize the importance of the phenomenon: privately farmed plots are but a subsidiary and temporary activity of the peasants, whose main efforts and interests lie in their membership and work in the kolkhozy, those large-scale, highly mechanized, and modern socialist enterprises. But there are also other arguments in the official views, appeals for vigilance and numerous campaigns organized by the government about and against these plots, which raise

---

* This chapter deals mainly with the period up to about the mid-1950s, or roughly, the period of Stalin's rule. Since then many changes have occurred in the ways Soviet agriculture works and in the position of the peasantry, but it is assumed that many important traits of the past persist.

some questions in our minds. The energy displayed by these campaigns betrays the government's awareness that the phenomenon may have been far more significant than is suggested by the idea of its transient and "subsidiary" character.

The history of these plots—the way in which it all began in the winter of 1929/30 with an all-out collectivization drive and the virtually whole-sale expropriation of peasant cattle, including small animals,[1] and then further zigzags of policy and stubborn peasant resistance—was certainly dramatic and violent and often led to bloodshed. Much of it revolved around the plot, the unwillingness to part with the horse, but especially the cow—the family's mainstay and the peasant woman's sine qua non. The first years of "collectivization" were full of massive and persistent riots of the womenfolk which were caused by what Stalin later called "our minor misunderstanding" with the kolkhoz women "about the cow"[2]— certainly an understatement trying to play down what really amounted to a major social contest between the peasantry and the state. The problem consisted of more than just these types of riots—but those were among the most direct and violent acts of opposition to the government during the first years of collectivization.

By 1935 the government seemed to have learned the lesson and have reached a decision to compromise with the peasants by legalizing the plot fully and guaranteeing in the new status of the kolkhoz the right to a certain number of cattle to be kept on the family farm.[3] Although this status was not openly challenged after that, the problem was far from over. The government kept a constant watch over this activity and engaged in counterattacks alleging the abuse by the *kolkhozniki* of the plots and accusing them of pursuing private commercial gain at the expense of the collective sector of the kolkhozy. One of the fiercest of such attacks occurred under Stalin just before the war (there were several more after the war and under Khrushchev), when a stern law of May 27, 1939, signed by Stalin and Molotov, claimed that the peasants, with the connivance of kolkhoz managements and local authorities, surreptitiously enlarged the plots and the number of cattle, minded their private interests, and tended to shirk in the kolkhozy. A vociferous campaign was instigated clamping down on the plot owners with new taxes and procurement quotas. Special government controllers were created to check the size of the plots and the economic activity on them, and a huge network of committees was set up to measure the plots, cut down the unlawful extra land, and return it to the kolkhozy.

The campaign was presented in the propaganda channels as an anti-capitalist drive, and it had at least two important results. First, as figures disclosed in the 1960s showed, the whole activity was one of the numerous exercises in aberration quite characteristic of Stalin's Russia; on the whole, the kolkhoz peasantry did not even fully use its statutory limits in terms of number of cattle and the legal size of plots.[4] Only 10.4 percent of the kolkhoz households might have eventually overstepped the limits by small amounts,[5] and much of the land confiscated from these transgressors was very poor or otherwise unusable, and the kolkhozy who got it "back" had no use for it.

The second factor was no less important: the clamping down on the plot caused the numbers of cattle to fall—something the country just could not afford in view of the tense situation with food supplies and the war already on the doorstep. Such blows to popular consumption and welfare were the constant and predictable result of every campaign against the plots.

It is not difficult to see why. According to one estimate, in 1938 about 45 percent of total farm output was produced on the 3.9 percent of sown area, which was worked privately by the peasant families (0.49 hectares per household). The kolkhoz family derived from this plot half of its money income, almost all of its animal foodstuff, and most of its potatoes and vegetables, while the kolkhoz supplied them mainly with grain.[6] The family plot, apart from producing 52.1 percent of the kolkhozy's potatoes and most of the fruit and vegetables, maintained over half of the country's cattle and most of the cattle available in the kolkhozy,[7] and they produced 71.4 percent of the milk, 70.9 percent of the meat and 43 percent of all wool.[8] At the same time these tiny enterprises, through sales to the city population on kolkhoz markets, contributed the impressive share of some 20 percent of all marketed food supplies[9] and supported friends and relatives in the city with gifts. They also provided the government with procurements and contracts, which became particularly exacting in 1939.[10] This performance was achieved through something like 6 percent of the labor input of adult males and 33.6 percent of the women's labor.[11] Not unexpectedly, as became clear very soon to the government's experts, the *kolkhoznik* earned more from the plot than from the kolkhoz,[12] and his workday on the plot gave him, in 1937 and again in 1938, twice as much as the day's work on the kolkhoz.[13]

This is not the whole story, but it is enough for us to conclude that the small plot fed the peasantry and contributed decisively to the country's agricultural output and to the food supplies. It was, despite its small scale, a major economic branch and an indispensable producer. It was also, as Soviet writers admit today, a factor sustaining not only the country but the whole kolkhoz system as well. Such facts bring us far away from the official image of an auxiliary and transitory activity. The private small enterprises look rather like a "giant dwarf," an important and vital producer, and this is why whenever the government tampered with it beyond a certain point, a worsening of the country's food situation followed automatically.

But why should the government have indulged in warfare against the plots? An exhaustive answer to this question will not be attempted here. However, the whole problem will get into proper focus if the general situation of the country's agricultural production is presented. During the years of the first and second five-year plans, till the bumper crop of 1937, agricultural production kept falling, animal foodstuffs and grain alike. Only the figures for the three and a half years of the prewar, unfinished third five-year plan showed an improvement. After 1934 the numbers of cattle stopped falling and together with grain production began slowly to increase. But, as corrected official figures published after Stalin's death have shown, there was no reason for jubilation. By 1940 the country produced less animal foodstuffs than in 1916, a war year. It did produce somewhat more grain than in tsarist Russia, although not much more than in NEP, and this was achieved through an enlargement of sown area without any significant qualitative progress. The average yields were only 7.7 quintals per hectare, still no better than under the precollectivization system, and still extremely low despite the vaunted benefits of modern large-scale organization, of kolkhozy and sovkhozy, with their hundreds of thousands of tractors and combines, with numerous ministries, and so on.[14] It was against the background of such poor results—in view of the growing number of mouths to be fed many would agree that they were indeed catastrophic —that the performance of the private plots in this overall output looked so outstanding. They were more efficient, more reliable than the kolkhozy and sovkhozy, and without them the peasants and the country would have starved. Thus the country needed this sector of private peasant activity.

But the government was not ready to interpret these facts as manifestations of a failure of its policies and an expression of the need to accept an open and frank compromise between the two sectors for the benefit of both: grain and industrial crops on the kolkhoz fields; cattle and vegetables on the private farms with state help in fodder, agronomy, supplies. Instead, a "rotten compromise" prevailed, unacknowledged and vociferously denied, which helped to transform eventually complementary activities on plots and in the kolkhozy into competing and contradictory, alien forces. State policies and ideology preferred it that way.

The kolkhoz system, as it emerged by 1933, represented a combination of three sectors locked in an uneasy, antagonistic coexistence. First, there was the large kolkhoz with its administrations. Second, the state-owned machinery and tractor stations (MTSs) were given work on kolkhoz fields in accordance with a contract signed with the kolkhoz. Finally, the third sector was formed by the multitude of private plots. On the face of it, a symbiosis was supposed to reign among the three. In fact, as has been said, the picture was less idyllic: in each of the three sectors there were serious discrepancies between ideological and constitutional statements and reality. The kolkhoz, being in theory a cooperative, was supposed to be run by administrations freely elected and supervised by the general assembly of its members. In fact, kolkhoz leaders were superciliously watched by local administrations and the police and were summarily dismissed and appointed at will. The cooperative principle was thus no more than a fiction.

The MTSs, state agencies that were created in theory to service their client kolkhozy and to do for them the job they wanted for a reasonable reward, were in fact the real bosses on the fields, geared to squeeze grain out of the kolkhozy, to "plan" and control them, and to exercise political and police supervision. This bureaucratic organization was created because the kolkhozy could not afford, or rather, the government felt, could not be trusted with agricultural machinery. The MTSs were inefficient organizations, often in conflict with and frequently mishandling the kolkhozy, which had little recourse against them and their power.

The plot, the most efficient producer of them all, was in theory a small supplementary device. But at the same time, the ideologists and the politicians magnified it into something quite unusual: its very existence was seen as a result of "survivals of a petit bourgeois mentality," its activity was basically motivated by the peasant's lust for private gain and his commercial spirit, and the whole sector was presented as an alien body in socialist society. Thus the peasantry as plot owners were ideologically illegitimate, deeply immoral, and barely tolerated for the time being.

The whole so-called collectivized agricultural organization thus resembled a peculiar awkwardly shaped cart with two huge wheels and one small, one big wheel dragging the peasants into a pseudo-cooperative, the other supplying them with machinery over which they had no say, and the small third one feeding them. At the same time the three disproportionate wheels, instead of really pulling in one direction, were badly coordinated and all too often blocked each other, each of them operating under different constraints and a different, often contradictory system of motivations. Without massive state coercion nothing of this kind could have existed for long in such a form. It did of course continue to exist, but the results of such husbandry, not unexpectedly, were extremely disappointing.

The government, frustrated by the weakness of what it had hoped would soon become a superior social and economic form, and seeing it easily beaten as producer by the dwarf plots, tended to present the plots and peasant greed as the main culprit of the poor results of the new agricultural system. It claimed therefore that the main problem consisted in "reeducating" the peasant and changing his mentality.

En attendant, the system did not look like a very "pedagogic" institution. It could not have been one with this kind of ideological attitude which distorted reality and produced faulty analysis. The problem with the plot was not so much a "backward mentality" as its simple economic necessity. The branch was not subsidiary or auxiliary but indispensable. The labor put into it was hard and honest and the motivations legitimate and fully comprehensible. To present this labor as somehow "immoral," suspect, etc., was the result of the ideologist's own distorting mirror, which prevented him from seeing things as they were. The conflict with the peasants was imposed on them by political constraints and ideological predilection, which were no more than an expression of an attempted rape of social realities. Moreover, the principles the government set out to inculcate were not the ones of cooperation, solidarity, and economic progress. Rather, they involved the imposition with iron gloves—anything else would not do—of the very different principle of absolute priority and superiority of the interests of the state over the interests of the producers. In practice, it amounted therefore to a system where state procurement rather than production became the central axis of the relations between the state and its kolkhozy, with a third or more of the output being extracted from the kolkhozy for no more than a nominal price which covered only a small part of their production cost. This was the central principle from which stemmed all the other traits of the system. "Material responsibility" instead of "material stimulation"—such is the highly critical verdict of a modern Soviet author, even though he uses, for obvious reasons, quite guarded terms.[15]

It all ended up in a system which could not be a rational economic proposition. Not surprisingly, terms like cost, profitability, material interests, and material incentives were excluded from official thinking. Forced deliveries, forced minimums of workdays to be spent on kolkhozy fields, detailed production plans imposed from above—a whole system, in fact, forced from above—justify the assessment by a Western scholar that the kolkhoz became "a system of forced labor."[16] Shadows of the past could be seen in this situation, ever more reminiscent of what was abolished in 1861. The peasant reacted by, as it were, splitting his personality as producer and employing two measures according to two different types of motivation, one when working "for them," the other when working for his family. This was similar to what happened in the system of serfdom, when there was nonchalance and neglect on the fields of the *pomeshchik*, and hard work on his own farmland. Behind the *pomeshchik* stood the might of the state; behind the kolkhoz and the MTS stood the state, too, but it had a more difficult task now than the old state, namely, to "reeducate" not only the peasants but the kolkhoz administrations as well.

The disquieting parallel with serfdom runs even deeper when it is realized that the kolkhoz regime under Stalin straitjacketed the peasantry into an economic and juridical system which discriminated against them in more than one way. Peasants not only had to suffer from the "normal" disadvantages of rural backwardness (which are still at work today)—bad schools, few cultural amenities, bad roads—but they were also declared an inferior class and treated accordingly. Their remuneration for labor was based on the "residual principle" without the guaranteed income which other classes enjoyed.[17] There was no social security system for them, no help for housing, a system of state duties to which nobody else was subjected, special higher prices to pay for goods, the denial of passports in order to control their mobility, and an elaborate and heavy system of taxation directed against their private plots.[18] The fact of having to run their plots could also be construed as a handicap, rather than some kind of privilege.

Thus the state, awaiting the abolition of classes in a very next historical stage, "told" the peasants quite firmly that they were a suspect and inferior class. The peasants knew it anyway. As the state stood over their heads and forced on them its "first commandment"—this was the Biblical term actually employed—"Supply the state first," the peasants responded quite audibly: "Supply yourself and your family first." The lesson they learned from experience taught them, in essence, that "if you don't take care of your family nobody will, it will starve." This was a fact of life which is freely admitted today by some Soviet authors. In this situation a deep and basic clash of interests was bound to develop: the state perceiving the peasant as dangerous to the foundations of the regime, and the peasant viewing the state as a menace to the survival of his family.

Only in the 1960s did it become possible in the Soviet Union to state some of these truths as well as the paradoxical fact that, despite the economic and ideological warfare conducted by the government against the plots during those years, "the private plot was in fact the only stimulus to participation in social production,"[19] and thus the system's savior *malgré soi!*

Nevertheless, for over a generation Soviet agriculture found itself locked in a vicious circle which did not allow it to advance this branch— a problem that is far from being resolved satisfactorily even today. In terms used by a Soviet author, kolkhoz production does not grow because productivity of labor does not grow, and this happens because the *kolkhoznik* is not interested in working in conditions of very low income. "But improving his income is impossible because production does not grow."[20] This author has in mind some of the backward kolkhozy in the 1960s. In fact, this diagnosis applies well to the whole system in the past as well as, to an important degree, the present.

In this situation of stagnation in agriculture, the position the peasantry found itself in—the position of an "estate" constricted "from above"— was strongly reinforced and perpetuated "from below" by the activity of the kolkhoz families on their private plots. Both factors, the state and private enterprise, helped to shape the social realities of the Soviet countryside in an unexpected way. The traditional peasantry was supposed to become "modernized" in the process of collectivization and industrialization of agriculture, to the extent of actually withering away and changing its social substance. In fact, the kolkhoz system developed a quite different tendency in relation to those peasants who remained on the land. They showed no signs of withering away. Quite the contrary.

As we have said, the state created a situation in which it laid a priority claim to what the kolkhozy produced. But the peasants were supposed to run this system themselves, although it neither fed them nor offered them any guaranteed income. In addition to laboring in the kolkhoz, they were supposed to take care of their families and much of the rest of the country as well. Their perception of the reality in which they found themselves reminded them of the duality experienced by their ancestors in serfdom, and they responded with the traditional diffidence toward the state—as was the case with peasants for generations. An old tradition was here simply continued and was fully reflected in the consciousness of a class identity shaped by conflicting forces.

To be sure, there was no longer an oppressive landowning class. Instead a new social force emerged: the bureaucracy of an industrializing state. But while the state rushed ahead into the age of machines and mass communications, its peasants were socially "frozen" in an earlier stage, if they did not actually move backward. There were, of course, tractors and combines on kolkhoz fields, but even with these there was a problem: this technology was implanted without enhancing the country's agricultural production for at least a generation. The factory system, where the machine does not belong to the worker, was the source of an immense rise in productivity, and this was the case with the Soviet system too, despite difficulties and impediments to innovation and technical progress. The kolkhoz, on the other hand, unlike the factory, was not the result of an organic development. It was "invented" and imposed by the state, and here the main means of production were expropriated. It was to become a botched up transplant, with clear elements of rejection. For a long time massive evidence pointed to the fact that kolkhoz fields were a cemetery for tractors. Peasants broke them, misused them, were not interested. And as far as the plot was concerned, this big machinery was entirely irrelevant. The activity of the plot was entirely outside the technological age. It consisted in the most old-fashioned, archaic, physical work.

But however small and technically backward the plot was, it was still a manifestation of a full-fledged, small-scale, private entrepreneurship. The dependence of the peasant family on the plot for its livelihood—which sometimes made the income from the kolkhoz look "subsidiary" rather than the other way round—gave a powerful incentive to work with zeal on the plot and to seek out other private sources of income whenever available, and to do the unavoidable minimum in the kolkhoz. This forced the government to undertake action against mass shirking by imposing legal minimums of workdays, coupled with penalties for failure to do so.[21] What was at stake, as the peasant understood it, was the survival of the peasant's household and of the family. In order to solve the problem the peasant resorted to his traditional form of economic activity: using and reinforcing the family as a unit of economic activity. It is immediately obvious that such an outcome ought to have had important consequences for the outlook of the Soviet peasantry.

Since the plot was a crucial economic sector, it served as a basis for the perpetuation of the traditional behavior and attitudes of the peasantry. Deprived of social security and a guaranteed income, the homestead and the plot and the efforts of the family became the only sources of such elementary and basic needs. The peasant hut offered lodging, and the farm offered support for the elderly and milk for the children. Behind the hut were the cowshed and other farm buildings, the form and substance of an old peasant household (*dvor*), with its sense of cohesion and mutual dependence. The position and role of women and children as well as the elderly continued as ever on the old lines, maybe even increasing the burden on women, who became the main factor in running the plot as well as doing work in the kolkhoz. This involved also the tedious and time-consuming business of traveling, often every day in suburban areas, to carry small amounts of eggs, meat, butter, or vegetables to the markets— the most important source of family cash.[22] But the trading on markets, apart from being a waste of time which modern methods of organization could have avoided, perpetrated an old dimension characteristic of the life of the peasant family: its dependence on and vulnerability to market fluctuations, Gosplan notwithstanding.

The serious activity on the plot thus added a burden of working hours which other classes did not share and deprived the peasant of many opportunities to broaden his cultural horizons. Modern Soviet sociologists have grasped the full implications of this factor. Some have pointed out that the private plots of even the sovkhoz and industrial workers, still widespread and economically quite important, influence the outlook and mentality of those involved.[23] The much bigger peasant plot is an even weightier economic and social factor. Although indispensable in order to bring the peasant's income to the level of industrial workers, it has in fact retarded the much-heralded fusion of social classes by perpetuating many classical traits of the peasantry,[24] and maintaining it as a family-based agricultural entrepreneurship. Moreover, the conditions in which this entrepreneurship has been exercised have impeded agricultural progress and encouraged the most archaic methods: primitive physical labor, rather ridiculous conditions of commercialization, and a very low level of consumption. In fact, well into Khrushchev's days the mass of peasants still suffered from underconsumption.[25] Thus, precarious economic conditions, characteristic of small peasants in many regimes, which left no energy for long-term calculations and risk taking, made family survival dependent simply on the next crop. The psychological traits which such a situation produced in the peasant mentality are notorious: conservatism and sticking to routine, fear of change, opposition to technology, distrust of the cities and of city dwellers, and alienation from the state with its officials, judges, and policemen.

In other words, the social effects of the functioning of the kolkhoz system, for a generation at least, consisted in reproducing backward

Russian *muzhiki* instead of the modern cooperative, industrialized farmers. If anything, these Soviet *muzhiki* might have become more interested in private property and private farming than they ever were before. Until 1906 the Russian peasants had a very vague concept, if any, of private property,[26] and the well-known efforts of Stolypin and his reforms between 1906 and 1910 were necessary to inculcate in them a degree of dedication to this concept. This was a conscious, not fully successful effort. One may ponder over the possibility that in its Stalinist stage collectivization, although aiming at uprooting such attitudes, went in fact a long way toward reinforcing and developing them.

There was nothing new for the *muzhik* when official Russia did not recognize his labor for what it was, when it was seen not as hard and honest but as some kind of a nuisance. This was an insult which the *muzhik* could take. He was used to being at the bottom of the social ladder and tried to make the best of it, which had significant, sometimes incalculable effects on the country's destiny. Here was a manifestation of what Russian writers called, approvingly or disapprovingly according to their ideological predisposition, the old *"muzhik* might" (*muzhitskaya sila*).

This vague concept had, nevertheless, a powerful content behind it, expressing the economic, social, and cultural influence of old rural Russia and its effect on the behavior and mentality of Russian society as a whole in the process of becoming an industrialized and urban country. On the one hand, powerful forces eroded large sections of the peasantry by absorbing them into nonrural employments; on the other hand, contradictorily, other forces reinforced and reproduced the *muzhik*. As long as this was true, the old *muzhitskaya sila* was bound to continue and mightily influence the nation and the state system. The fact that these influences and interests of the peasantry were not allowed open forms of expression, through literature or other free channels, did not prevent the operation of deep-seated trends. The moralizing propaganda against petit bourgeois mentality and *mel'kosobstvennichestvo* or, for that matter, against religious beliefs, would fill out the editorials and speeches, but real cultural and social processes would of course go on unabated, forming widespread subcultures and distinct modes of behavior. The dictatorial method of *zagonyat' vnutr'* (driving inward), instead of letting interests and ideas out into the open, had a distorting effect on national development, with many subterranean streams of unacknowledged force quietly taking over the minds of masses of people away from the official clichés, though not always in the most palatable directions. But such considerations bring us far beyond the scope of this study.

To reiterate briefly the gist of our argument. The private plot had a paradoxically disproportionate influence: it was an economically restricted but socially powerful force in the shaping of a class. It made the social history of Russian under Stalin, as well as after him, a more complex affair than appearances and clichés would suggest. It entailed the preservation of a rather backward peasantry in an otherwise very dynamic setting. But this was only one instance of a broader phenomenon in Stalinism, in which the dynamism of industrial development and social restructuring went hand in hand with the baffling phenomenon of perpetuation and re-creation of much of the imperial past.

·3·

DIFFERENT LENINISMS AND SOCIAL CHANGE

8

LENINISM AND
BOLSHEVISM:
THE TEST OF
HISTORY
AND POWER

▪ THREE CORROSIVE FACTORS

As the Romans said of books, "habent sua fata libelli," we may say that ideologies have their own destinies, their history and sociology. Much remains to be done toward understanding the fortunes of Leninism and bolshevism and making them known; this brief presentation offers just a few ideas for discussion.

The two notions are not identical. "Bolshevism" applies to the party as a whole, which espoused Leninism by and large as its ideology of struggle, but bolshevism included factions which often proposed divergent interpretations of the Marxist canons as well as of the theoretical and strategic positions that derive specifically from Leninism. This has already been said by others: the Bolshevik party was, and between 1919 and 1929 fairly clearly remained, an alliance of factions. To be sure, it was more strongly unified than other parties were, but nevertheless it did not constitute a monolithic bloc cast in a single mold, as would be alleged later on, even by specialists. Leninism, one of the Russian versions of Marxism, developed by Lenin, was shared by the Bolsheviks who had acquired their ideological formation before the revolution and who maintained an openmindedness, an institutional flexibility in pursuing the struggle of ideas in particular, but not exclusively in the areas of strategy and tactics that made up the core of Leninism. It is important to recall that bolshevism had gone through quite a number of internal debates before 1917, that it had functioned in a multiparty environment, especially after the revolution of 1905, and even after the takeover of power, until 1920. Starting with the revolution of February 1917, in particular, and until the prohibition of factions by the Tenth Party Congress in March 1921, various wings and tendencies, opposing factions and platforms presented before and during the congresses, coexisted within the party; these were not only tolerated but were actually used as widely accepted *modus operandi*. Bolshevism, then, was factionalized; Lenin himself played the game, during and after 1917, according to these rules, although he did not always show much fondness for them.

Let us recall a few pertinent facts. Before the takeover, bolshevism was a young faction. It was definitively established as a party in 1912, and thus it found itself in power a scant five years later. Moreover, up to 1945 its activity was marked by two wars, two or even three revolutions, an atrocious civil war accompanied by symptoms of the breakdown and fragmentation of the social body, by the near disappearance of the state after 1917—a phenomenon whose depth and effects have not been fully grasped even now—and by its recomposition, followed by other social crises such as industrialization and forced collectivization, the great purges, all this topped off by another world war. One would be astounded not to find an ideology and a party profoundly tested, transformed, or even destroyed by events of such magnitude. This is an issue worth exploring: far more than transformation or degradation is involved. From the time of the takeover, international conditions and the structural conditions of the country imposed unavoidable changes which led finally to a total transformation from top to bottom that modified the very essence of the phenomenon. In short, the international situation, the test of power—which always has a conservative effect—and finally the structure of the society define the principles underlying the dissolution of this bolshevist–Leninist compound.

▪ LENINISM AND THE WORKING CLASS

Rather than try to give an exhaustive definition here, let us settle for a few characteristic features of Leninism.

First, the theoretical base of Leninism was unquestionably Marxism. The theory of capitalism and the ideas of Marx and Engels on socialism were more or less completely accepted by Lenin, but often with additional elements contributed by Kautsky and Plekhanov.

Second, although he remained within the framework of Marxist thought, Lenin added to this base the anticipation of revolutionary crises, in the West as well as in Russia. This outlook was based on his concept of imperialism as the last stage of capitalism, although Lenin's view does not really constitute an original contribution.

Third, in revolution, the proletariat was assigned to the front lines; in particular, it was supposed to play the role of collective dictator while awaiting the dissolution of the classes and the withering away of the state.

Fourth, a specifically Russian problem, the question of the development of capitalism in that country, was the subject of lengthy discussions. The speed and depth of capitalist developments were considered first; but adjustments had to be made, and under the pressure of facts, concern shifted to the difficulties and delays of the capitalist advance.

Fifth, in the context of backwardness specific to Russia, Leninism granted an important place—although with divergent implications—to the role of the peasantry in the revolutionary process, and it was finally convinced of the need for alliances either with the peasantry as a whole or with its poorest strata.

Sixth, it is certain that the peasantry—a class made up of worker-owners —did not share the socialist objectives of the proletariat and that a collision with that immensely populous class was always to be feared.

Such a collision was even, or especially, to be feared after the establishment of a common government, which was one possible result of a bourgeois-democratic revolution, according to Lenin. This phase was foreseen, but in different terms, by the Mensheviks, according to whom the liberals would be the ones to spearhead the revolution. Lenin's post-1905 version predicted that the bourgeoisie would no longer be interested in overthrowing tsarism, and he proposed a formula for a worker-peasant bloc and government to assure the success of a bourgeois-democratic revolution. A latter-day clash between the partners or any other development remained unspecified. The formula was never really articulated.

This is a highly important element in the Leninist strategic outlook. It shows very clearly that prerevolutionary Leninism conceived its strategy in terms of a democratic revolution, within a multiparty perspective. It thus led the party at the very most toward participation in power, and not toward a single-handed conquest of power. Such a task was left for later; it did not seem timely.

Seventh, the view of the party as the seedbed of professional revolutionary cadres, highly structured and disciplined, was the most original aspect of Leninism. This conception went hand in hand with the idea of relations between the party of clandestine political professionals and the working class which, according to some, was sharply revising Marxism in a voluntarist and highly authoritarian direction. Many authors already saw this as the sign of particularly ominous future developments. Others simply saw a realistic adaptation to the political and social conditions of tsarist Russia; still others saw only the expression of a realism lacking in any troubling overtones.

It is an interesting debate. Let us nevertheless note one striking fact— for it is a fact. Before the revolution, the hope of Leninism was vested in the Russian proletariat, and stress was often placed on its unique aptitude for combat; this gave way more and more frequently, after the revolution, to a discourse on the vulnerability of the proletariat to the influence of the petite bourgeouisie and especially of the peasantry, even though this latter group was supposedly an ally.

Here, no doubt, we may find a certain foretaste of things to come. Glorification and suspicion of the working class are found side by side in Leninism, even during the period of the seizure of power. The support of this class was indispensable and actively sought. But Lenin stated insistently in October 1917, going against the views of many Bolsheviks, that the party alone should take power, while following the decisions of party agencies and not those of the class in the broad sense. For it was impossible to know, said Lenin in October 1917, whether the Second Congress of Soviets, about to be convened on the twentieth, then delayed to the twenty-fifth of that month, would have a pro-Bolshevik majority. The congress, already convoked, thus had to delay its opening until the seizure of the Winter Palace, in spite of the fact that a pro-Bolshevik majority had gathered there after all. Would Lenin have returned the power his party had decided to seize to this working-class assembly if this power had been denied him? Or would he have dispersed it, as he did with the Constituent Assembly? It may be supposed that in October 1917 he would still have accepted the verdict, particularly because the opposition to the seizure of power by the Bolsheviks alone was more significant within his own party than is commonly thought. All this is debatable and warrants discussion. But one thing is certain: Lenin did receive a mandate from the Second Congress of Soviets, which means that the idea of the "political void" which supposedly permitted a Bolshevik victory has to be revised. Let us not forget that until October there was a dual power in Russia, a dyarchy, and this was true as early as February–March 1917. The void was created in only one of the two branches, the weaker one, while in the other the Bolsheviks carried the day.

■ TOO REAL A REALITY

Seen from the perspective of three or four years in power, the first months of the new regime, in spite of their victory in the civil war, must have looked to the Bolsheviks like a golden age. For in the interval doubts had already arisen about the Leninist forecast concerning the crisis of capitalism and proletarian revolutions in the industrialized countries.

It was some time before these doubts could be assimilated and used to spur the necessary adaptations. From this period on, the hope of being towed along in the wake of a victorious revolution in the West began to fade. Bolshevik power, then, was about to find itself all alone, in an underdeveloped country, left with no forces but its own to count on—and these seemed far too meager for the task at hand.

This brings to mind the debate between Lenin, Zinoviev, and Kamenev in 1917, in which the latter two figures opposed the seizure of power on the grounds that it was premature. Most of their tactical arguments proved mistaken in the short run, but they had the better of Lenin in their analysis of the international situation and the consequences that would follow upon the Bolshevik takeover. Thanks to his tactical sense, Lenin carried the day against them in the Central Committee and in the field. But once the decisive act had been carried out, it was discovered that a number of strategic factors of prime importance which were being counted on were lacking, and sometimes cruelly so. Rarely had a victory—a brilliant one as it happens—been won on so many false assumptions.

The unexpected isolation of the Russian revolution had a particularly heavy impact. One must realize that Leninist thinking about future revolutions and the role of the proletariat was based in large part on observation of the developed countries and on an analysis in which the behavior of the classes played a major part. Within this perspective, first of all, capitalist development was supposed to pave the way for the conditions required for the rise and success of the future proletarian power and to bring these conditions into effect. Second, owing to the dictatorship of the proletariat, by definition a transitory stage, the class was to become the state, and this state ipso facto was to begin to wither away. We can understand why views of this type originating in the West were very useful to people thinking about seizing power in the course of a revolutionary crisis, while at the same time they did not prepare very well, if at all, for the realities of the exercise of power, especially in a country like Russia. The degree of capitalist development in that country, although significant, was highly exaggerated by impatient revolutionaries, and the work of preparation that capitalism was supposed to accomplish did not take place. This was equally true for the working class, for almost immediately after the seizure of power, and especially after the civil war, it was clear that the absolutely crucial support of the working class had its limitations. Not very numerous and barely educated, this class was not capable of managing or even comanaging the factories, and it could not supply enough cadres to manage the state. It was too weak to bear up under the combined devastations of the war, the burden of service and losses in the Red Army, depletion at its core (extractions of the most gifted elements of the working class to the benefit of the administrative apparatus), and at the same time to survive the destruction of industry, unemployment, and famine. Toward the end of that fateful civil war, we hear Lenin utter a cry of alarm: "The working class, devastated, declassed, dispersed in the countryside in search of bread, has disappeared!" Power remained suspended "in the air," as it were, for it had lost its social base.

It can almost be taken for granted that the working class should lose what seemed to be the chief October gain—control and worker management of the factories. These were soon replaced by the increased power of the unions, which were centralized and more easily integrated within the mechanisms of the state, especially by virtue of the "one-man management," within industry, of directors appointed by a state organization, albeit with a strong say reserved to the unions. It is true that it took some time for this "autocracy in the factories" to take hold. It was decreed again in 1929, and from that point on it was successfully imposed. The tendency toward a strong regime in industry had as its counterpart an accompanying favorable orientation toward the cadres and technicians; that reorientation, which was just getting under way in April 1918, was to take on increasing emphasis in the 1930s, when it hardened into a system.

Alongside the weakness that was showing up in this way in the factories, the new regime discovered that it had a critical need for specialists —who were almost all members of the bourgeoisie, in more or less open opposition to the new regime. It is clear why Bolshevik power, with its proletarian orientation, was taken by surprise. For these strata could not be conquered by force alone; it was necessary to offer them some material privileges. Furthermore, they were needed at the pinnacle of the hierarchy, where proletarians newly promoted to high responsibilities by the revolution were often ineffective, owing to their lack of training, and were ultimately at the mercy of more or less hostile experts, at least at the outset.

But these positions inevitably conferred supplementary privileges in addition to the economic ones. The difficult relations established with these strata of experts, hostile but indispensable to the success of the regime, were coupled with genuine drama when the so-called popular intelligentsia, the traditionally leftist primary and secondary teachers in particular, opted out as soon as the new regime was installed by engaging in a massive strike. That bitter pill had left deep scars, and it implanted a paranoia against the intelligentsia, the only educated group in a backward country, but one which took exception to a proletarian revolution, even a popular one. The decision to form "our own intelligentsia" was to be transformed in the years to come into a large-scale action, impressive in its scope and results, but the paranoia was to persist and turn later even against the new strata of the intelligentsia, those faithful to the system, particularly in the murderous purges of the 1930s.

But no matter. Through these disappointments, whether with the so-called bourgeois specialists or the artistic intelligentsia or the tsarist- or Soviet-trained educators, the tendency to lean more and more on the educated strata, so necessary to the smooth operation of the economy and the state in general, increased in scope and began to be perceived as a complete change in orientation, capable of transforming the face of the system. (The philosopher A. Bogdanov, for example, who was a Bolshevik but was expelled before the revolution, said during the earliest stages of victorious bolshevism that despite the sincerity of bolshevist convictions the proletarian character of the system was only an illusion. The system was nothing but an enterprise led by and in the interests of the intellectuals.)

In the early years, the anxieties of the highly politicized party circles were attenuated by the significant presence within the system of a proletarian will and orientation that were to allow those in power to make use of former representatives of the opposing camp, while making concessions on one or two points of principle. Didn't this work in the army, where nearly 50,000 White officers, few of whom had undergone an ideological conversion, were helping to build the Red Army, and to defeat their brothers in the opposing camp? The reasoning according to which the regime had no other choice but to build communism with bourgeois hands, without this being dangerous in the long run, was reassuring. But another problem which was mixed up with the problem of specialists had to be added to the list of "surprises" for which Leninism and bolshevism were unprepared: the bureaucracy. At the beginning of the regime, tsarist functionaries demonstrated great solidarity: they completely rejected their new masters, going on strike and denying their services by other forms of sabotage as well. The Bolsheviks rapidly wiped out this resistance, but they quickly discovered that the state apparatus in which they had formerly shown little interest—for it was destined to be shattered, at least in large part—was a formidable force. Lenin was to say later that the trouble was not so much the strike but the fact that the tsarist functionaries, their resistance broken, returned in droves to serve their new employers in more or less lukewarm fashion.

The countless difficulties that ensued, in particular the weakness of the state apparatus, were too often attributed to the origin and training received by these *"chinovniki"* inherited from the tsarist system. Many people, notably Lenin himself, thought that bureaucrats and the bureaucracy were a legacy that would be overcome in the long run by the economic and cultural development of the country. But there, too, an analysis carried out solely in terms of classes was not relevant; in the later phases (which were moreover very brief) of the history of the system, the bureaucracy was to become a Soviet phenomenon par excellence, independently of the social origin of the functionaries involved. As certain critics inside the party began to be suspicious of it, "the dictatorship of the proletariat" ran a great risk of leading toward an entirely different configuration of power.

In our brief glance at these essential factors, which were causing unexpected problems for bolshevism and its ideology in the social structure of postrevolutionary Russia, we must also mention the peasantry, that is, the vast majority of the population. It played a dual role in the revolution: as producers in a state of rebellion who destroyed the old regime, through the confiscation and redistribution of lands belonging to the nobility; and as soldiers who refused to serve the tsar and to a large extent placed themselves at the service of the revolution and the new regime. Without this factor, the October revolution and the Lenin government would have been unthinkable. The role of the peasant-soldiers in the consolidation of power deserves more extensive discussion than we can give it here. Still, going back to the land-hungry peasantry, let us mention a few of the consequences of the agrarian revolution that contributed toward changing the social landscape of the new Russia. Lenin and his party hoped to obtain the support or the benevolent neutrality of the peasantry as a whole, or most of it, by adopting the agrarian program of the Social Revolutionaries (SRs). That strategy fully justified itself. Later on, the Leninist analysis counted rather more on the poor peasantry, an ill-defined social category but one whose existence in the countryside was nevertheless quite real, in order to carry on the revolution and control the capitalist tendencies of the rural petite bourgeoisie. But at the very moment when Lenin was calling upon the poor peasants, through the "committees of the poor," to go on the offensive against the kulak class and obtain the grain necessary to feed the cities, the agrarian revolution was changing the social character of these same "poor peasants" and of the peasantry as a whole. For the distribution and redistribution of land was transforming the poor peasants (*bednyaki*) on a broad scale, at least in their dreams, into *serednyaki* (middle peasants), whereas many kulaks were at the same time being reduced by redistribution to the status of *serednyaki*. The peasantry was moving away from social polarization toward homogeneity at the very time when Lenin, in one of his least prudent declarations, announced that the "poor peasants" were transforming the October revolution into a genuine social and socialist revolution in their assault on the wealthy of the countryside. These major social phenomena within the peasantry were to have important consequences in the long run, but certain results were already visible in the conduct of the civil war, for these phenomena are the cause, as early as March 1919, of a change in the pro-*bednyaki* strategy, in favor of an alliance with the middle peasantry.

▪ THE FACE THAT DISTORTS THE MIRROR

But did the party itself live up to expectations? Was it the perfect political tool and nothing more?

It is important to realize that the "tool," which was working in fact remarkably well, was not and could not be exempt from historical and sociological influences. Appearances and aspirations notwithstanding, politics could not float serenely above the realities of the country. The party, faced with the recalcitrant realities, was thus bound to cause problems for its leaders in turn, chiefly by undergoing numerous and abrupt transformations that affected its very nature—and that have not been adequately examined. The customary understanding of the role of the regime and the party in the fate of Russia has to be supplemented with increased attention to another horizon: the role of Russia in the transformation and the fortunes of the party and the regime as well. For bolshevism, which had set about to restructure the country, now had to undergo restructuring itself. The consequences of this shock were necessarily profound. Let us see what was at stake by sketching out the essential phases and features in this development.

First let us consider the historical stages, which shifted quickly with the highly volatile circumstances, so volatile indeed that they left those in power little time to reflect and reorient themselves. The prerevolutionary party, small, illegal, frequently decimated by the police, was a network of very active committees, with well-maintained contacts in the factories, and with little experience, historically, of the rural world. It had some influence among students and those circles of the intelligentsia who were open to the appeal of Marxism. This party—which in the period in question may be said to be close to the model proposed in "What Is to Be Done?"—was perhaps better able to resist repression than other groups (this remains to be proved), but it adapted easily to the fluctuation of political mobilization, especially in the working class. During the war it was decimated nonetheless; its principal cadres lived abroad or found themselves in exile in Siberia.

In 1917, the party underwent a rather astonishing change in structure and nature: the number of its cadres, which had not gone beyond 20,000, increased toward the end of the year to 300,000 or more, so that it became an authentic party of the urban masses, a legal, democratic party made up of people from diverse social strata and heterogeneous ideological horizons.

After his famous "April Theses," in 1917, Lenin succeeded in convincing the party to change course, although not without difficulty, and toward the end of the year, after a new effort that was equally if not more strenuous, he convinced the party to make an all-out attempt to seize power. Lenin's leadership was based at that time on the unrivaled prestige he enjoyed within the party, but he was not alone at the top; among the leaders grouped around him, each was capable of contesting his theses and did not hesitate to do so. The party also had at its disposal a second echelon of local leaders, who played an important role in party politics and whose opinions were often solicited, for these people were indispensable, and they would have made their voices heard had they not been consulted. Thus it was indeed a political party, better structured and better directed than all the others on the national scene, although strongly democratic, even factionalized, and accustomed to bitter political debates. This party, then, was moving toward the moment of its greatest glory, and even though it acknowledged Lenin as its historical head, it was not a party of the "Leninist" type.

The years of power, and especially of civil war, subjected this party to pressures too numerous to be listed here. Let us simply note an enormous fluctuation in its membership, a constant mobilization for the army and state service, a heavy rate of attrition (owing to death, physical exhaustion, or desertion), but at the same time, at its middle and higher echelons (most of which were of prerevolutionary vintage, with many recent cross-overs from other parties on the left), the permanence of a certain political life, with debates, factions, and platforms that were presented to the press and to the regularly held assembles of the higher agencies (congresses, annual conferences). In short, although in power and militarized, it was still a political party. Now toward the end of this period the social parameters we have already mentioned, such as the weakening of the proletariat, the changes in the structure of the peasantry, the painfully felt deficit of educated cadres, the slow but almost inexorable trend toward centralization and bureaucratization (even though this latter inspired a deep aversion), these factors weighed upon the entire system and did not spare the party. One of the factors of profound change within the party which led it in unforeseen and disquieting directions was the shifting nature of its social composition and its membership. A few figures, which do not purport to be at all precise, already give a sense of the process in question: thus there were 24,000 members at the beginning of 1917; 300,000 by the end of the year; 150,000 at the beginning of 1919; twice that many by the end of that year, going up to more than 500,000 in 1921, soon cut by some 180,000 in the first purge; and next, a mobilization of around one-quarter million workers in the context of the "Leninist enrollment" after the leader's death. All this led to a membership of 1 million in 1927, and about 3 million in 1933.

These figures are highly significant, for they are the expression, first of all, of the working-class accession, by means of the revolution, to the party, to administrative positions, and to power. Other groups emerging from the various nonproletarian strata, a large number of peasants, a quite considerable number of turncoats from other parties, but most of all a ground swell of people of popular origin, ill-educated, often illiterate, politically innocent if not indifferent, elements that knew nothing of Marx (who was discussed in the "circles") and would most often never know anything about him—this was the legitimate result of an authentic popular revolution in an underdeveloped country. The underclasses enjoyed their right to social advancement and took advantage of the most important channel in order to participate in power from the bottom, if not from the top.

The positions at the top of the party were still firmly held by the old guard, but for how long? During these years, the intellectual and cultural level of the party had fallen very low (the political reeducation and assimilation of such large and unschooled masses was not an easy task, in some ways even quite unmanageable), and one can understand the cry of alarm uttered by certain party leaders and veterans who felt threatened, if not inundated, by this tidal wave of new memberships. The influx was prompted, in fact, by the will to mobilize in order to assimilate, but there again, no one knew who was assimilating whom. Indeed, in conjunction with other factors already mentioned, the party found itself leaning toward transformations so profound that it was already possible during NEP to envisage the dissolution of bolshevism and, if not the complete destruction of Leninism, at least its reduction carried to the point that it would become a fiction: the apparatus would gain total control over the party— which was already quite "unpolitical" in any case—so as to transform the organization into an arm of its administrative structure.

Some people believe that the civil war was responsible for administering the fateful impetus. This thesis deserves consideration. After Wrangel's defeat, at the end of 1920, the triumphant regime had nothing to boast about. The country had been bled dry and remained literally prostrate; industrial activity and communications represented only a fraction of their prewar levels; a famine had broken out and was spreading throughout the country. The proletariat, as we have already seen, had been decimated; the threat of a *jacquerie* was widespread; it was a period of extreme economic and psychological exhaustion, among the population as well as within the organs of power, and the party felt isolated, cut off from the masses, socially "suspended in a void." It is significant, all the same, that this metaphor is not entirely apt. The party still had one important source of support at its disposal, and it was the least desirable, indeed the most embarrassing support, although under the circumstances it was effective. This consisted of the army, the police, and major sectors of the bureaucracy, which, even though hostile to the Bolsheviks, had no other masters to serve. There was no serious alternative on the horizon, and it was this combination of the lack of a credible alternative after the defeat of the "Whites" and the control by the party of the most coercive sectors of the state apparatus (destined by definition to an assured withering away well before other sectors of the state machine) which saved the regime. The spectacular effects achieved by the sudden turnabout of the NEP did the rest.

But it was at this highly dangerous moment, when the turnabout was being declared, right in the middle of an economic and social catastrophe, that the party seemed to go into a profound crisis. The party, too, threatened to succumb to the fragmentation of the social system, and its capacity to act and to govern were what seemed to be in question, in the face of the phenomenon of depletion and decomposition that threatened the country's existence. It was in the course of the 1920–21 general debate over the role of the unions within a state—a debate that turned out to be more symptomatic than significant—that the party seemed to break up into a multitude of groups and platforms—a state of affairs that Lenin, having become deeply disturbed by this spectacle, diagnosed as a "feverish condition." The medicine he prescribed in this situation, in which the major instrument of his strategy was about to lose its footing, was characteristic: the leader called a halt in authoritarian fashion, by prohibiting factions!* No one protested, so far as is known, for the diagnosis was widely agreed upon. However, Lenin's move was seen by many as no more than a stopgap measure. Now this occurred at a time when the vestiges of other political parties had also been suppressed. The factions, as we know, lasted a few years longer. But Lenin's decisions facilitated the task of the "monolithizing" wing of the party and of that administrative and disciplinary tendency that hoped to overcome the difficulties through a "realism" that others feared as the sign of the end of a dream. It stands to reason— as stated in the Introduction—that this wing was a creation of the civil war, carried by the numerous cadres that joined the party after 1917 to become its overwhelming majority and partaking of a political culture that emerged, unavoidably, during those years.

▪ LENINISMS IN QUESTION

The process described is one in which the party stops being the avantgarde organization and becomes a master, even as it bows to its own apparatus. The process is facilitated, curiously enough, by the rise of new more or less "nonideologized" strata, which appreciate social mobility (advancement) more than political programs. This rise took place against the background of a country that had seen its social structure regress by half a century, revert to a level far behind the threshold reached in 1914 and 1917. That extraordinary regression was the price of the revolution and the civil war, but it was not the ultimate price to be paid. It was thus incumbent upon the party, from the very beginning of the NEP, in the face of an emaciated social body, to undertake the work of resurrection of the economy and society—an enormous task over which the party alone could preside, for it held the principal power, the state and the organized bodies, and the life-giving resources, very rare and precious in a situation of widespread penury, that were represented by the monopoly of privileges to be redistributed.

How did the Leninism that reigned over this immense, desolated country react to the shattering of its hopes with regard to the international arena, the behavior of the social classes, or the catastrophe caused by the civil war? It was clear, as Lenin and many others recognized, that Russia no longer corresponded to most of the models of behavior devised before or just after the revolution. The country seemed, on the contrary, to be pushing the revolutionaries and the new regime in frightening directions. We know that at the beginning of NEP Lenin deplored the fact that the "machine" (he surely meant to say "regime") was not responding to the

---

* We do not mean that Lenin just ordered this; he didn't have the power. He arranged to have the decision adopted by the appropriate party channels who had the full freedom, at that time, if they wished, to vote against it.

helm and was headed in quite another direction. Reacting to each of the countless crises, trying to navigate and maneuver among the pressures and shoals that threatened the entire enterprise, his ideological production was ample, and even feverish. Already in April 1918, Lenin had forcefully tried to change course in an effort to dominate a chaotic situation, when he had worker control in the factories halted and replaced by "personal power"— Lenin's term was "dictatoriat"—on the part of the heads of industry. To achieve a higher output, Taylorism and even piecework were advocated. All this sent shudders through the party's left wing. It was new indeed. But the real innovation that torpedoed the "April Theses" of 1917 was the idea—the goal—put forward by Lenin of setting up a "system of state capitalism"—although under strict control by the proletarian government. It is interesting to note that the idea was very poorly received within the party and poorly understood, all the more so because it never went into effect: the capitalists rejected the very idea. But this shows how Lenin's thought was seeking a response to the problem of underdevelopment and what content can appropriately be attributed to the strategy of that transition period. Clearly, since capitalist development was lacking in Russia, and because that was the only force known up to that time to be capable of developing industry, one solution was to put capitalism to work so it would help socialist Russia acquire the missing link in the developmental chain.

Let us note that Lenin later tried to advance that idea again at the beginning of the NEP, then he abandoned it once again to look for something else. State capitalism was seeking an alliance with the forces of big capital, against what was considered the principal enemy—the anarchistic, dissolute, and rapacious petite bourgeoisie. But during the NEP a very different language is heard, an appeal for an alliance with the same rural petite bourgeoisie, against capitalism.

Another ideological innovation, this too an authentic revision, was connected with the way Moscow directed the Comintern. It very quickly began to seem normal that Moscow should become the center of the international revolutionary movement—instead of being a rather modest contributory force, a role that fitted a *muzhik* country, as it was seen before. But it went even further, rushing through stages with less and less compunction: the Soviet party, and in fact the Soviet regime, were soon to be offered as obligatory models to the industrialized countries, with no allowance for the slightest deviation. Of course, the success and the revolutionary boldness of the Russians seemed to justify such claims. In reality, we are witnessing here one of the major consequences—even though it was not immediately understood by its chief actors—of the isolation of the Russian revolution and of the reduction of its base to a single country (which, as we know, had already liquidated the worker councils and in which the Soviets, by official admission, had already lost any trace of independence).

Unwittingly, the most authentically internationalist ideology, by becoming "nationalized" within the limits of Russia alone, projected its own mode of existence as a standard of internationalism. For an informed observer, these agitations and slogans, by distorting the phenomena in question, as ideologies often do, were reflecting a new reality and a major constraint within which the new regime had to maneuver from then on.

The inevitable adaptation—not immediately perceived as such—to the new developments gave rise to dangerous illusions as well, which were magnified by many problems of the same order coming up again in connection with another major innovation which was quite different in nature but which also blended the inevitable with dangerous utopian behavior. What is involved here is the set of ideas and actions joined together in the expression "war communism." These, moreover, appear after the events, when this concept has already been rejected as erroneous. In this case, we find attached to a series of war and rationing measures—which are egalitarian as a result of the prevailing destitution—the global concept of 'instant communism," capable of being achieved by "cavalry charge" methods, on the strength of militarization, terrorism, suppressions, and prohibitions. The suppression of the markets and the nationalization of a dilapidated economy undertaken during these years also led to the suppression of commerce and budgets, banks and salaries; it led to payments-in-kind and to offers of free services to workers and state employees. It was imagined that a magic remedy had been found in this way, one which would make it possible to throw overboard all the "transition strategies" that up to that point had given the impression of being a *conditio sine qua non*.

Was this still Marxism? In any event Leninism, through certain of its attitudes and still more through impulses generated in it by the situation, encouraged voluntarist hopes of this kind.

We note that the bolshevist camp, from its earliest days in power, included a significant number of groups pushing for strategies of assault; others were inclined toward strategies of extreme prudence, labeled "menshevist" by the left wing. Along with some others, finally, Lenin maneuvered between the two poles. In situations of disequilibrium, he seemed to believe in freedom of maneuver almost as a system of action, and he saw salutary possibilities in abrupt reversals. That is why he could be seen to encourage opposing policies. Thus in particular (here is another innovation, and certainly an important theoretical revision of Marxism), in opposition to former left-wing Menshevik Sukhanov (the famous chronicler of the 1917 revolution) he envisaged the possibility that in a country without the necessary economic bases for socialism one could first seize power, given a revolutionary crisis presenting favorable circumstances, and later on construct the economic base it lacked. Although this idea is quite characteristically Leninist, it was set forth at the moment when an older and wiser Lenin was proposing a new and final series of innovations knowns as his "testament." Lenin was known to have consistently advocated keeping one's powder dry and not hesitating to use violence if the revolution were in danger—and he himself christened this method "revolutionary terror." But the testament does not mention either the "dictatorship of the proletariat" or "revolutionary terror" of any sort. Its message is very different: no violent measures as a way of transforming the social structures of the country! The cultural revolution first, an understanding with the peasants, and—an eminently necessary measure—slowness as the supreme virtue; in addition, an important discovery, a new vision on Lenin's part of socialism as a "regime of civilized cooperators."

These theses, and many others, are well known. We are also reminded of an idea expressed by Lenin in 1920, during the debate on the role of the unions, at the Ninth Congress of the party. Seeking a formula to soften the rigorous military statization that characterized "war communism," Lenin proposed a definition of the Soviet state that astonished his audience. We are not, he said, a proletarian state, but a worker and peasant state, with in addition a bureaucratic deviation. It seems that later on Bukharin succeeded in getting Lenin to make a concession: he agreed to withdraw the phrase "and peasant" from this definition of the character of the state. Lenin never elaborated upon that formula; the strictly theoretical phase of his activity was already almost over, and the strategies that ensued were proposed without adequate theoretical reflection. Lenin was being devoured by direct action under dramatic conditions. But the formula, a very interesting one, shows concern for taking into account the real social structures in which the dictatorship was operating in order to develop realistic transition strategies. The formula did not mention the experts—perhaps they fall within the bureaucratic component—but the peasantry is there as a component of the statist system, and the bureaucratic phenomenon, although included under the inadequate term "deviation," appears here for the first time in a basic formula.

It seems legitimate to include this reflection in the overall program expressed in the "testament." Lenin was now aware of the forces and pressures that were tugging at his movement and his system, pushing it "not at all where we wanted it to go."

In order to break free of these fateful pressures, in order to avoid the extremism of dangerous strategies, he seemed to be saying in substance that it was necessary to reduce ambitions rather than to raise the stakes, to adapt to the reality of the *muzhik* country, although without losing sight of the objectives cherished by the revolutionaries, in order to save them. Contrary to the tendency of one segment of the party to react by rushing ahead in spasms of voluntarism and violence, Lenin closed the book on Leninism(s) by suggesting that it was the desire to hurry things along that now seemed to him most dangerous.

It is well known that that set of ideas was disdainfully labeled "liberal-ism" by Stalin himself—at the very moment when Lenin was writing his final notes, whose content Stalin vaguely suspected.

▪ LENINISM EMBALMED AND THEN . . .

A country of reduced potential, which was beginning a painful climb back and up with the arrival of NEP, with a social system basically consisting of a sea of peasants holding small parcels of land (often tiny or minuscule parcels) in which an urban sector was swimming, this sector also dimin-ished by the civil war, sheltering a dilapidated industry; here in general terms is how the social landscape looked after the civil war. A statist system seeking to pass as socialist seemed to float above this rural mass and the production system from another century, unable to take root in it without getting swallowed up, unable to change it all without taking root. We have already mentioned the tendencies and factors that were more and more strongly felt as structural givens: the isolation and reduction of the system to Russia alone, thus its dependence upon Russian society, which weighed more and more heavily and entailed constant concessions. The bureaucratization of the system, its increasingly accentuated statization (that is, the almost exclusive recourse to the state and its agents to make the country function), the pressures that were brought to bear to reorient the system of privilege and social status, all these pushed the initial values of the revolutionary movement further and further into the back-ground. This, then, is what the social realities looked like. Furthermore, it was necessary to keep on creating ideologies in order to express these realities, to formulate new paths or camouflage embarrassing changes.

These sorts of pressures and imperatives were increased by the fact that the system, even during NEP, rejected the independent economic initia-tives of the population and vigilantly prohibited a plurality of political expressions. But this obstruction of private initiative accentuated the bureaucratization and the dependence of the system upon state action. The party itself, extremely busy building and supervising the state bureau-cratic machinery, was conscious of, but not sufficiently vigilant against, the dangers that this machinery held in store for the fate of the regime; it eventually found itself more and more "contaminated" by the object of its action and was subjected to the profound effects of its own "statiza-tion." We have already shown how the circumstances, outside and inside the country, favored the process of the party's submission to its own apparatus, which, moreover, had only begun to take shape in the middle of the civil war.

The circumstances we emphasize, taken alone, allow us to do no more than set forth the problems and sketch out some perspectives. They do not yet dictate categorically the ultimate results. During NEP we see ideas in combat and a political struggle over the party's strategies and objectives, with several notable ideological innovations and elaborations. But we know the outcome of these struggles and the new paths that the regime has followed since.

In our view, although the same term continues to be used, the metamorphoses of the regime after 1918 included an ideological change so profound that the term "Leninism" was to lose its meaning.

We find it useful, for the purpose of discussion, to posit the existence of a more or less coherent prerevolutionary Leninism, version "A." But the set of innovations, explicit or implicit, that came about after the takeover of power would constitute a separate version composed of new elements that make it a version "B," very different from the first. In the interest of brevity, we are leaving aside here the period of NEP—it is the best known of all the periods—which brought about the transition from Leninism to Stalinism, in order to posit two subsequent phases of ideological development, corresponding to the period of accelerated industrialization and forced collectivization. It is obviously necessary to add that this too was a further stage of reinforced bureaucratization, of statization carried to the extreme, and of unprecedented police violence, which ended up in the creation of a leviathan state and a system known as "Stalinist." Now with respect to the original Leninism, Stalinism not only changed strategy but also reoriented the system toward quite different objectives. It was no longer a matter of constructing a society in which the classes and the state would disappear, passing through a stage of "socialism," as that term had been understood by Marx, Engels, Lenin, and also many Western socialists. It was now a matter of "statizing," that is, of crowning the whole with an all-powerful, dictatorial state in order to preserve the class system and such privileges as had been put into place during the period of forced industrialization. It is thus possible to speak here of a break, not only with the prerevolutionary period of Leninism but also with the very different postrevolutionary version, which proposed an authoritarian political system, a dictatorship, but which nevertheless aspired to acquire a broad and varied social base, and which in the end rejected the path leading toward a superstatism deemed antisocialist—an attitude and program taken up later by Bukharin.

In conclusion we may perhaps add a note concerning the phases of Stalinism, which also correspond to phases of its ideological development. During the period 1928–34, broadly speaking, and paraphrasing the definition that Lenin gave in 1920, one can see a state made up of the bureaucracy and specialists, along with what was labeled a "working-class deviation." This was to give way, after 1935, to the period that saw the apogee of Stalinism. The party and the system were then subjected to a personal despotism, in an alliance with the police, seeking and receiving support from a conglomerate of heterogeneous and changing social forces, including a certain *lumpen* bureaucracy, population groups uprooted by the great whirlwind and glad to find even temporary security and a certain measure of advancement, as well as the psychological security afforded by the cult of a leader for those who accept him. In addition, functionaries of working-class and other origin, newly promoted to important positions, scarcely if at all politicized, lacking in ideological convictions, were called upon to replace cadres who were often Marxists and Leninists from the pre-revolutionary period and who had in the past belonged to a party that was still bolshevist. This problem of the social understructures of Stalinism demands more thorough investigation. What we can say about it here remains provisional. But what is more certain is that the Leninist formulas of the preceding phase could no longer suffice, nor could they even be adapted to the Stalinist change of course and to a practice that was producing a leviathan state punctuated by social wars, sometimes against workers and peasants, sometimes against the cadres faithful to Lenin, also in the end even against those cadres faithful to Stalinism, which had burned almost all the bridges that connected it with the old ideology. For that ideology, except to the extent that it had been rendered harmless by the process of transformation into a catechism, had become an embarrassment.

(Translated from the French by Catherine Porter)

9

SOCIETY, STATE, AND IDEOLOGY DURING THE FIRST FIVE-YEAR PLAN

The period 1929–33 is probably one of the most momentous quinquennia in the history of Russia, indeed, in modern history. The scholar is astounded by the incredible intensity and scope of the transformation of society, not to speak of the bewildering effect those years had on contemporaries. This was a unique process of state-guided social transformation, for the state did much more than just "guiding": it substituted itself for society, to become the sole initiator of action and controller of all important spheres of life. The process was thus transformed into one of "state building," with the whole social structure being, so to speak, sucked into the state mechanism, as if entirely assimilated by it.

The pace and violence of the changes were breathtaking. In a matter of a few years much of the previous social fabric, tsarist and Soviet, was dispersed and destroyed. With the destruction came the creation of new patterns, which, although they emerged very rapidly, became permanent. The sense of urgency in the whole upheaval is baffling: the pace imposed suggests a race against time, as if those responsible for the country's destinies felt they were running out of history. The appearance of a new social hierarchy in the 1930s was a similarly speedy and contradictory affair: the emerging ruling strata were kept in a state of perpetual tension and were several times knocked out and partly destroyed before they were allowed to settle down. Most of the makers of the upheaval were themselves transformed, engulfed, and annihilated in this prolonged Walpurgis Night, thus giving to those years the traits of a real "total drama": nobody was left unharmed, and all the survivors became thoroughly disfigured. This was not surprising. The new world being built was not the better and freer world of the dreamers but a Caliban state. That a progressive ideology, initially intended to enhance human freedom and to create higher forms of community, came to serve a police state is one of the peculiarities of the period and an important phenomenon to study.

■ BEFORE THE PLANS

THE TSARIST HERITAGE

The strictly dramatic point of view would suggest that our study should begin at some idyllic moment before the storm, perhaps 1926. But more prosaic scholarly interests will be better served by starting at about 1922, immediately after the great famine that was the culmination of years of war, revolution, and civil strife. This starting point serves to highlight the fact that the lull between the end of one catastrophe and the onset of a new one (quite different in character) lasted a mere seven years: Russia's body social, shattered in our century by a series of cataclysmic events, has shown an amazing capacity to recover.

The period 1914–21 was unquestionably a demographic earthquake. At the end of it, Russia's population was about 30 million less than would normally have been expected: the shortfall included about 16 million dead in war and civil war, famine, and epidemics, with the remainder accounted for by the calamities that befell potential parents.[1] These figures are relevant to an understanding of the stresses of the 1930s, for the 30 million missing out of the 1923 population contributed to the later serious gaps in the labor force and military manpower.

Before war and revolution, tsarist Russia had seen a significant advance in industrialization and urbanization, with its cities growing faster than the total population. But the whole urban sector comprised no more than about 18 percent of the population, and the modern industrial sector was even smaller than that: less than 1 in 5 of the population lived in towns (most of which were quite small provincial backwaters), and only 2 in 100 were employed in manufacturing and mechanical industries, compared to 11.6 in 100 in the United States.[2] Thus most of the cities were dominated by rather small producers. The educated professional and intellectual segment was also small, and it included more bureaucrats and officers than managers, teachers, scientists, and artists.

Rural Russia was bedeviled by poverty, land hunger, and irritating remnants of the old regime of serfdom and was in the throes of the social unrest created by the Stolypin reforms. These reforms led to the development of a consolidated smallholder class among the peasantry and to the shattering of the communal system, but the hardship they caused the peasants had painful effects.

Official and educated Russia was notoriously detached and isolated from illiterate and semiliterate rural Russia, although the peasants came to the towns in millions in search of seasonal or full-time employment and formed the bulk of the armed forces. This was a symptom of Russia's "underdevelopment," and one of the most profound.

The top layers of the Russian social and political structure, some 4 percent of the population, presented an intriguing and complicated pattern. They included the top bureaucracy, considered by some (including Lenin) to be the real rulers of Russia—organized, socially cohesive, and highly instrumental in ensuring the stability of the state. But there was a fundamental weakness: decisions on who was to head the bureaucracy and the government were made by a quite antiquated institution, the imperial court. The court, a product of centuries of absolutism, was incapable of making the most of the talent, growing experience, and skills accumulating among the abler elements of the bureaucracy. An important social prop of the system, the nobility, was a decaying class, heavily dependent on the favors of the tsar and his officials (themselves part of the top stratum of the nobility), deeply in debt, and constantly losing its lands and its economic and political power.

The entrepreneurial classes, developing before and during the war in the wake of an impressive industrial expansion, came to play an important role, especially during the war, but were still inhibited by their low culture, dependence on state tutelage, and political immaturity.

THE CIVIL WAR

Revolution and civil war brought economic life almost to a standstill and destroyed the old social structure. The landowners, bourgeoisie, top officials, and, on the whole, army officers ceased to exist as classes or groups. Death and emigration also carried away much of the middle class—the administrative, managerial, and intellectual talent that Russia had begun to develop and use before the war. The whole modern sector of urbanized and industrialized Russia suffered a severe setback, as becomes obvious from the population figures. The entire population of the country fell from its 1917 level by many millions, but the cities—still only a modest sector in Russia—were particularly badly hit. By 1920, the number of city dwellers had fallen from 19 percent of the population in 1917 to 15 percent. Moscow lost half its population, Petrograd two-thirds.[3]

The social structure of the cities also changed. Moscow and Petrograd population figures for 1920[4] show that the middle classes and small producers—members of the free professions, merchants, artisans, and craftsmen—were depleted, while déclassé elements, such as servants of masters who had fled or been killed, stood almost untouched, and with them the quite indestructible criminal and demimonde that could not but thrive on the prevailing conditions of dislocation. Two groups now stood out as strongest in these towns: the working class and the category described as state employees (*sluzhashchie*). In the latter, probably, was a mass of lower tsarist officials who had flocked into the new Soviet offices, as well as many new recruits from the former privileged classes who, being literate, could get office jobs and some kind of haven. A survey prepared for Lenin[5] claimed that in 1920 a typical Soviet institution would shelter, for every 1,500 officials, some 900 from the former "working intelligentsia," 250 former workers, and about 300 former landowners, priests, officers, top managers or "bourgeois specialists," and high tsarist officials. All these people got into a lot of trouble in later years; the label *byvshie lyudi* (has-beens) turned out to be ineradicable for quite a time to come.

The working class, especially the hard core that the Soviet system considered its mainstay, dwindled by more than half. Some 600,000 served in the Red Army, 180,000 were killed, many went into the state and party *apparat*, and others—some 75,000—into food squads. Many more returned to their native villages in order to survive, or became déclassé in various ways.[6] Those who remained in the factories were diluted by an influx of "foregn elements" from other social strata conscripted for labor. This admixture contributed to the general industrial demoralization and unrest, *volynki* (disturbances) and strikes which, as Soviet writers stated, raised "purely peasant" demands for an end to the forced requisition of grain and cattle and the confiscation of "peasants' domestic objects."[7] It was alleged that this was a result of the "corrupting influence of petit bourgeois anarchy [*stikhiya*]" on the working class.

As industry came to a standstill, some 3 million people were fired in an enormous purge of offices and factories. The state could not employ them and could offer them no rations. They included 260,000 industrial workers, 27.7 percent of the Supreme Council of the National Economy of the USSR work force.[8]

The peasantry was the class that survived the upheaval best. It absorbed many of the fleeing city dwellers, quite a number of whom—characteristically for Russia—had not yet severed their connections with their native villages. It is important to note the so-called leveling out (*poravnenie*) of the peasantry. Many of the richer peasants disappeared, or lost part of their farms and economic strength, and many poor peasants received land and, at least for the statistician, moved into the category of the "middle" peasant.

The civil war left the cities shattered. Russia became much more rural and smallholding than it had been before the storm—a considerable setback in terms of social and economic development. Significantly, Russia's historical "heartland"—the most developed and populated central regions—was also badly battered. As Lenin's stronghold, the "heartland" survived the onslaught of the peripheries, but it was bled white and in great need of a respite to recover from the bleeding.

THE NEW ECONOMIC POLICY

The respite was provided by the New Economic Policy (NEP), which allowed a limited restoration of private enterprise and reestablished market relations between town and country. This helped restore economic activity to prerevolutionary levels and bring the population figures up to and above those of old Russia. It was the tide of robust peasant fertility that made it possible for the country to recover from the war wounds. The cities also grew, regaining or surpassing the prerevolutionary population level by 1926. Working-class numbers were back at, though not above, prewar level by the end of NEP.

Restoration of the country's industrial-administrative stronghold earned the new political system a breathing spell, but without producing any important structural changes that might have overcome Russia's backwardness. If anything, this structure was less developed than the tsarist one. Eighty-two percent of the population still lived in rural areas, and 77 percent earned a livelihood directly from agriculture; 86.7 percent of the employed population lived on agriculture. This was, in crude terms, the level of development of India or Turkey, although Russia was better equipped in terms of administrative and industrial experience. The social structure that emerged in the NEP period was characterized, first of all, by nationalization of the key sectors of the economy, hence a larger role for the state. A parallel novelty, in the political sphere, was the party and its leadership. This new factor had important social implications, too, as the role, status, and well-being of individuals and groups would increasingly be determined by their place in the state apparatus and the party, not by wealth or birth. This utterly new and momentous fact was not yet fully perceived because of the continued existence of private sectors and people with money.

The party, the new linchpin of the system, was in the process of transformation. The old revolutionary organization of political intellectuals and politically active workers (there were no peasants in the Bolshevik party before the revolution, and not many just after) was steadily being eliminated, and a "secretarial machinery," reflecting the impact of civil war and NEP recruits on the social composition of the party, was coming into the ascendant. The lower and middle ranks of the party, and to some extent the upper ranks, began to draw in semieducated recruits from the milieus of industrial workers and junior government employees, and this important new pool of officials could not fail to make an imprint on the outlook of the party and to penetrate the higher echelons. For some time to come, the very top party posts would still be held by the former professional revolutionaries, but it was precisely this category that was continually weakened by dissent and pushed out. A crucial role in the state machinery was played by professional experts, the so-called bourgeois intellectuals, who had acquired their skills before the revolution. Only the few who joined the party before or during the revolution had the privilege of having the "bourgeois" stigma removed. Their weight was a tribute to the strength of the pool of professional talent that tsarist Russia already possessed but had not managed to put to full use. Their important role in restoring industry, organizing the state administration, and teaching Russia's youth was parallel to the role peasants played in restoring the country's livelihood and human stock. They would soon, however, have to play the very different role of scapegoat.

The urban population of NEP Russia was made up of a growing working class (estimated at 4.5 million in 1926/27), an army of unemployed, reaching well over the million mark, and the increasingly large and influential group of government employees (reaching 3.5 million at the same period), partly composed of former tsarist officials and refugees from the former privileged classes. Some 700,000 artisans and 500,000 small merchants, mainly self-employed, formed a fairly small supply-and-services private sector. To complete the picture, there was a maze of smaller, picturesque underworld elements; an amazingly large number of "servants" (339,000), middlemen, and speculators (the heroes of Zoshchenko and Ilf and Petrov*); and a very small but immensely creative artistic intelligentsia. As for the Nepmen or "bourgeoisie"—entrepreneurs and merchants employing hired labor—they constituted only 75,600 people (284,000 together with their families), according to one source.[9] Such figures could be inflated by including the small merchants under the heading of "bourgeoisie,"[10] giving the still unimpressive total of 855,000 people (2,705,000 with families). This shows how small the private sector was, even after the quite inadmissible inclusion, common in the official statistics, of peddlers and people renting out a room in an apartment in the category of "entrepreneurs."

An assessment of the taxable earnings of all groups and classes of NEP society made by a special committee of Sovnarkom[11] showed that the category called "small, semicapitalist entrapreneurs" earned per capita only slightly more than Soviet officials, and even this figure was pushed up by the numerically smaller but richer group of merchants belonging to the "big bourgeoisie." Artisans employing hired labor similarly earned per capita slightly more than workers or officials. But it was only the few big entrepreneurs and merchants who earned considerable sums although

---

* Mikhail Zoshchenko (1895–1958) was the author of many humorous stories of life under the NEP. Il'ya Ilf and Evgenii Petrov were joint authors of the satirical novels *The Twelve Chairs* (1928) and *The Little Golden Calf* (1931).

these were certainly less impressive after tax. The scope of private entrepreneurial activity under NEP can further be seen from figures on the labor force employed by the bourgeoisie. The bulk of private employment was concentrated in the small, basically craft industries, which had 230,400 workers, while the big capitalist entrepreneurs employed only 67,200 people.[12] One would not quarrel with the Soviet statistician who stated that the NEP bourgeoisie was "cachectic" (khudosochnaya).[13]

Under NEP, the peasantry was to a great extent left to its own devices, coming into contact with cities through the usual ways of the marketplace and part-time work, and with the state at the time of tax assessment and payment. Grain procurement was another area of contact fraught with potential conflict, but in the heyday of NEP this was still a commercial operation. The peasantry was relatively peaceful and not particularly anti-Soviet. Nevertheless, the Russian peasants, true to their traditions, distrusted the state and its officials—particularly the tax collector, who was for them the symbol of the state. For the peasant, what was "state" (kazennyi) came to be seen as the product of a foreign, soulless, and oppressive force.[14]

The phenomenon of otkhod—seasonal departure of peasants in search of work—reappeared with NEP after a prolonged absence during the civil war and grew to a stream of several million otkhodniki per year. This put pressure on the towns and increased their unemployment rate, but helped the peasant family make ends meet and allowed the cities to get the indispensable labor force for many difficult jobs. The otkhodnik, a product of rural overpopulation, occupied an intermediate rung between the farmer and the urban worker or artisan; and in this category, probably, were many of the most literate and competent elements of the peasantry.

The social "leveling" that the revolution caused in the countryside was not significantly disturbed during the NEP years. The most cautious assessments[15] show 2,300,000 farmhands, but of these only 44 percent—about 1 million people—worked in the private farms, the rest working for the state or for peasant communities. At the other pole of rural society were the "rural entrepreneurs" (kulaks), holding 750,000–760,000 homesteads, or about 3.4 percent of all farms. By definition, they were supposed to have prospered through systematic exploitation of hired labor.* However, the "systematic exploitation" was hardly impressive, considering that 750,000 rural entrepreneurs were employing only about a million laborers. The most prosperous peasants, according to a large 1927 survey had two to three cows and up to ten hectares of sowing area, for an average family of seven people.[16] Sovnarkom's taxation committee computed that such an entrepreneur made 239.8 rubles a year for each member of his family, compared to a rural official's 297 rubles. Although the kulak still made twice as much as the middle peasant,[17] Soviet rural "capitalism" barely existed. The state

* See Chapter 5, "Who Was the Soviet Kulak?"

could curb the richer peasants at will; indeed, it did so in 1928/29, when, under pressure of taxation and forced procurements, this stratum shrank very substantially,[18] and rural "capitalism" began to melt like wax. In defiance of the official class analysis of the peasantry, the attempt at the end of NEP to identify and squeeze out kulaks immediately had adverse effects on the peasantry and agriculture in general; many "middle" peasants were badly affected, and their economic activity began to dwindle.[19]

THE CULTURAL LAG

NEP and its class structure, although quite aptly characterized as a "mixed economy," was not a mixture of "socialism" and "capitalism." Basically the society and the economy were dominated by the rural sector and small-scale producers and merchants, with a small, highly concentrated, and influential large-scale industrial sector and a state administration employing quite a cohort of officials and putting to good use a smaller administrative and professional stratum.[20] This society was spared such familiar phenomena of underdevelopment as absentee landowning and moneylending classes with a plethora of servants and luxurious, conspicuous spending. But it had its own stigmata of backwardness—a greedy, uneducated, and inefficient officialdom and a maze of offices in which a simple citizen, especially a peasant, felt entirely lost and quite unceremoniously mistreated. "Bureaucratism" was officially attributed to "survivals of the past" and was combatted under this heading. Linked to the bureaucratic source of corruption were the "seats of purulence" (*gnoiniki*) resulting from unholy alliances of officials (especially in the supply networks) with private merchants in big illegal operations with government goods. The press was full of such stories of large-scale corruption, and now and again the whole leadership of a district or even a republic would be purged for having tolerated or participated in such affairs. NEP thus had its share of venality, crooked business deals, and ways to spend the profits, including nightclubs, *cafés chantants*, gambling dens, and houses of prostitution.

In the background lay discrepancies very menacing to the system's future. There was the disparity between the party's ideology and aspirations and the frustrating reality of a petit bourgeois country, aptly described by a recent historian as "large-scale theories versus small-scale realities."[21] As the government, not unnaturally, strove to revive and develop the economy, it allowed the cultural front—mass education and the fight against illiteracy—to trail dangerously: the economic recovery had not yet become a cultural one as well. Although the industrial specialist was relatively well off and the white collar employee in big industry earned almost twice as much as the worker in the period 1926–29, teachers—lowest on the pay scale, especially in elementary schools—were the most neglected part of the "intelligentsia" in income and status[22] and earned no more than 45 percent of their prerevolutionary salaries.[23] Investments in "culture" were lagging heavily behind investments in the economy, and Lunacharsky complained to the Fifteenth Party Congress that he had at his disposal less money for schools than the tsarist educational system had. Some of the top leadership were painfully aware of the problem. Rykov stated at the same congress that without sufficient cultural advance further economic progress would become blocked.[24]

With the proportion of elementary school pupils per thousand inhabitants even lower than that in many poorly developed countries—and with lower per capita expenses on culture and lower average duration of schooling in the countryside and in towns[25]—the current expression "Asiatic lack of culture" (*aziatskaya beskul'turnost'*) had its justification. "Vodka is squeezing out culture!" a party writer exclaimed dramatically,[26] although he still did not admit that it was too early to talk of a "new culture," let alone a proletarian one. It was one of the peculiarities of party life that obvious facts about society became distorted in the mirror of party struggles and ideological juggling. Trotsky had to be attacked for having stated the truth that as long as the "clutches of dictatorship existed" no new culture would emerge.[27]

The "clutches of dictatorship" would soon be used to spread popular education, but the higher levels of culture, as well as the bearers of that culture, were to go through serious troubles. The party had made a concerted effort, partly successful, to get more workers and peasants into higher education. In 1926, however, limitations on university entry for white collar and other nonproletarian social groups were eased, and the university became relatively accessible even to sons of "alien classes," especially those of the "bourgeois intelligentsia."[28] But the NEP world, dominated as it was by the mass peasant background, the rapacious, moneymaking Nepman, the sternly ideological party militant, and the conniving, corrupt state official, did not make for any buoyancy in intelligentsia and student circles. Vodka was widely used among the moody Russian educated people; and among student youth in particular there were "manifestations of despair culminating in suicide" at and after the time when the poet Esenin took his life, and "mischievous behavior culminating in crime," as Lunacharsky put it.[29]

In contrast to the oversensitive intellectual Oblomovs* and talented but gloomy Esenins was the current urban type of the ordinary "Soviet lad"—poorly educated, but dodgy and shrewd, semicynical, and semiparasitic. His collective portrait was sketched by Bukharin as follows: a good drinker and a good fighter who can raise hell and swear like a trooper; a lad who won't work too hard and knows how to look after himself.[30] These "smart fellows" were products of a semideveloped society, on the

---

* Oblomov is the hero of a nineteenth-century novel of that title by Ivan Goncharov. He personifies the "superfluous man" who sinks into idleness and lethargy on his provincial estate.

border of a static and uninspiring rural world and a corrupting urban (usually small-town) world of petty affairs. They were to flock into the clean and unexacting jobs of lower (and often higher) officialdom, into the supply networks, into the criminal world and—why not?—into jobs as police investigators.

In sum, the cultural deprivation of the NEP population—with its working class crammed into a diminishing living space, its massive illiteracy, its tricksters and Oblomovs, its brilliant top layers and crude and ambitious rulers—gave substance and lent credibility to the fears for the fate of the revolution and the future of the state. The danger of degeneration (*pererozhdenie*) of the party and its leadership—a cry raised by the party oppositions—was taken up by Bukharin, although somewhat ambiguously since he himself was still one of the leading official spokesmen: if there was no cultural rise of the masses, no constant influx of workers to universities, degeneration was to be feared, as this would certainly push the leading cadres "to close in upon themselves, to harden into a separate layer, with a tendency to form a new ruling class."[31]

Bukharim's suggestions for avoiding such an outcome were clearly insufficient. Speedy and half-baked mass education may tend to make people more vulnerable to propaganda and indoctrination[32] and enhance the grip of the leadership and the controllers, rather than make the leaders more open to the pressure of the masses. This was, in fact, what happened after the shattering of NEP society and its furious reshaping during the subsequent "revolution from above," when mass schooling and crash courses did not prevent the hardening and self-seclusion of the ruling groups, or an uuprecedented degree of alienation of state from society.

▪ THE BIG DRIVE

RURALIZATION OF THE CITIES

The all-out drive for industrialization from 1928 opened a period in which so many things happened simultaneously that one could aptly describe it as the birth pangs of a world. There was, to begin with, a huge population movement, with millions milling around the country, building and rebuilding, flocking to towns, searching for a way out of material and other miseries, and with many ending up in the growing concentration camps. At the same time, a massive cadre formation process was launched, bringing in its wake a hectic restructuring of society—a growing industrial working class, sprawling bureaucracies and offices, managements, a scientific establishment, a new hierarchy of status, privilege, and power, and an ominously growing security and coercion establishment that tried to match the energy of the builders by furiously ferreting out and destroying numerous social categories of the past as well as many of the newly formed groups. In the countryside, it was an upheaval as elemental as a hurricane—the old rural structures and ways of life were shattered to their very roots, with uncountable consequences for society and state alike.

The whole explosion was, once more, damaging for population growth. Population growth did not stop, to be sure, but was certainly slowed down, especially in the countryside, by the collectivization terror and the famine in the southern parts of the country in 1932/33. The rural birthrate fell from 49.1 in 1913 (31.7 in cities) to 42–43 in 1923/24, and, finally, to 32.2 in 1935 (24.6 in cities). Material hardship and the turmoil of collectivization were among the main reasons for the trend,[33] and according to a number of sources, Gosplan expected by 1937 a much greater population than was actually found in the 1937 census.[34] Without entering into the complex problem of how high a price in human lives was paid for Soviet development policies, there is no doubt that it was heavy, compounding the losses that occurred between 1914 and 1922.

Industrialization was launched on such a scale that the sudden demand for labor flooded the planners and government offices and for a long time threw the whole machinery out of gear. The peasantry had to provide, at short notice, millions of people for the construction sites and the new cities. This in itself was no problem for the notoriously overpopulated countryside. Peasants were used to the quite unorganized but fairly steady *otkhod*, the seasonal departure for work along well-trodden historical routes. But at first the newly created and shaky kolkhozy (collective farms) tried to retain the labor force, fearing the prospect of remaining without the labor indispensable for the still unfamiliar tasks of a collective organization. However, governmental measures and the urge of the peasants to leave the kolkhozy soon broke down all impediments.[35] During the years 1926–39 the cities grew by some 30 million people at least, and their share in population grew from about 18 percent to 33 percent (reminding us that by 1939, 67 percent of the population was still rural). During the first five-year plan alone the cities grew by 44 percent, almost as much as during the whole period 1897–1926, and the salaried labor force (workers and officials) more than doubled, growing from 10.8 to 22.6 million.[36] There is no doubt that the bulk of this growth was made up by peasants. If during the years 1928 and 1929 about 1 million new migrants came to live in the cities, during the next three years 3 million came each year. The Moscow and Leningrad regions alone each received 3.5 million new inhabitants during the first five-year plan. In 1931 a staggering figure of 4.1 million peasants joined the city population; and for the years 1929–35 the total was 17.7 million.[37] This does not yet give the whole measure of the mass movements and changes, since in addition to those peasants who came to stay in industry, cities, and construction sites, millions of seasonal *otkhodniki* went, with or without contracts, to build roads, canals, and factories. In the remarkable year of 1931 alone, about 7 million *otkhodniki* moved around the country.[38]

In the cities, the inordinate and unanticipated growth transformed a strained housing situation into an appalling one, creating the specifically Soviet (or Stalinist) reality of chronically overcrowded lodgings, with consequent attrition of human relations, strained family life, destruction of privacy and personal life, and various forms of psychological strain. All this provided a propitious hunting ground for the ruthless, the primitive, the blackmailer, the hooligan, and the informer. The courts dealt with an incredible mass of cases testifying to the human destruction caused by this congestion of dwellings. The falling standards of living, the lines outside stores, and the proliferation of speculators suggest the depth of the tensions and hardship. Soon the cumulative results of such conditions were to cause widespread manifestations of neurosis and anomie, culminating in an alarming fall in the birthrate. By 1936, in fact, the big cities experienced a net loss of population, and a high infant mortality rate, which explains in part the alarm in government circles and the famous laws against abortion proclaimed in that year.

Once the initial urgent need for labor was satisfied and the authorities realized the damaging effects of the chaotic influx into cities, passports and the *propiska* system of obligatory registration with the local police were introduced (by law at the end of 1932 and in practice during 1933). These were methods of controlling the movement of the rural population, especially during the hungry winter of 1932/33, when starving peasants trying to save their lives crawled into the cities without permission. A peasant received a passport only if the authorities were satisfied that he was needed in some employment and the kolkhoz was ready to let him go.

It was during those years of mass mobilization that the government and managers acquired the characteristically Soviet habit of shuffling the labor force around like cattle. With their eyes fixed only on their targets, they tended to neglect elementary human needs of workers. This attitude, which was not born in the camps but predated them, served as a background to the growing camp system of the GPU and the "reeducation through labor" of its inhabitants.

A single term to characterize the process would be "ruralization" (*okrest'yanivanie*) of the cities. One of the results of this ruralization was the breakdown of labor discipline, which saddled the state with an enormous problem of educating and disciplining the mass of the crude labor force. The battle against absenteeism, shirking, drinking in factories during working hours, and breaking tools was long, and the Soviet government played no "humanistic" games in this fight. Very soon, methods such as denial of ration cards, eviction from lodgings, and even penal sentences for undisciplined workers were decreed. The same harshness was recommended in the fight against deterioration in the quality of industrial products (*brak*); here the fight was directed not only against workers but also against managers and technicians, and special laws gave the prosecutors the means to prosecute transgressors.

TEKUCHKA

As traditionally happened in times of stress and catastrophe, peasant Russia was turning into *Rus' brodyazhnaya*, a country of vagrants. Massive and rapid labor turnover (*tekuchka*) was characteristic of the early 1930s. The factory labor force, hard pressed by working and living conditions, moved around to find something better, encouraged by real or fictitious differences in pay or food. The workers were often (illegally) lured by promises from the managements of construction sites and enterprises, who were forever anxious to have labor reserves needed to meet crises of plan fulfillment.

It was all too easy to explain this phenomenon by insisting on the petit bourgeois character of the new working classes, with their concomitant anarchism, self-seeking, lack of discipline, attachment to property, and slovenliness, to use the morally charged vocabulary of Soviet sources. That it was the same petit bourgeois mass of parasites which actually built the country is one of the paradoxes of this type of class analysis. Factories and mines in these years were transformed into "railway stations"— or, as Ordzhonikidze exclaimed in despair, into one huge "nomadic gypsy camp."[39] The cost of the turnover was incredible. Before they had managed to learn their job, people had already given their notice or done something in order to get fired.

But more: the same process, and on a large scale, was going on among managers and administrators, specialists and officials. At all levels of the local administration and party *apparat*, people adopted the habit of leaving in good time, before they were penalized, recalled, brought in for questioning, downgraded, fired, or arrested.[40]

Thus workers, administrators, specialists, officials, party apparatus men and, in great masses, peasants were all moving around and changing jobs, creating unwanted surpluses in some places and dearths in others, losing skills or failing to acquire them, creating streams and floods in which families were destroyed, children lost, and morality dissolved. Social, administrative, industrial, and political structures were all in flux. The mighty dictatorial government found itself, as a result of its impetuous activity during those early years of accelerated industrialization, presiding over a "quicksand" society.

It is not difficult to imagine the despair of the rulers and their fierce resolution to put an end to this situation and introduce law and order into the chaos. The stern traits of the disciplining effort soon became viciously contorted. That the drive pressed hard on the judiciary—itself "leaking" like everything else—was a foregone conclusion. The secret police (GPU) was allowed to swell its empire to enormous proportions. Constant purges (*chistki*)*—a paradoxical method, not unfamiliar in medicine, of dealing with an illness—were undertaken and contributed considerably to the flux. After the early period of "proletarianization," two additional strategies were used to stabilize the body social: first, creation and consolidation of a network of supervisors in the form of hierarchies, apparatuses, and elites; and then, from about 1934, the adoption of policies that the sociologist Timasheff[41] described as "The Great Retreat"—a set of classical measures of social conservatism, law and order strategies complete with a nationalist revival, and efforts to instill values of discipline, patriotism, conformism, authority, and orderly careerism. That such a policy should be accompanied by another shattering set of purges (this time, bloody ones), in the later 1930s, is one more enigma, amazing even for one who is already well versed in the vagaries of Soviet history and policies in those years.

During the first five-year plan frenzy (1928–32), all social groups and classes were in a state of flux and shock, partially or totally "destructured" and unhinged. One can say that for a short span of time, some years ahead of the happy announcement on the coming of a socialist society, Russian society was indeed "classless": all its classes were out of shape, leaving a free field for the state and its institutions, themselves very considerably shaken, to act and grow.

▪ CLASS WARFARE

THE "ALIENS"

Industrialization, collectivization, and the formation of cadres were not the only factors in the shaping of the new social structure. Social policies of a quite complex and often contradictory pattern were factors, too. One can tentatively speak of an initial period of "proletarianization," which could also be called the "production" (*produktsionnyi*) period, when workers were given preference and drafted through special mobilizations into universities, schools, and administrations. Parallel to this process went *spetseedstvo* (specialist baiting), ovewhelming emphasis on social origin, and the transformation of academies and universities into "production brigades." The frenzied "proletarianization" often emptied the factories of their most experienced and reliable workers and pushed many of them into a hostile environment of officialdom or, on the basis of social origin or party loyalty alone, into the stressful situation of being enrolled in institutions of higher learning without appropriate academic preparation.

---

* Here, purges of party membership or state employees meant expulsion from the party or job—essentially not a criminal offense. Not to be confused with the arrests and shootings that happened in the later 1930s, which were also called "purges" in the Western literature.

From 1931, this line began to change. Recruitment of workers to offices was formally forbidden at the end of 1930, and somewhat later university enrollment returned to a basis of some ability and academic preparation. A temporary halt to the cruder forms of *spetseedstvo* also occurred at this time. With the fight for labor discipline in factories, kolkhozy, and offices, a new strategy was adopted for instilling stability and productivity, which entailed creating a new and strong layer of bosses. This kind of "elitist" policy would continue, not without some baffling reversals throughout the 1930s.

That mass terror was permeating all these phases is a well-known fact. The first target of the security "organs" were those who had belonged to the former privileged classes before the revolution ("class enemies"). Later the terror would be turned against the growing elite itself: most of the top layers in party and state administrations were to be totally renovated by an influx of new recruits from the universities or the lower ranks of the bureaucracy.

One important factor that ought to be strongly emphasized is that for millions there was upward mobility and social promotion in the midst of the whole upheaval. This statement needs to be qualified. Peasants going to factories could not see it then as promotion—for many, the factories meant a drop in their standard of living and self-respect. But it may have been different for the great number who became officials, however low the rank and however bad the pay. For those who went to universities and to responsible jobs, or acquired new skills, the social advance was undeniable, and the new possibilities were seized on eagerly.

Urban social groups and classes, freshly formed to a great extent, were obviously not yet stabilized in their new jobs and settings, and it would take some time for the new patterns to solidify. Flux remained part of the social landscape for most of the Stalinist period. No wonder that the state, which turned into a Leviathan and kept extending its domination, met no countervailing forces or checks. The state presided imperiously over the social changes and ruled society—but this does not mean that the influencing and shaping was a one-way affair. Although the mighty state machinery was in no direct way accountable to the masses, the social milieu, however passive and defenseless, might exert an influence not unlike that which the conquered sometimes have on their conquerors. But this is a problem that must be left open for further discussion.

Of all social groups, the most defenseless were those destined for "liquidation as a class." This could mean anything from simply being squeezed out of one's business and allowed to hide in some office or factory to imprisonment in camps or shooting. The biggest such group, with more than a million homesteads, was that of the kulaks. "Dekulakization," which consisted of exiling the kulak families to uninhabited territories (plus some straight prison sentences and shootings), was equivalent in its scale to the uprooting of a small nation. It was an economic disaster, with incalculable long-term effects and insignificant, even ridiculous, immediate gains: officially, 170 million rubles' worth of property (or up to 400 million, according to a reassessment)[42] were confiscated, that is, between 170 and 400 rubles per household. What meager assistance the kolkhozy gained from the destruction of "rural capitalism"! It is probable that even the uncharitable but unavoidable expenditure on resettlement of these people, after shattering them and thinning out their numbers, cost more.

But kulaks were not the only victims of the "anticapitalist revolution." All members of the relatively modest sectors of private activity and initiative under NEP now fell into one of the imprecise categories of "nonlaboring," "alien," or "déclassé element," or were *lishentsy*—deprived of civil rights. In the Russian Republic alone, 1,706,025 people, or some 3.9 percent of all potential voters, were *lishentsy*, and in 1932, 3.5 percent were still on the black list.[43] But these figures probably do not express the full numbers of those who got into trouble by virtue of belonging to one category or another of "has-beens" listed in the edict that instructed authorities on who should be deprived of the right to vote.[44] The methods of dealing with these groups were not restricted to the quite platonic deprivation of the right to vote. Such deprivation was often followed by denial of lodging, food ration, and medical services,[45] and especially by exile. One of the better-known aspects of the antibourgeois campaign was the mass arrest of people supposed to have possessed valuables like gold and silver. Another was a huge purge of "undesirable persons" from the cities in 1932, just before the introduction of passports.[46]

The "squeezing out of the private businessman" (*vytesnenie chastnika*) consisted of the eviction of about a half a million ex-merchants (1.5 million with families), most of whom were small-fry working without any employees. Their shops in the countryside, where most of them operated, were assessed in 1927 as having a capital value of 711 rubles per shop.[47] The effects of this eviction, as well as similar action against artisans and craftsmen, were momentous. As merchants closed their shops and went to factories, offices, and camps, there arose a deplorable situation of "commercial deserts," a development the state and cooperative sectors were not equipped to cope with. Even the meager goods available could not be distributed. New shops and commercial organizations were quickly founded to cope with the emergency, but their quality remained lamentable and their numbers insufficient for more than a generation. As the lines outside the stores grew, so did the plague of speculation, black markets, and rackets. The fight against speculation—now counting among its victims many people with impeccable class origins—brought a mass of new criminal offenses into the overcrowded and overworked courts: personal and mass embezzlements, theft in supply networks, fictitious accounting, illicit dealings in ration cards, and so on.[48] A fiercely repressive law of

August 7, 1932, against theft in kolkhozy was later broadened to embrace all other sectors and became the state's main weapon for protecting its property. Mass thefts were in fact taking place as the economic situation, especially food supplies, deteriorated. The GPU could help neither in supplying food nor in rooting out theft. The nation, disrespectful toward state property, seemed to have been transformed into a nation of thieves.

THE WORKING CLASS

For the development of the working class, some figures can provide a telling picture (Table 9.1). Growth was phenomenal in the first five-year plan period and still considerable in the second, but slowed almost to a standstill as far as industrial and construction workers were concerned in the years 1937–40 (when the increase was mainly in the "employees" sector). This growth, as already stated, was based to a large extent on a mass influx of peasants. But even in the preplan period the peasant influence in the working class had been strong, especially in the Ukrainian mining regions. A survey of industrial labor carried out in 1929 showed that 42.6 percent of the workers were of peasant origin, and 20.6 percent had land in the countryside.[49]

Not unexpectedly, the professional level and educational standards of the crude labor force were extremely low. As late as 1939, when things had largely settled down, only 8.2 percent of the workers had an education of seven grades or more.[50] The working class had also become much younger. It included not only a mass of inexperienced and often bewildered peasants but also many women new to industrial jobs: by 1936 women constituted 40 percent of the work force.

For the managers, for the state, and especially for the workers them-

TABLE 9.1

GROWTH OF THE WORKING CLASS, 1928–40
(in thousands)

	1928	1932	1937	1940
Total employment (workers and employees)	10,800	20,600	26,700	31,200
Workers only (total)	6,800	14,500	17,200	20,000
Workers in industry	3,124	6,007	7,924	8,290
Workers in construction	630	2,479	1,875	1,929
Workers in sovkhozy and other state farms	301	1,970	1,539	1,558

Sources: A. B. Mitrofanova, in D. L. Baevskii, ed., *Izmeneniya v chislennosti i sostave sovetskogo rabochego klassa* (Moscow, 1961), p. 220; and R. P. Dadykin, ed., *Formirovanie i razvitie sovetskogo rabochego klassa (1917–1961)* (Moscow, 1964), pp. 55–56.

selves, the problems arising from such rapid growth were formidable. At the beginning, many of the newly enrolled peasants experienced cultural and psychological shock, manifested, for example, in drinking, hooliganism, criminal behavior, breaking the expensive and unfamiliar machinery, and "a colossal growth of industrial traumatism."[51] The problem of labor turnover has already been discussed. The bewildered administrations sometimes tried to placate the workers and sometimes reacted with "administrative methods"—a flood of fines, dismissals, and repression.

The constant seesaw of short periods of liberalism and long waves of *goloe administrirovanie* (crude administrative methods) was by now firmly embedded in Soviet politics. Mass repression was not, as the party liked to put it, some aberration of local officials, but party policy. The harshness of the methods used against absenteeism can be illustrated by a law of November 15, 1932, supplemented a few months later, prescribing dismissal, denial of food rations, denial of access to food shops, and eviction from lodgings* regardless—as the text emphasized—of the time year.[52] Factory administrations were now allowed to starve people in order to ensure their presence in the factories. A single day of "unjustified absence" was defined as absenteeism, punishable according to this law (in 1938, 20 minutes' absence or lateness would constitute absenteeism).

The overall strategy, of course, was more complex and included more than sheer repression. Trade unions and party cells were mobilized to serve the needs of production and of the plans, and this was supplemented by inculcating in the managers a taste for power. Tough leadership became the style preached by the party, with M. Kaganovich teaching the manager to behave in such a way that "the earth should tremble when the director walks around the plant."[53] The NEP "triangle" of party, trade unions, and management was abandoned in 1929 and replaced by a fierce one-man rule (*edinonachalie*). A further method in the struggle to raise the productivity of labor was the enforcement of piece work, spreading of the pay differential, and promotion and offer of better food and priority in lodging, vacations, and school admission for the outstanding worker (*udarnik*) and his children, and for those who stayed long enough on the job. It never seemed sufficient, however, and the fight against the proponents of new categories of morally reprehensible behavior (castigated by the propaganda as "flitters," "idlers," "disorganizers," "absentees," and so on) always included those "indiscriminate mass repressions" that L. Kaganovich, the chief architect of the strategy, pretended to regret in 1936.[54]

From time to time, almost as an afterthought, an Ordzhonikidze or Kirov would appeal to the managers to stop neglecting their workers and to improve their attitude toward them.[55] But the fact was that once the

---

* Enforcement of this law was, however, impeded by the inability or unwillingness of many managers to antagonize the workers to the point of making the factories unmanageable.

"triangle" was gone and the party and trade union turned their "face to production," they had to turn their face against the workers.

THE PEASANTS

In the countryside, a state of major crisis and warfare existed between the government and the peasants. There was nothing like "dekulakization" in regard to the workers, even in the heat of the ruthless fight to instill discipline in their ranks, and (except in the prewar period) even the most repressive bills against labor absenteeism did not abolish the freedom to leave the workplace after giving due notice, although many obstacles were put in the way of doing so. Salaries and social benefits paid out to workers, however meager, nevertheless remained an obligation that the state accepted and fulfilled. In the cities, the government's effort to stem disorder was to some degree bearing fruit, and workers, however sluggish and apathetic many of them might be, did learn trades, improve productivity, and yield to more orderly patterns.

In the countryside, the effects of collectivization were of a different kind. For the peasants it was a revolution that was imposed upon them, a violent destruction of a system of production and of a life pattern, although even here, after an initial period of shock lasting, probably, from 1930 to 1934, the peasants began to acquire some working habits and accepted some routines. But long-term negative phenomena persisted, and some have not been overcome even today.*

At the root of the difficulty of the kolkhoz system lay the fact that the peasants' previous experience, way of life, and educational level in no way prepared them to accept and run the system that was now being imposed on them. It was this contradiction, a Soviet writer stated, that made imperative the state's interference in[56]—or rather takeover of—all aspects of running the kolkhoz system. In addition, the strains caused by forcing on a conservative and mostly illiterate people[57] an abrupt change of age-old life patterns were compounded by an attack on their religion—an act of incredible folly, and quite irrelevant to the problems of kolkhoz production. Its futility was demonstrated by the later admission of the head of the antireligious crusade that by the end of the 1930s two-thirds of the peasants were still believers.[58]

At the very beginning of the process some leaders, honest enough to raise a fuss in public, predicted the essence of things to come. S. I. Syrtsov, premier of the government of the Russian Republic, sounded the alarm.[59] There could already be observed, at the beginning of 1930, a dangerous "explosion of consumerist moods": as the regulators and stimulants of his previous life and production were lost, in fact violently repudiated, the peasant's usual urge to save and accumulate was replaced by an equally

* In Chapter 6 the mechanism of the procurements and their effect on the development of the kolkhozy is described.

strong urge to consume everything (*proedat'*); his usual care and worry about the state of affairs on his farm was replaced by apathy and "a nihilistic attitude toward production" (*proizvodstvennyi nigilizm*). The peasant was now waiting to be guided, expecting to be told what to do. But the state did not know what to do or how to do it, and its agencies in the countryside were in confusion and disarray.

Loss of interest in production was part of the larger problem of loss of identity and self-respect. In the previous system, the peasant was the master (*khozyain*) on his farm, and with this, however poor the farm, went the sense of dignity of a free agent. The new situation deprived the peasants of status and freedom. Their main objection to the kolkhozy was that they would be "put on a ration system" there, which would mean a loss of independence. When this did in fact happen, the peasants, as we have seen, became eager to get away from the kolkhoz into towns—a reaction, among other things, against the phenomenon of "statization" (*okazenivanie*).[60]

The first steps of *okazenivanie* were not part of a deliberately planned strategy. The government was forced, or felt itself forced, to undertake salvage operations that led it ever deeper into the trap of growing interference in all phases and details of agricultural production and organization. The one big step that can be regarded as strategy was the removal of machinery from the kolkhozy to the government MTSs (machinery and tractor stations),* but much else in government policy at the beginning had the character of ad hoc reactions.

Because the state'a needs in grain and other products were urgent and immediate, it pressed on its officials and local administrations to get what was necessary from the peasants. Quite soon the *kolkhoznik* and kolkhoz managements found themselves gagged and at the mercy of an all-powerful network of local officials making searches and seizures, judging, punishing, expelling, and, in particular, arresting freely, making liberal use of the meaningless label of *podkulachnik* (kulak's hireling). Ia. A. Yakovlev, the commissar for agriculture, formally protested, apparently, at the Central Committee meeting in July 1931 against what he called the "mass of antikolkhoz actions" by local administrations ,saying that the *kolkhoznik* had become "an object of sheer arbitrariness." But in the same year one of his Central Committee colleagues, B. P. Sheboldaev, gave the key to the situation and to the policy of the hardliners who were more powerful than Yakovlev. The kolkhozy, he stated, "have too little goodwill toward the interests of the state," and there was no justification for "idealizing the *kolkhoznik*." The old wisdom of rulers—coercion—had to be resorted to without qualms.[61] This attitude totally disregarded the interests of the many millions of peasants. The concerns of the government was epito-

---

* Machinery and tractor stations (MTSs) were set up in 1929 to consolidate tractor and machinery holdings and to service the kolkhozy. Later they also assumed functions of political supervision over the kolkhozy.

mized in the procurement (*zagotovki*) squeeze, "that touchstone on which our strength and weakness and the strength and weakness of our enemy were tested," as L. Kaganovich said in a sentence crucial to the understanding of government strategy and the relations between kolkhoz peasantry and the state.[62] "The enemy" here were truly legion. Hence the shrill demands coming from the Central Committee to punish "without mercy" not only reluctance to part with grain but also what was called "a maliciously careless attitude to work";[63] hence the suggestions to local authorities that bad work should be called "kulak sabotage" and that lenience toward transgressors would be considered as help given to the enemy.

Krylenko's* typology of "contravention of socialist legality" in regard to peasants and the kolkhoz included such "arbitrary treatment of the peasantry as . . . illegal searches and arrests, confiscations, preemption of property, illegal fines, and the like."[64] The capriciousness of the accusations of "sloppily careless work" and sabotage becomes clear when we examine the kind of "guidance" the state was giving the kolkhozy. Obviously the local party committees knew nothing about agriculture in general, and even less about their pet idea—large-scale agricultural production. Stalin taught that, since the kolkhozy were inexperienced, they had to be run from above by minute party interference. But as Kirov stated in a moment of despair and truth: "I myself, sinful man, don't see clearly in agricultural matters"[65]—this after having given the most ignorant orders to peasants and then ordering or approving mass arrests of those who refused to comply[66] before discovering that he was on a false track.

The more honest Stalinists were more and more despairing of the state of affairs and were groping for changes. Kirov, who sometimes seemed utterly disappointed in 1933, called for change and made an appeal to go and learn from the *kolkhoznik*—a telling statement of the failure of government methods. But it was at about the same time that Stalin issued stern instructions to meddle, in effect, with every detail, because the *kolkhozniki* did not know how to run their affairs.[67]

The peasants were fettered and "bureaucratized" and well knew that they had lost the independence they had had as producers and citizens under NEP. There was a whole system of discrimination, amounting to a special legal and social regime for the kolkhoz peasantry. If lack of legally guaranteed rights was to be for a time the trait of the system in regard to all classes, the peasant was particularly vulnerable because of the ideological formula of the regime, which considered him suspect in terms of his class origin, in terms of the inferior status of kolkhozy, in terms of the purity of socialism in comparison with state-run institutions. Whereas the worker earned a salary—more or less state controlled, but independent of the total output of the industry or of the industry's efficiency—the

---

* Nikolai V. Krylenko was commissar of justice of the Russian Republic.

kolkhoznik was paid from the residual of kolkhoz income after the crop had been gathered and the state had taken its share. This income was both insecure and, as was formally acknowledged, insufficient to feed the peasant's family; hence the concession to the peasant allowing him a private plot and a cow (small enough not to make him too happy and forgetful of the kolkhoz, but big enough to provide for some of his family's, and the whole country's, essential needs). This allowance, of course, was one of the factors keeping the old peasant alive in the *kolkhoznik*, thereby providing an additional argument for doubting his socialist credentials.

In addition to insecurity of income, the peasants were denied the benefits of social security that the state guaranteed its workers and employees.[68] The peasants were subject to several state corvées—road building, timber hauling, and so on—whereas city dwellers had long ago forgotten this remnant of the Middle Ages. The peasant did not have the freedom of movement, however qualified, that the worker had. His travels were controlled by the passport system and the *propiska* (the document indicating registered place of residence), and also by the law of March 17, 1933, stipulating that a peasant was not allowed to leave the kolkhoz without a contract from a prospective employer, duly ratified by the kolkhoz management. At about the same time, USSR Prosecutor Akulov ordered peasants to be punished by up to six months in prison for not respecting a contract with a state employer. Akulov was reminded by one writer (with unknown results) that introducing criminal law into a basically civil transaction like a labor contract was contrary to the principles of Russian and European labor law.[69] But this was precisely the point: disregarding the interest of "the state" was all too easily becoming a criminal or, even worse, a political offense. This was one of the attributes of "Stalinism."

Here, then, was the system of "military-feudal" exploitation of the peasantry that Bukharin had fearfully anticipated in 1929, and "statism" at its purest. A producer (not to say citizen) so strongly fettered and discriminated against could not be efficient. On the contrary, he lost the incentive to exert himself on the job, unless this happened to be his own plot, and became demoralized both as a producer and as a person. "We are not our own men but the kolkhoz's," the peasants often repeated. This summed up the whole process. Before they had been "their own men"; now they belonged to the kolkhoz, but the kolkhoz did not belong to them.

Over the years, slow and not unimportant changes took place within the kolkhoz peasantry, such as the emergence of numbers of managers and administrators who had not existed at all in NEP agriculture. Growing numbers of tractor drivers made their appearance, as did a sprinkling of "rural intelligentsia." But according to a Soviet sociologist, by the end of the five-year plans this so-called rural intelligentsia was as yet barely distinguishable by its level of education from the mass of *kolkhozniki*.[70] The mass was still composed of peasants, and they were at the bottom of the social ladder, just as the *muzhik* had been in former times. The only means of social promotion was to move out. Millions did so whenever they could, and in so doing probably influenced Soviet society, culture, and the state much more deeply than is sometimes realized.

▪ THE EDUCATED AND THE RULERS

SPETSEEDSTVO

The so-called intelligentsia is a problem of considerable complexity, and its story during and after the "big drive" is crucial for understanding the social structure that was in the making. Here too we have a state action carried out with great speed and urgency. The first five-year plan created an enormous demand for technicians, administrators, and scientists of all sorts, and the existing training faciles and governmental institutions were overwhelmed by the task. It is significant that very soon the whole problem of the "intelligentsia" became a problem of "cadres" in the hundreds of thousands and even millions, administered and bureaucratized by a network of "departments of cadres," established "as we go along," as Ordzhonikidze put it.[71] Improvisation of a social and professional process of such importance is a trait we keep meeting in this period, not only in the domain of cadres.

The attitude toward the intelligentsia in this and previous periods was shaped by contradictory factors and under changing circumstances. From the very first days of the regime, the party needed educated people to run the economy and the state (a dependence that was somehow not anticipated: the party leaders, intellectuals themselves, were busy understanding "history" and political strategy, not running an economy). However, the intelligentsia en masse, including the so-called popular (*narodnaya*) intelligentsia, actively opposed the Bolshevik takeover, in the massive strikes of late 1917/early 1918. This opposition, in its overt forms, was quite quickly put down, but the shadow kept hanging over relations between the party and the intellectuals.

With all the disdain for Oblomovs and *intelligenty* that Bolsheviks sometimes encouraged (the notorious "Makhaevite tendencies"), an urgent need arose to foster respect for members of the intelligentsia. It was not an easy task. The conundrum can be studied in two statements by Lenin: he declared, on the one hand, "they must be given work, but they must be carefully watched; commissars should be placed over them and their counterrevolutionary schemes suppressed": he appealed, on the other, for respect for culture and those who possessed it and issued the injunction to "command less, or rather not to command at all."[72] That this con-

tradictory attitude would produce zigzags in political tactics and mar
relations is obvious. Lenin knew that he could not take a step without
experts, and he acknowledged frankly after the civil war that the Red
Army, for example, would not have existed at all without the ex-tsarist
officers who helped create it.[73] But the same was true of the universities,
the State Planning Commission (Gosplan), and all the important economic ministries as well. The great dream of preparing "our own" intelligentsia could not be achieved without the old one cooperating in the
job.

NEP settled down to an uneasy acceptance of this situation. The intelligentsia was basically still, at the end of NEP, the "old" one, non-Bolshevik
in its majority. In October 1929 a third of all specialists working in the
national economy and a majority of those with higher education were
from the old intelligentsia, as were 60 percent of teachers in higher education. The mass of new specialists being prepared under Soiet rule would
not just be trained by these instructors but also undoubtedly politically
influenced by them.[74]

The Shakhty affair* came as a warning and a demonstration that the
"old" would not have it their way in shaping the profile of the immense
mass of new trainees. It opened a period in Soviet history that was not
only a tragedy for the old intelligentsia but also amounted to a furious
destruction of many cultural values. The hectic creation of instruments for
the diffusion of culture—schools, higher schools, universities—was to be
accompanied by an unbelievable display of obscurantism and attacks on
anything sophisticated or refined. The universities, for example, were almost completely destroyed before a new approach, from about 1934,
helped to save them.

During the Shakhty trial and thereafter intellectual circles were panic-
stricken and depressed, in a not unjustified expectation of a wave of
spetseedstvo and mass repressions.[75]

One central idea that the key leaders wanted to "explain" by the
Shakhty trial was that neutrality in politics—that is, toward party policies—could lead to sabotage. This message was now presented in a new
way: by a stage production with a recognizable signature on it.

Lenin had earlier been irked by the attitude of educated specialists who
claimed noninvolvement in politics as part of a moral and professional
ethic. This implied, from Lenin's point of view, that they would work as
specialists for the new regime without endorsing it or identifying with its
aims. Lenin was prepared to accept this compromise, but Stalin's policies
refused any such accommodation. His objective, in common with that of
the Inquisition, was to force thinking people to desist from their independent thoughts and moral principles and to identify with a party and with

* The Shakhty trial of engineers for wrecking and sabotage was held in May–June 1928.

policies felt to be unacceptable or questionable. The most unacceptable was precisely what they were asked to do: to prostrate themselves, to turn their guts out in fervent repentance—or else be declared treasonable. The formula "doubt equals treason" was one of the deadliest tools of the moral and cultural reaction that hit the country at the height of its economic and military construction. Why this presumably optimistic surge of creativity was darkened by such a deeply pessimistic attitude to men and culture is one of the unanswered questions. In any case, the quasi-mystical "disarm yourself before the party and repent" was self-defeating. Even the most dedicated and blind followers of the party line could not prove that he had really never had any doubts.

The singling out of the "bourgeois intelligentsia" for this treatment was a catastrophe. The country's development could not proceed without the participation of the best professionals, who were badly needed amid the now enormous mass of inexperienced and ignorant newcomers and with the deficit of specialists still growing. Some were mercifully allowed to "redeem their crimes"—that is, their alleged sabotage—by working "honestly," inventing or designing in their prison cells or on the site, but with the status of convict. To encourage them to invent machinery and weapons, big salaries and the best food in a hungry country were sometimes given to these men, but at the same time they were kept as prisoners and promised freedom at the price of compliance.

The policy certainly did not have the full approval of all top leaders. Within the framework of a new line initiated in 1931 to stop some of the damage of *spetseedstvo*, Y. E. Rudzutak explained officially that many lower technicians were too ignorant to be able to distinguish "wrecking" from the normal professional risk taken by an engineer,[76] but he certainly knew that the problem was not one of "ignorant technicians." It was a problem of party policy throughout; otherwise the excesses of the "proletarianization" period could not have taken place. There were waves of purges, dismissals, and arrests of "alien elements" and, in particular, of their children taking place in universities and institutions. The numerous "social purges of students" enhanced the anxiety and panic among the intelligentsia and even produced suicides—not to speak of candidates to build canals.[77] Mass expulsions of students drew a protest from Lunacharsky, who, in a letter to Stalin that was found in the Central Party Archives, considered it unacceptable to persecute sons for the sins of their fathers, especially when the sin was no more than the wrong "social orgin."[78]

The treatment meted out to old specialists was scarcely beneficial to the rest of the engineers, including the party members, who were not under suspicion. The onslaught on the old engineers hurt the system across the board. Lack of initiative, a tendency to avoid responsibility and hide behind somebody's back, putting the blame on somebody else, and the philosophy that "it's no business of mine" (*moya khata s krayu*) came to permeate institutions and whole layers of society.

THE INTELLIGENT AND THE LESS INTELLIGENT

The figures on the growth of the "intelligentsia" during the 1930s are staggering. From modest beginnings at the end of NEP it is claimed that there was a leap by 1939 to 10 or 11 million employed, amounting to 13–14 percent of the whole population[79]—in itself an important structural change. Numbers of university students grew from 169,000 in 1928/29 to 812,000 in 1940/41, and there was an impressive growth of students in secondary technical schools. In the early years, however, it was not the school system that supplied students for the university and men for professional jobs: in the "proletarianization" period this was done by mobilization of party members, workers, and peasants through short courses, workers' faculties, *vydvizhenie* (advancement of workers to positions in the *apparat* or higher education), and so on. In fact, like everything else, the school system was in turmoil during these years, and the quantitative strides were not the whole story. This was especially true of institutions of higher education, whose hectic expansion and initially lax admission standards created large numbers of unviable institutions producing graduates whose level of qualification was no higher than that of a secondary school. The crash campaign for cadres was costly and to some degree ineffective. Later, measures were taken to stabilize the system, and, with the development of secondary schools, mobilizations and discrimination on class grounds ceased. But the effect of such measures on the quality of specialists and officials subsumed under the label "intelligentsia" could not be felt quickly. In 1930 a survey of industrial cadres showed that more than half the engineers and technicians in industry were *praktiki* (persons working as engineers and technicians without the appropriate formal training and diplomas) with little education and sometimes without even a crash course. Only 11.4 percent of the engineers and technicians had higher education. The same applied to the whole mass lumped together into the category of "leading cadres and specialists" in industry at large. A survey taken in 1933 showed that of 861,000 people that were surveyed in this category, some 57 percent had neither higher nor specialized secondary education.[80]

We should examine the general problem of the "intelligentsia" from yet another angle. The statistical concept used by official publications was faulty and did not express social realities. The term itself glossed over complexities and a maze of special groups comprising (1) the creative intelligentsia, old and new; (2) the specialists, old and new, covered by the concept "engineering and technical workers"; (3) lower officialdom in the various *apparaty*; (4) the higher administration; and (5) the top ruling oligarchy. The last two can be grouped together in the somewhat larger concept of a sociopolitical elite.

This classification makes it clear that the story of the intelligentsia involves more than creating a layer of educated professionals. Hiding or camouflaging the realities of power in statistical or ideological constructions —not an exclusively Soviet phenomenon—takes on different forms in different circumstances. Categories like "employees" (*sluzhashchie*) or "intelligentsia" may conceal far more than they disclose.

The millions listed as "intelligentsia" also included—as said—an overwhelming majority of officials with little education and a low level of professional skill—three such officials to one educated professional.[81] The lumping together of these unspecialized and poorly educated people with the educated specialists and literati was intended to create the impression of a cultural leap and grossly overstated the true situation. In reality this mass of badly paid officials was an addition to the social structure that did not necessarily elevate it but, on the contrary, provided a convenient milieu for the spread of irrational and obscurantist tendencies. This category of lower officials overlapped only partly with that of *praktiki*, many of whom, although not formally educated, were men of ability. The majority of those low officials were, as a Soviet sociologist put it, quite "unpromising" (*besperspektivnye*), although many of them filtered through the party into quite high places in the influential *apparaty*. Many such people were incorporated into the category of party members listed as "employees," and they certainly contributed to the moral and cultural decadence of the party in these years.

Our intention here, it should be said, is not to link degrees of education with moral standards. But we are dealing with a political climate that promoted or appealed to irrational and baser instincts and that probably received a better response from an inexperienced, uninformed, untrained, and disoriented mass than it would have from a more cultivated, politically alert population.

Exalting this mass that was overcrowding the offices to the glamorous category of "intelligentsia" was a spurious gesture. The junior officials in any case did not gain much from the policy of promotion and improvement in salary and prestige that was applied to specialists. This policy gained momentum in the process of the fight against wage leveling (*uravnilovka*). The spread in salaries increased, first among the workers themselves, on the basis of skill and piece-rate norms, and second (at the same time, from 1931 on) when the average salaries of engineers began to grow and to move away from the hitherto privileged norms of industrial workers' earnings. In August 1931 an important formal step was taken to remove discrimination against the technical intelligentsia: full equality with industrial workers—including admission for them and their children to higher education, food norms, and rights to sanatoriums—was introduced in areas where the industrial workers had had priority. The technical in-telligentsia was also given the all-important right to accommodation on equal priority with industrial workers, with the further right—hitherto reserved only for the privileged category of senior officials (*otvetrabotniki*) —of extra space for a study.[82] A year later, a special government committee was created to watch over the construction of housing for engineering and technical workers and scientists.

The position of equality with industrial workers did not last for long. since the status of technical and other specialists continued to rise. During the "proletarianization" period, the social composition of the university student body had included over 50 percent from the working class, with the "employee" category falling to 32.8 percent. But in the course of the 1930s, class limitations on entrance to universities and the party were removed, and the sons of employees (including specialists) came back in force. In universities, the employee group allegedly rose to 42.2 percent, with the workers dropping back to their position under NEP, namely 33.9 percent.[83] Obviously, sons of workers and peasants were now in the uni-versities in great numbers. But the growing trend in favor of the children of the already educated was unmistakably part of a new scale of values of the policy maker and of society at large.

From 1934 on, the professional, the specialist, and the administrator would begin to get orderly and guaranteed fixed monthly salaries; and after the quiet removal in 1932 of the *partmaksimum*, which kept salaries of party members at about 250 to 300 rubles a month, the gate would be open for the creation of a real pyramid of income and privilege.[84]

THE BOSSES AND THEIR *APPARATY*

The cadre problem was not just one of getting enough specialists and managers, but of promoting a powerful class of bosses—the *nachal'stvo*, composed of top managers in the enterprises and top administrators in state agencies. The *nachal'stvo*, the state's ruling stratum, was the prin-cipal group that the system kept fostering—although we must not forget that in Stalinist terms "fostering" always meant, even for the most priv-ileged, constant beating.

Nevertheless, the rewards for being admitted to this group were very considerable, especially in a country in a condition of penury, and their power over subordinates was very great. Some privileges—a car, a special pension, separate eating places—were public knowledge. But much was hidden, like the special stores, special warrants, graduated scale of expense accounts, housing privileges, special well-sheltered resorts, and finally the "sealed envelope" with money over and above the formal salary. All these slowly developed into a formally stratified and quite rigid ladder of impor-tance and power.

The *nachal'stvo* class was born of the principle of one-man direction (*edinonachalie*) as it developed after 1929. The creation of hierarchical scaffolding of dedicated bosses, held together by discipline, privilege, and power, was a deliberate strategy of social engineering to help stabilize the flux. It was born, therefore, in conditions of stress, mass disorganization, and social warfare, and the bosses were actually asked to see themselves as commanders in a battle. The party wanted the bosses to be efficient, powerful, harsh, impetuous, and capable of exerting pressure crudely and ruthlessly and getting results "whatever the cost." Rudeness (*grubost'*) became a virtue and, more significantly, the boss was endowed with quasi-police power in the work place: among his prerogatives were fines and dismissals, which would mean deprivation of lodging and food, and he had the further resource (even more corrupting) of the local security organs and the public prosecutor. The formation of the despotic manager was actually a process in which not leaders but *rulers* were made. The fact that their own jobs and freedom were quite insecure either made the tyrannical traits of their rule probably more rather than less capricious and offensive.*

THE FLOOD OF PAPER

All the *apparaty*—central and local, party and state—were affected by rapid growth and rapid turnover, purges, low educational and professional standards, and the dysfunctions associated with overcentralization and "administrative methods."

Centralization of decision making, coupled with concentration of power, prerogatives, and resources in a few hands at the top, was paralleled by similar tendencies in every single administration. At all levels power went to the top few, and often into the hands of a single boss. We have already discussed this creation of "small Stalins" in the factories. The phenomenon became all-embracing. But its overall results were only partly calculated and sought for. The policy makers were guided by the idea that in conditions of scarce resources, scarce talent, and not too much commitment in the growing socioeconomic organism, one should concentrate power in fewer, but more competent and reliable, hands. This was reflected in the fostering of the *nachal'stvo*, *edinonachalie*, and, at the summit of the edifice, the "cult of the individual." But much of the trend was spontaneous, under the combined impact of policy and those numerous unplanned but tenacious elements, inherent in the bureaucratic world of a

---

* The preference for "crude leadership" does not mean that every manager actually was a despotic type. There certainly were many of the traditional Russian "paternalist" type and some, a minority, of "businesslike" frame of mind and style (*delovye*), compromising and conniving. Whatever the typology, their power and privilege were common to the whole category, especially in the more important enterprises and establishments.

dictatorial state, that fitted no strategy and nobody's intentions. These elements might separately be identified as "deficiencies" by Politburo members, journalists, or inspectors of the *apparat*; but in fact, the "deficiencies" were so persistent that there was no escape from the conclusion that they amounted to permanent features of the system.

Among them were the "flood of paper" (*bumazhnyi potok*), the proliferation of officials and offices, and (incredible as it may sound for such a centralized state) multicentrism. A study of Mikoyan's Commissariat of Foreign and Internal Trade, to take an example, found the whole ministry to be, characteristically, in a state of crisis in 1930. But submergence in details, a flood of 2,500 "papers" a day, and loss of control over essential policy matters and over their coordination[85] was not only young Mikoyan's problem. Another study[86] of the *apparaty* of local soviet executive committees found the following unpalatable traits: firmly entrenched distrust in the upper rungs of lower organs, lack of clarity in the division of functions, multicentrism, parallelism, enormous multiplicity of channels all the way down the line from Moscow to the *raiony*, harassment and pettifogging in supervision of the lower level by the higher, and constant delays.[87] Red tape and the bureaucratic style of operation, castigated by the top leaders themselves as "formalistic paperwork" (*kantselyarshchina* and *formal'no-bumazhnoe rukovodstvo*), became phenomena from which there seemed to be no escape. The leadership and the public alike were bewildered and, in fact, helpless. Stuchka (a leading jurist, theoretician, and Supreme Court judge), for instance, seemed quite astonished to discover what every official knew already, that government departments were engaging in fierce infighting: it was real "class warfare," he said, in which the parties behaved like enemies and genuine competitors.[88] He could only sigh.

The leadership clearly did not understand what was happening inside the bureaucracy or why. Ordzhonikidze, when still head of the Commissariat of State Inspection, lamented that every time reductions of personnel and financial economies were decreed the result was bigger expenditure and an increase in the number of officials.[89] It was impossible, he went on, to get through the maze of cumbersome and top-heavy *apparaty* and wrench realistic data out of them,[90] and he appealed for a study of the tendency of the *apparaty* to distort government decisions. It was, in fact, an impossible task. Officials formed "families" and engaged in every kind of mutual protection.

The growing bureaucratic Moloch not only menaced the country but terrified the top leaders as well. They reacted, true to style and tradition, by pressuring and purging the *apparaty*. The general idea was to make the officials felt compelled to defend themselves by padding, cover-up, and down hard on some, as an example to the others" (*bol'no stuknut' kogo sleduet, v primet i nauku drugim*).[91] As the leadership increased control and terror, "centralization" was also strengthened and kept breeding more and more of the same phenomena. Facing such pressure from above, officials felt compelled to defend themselves by padding, cover-up, and "hand in glove" policies—and by redirecting the pressure downward to get some results.

In this atmosphere, the type that thrived and prospered was precisely the cunning and dodgy character, unscrupulous and conformist, who had learned the hard way the disadvantages of taking any initiative without orders from above. Soon the habit would become second nature, and the system of "counterincentives" would mobilize more energies to blocking orders and plans from above than to fulfilling them. Syrtsov, chief of the state machinery of the Russian Republic, knew what he was talking about when he commented. "We bind a man hand and foot with all kinds of rules; we drive him into a bottle, cork it up, and put a government stamp on it; and then we go round saying: 'Why doesn't this man show any energy or any initiative?'[92] He did not mention terror, but this was obvious. His appeal to solve the problem "by letting people out of the bottle" led him too into trouble the very same year.

Four years later L. Kaganovich, one of the promoters and practitioners of the method of "coming down hard," listed the factors responsible for the devastating turnover of personnel in the party and other *apparaty*: those at the top "hit from the shoulder," and dismissals and punishments were so frequent that many local party officials, even if highly successful for some time, took it for granted that normality could not last and, in order to avoid catastrophe, decided: better clear out (*nado smyvat'sya*) while the going's good.[93]

The "logic" of the centralized machinery led to putting the blame only on the lower ranks: if only the oblast committees knew more about their cadres and looked after them better, a Kaganovich would complain. But he could also resort, when necessary, to a broader view: the "class analysis." Tsarist officials still in service and all the other "socially alien, . . . bankrupt, degenerate hangers-on" could be invoked to carry the blame.

These were, in fact, the terms used to guide the mammoth purge of the state *apparaty* ordered by the party in 1929.[94] To purge (*chistit'*, or, more lovingly, *podchistit'*) became another expression of the current "art of ruling" and had far-reaching and well-known effects for everyone. The purge of officialdom begun in 1929 dragged on for a full two years, disorganized and disorientated the administrators, dismissed every tenth official who was checked—and then petered out with a decision to stop the whole thing and never return to the method of "wholesale purges" (*poval'nye chistki*).[95] As the 160,000 purged officials left (many probably found their way back later) and all the disturbing phenomena remained, including inflation of personnel, the government decreed a new move: not a purge but a "reduction of personnel," in which a further 153,000 officials were apparently fired in the winter of 1932/33.[96]

This was not going to be the last word. The *chinovnik*, Trotsky thought, was going to swallow the dictatorship of the proletariat if the dictatorship did not swallow him in good time. The prophecy was not quite accurate. The *chinovnik* was "swallowing" the masses, the state was swallowing those same *chinovniki,* and the proletariat was quite irrelevant to the question. The whole thing was simply the *modus operandi* of a police state, beating the country into a modernity of its own definition and catching some morbid diseases in the process.

10

SOCIAL RELATIONS
INSIDE INDUSTRY
DURING THE PREWAR
FIVE-YEAR PLANS,
1928–41

The period under consideration—circa 1928–41—saw deep changes in the social and political setting of the USSR. Our focus here is on social relations in industry, mainly in the category of large-scale industry, and it can be stated that these social relations were part of a whole new industrial system which emerged in those years. It is true that the period is indeed very short and it is not always easy to distinguish in it the transient from the more permanent traits, many of which are still essentially in place to this day. For a historical consideration though, some of the shorter-term phenomena—especially the speed and intensity of change, the unprecedented human flows into industrial employment, characteristic of those years—were crucial for the social and human relations of the day and also affected the character of the political system. Both the industrial and the political components of the regime were in a state of flux, to which an excessive rigidity and severity, as well as the capricious quality of power wielding can be related for purposes of analysis and explanation.

During this period the industrial labor force tripled, the number of workers grew 2.5 times, some 8,000 new big enterprises were built, whole new branches of industry emerged, and of course, in this process, whole new groups entered the industrial social sector in a rush, and this surge of industrial development and assimilation of a huge labor force generated powerful tensions. No doubt the term "social crisis" can justifiably be used to describe the social tensions of the period. Scope and speed were at the root of the crisis, and in particular the phenomenon of "telescoping of stages" that occurred in those years when a semiliterate if not illiterate, predominantly rural labor force had to be broken into the industrial world and taught, simultaneously, to use machines, to get used to an unfamiliar, complicated organization, to learn to read, to respect authority, to change their perception of time, and to use a spitoon. It goes without saying that such tasks would take much longer than a decade, and they inevitably got complicated by a parallel effort in training, often from scratch, engineers and administrators as well as teaching teachers who would profess in the hundreds of new institutions of secondary and higher learning that mushroomed in those years. The phenomenon of the so-called *praktiki*—people without any specialized, and rather poor general education, who took up technical and administrative jobs—were and remained an aftereffect of the "big drive." In fact, such effects were actually deeper and longer lasting than just *praktiki*—some of whom, it must be added, were certainly able individuals.

But we are talking about a "social crisis" and not just a process of learning, teaching, and heroic belt-tightening, as some old-fashioned writers still want us to look at it. The decade—if we may so call the period for brevity's sake—was marked by waves of social warfare, and notably, three stages or three social wars are worth singling out. In the years 1928–31, beginning with the Shakhty trial,* an assault on the "bourgeois intelligentsia" seriously perturbed the world of industry; thousands were arrested, with or without show trials, and went on to camps where an adumbration of what later would come to be called *sharagi* made its appearance: captive technicians inventing and constructing complicated pieces of equipment, under the whip of the GPU and the spur of promise of freedom and high pay. This rather "pharaonic" method of using twentieth-century technicians permeated the period in many other ways—an illustration of the "telescoping of stages."

As persecutions of the technicians were subsiding, relations with the working class worsened, a catastrophic dip in labor discipline occurred, with its *proguly* (absenteeism), horrendous turnover (the *tekuchka* we read so much about), drinking, hooliganism and machine breaking, and very "ugly moods" among the workers (from a 1932 speech to the Ninth Trade Union Congress by Postyshev, who said, *skvernye nastroeniya*).

The regime responded by a volley of draconian measures using dismissals, deprivation of bread cards and of lodging with the party—government decree making it specific that the eviction from the home had to take place "independently of the season." This was the second social war, which was to last, with fluctuating intensity, and especially a new flareup, during the third five-year plan. The 1931 efforts of

---

* In the spring of 1928 about fifty engineers and administrators of the Donbas mining industry in the Ukraine were put on trial for alleged sabotage. Most of them were sentenced to prison, and there were also some death sentences.

reconciliation with "bourgeois" (and other) specialists might have a lot to do with this warfare, and not just with the debilitating deficit of technicians.

The effects of the two wars still lingered on when a third wave came to the fore that can be called "the war against the cadres"—political, military, administrative, technical, and scientific—with the flower of them getting swept away in the purges of 1936–38.

Our background sketch would be incomplete without mentioning the fact that the orientation on heavy industry and the investment policy created inflationary pressures, with a push in 1928/29, a long wave in 1931–34, stabilization of prices 1935–37 and a new inflationary wave from 1938 on—to last all through the war period.[1] Real wages dropped during this period—despite some improvements during the inflationary lull— well below the level of 1928 and 1913, and stayed approximately on the same low level till sometime in the early 1950s—as some Soviet studies asserted.[2]

It is with this background in mind, pertaining to the "primitive accumulation" era, that the examination of the social structure can proceed.

▪ THE PROFESSIONALS AND THE OFFICEHOLDERS

The figures of industrial employment that rose from 3,779,000 in 1928 to 10,967,000 in 1939 show convincingly a quick process of physical renovation of the personnel and a rather recent entry into industry of the bulk of the employed. As one source had it, in relation to employment in the national economy at large, 80 percent of those employed by 1940 joined the labor force at the beginning and during the "reconstruction period." A similar order of magnitude applied to industry, too, and this brevity of *stazh* (length of service) applied equally to all its categories and social groups. Our survey begins with the category of *rukovoditeli*, the administrators, although difficulties emerge in discerning the managerial, or administrative, from the engineering-technical components. From a document from the Central State Economic Archives (TsGANKh), dated March 29, 1941, we learn that the total number of "leading cadres and specialists" was 589,049, with about 175,000 of them working in the *zavodo-upravleniya*, and the rest on the shop floor.[3] As said, a minority among them—from the factory directors, 13,530 in all, to the foremen (*mastera*), 138,363 strong at the lowest rung—were the administrative ladder or scaffolding; the rest, rank-and-file engineers and technicians. The real *nachal'stvo* (bosses), though, would include, to my mind, some 75,000 from the plant-management level and 43,888 shop superintendents (*nachal'niki tsekha*), the first group belonging, in the accepted militarized language of the day, to the higher command structure (*vysshii komandnyi sostav*), and the shop superintendents with their deputies and chief shop engineers assigned to the middle ranks (*srednii komsostav*); finally, there were the foremen, who counted as NCOs.

The party saturation of this whole category of managers and specialists was quite high, with about 30 percent in the party and 10 percent in Komsomol; 81 percent of the directors, 48 percent of the shop superintendents, and 30 percent of the foremen were party members, a smaller percentage were members of Komsomol.

The *mastera*, the lowest representatives of the administration, caused many headaches for the authorities. They were a crucial segment in the industrial administration, but they were often, at the end of the NEP and for some time thereafter, a rude and crude lot, hovering between the world of the workers and of the ITR (engineering-technical ranks), without adhering to either of them.[4] The *master* was too rough for the workers to accept (and, after all, wasn't he the administration's eye?) and too primitive to be accepted, socially and even professionally, as one of their own by the ITR.

In due course, the foreman would become, not just formally, a part of the ITR, which at the end of our period would be composed of 264,736 engineers and 222,557 technicians, some of those engineers, obviously, belonging to the administrative scaffolding mentioned above. The proportion between engineers and technicians, so obviously inadequate, cannot detain us here despite the fact that it had many important consequences, including for the self-image of the engineers. But we cannot overlook the fact that only 38 percent of the engineers had higher education. About 20 percent had a specialized secondary training, and over 41 percent were *praktiki*. Among the technicians, a huge 60 percent were *praktiki* and the lack of appropriate training concerned all the ranks, including, especially, almost 27 percent of the factory chief engineers—probably an improvement over what obtained at the beginning of the plans, but only modestly so. And the foremen again, before World War II, were *praktiki* overwhelmingly—almost 89 percent of them.

According to Seniavskii, industry could boast only of 310,000 people with higher and secondary education, a very inadequate proportion, due in part to a still rather modest supply of trained people in the country by 1941 (not more than 2.4 million), but due even more to a social trend among the educated away from industry, and if inside industry already, away from the direct production process and toward the offices of management and commissariats.[5] This phenomenon belongs to the sociological realm of status patterns in Soviet society and inside industry, and more will be said about it later. But we note that the country's leaders constantly deplored the inadequacy of the cadres, in numbers and quality, which constantly blocked the development of the country, in particular during the second five-year plan, as one source hinted.[6] But why not also in the third, after the purges engulfed so many of the cadres, probably some of the best, when only 8 percent among those who were university trained belonged to the former "bourgeois" category? Those purges certainly influenced the length of service of the engineers. Almost half of those so-called engineers had less than three years of service, 65.6 percent less than five. Thus the experience of the mass of engineers was at that time low. They were, in a real sense, as "raw" in their position as many workers were in theirs, and the same applied to the administrators. No one will be astonished to discover that the thin layer of the "bourgeois specialists"—who after some measure of reconciliation from 1931 on weathered the storm of the purges much better than party-affiliated cadres —was still immensely important for the new industrial giant. They still held the majority of crucial jobs as technical directors and chief engineers.

The next layer, socially and numerically important inside the industrial realm, was that of the "officials"—*sluzhashchie*—or "clerical workers," whom some authors and statistical sources in the USSR still place in the unified category of salary receivers, or in the intelligentsia; some even lump them together with the workers, but others, happily, allow us to single them out and distinguish them from the workers and the ITR. A small table from a 1964 statistical handbook offers a helpful picture of and a sense of trend in the different groups inside the industrial personnel (see Table 10.1).

These figures show that this officialdom was growing very fast and was even for some time the biggest group (after the workers) in industry. The ITR caught up after 1937, when the officials were curtailed, but later went into faster growth again, less so than the ITR, but much faster than the workers. One source showed that whereas the numbers of workers in industry fell by 2 percent in the period 1937–39, the *sluzhashchie* expanded by over 15 percent.

The figures seem to confirm a relative slowing down, resulting from efforts to check their growth, but this may be partly misleading. When administrators complied with stringent demands from the government to reduce the *shtaty* (staffs), they either engaged in some of their "cosmetics" to seem like doing as ordered or rather increased the numbers of ITR and burdened them with extra nonprofessional office work and chores, which

TABLE 10.1

	Industrial Personnel, 1928–40 (in thousands)			
	1928	1932	1937	1940
Total personnel	3,773	8,000	10,112	10,967
Workers	3,124	6,007	7,924	8,290
Apprentices	135	560	335	351
ITR	119	420	722	932
Sluzhashchie	236	700	649	768

Source: *Promyshlennost' SSSR* (Moscow, 1964), p. 84.

was, in fact, one of the sources of inefficiency in industry, when engineers wasted more than half of their time on this type of busy work and complained bitterly about it.

Officials did not enjoy much respect among workers and did worry the authorities a good deal. It is their growth that used to be identified with the plague—in industry and elsewhere—of "the ballooning (*razbukhanie*) of the *apparaty*." Indeed, they were seen as the epitome of "bureaucratization" and "bureaucratism." The causes of this ballooning were analyzed by an interesting study of this layer by the Gosplan.[7] The authors point to such traits of the system, including the industrial sector, as "the method of petty tutelage," a complicated management chart, tangled pay systems, exaggerated reporting and paperwork, distortions in personnel and job description, growth of supply *apparaty*, poor mechanization of office work —all contributing to the number of poorly trained officials multiplying sometimes quicker than the rate of economic growth. (Scott proposed an additional factor for such multiplication: the prevailing piece-rate system, which demanded complicated calculations of wages to be paid out.[8]) We see why Gosplan complained that the expenditure on *apparaty* financed by the state budget grew in 1938–39 by 27 percent, and the ones financed by economic agencies themselves by almost 29 percent, when figures for industrial growth and growth of national income were more modest.

We are here at the hub of the apparatus and bureaucracy woes in the USSR, although we have to keep in mind that part of the problem was often misunderstood because of underestimation in Soviet theory of the "nonproductive" spheres of activity, leading to an exaggerated fear of "officials." But the problem was nevertheless very real, including on the social plane. These officials—then and much later, too—were not "specialized," not trained in anything particular, and very poorly educated; many of those so-called "accountants," or more pretentiously, "economists," got these professional labels mainly for knowing how to read and write, and in order to be given a salary for them.

This milieu, often of popular origin, was held in low esteem by ITR and workers alike, and frustrated by this, they were, in fact, an "aggressive class of people, craving material goods and status greedy, without any high performance to justify their appetites. More studies of this Soviet "lower-middle-class," or lower "white collar," segment would probably show that they harbored backward moods and conceptions of life and politics— notably nationalism—and were the carriers of all kinds of "petit bourgeois" tendencies, even if they did not possess land, shops, or artisan ateliers. It was therefore quite astonishing to discover that Soviet authorities, notably Molotov in his 1939 data on the Soviet intelligentsia, included these poorly trained and quite unglorious social by-products of industrialization in the glamorous "intelligentsia" graph. Was it done in order to substantiate the claim that "a cultural revolution" had actually occurred in such a short time span, with some 16 percent of the nation's employed pronounced "intellectuals" (*intelligenty*)? The fact was later quite emphatically diagnosed by Soviet sociologists that no more than 3 percent of the employed qualified for the intelligentsia category, the other 13 percent being a quite backward mass of petty bureaucrats whom Seniavskii characterized as "a prospectless (*besperspektivnyi*) layer."

Unfortunately, the inclusion of the *sluzhashchie* in the intelligentsia category then acquired the ring of government status policy, which certainly sounded offensive to others on the social landscape.

▪ "THE RULING CLASS"

Industrial workers, in tsarist and Soviet Russia, had a rather short but difficult and convulsive history, with ups and downs in their well-being, political involvement, and ideological battles in and outside their own ranks. We know of the workers' important role in the 1905 revolution and the two stages of 1917, and of the ravages the civil war and "war communism" caused to them. During the NEP came a peculiar process of "reassembling" of the workers, from the countryside, the army, and whenever possible—from the ranks of the déclassé vagrants and others. But, of course, war casualties, social wrecks, and the upwardly mobile who went into administrations and schools, not the worst of its representatives, were lost for good. They had to be replaced, as ever, primarily by recruits from rural areas, where the majority of Russian workers came from. A much smaller contingent of urban origin, growing with the growth of the cities —from artisan and small trader families, from the ranks of children and wives of workers—also contributed a share.

NEP was a time when the workers, although quite poor and far from happy when facing the new breed of Nepman or state bosses ostentatiously enjoying the better things in life, were still the regime's favorites. They enjoyed preferential treatment in access to schools, they were subjects of promotion campaigns (*vydvizhenie*) to offices and higher positions, and a clear preference was also reserved for them in admission to the party. Theirs was still "the right social origin," although other groups worked hard at eroding this position. Witness to this, as well as to the preferential treatment accorded to workers, was the drive in many nonlabor quarters to gain access, by hood or by crook, to some factory employment and trade union so as to advance even higher—to the metal industry and metalworkers union—in order to acquire this kind of coat of arms and open up other avenues to the regime's favors.

Grievances and causes for complaint were not absent in the ranks of the workers; among them was an unemployment rate reaching almost the 2 million mark and the growing power and numbers of party and state bosses, powerful, arrogant and obviously privileged in many visible and invisible ways. Even the Central Committee complained already in 1926 that the *vysshie chiny* (upper ranks), in industry were being pampered by covert bonuses and perquisites, including all kinds of lucrative *komandirovki* (business travel).

The worker with some industrial experience, especially a prewar *kadrovyi* (cadre), often resented this growing inequality, outside and inside his own ranks—a far cry from those difficult and hungry but more just and equal relations of "war communism."

As the NEP unfolded its economic consequences, the internal differentiation and stratification inside the working class kept growing. The wage differential was almost one to four in 1926, and kept growing, so the trade unions adopted a policy of closing those differentials and engaged in a 1927/28 wage reform with this object in mind. Even with some achievement to their credit, Dogadov's figures published in the minutes of the Eighth Trade Union Congress, the working class showed a one-to-six differential between the 10 percent of the poorest versus the 10 percent of the highest earners. With the average wage still very low, although about 15 percent above the 1913 level, the considerable mass of workers who did not make the average wage lived in great poverty. Workers were known to have reacted angrily to what they felt to be exaggerated income differentials, which actually reached even one to ten, if smaller groups than 10 percent are considered. But they also distrusted every *nachal'stvo* and disliked, even actively baited, "bourgeois specialists," in whom they still saw their former exploiters. This "specialist baiting" did worry the leadership during the NEP, and it did, in fact, have much to do with the very low cultural and living standards of the workers. Some would even put such backward anti-intelligentsia attitudes at the doorstep of the workers' rural origin and outlook.

It would not have been far from the mark to say, to paraphrase a contention by Sukhanov made before the war, that one had only to scratch a Russian worker to find a peasant, ready to return to his origins, especially in times of stress. Such a statement would be exaggerated: a growing number of people, and even their parents, lived in towns and some worked in factories in which their own parents had worked. But those groups were constantly flooded by newcomers, and the diminishing links with the land and weakening of relations with the countryside of some groups would be more than compensated by the influx, which would also lower again the statistical averages of educational and professional standards of the working population. Internal cohesion, or some modicum thereof, would suffer, internal cleavages and stratification would also get exacerbated by the raw recruits, especially when they came in great numbers; and it is known that qualified workers, and even *chernorabochie*, who themselves had come in quite recently from similar surroundings, would despise and shun the rurals, the *derevenshchina*, as the latter were commonly called.

Thus newcomers would always form, for a period, a quite discernibly separate social stratum in the factories. Socially lower than those stood other rurals who were still seasonal workers, not really protected by trade unions, and a further subcategory of the seasonal ones, especially at tough times, who would appear as *brodyachie*—tramps or *lumpen* workers, mainly miners, who would wander off back home, or just to work at peak times in agriculture anywhere, easily severing their industrial ties and as easily restoring them.

Above these groups, stood a large layer of unskilled workers of longer standing; higher yet, the qualified; finally, the highly qualified, not infrequently called aristocrats or kings by the workers themselves. And it must be mentioned that women, recently recruited from rural areas like everyone else, or even from among city dwellers, constituted for a variety of reasons a separate layer among workers—one could even say they formed an underdog group inside the industrial proletariat.

The industrial drive that began in 1928/29 introduced very deep changes in the life of the working class. Many traits of their environment as well as of the whole system were transformed quite drastically. One of the paradoxes of this developmental effort was that during the short period, especially during the first five-year plan, the economic situation worsened and all social relations sharpened to such an extent that a multifaceted crisis ensued for all involved, but was particularly harsh on the workers. The numerical growth of the workers from 3 to 8 million in 1940 is in itself a phenomenon of importance, but this growth was neither uniform nor smooth. The numbers of workers even dropped twice—by 4 percent in 1933, and by 2 percent in 1938/39. The fastest growth occurred during the first plan and later slowed down, coming to almost a standstill toward the last plan, when most of the growth in industrial employment concerned mainly the ITR and officials.

During the NEP, 57 percent of the workers were employed in small-scale industry. Toward the end of the period only 14 percent remained in such branches; 76.5 percent were employed by factories with over 500 workers; 63 percent, over 1,000; a third, 10,000 and more. In addition, the majority of all workers and other employees worked in the new plants built during the plans. Many of the old factories were considerably enlarged and renovated, and the technology, thanks notably to intense importing of machinery, was now new and up to date, and the mass of workers, whether *kadrovye* or just fresh from the fields, now faced a technical challenge which it was not easy for them to meet. Nor were there many qualified people around to teach them how to handle things. Machine and limb breaking in these conditions became a massive and everyday phenomenon, not to mention the poor quality of products, notably the constant flood of *brak* (defective products).

The reason for this was simple: the average Russian worker, at the beginning of the plan era, had no more than some 3.2 years of schooling— often not enough to prevent a man from relapsing into, at least, semiliteracy. In the NEP, 20 percent of all the workers worked with machines and had a skill; 80 percent were semi- or unskilled, which meant that they were engaged in simple physical labor. The new machinery, therefore, without proper time and conditions for training and teaching, was a bewildering task—exciting for some of the younger Komsomols, no doubt, but a real strain on others.

The specifics of what historians of labor organization call the partial mechanization of those years[9] begot two phenomena. First, this mechanization created an additional demand for auxiliary nonskilled labor, and therefore the sought-after reduction of sheer physical, unskilled labor was very slow. Except for a few branches, a rather unsophisticated, poorly trained labor force still populated those new factories in great masses.

Second, to enable such workers to deal with machines and get skilled, a process was partly promoted, partly drifted into, of a fragmentation of professions and specializations which devalorized many old and, to some extent, the newly acquired expertise, too. For example, the profession of metal craftsmen (*slesar'*), which was subdivided in 1930 into 12 specialties, featured by 1939 176 such specialties. For a turner this development went from 10 to 109; for an electrician, from 3 to 188. Not unexpectedly, both the phenomenon of "dequalification" for some who had difficulty learning new skills and the fragmentation and splintering of the labor process produced unavoidable effects, some positive and many quite negative, especially stress phenomena, which were little studied in those years but certainly deserve our attention .

Thus, by the end of the 1930s, as a result of much effort put into schooling, the average school attendance per worker climbed to 4.2 years, and some 90 out of 1,000 now had 7 years or more. Reversing the order, 910 out 1,000 had just an elementary schooling experience and, consequently, very low standards of skill and culture. In 1928 Tomskii complained that "we"—i.e., the trade unions and the party—had managed to cater to the cultural needs, through the clubs, of some 20 percent of the workers; 80 percent preferred the tavern. The situation by 1940 was certainly much better, but hardly dramatically so. Several family budget studies even showed that workers dedicated less time to books and cultural pursuits in the mid-1930s than in NEP and that vodka, not unlike NEP, was still a bigger item than the expenditure on "culture." And no wonder. The standard of living, real wages, the lodging situation—all worsened dramatically. And the mighty influx of millions of peasants kept lowering all the good averages and raising the bad ones. But the same flood also was responsible, to a large extent, for the fact that the working class underwent a considerable rejuvenation: a huge percentage of the workers was now under twenty-nine years old, and a considerable contingent was twenty-three years old or younger. At the same time the length of service and industrial experience of the work force was now very short. About 80 percent of the workers had five years of service and less; 38.6 percent, a year or less!

Such youthfulness had, of course, many social and political implications. We should add that the percentage of women among workers grew from 28.8 percent in 1928 to 43 percent in 1940, and they, too, were rather young and mostly rural. They worked in the most unskilled and badly paid jobs and had no time to study because of an enormous additional workload at home. Here was another subgroup in the working class in a visibly inferior, "underdog" position.

All in all, before the war the internal social structure of the workers changed little in terms of the big components. The main strata remained the same, but governmental policies and social strategies and just plain social drift and inertia introduced a larger range into the differentiation and a more pronounced wage (and other benefits) rift between the Stakhanovite top and the underpaid bottom.

• SOCIAL POLICIES AND THE AUTHORITY STRUCTURE

The preceding sketch of the components of the labor force allows us now to treat two interrelated processes that deeply influenced the internal social relations among them in industry: the reshaping of (1) the authority structure and (2) the whole social pyramid.

The so-called *edinonachalie* (one-man management) principle that Lenin began to precognize in 1918 when he concluded that workers control had been a disaster, was officially in place during the NEP. But despite the important role played by the "Red directors," the system was strongly diluted or incomplete because of two countervailing factors. First, the "Red director," even if strong-willed and often able,[10] had no technical training and was therefore dependent on his deputy or chief engineer, who, in most cases, was "a bourgeois specialist." This dependence was too strong not to mar, however informally, the *edinonachalie* principle. Quite often, the pattern resembled more a duumvirate rather than a one-man power.

But there was yet another subsystem which created an additional check on the top manager's power: the official, or de facto, role played by the *treugol'nik* (triangle). The *treugol'nik* composed of management, the party cell, and the local trade union chapter—sometimes in tandem, sometimes in conflict—presented a set of brakes on the manager's freedom of action. The lower levels of the managerial network, especially the foremen, were even more fettered than the top by the two other partners. Foremen often were almost nominees of the trade unions and were thus forced to split their loyalties between their hierarchical superiors and the *zavkom* (factory committee) with its shop floor representatives. The line of command was thus partially broken.

With the growing labor unrest in 1929—and the premonition that more was to be expected—the government began a forceful strengthening of the authority and power of the director. First came, in March, a decree allowing the director to use all the penalties allowed by the disciplinary code, including firing, without first going to the conflict and arbitration machinery—which meant without the sanction of the trade unions. This was a blatant breach of the 1922 Labor Code, a breach that had already been attempted by a 1927 decree, but the trade union had successfully blocked it then. There was nobody now, after the shake-up of the trade unions in 1928/29, to keep on this kind of sabotage. In September 1929 came another decree on *edinonachalie* which attacked the whole triangle principle and set out to break it up. Although it took some doing, during the next two years the position of the trade unions and of the party cell inside factories, and their relations with management, changed significantly. All had to turn their "face to production," as the party's slogan now proclaimed, and from now on productivity, the plan, and discipline became the central tasks, as well as strengthening the power and authority of the director and of management in general.

The *edinonachalnik* (director) was not meant to be some *primus inter pares* or a simple chairman of the board. The aim was to create a real autocrat. M. Kaganovich made it clear in a 1934 address when he explained that "the earth should tremble when the director is entering the factory"— as it did tremble indeed when Kaganovich himself entered. The policy was geared to promoting tough leadership (*zhestkoe rukovodstvo*). Obviously, for this to happen, the trade unions had to be shorn of the prerogatives they previously enjoyed, become fully integrated into the managerial structure, and deal with what was assigned to them—responsibility for social security payments, social competition, and preaching of discipline and submission to managerial authority. The role of the trade unions in shaping wage and salary policy was curtailed, and the signing of collective agreements, nationally, was discontinued from 1935 on. The outcry— including, rather hypocritically, from above—against the trade unions getting "detached from the masses" and bureaucratized was now obviously, louder than before—and more justified.

The party cell—a more powerful organization because of its privileged communications with the ruling party—would nevertheless end up, in fact, as the manager's supportive lobby, his *tolkach*, thus losing its leading position in the factory when at the same time the party's higher authorities were strengthening their own grip on affairs nationally.

But for the leadership in factories really to get tough, in tune with the tasks of those days, additional tools had to be put at their disposal so that they could cope with a drop in labor discipline during the first five-year plan, which some Soviet sources called "appalling." The 1932 decree on discipline now authorized not just dismissal of the transgressor but depriving him and his family, on the spot, of their ration cards and evicting them from their lodging. Giving the director's power over the workers' food, lodging, and other supplies in times of hardship and (it is 1932) famine was a very awesome tool indeed for disciplining and motivating. In 1938 these powers were supplemented by including social security payments into the strategy, and in 1940 by adding criminal prosecution for *proguly* and other forms of indiscipline, although in other forms this factor was always available during the 1930s, when any breakdown of a machine was easily interpreted as "sabotage." Thus, introducing criminal intervention in domains which elsewhere, and during the NEP, belonged exclusively to the sphere of the Civil Code, closed the full circle of the *edinonachalie* principle.

Space does not allow me to show here how this principle was nevertheless cautioned in reality by different social and economic constraints and how the despotic manager, so powerful when seen from below, was himself vulnerable and easily a victim of his superiors' whims. This was, after all, the time of "little Stalins" everywhere—a very meaningful description. A. Bek's novel, *Novoe naznachenie*, gives a convincing insight into a situation and psyche of a powerful hierarch who was almost a serfowner in regard to his subordinates, and in life-and-death bondage in regard to his superior—in this case Stalin himself. The most despotic leadership, though, and an administrative pyramid of command could not have operated without being embedded in a broader social milieu, intertwined with the administrative scaffolding and stratified hierachically itself. Such a social hierarchy was already emerging earlier, but now it was going to be developed further and acquire a more pronounced pattern. We can use the term "status revolution" to characterize this process and strategy.

Broadly speaking, the policies applied in this area—the combined strategy of wage differentiation and social stratification—was aptly called by one Soviet author "deep differentiation"—even if he did not give it our twist—and was pursued during the whole Stalinist period. One part of this policy concerned the widening of differentials in wages, through widespread piece rate, especially the *progressivka*, bonuses and preferential treatment of groups of workers, *udarnichestvo* (shock work), Stakhanovism, special food and goods supply and prizes.

These policies were pursued through persistent campaigns, using campaign methods. This meant fixing targets and demanding fulfilling quotas, like a share of piece rates in overall pay structure, percentages of Stakhanovites among the work force, maybe even soliciting some records to be broken. Later studies complained against such imposition from above of piece rates, without considering local conditions which made these pay methods very often counterproductive. The record mania of the first stage of the Stakhanov "movement," which so excited Stalin, showed very soon its disorganizing effects and met with enormous resistance from workers and managers alike. It was Stalin, I think, who tried to force things through by mobilizing the criminal arm, but Ordzhonikidze, before his death, quite clearly resisted the whole trend of "spectaculars" in production and the prosecution of managers who were lukewarm or opposed, and although Ordzhonikidze committed suicide, his opinions won out. From 1937 on, the content of Stakhanovism was changed, although the term was retained.

▪ THE STATUS REVOLUTION

The broader differentiation, concerning the whole social canvas, proceeded by stages. First, steps were taken, through a series of decrees, to remove the limitations on different intelligentsia groups, including the ITR, in access to schools and lodging. The decrees demanded they be allowed "equality with workers" in access to those benefits. In later years, the same became true in regard to admissions to the party. All the stringencies imposed on others than workers were removed, and it was a clear measure of the reversal of roles we are talking about: the party from now on became firmly—one would say officially and predominantly—a vehicle for officialdom and specialists, broadly speaking, even in terms of numerical strength.

This, of course, was not anything like putting them "on an equal footing" with workers. A constant improvement in salaries and living and working conditions soon produced a stratification, with the workers now at the bottom of the scale, above them the *sluzhashchie*, higher the ITR (with their own internal differentials), next the management and at the top, *otvetrabotniki* or *rukovoditeli*, especially the directorate, now endowed with immense power and privileges. The pay scales, even at the first glance at the averages alone, showed the strata quite clearly. The averages of *sluzhashchie* exceeded those of the workers, those of the ITR were 2 and 2.5 times bigger than those of the workers (according to branches). But a more probing inquiry could show a one-to-ten relation between a good average wage of a worker and his director's and technical director's. And it would easily become one-to-twenty if the lowest paid group of workers is considered.

That much transpires even when salaries and wages alone are considered. Observers, among them André Gide, noticed this ruling elite and also deplored the widespread poverty at the bottom of the pyramid. But he probably did not know about "perks" and payments given covertly, enormous bonuses bigger than the formal salary offered in special sealed envelopes, from safe to pocket. All these were official though unpublicized practices. We have it, e.g., from a biography of Likhachev, the famous director of the Moscow car factory, at one time commissar of transportation machinery, calling in executives from his former plant and asking them to solve urgently some technical problem. He opened the safe, showed a huge bundle of notes, and said: "It will be yours . . ."

Seen from below, from the worker's position, all this constituted a fall from grace. Their position during NEP, however modest, was nevertheless one of preferential treatment; they had freedom of movement and of job selection, a quite effective litigation system against management, an opportunity to criticize managers, a labor code that meant something. Most of this was now gone. They had become inferior to other groups and, most irritatingly, to the pettiest officials. We have the testimony of Postyshev (Ninth Trade Union Congress) who said in 1932 that the workers, when facing Soviet salesclerks, felt like defendants in court. The same applied often to any other officeholder. And the Labor Code has now become a bibliographical rarity.

As to the management that ruled over them, the popular origin of many of them did not change anything in the fact that the powerful *nachal'nik* wielded power over the worker's pay, food, lodging, health, and even over his freedom of movement and freedom *tout court*.

It was all symbolized by the rude and unceremonious *ty* (the familiar "you") used in addressing the worker, who would respectfully answer *vy* (the formal "you")—not unlike the tsarist *zemskii nachal'nik* talking to the low rural volost official—an old tradition, now reconstituted, although without "your excellency."

The other action, also symbolic, was the introduction of another old tsarist practice, the "labor book," starting in 1939. Criminal prosecution for absenteeism or for leaving the factory without permission capped the whole system. Workers became a fettered class, more so than others, despite the bad times all social groups had experienced during those years of terror.

A reliable documentation shows that workers fought back. The idea of some meekness supposedly ingrained in the national character is false. Workers not only disliked excessive inequality, piece rates, Stakhanovism, and bureaucrats, distrusted the *nachal'stvo*, and hated abuse of power, they also let it be known. They complained in thousands of letters to the press and to all the relevant institutions. They protested verbally and physically and looked for all possible and impossible ways of self-defense. Strikes probably kept occurring, but they were now very dangerous. The *tekuchka* now became a form of mass reaction and protest, "a substitute for strikes" and "a barometer of the social climate," as Kerblay suggests.[11] Workers also sometimes killed *udarniki*, jeered Stakhanovites, attacked foremen, and, to finish this list, *kryli gustym matom* ("swore most foully").

They often gained concessions of all kinds, especially because of another powerful weapon, "the refusal of zeal" (my paraphrase of Veblen's "withdrawal of efficiency" which is, probably, even better). Workers also reacted positively to any improvement in their lot—if this happened, but it was not too often during those years. The constant outcry from the workers: "*Snachala nakormi, potom sprashivai*" (Feed us first, then ask) expressed very well the elementary and basic character of their plight.

In those years, an attitude appeared among workers which, when asked to do more than their usual, they expressed in the often heard: "*My lyudi malen'kie, nachal'stvu vidnee*" (We're small fry; the bosses can see it better). On the face of it, an old national tradition of acceptance of authority and submission to it. At a closer look, here is an illustration of a "withdrawal of initiative" common among, probably, quite broad strata of workers still in our days and deeply deplored in many texts.

▪ GENERAL POINTS TO CONCLUDE

We are aware that a concentration on the short term, which was unavoidable in view of the theme itself, may introduce a considerable distortion into the presentation and interpretation of facts. The emerging industrial system, its social structure, its authority pattern, had much that was transient and much else that was here to stay; much that was characteristic of any industrial system, and much that was specifically Soviet. All this is a matter for further study and debate.

There was a considerable rift (*otryv*) between the workers and the higher-ups, especially during the first five-year plan. This *otryv* was the obverse of the so often deplored *otryv* of the trade unions or party officials from the masses, or the neglect of workers' needs by these organizations and management.

All this can be eloquently documented, although we are aware that the intensity of the breakdown of "the common universe of discourse between superiors and subordinates" was fluctuating. It could not have been otherwise, in view of the following three facts.

First, the whole system operated in jolts and tilts that irritated workers and others and produced a constant, nerve-wracking *dergan'e* (harassment), through "storming," forced overtime, endless *perestroiki* (restructuring) of pay scales, broken promises, and changing of norms.

Second, the system in those years considered complaints to be an expression of counterrevolutionary behavior (for instance, the demand "*Snachala nakormi . . .*"), the fight for discipline was treated as class warfare, and the abusive concept of "petit bourgeois vacillations" was a tool to engage in warfare against the workers at a moment's notice.

Third, in view of the low cultural level of all involved and the falling standards of living, the regime had no cultural models at its disposal to offer and share with the worker. The privileged of those days tended to turn to any styles compatible with their means—which would often turn out to be an unpalatable *meshchanstvo* pure and simple. But this includes a disdain for the very condition of workers, and the contradictions that this constituted with official language did not escape the attention of those interested. They now firmly learned the difference between a *rabochii* and a *rabotnik* and, next, the *otvetrabotnik*.[12] These points, of course, demand debate and elaboration.

The material we have brought—and more could be added—showed the appearance of cleavages and rifts and also allows us to reason why the social cleavages did not turn into political ones. Repression and terror alone could not explain the phenomenon. Factors like the cultural level, the relatively short industrial experience of the bulk of the employees (and the fact of upward social mobility for many in the system), the existence inside the working class of large unintegrated segments of newcomers, women, youth, a kind of workers' aristocracy, too, as well as a large differentiation span, all those explain social tensions, crude language, vodka and hooliganism, *tekuchka* and dirt, but may also serve as an explanation for the lack of any direct political challenge to the regime. Such a mass was probably difficult to rule—but easy to control (we remember that labor flows were constantly refractory to planning and organized recruitment, but as to politics, people mainly talked or cursed).

The freshly erected pyramid, social and administrative, of officials, ITR, and administrators was still too unsteady to defend itself from police arbitrariness, but they were sufficiently interested in their social position to lend a hand to the regime's survival.

The "telescoping of stages" and another factor, "the accentuation of backwardness" due to the scope and suddenness of the influx of new machinery, help explain some of the specifics of Soviet development during the plan era and later. The crudity of social relations and social policies, the despotic traits of the system and of the management, their control and stimulation by manipulating hunger or by administrating overdoses of privileges, favors, and perks in an overt or covert manner, the exaggerated material benefits for the powerful coupled with terror against them or others, and in general, the direct correlation and proximity of the carrot and the stick marked Soviet industrialization and the style of the regime deeply.

—11—

THE SOCIAL
BACKGROUND
OF STALINISM

- PREREQUISITES

The examination of social factors that were crucial in shaping or favoring the Stalinist phenomenon can safely begin from a study of the situation in which Bolshevism found itself at the end of the civil war and the self-perception, or rather the ideological (theoretical, if one prefers) terms in which the leadership analyzed the situation at this point.

The minds trained to think in Marxist terms about social development and policies were accustomed to a framework which provided some safe departing points and certainties. Socialism, even if its appearance demanded conscious effort and a revolution, could nonetheless be perceived in some essential contours in the womb of the developed capitalist system—the more developed the latter, the more precise the former. Even for somebody like Lenin, who clearly liked the quotation from Napoleon, "On s'engage et puis on voit," and often acted upon this maxim, voluntarism and idealism were nevertheless built on a sense of historical process that gave the indispensable backing to conscious intervention and ensured that the revolution was not a leap into the unknown but was to some extent a continuation of previous trends.

Russia, by general consent, was a backward country. If before the revolution the quick development of industry encouraged some impatient socialists to exaggerate the growing readiness of Russia for a socialist takeover, there could be no illusions about any such "readiness" by the end of the civil war. The country was devastated, its not too numerous higher and middle classes destroyed or dispersed, its working class depleted or déclassé, and its peasantry seething with unrest. At this moment there were no social forces, no discernible trends in Russian reality which could clearly be counted upon to generate an internal dynamic in the socialist direction—except the pure political will of the leadership. The state machinery, as far as the basic mass of its *chinovniki* (top officials, or rather, "bureaucrats") was concerned, seemed unreliable; the quickly changing party membership was often raw, soon to some extent purely adaptive in its motivations to join rather than ideologically motivated, and not fully reliable either; it had to be reeducated and indoctrinated first, as the original ideals of the Bolsheviks were not originally and naturally shared by the newcomers who soon became the overwhelming majority.

The post-civil war Marxist found himself thus on entirely unfamiliar ground where there was no visible backing "of a process" for the party's long-term ideological aims. On the contrary, the party found itself in a rarefied atmosphere of unpredictability and contingency, generated by chaotic, socially hostile petit bourgeois tides.

Lenin, in a number of pronouncements, showed that he was perfectly aware of the isolation of the Bolsheviks in the country they had conquered. The working class had almost vanished: the ex-tsarist officials who populated the offices were alien; the peasants were deeply dissatisfied and did not want to hear about *kommuniya*—their term for communism; the party membership needed purging; the top layers and the whole old guard were exhausted and weakened by wear and tear.[1]

This self-perception among the leaders of "isolation," of the lack of an appropriate social basis, was crucial. With it went an acutely neurotic fear of dangers for the movement, of its being either swept aside or, more perniciously, losing its identity. In fact, in a situation in which the commitment to their basic ideals was not shared by the masses and was confined to a relatively small layer, this layer found itself under inexorable pressures, causing not only physical wear and tear to individuals but also hesitation and ideological dilution, and thus increasing their vulnerability to dangers inherent in the transformation of dedicated revolutionaries into rulers. They had always known that they might be in power one day—but they had not anticipated that this would occur in social isolation. They hoped and were accustomed to see themselves as leaders, not rulers.

As we shall see, there could be different ways of overcoming, or of interpreting, this essential fact—different leaders would offer different remedies to the basic diagnosis—but one important explanatory factor is worth mentioning here: the sociological dissertations about the class essence and potential of the peasantry, taken *in abstracto*, were probably as true for Russia as they were, e.g., for China. Nevertheless, when Mao took over in 1949, he was certainly not pestered by a sense of isolation from the masses. He took over with the overwhelming support of the peasant multitudes amid whom he and his party had operated successfully for some decades. When Lenin took over, not in 1917, that is, but after the civil war, the country, and especially the bulk of the peasantry, was against him.

One of the important factors behind such an outcome, which was rarely analyzed or admitted by the Bolsheviks, was that they never constituted a real political mass movement, particularly not in the countryside. They were, in fact, and as a matter of strategic preference, an organization of committees, of leaders, professional revolutionary cadres. Although this form was a source of strength and a factor in their success at gaining power, it was at the same time a factor of isolation after power was gained and the civil war won. This does not mean that there was a lack of support from important social forces, including many peasants, during the civil war. The leadership exhibited great skill in gaining such support, isolating some sections, neutralizing or convincing others. But this was support for tactical moves and on the basis of tactical reasons—not a result of identification with the basic, long-term aims and the ideological framework, as would be the case in a genuine mass movement. The party did gain a membership of millions, but this happened much later, after it was already safely entrenched in power, when the circumstances and reasons for joining were very different. And even then the party would still remain weak in the countryside and would continue to suffer from this basic deficiency: its quasi-nonexistence in and lack of experience of the rural world.

▪ THE "SUPERSTRUCTURE" ... IN THE AIR

Lenin diagnosed the situation, not unexpectedly, in terms of relations between the "basis" and the "superstructure." The baffling thing for the revolutionary leaders was that they found themselves in the reverse position to that of Marx in regard to Hegel. Where Marx had put Hegel's dialectics on its feet, Lenin found himself—but without any reasons for self-congratulation—putting Marx on his head: his "superstructure" came before the "basis." The former was supposedly socialist, but suspended temporarily in a kind of vacuum, and the problem consisted not, as it was hoped, in adapting the recalcitrant "superstructure" to the basis, but in first creating and then lifting up the basis to the lofty heights of the most advanced political superstructure.[2]

As long as hopes persisted that the revolution would spread to the West the problem could be disregarded. But now, in the hungry and anguished years 1920–21, it had to be faced.

The elements of a solution were suggested by circumstances rather than by theoretical anticipation. First, the civil war brought with it a fully fledged practice and ideology of "statism," which was undoubtedly quite new to Leninism. Direct and wide-ranging state intervention, mass coercion, a centralized administrative machine as the main lever of action, an enthusiastic apology for statization (*ogosudarstvlenie*)—all were well-known aspects of "war communism" (the other was extreme egalitarianism). Trotsky's statization policy in regard to the trade unions was one example of it. Osinsky's "sowing committees" (*posevkomy*), which became party policy in 1920, grew out of a less-known but widespread and characteristic attitude. Direct state intervention was recommended and justified by different party authorities not on grounds of emergency, but as a socialist principle *par excellence*. According to numerous documents from the archives, state takeover, detailed planning, etc., were seen as ways of displacing the capitalist market (and not just speculation), and *ogosudarstvlenie* was prescribed as the best measure for overcoming the acquisitive nature (*sobstvennichestvo*) and capitalist impulses of the peasantry.[3] Thus it was not a social class anymore—not the proletariat—that served as the epitome and bearer of socialism through the state, rather—imperceptibly, for some ideologists—the state itself was now replacing the class and becoming the epitome and carrier of the higher principle with, or without, the help of the proletariat.

There was here, in embryo, an entirely new orientation and ideology. It certainly was not present in what "Leninism" was before. Although the desirable social backing might be missing, especially because of the whittling away of the working class, the party did not and could not operate in a void: having begun to rely ever more on the state, ever less on the unreliable masses, the state apparatus, whatever the social composition of its officialdom, was gradually taking over the function of principal lever for the achievement of the desired aims.

In such a way, bolshevism acquired a social basis it did not want and did not immediately recognize: the bureaucracy. This was becoming, quite early in the process, a key factor in shaping the whole system, but it needed some evolution and dramatic internal fighting for this fact to sink in, to become fully acceptable and later extolled. The whole turn of events was, in any case, misunderstood by the Bolsheviks, who were not adequately prepared to comprehend the state they themselves were building. The available theory was very inadequate on this score. It was becoming important to study not only the social potential of the proletariat, or the peasantry, but the potential, interests, and aspirations of the growing and changing Soviet state machinery. It is doubtful, however, whether such an analysis is available in the Soviet Union even today. The idea of "lifting up" the basis to the superstructure fostered not entirely unjustified hopes that this would "'normalize" the situation but missed the point that the state system which presided over the building of the basis could influence deeply the very character of this basis and thus of the whole system. In terms of the metaphorical thinking which pervaded this type of analysis, it might have looked ridiculous that the roof should shape the foundations, and not vice versa. But there was nothing ridiculous in such a supposition. It was, on the contrary, very realistic—as events would prove.

▪ WHY THE SCALE WAS TILTED

The statism of the civil war period had to be abandoned and was soon repudiated as an ideology of extreme administrative and coercive policies conceived as the main lever of social change. The New Economic Policy (NEP) was thus to be introduced on the basis of the negation of what was at the very heart of the previous stage, and it produced a remarkable set of compromises, between plan and market, political monopoly and social and cultural diversity, state and society, ideology and expedient. Once it was set in motion, the new policy soon turned into an interesting experience and a model and began to beget appropriate ideologies. The attitude toward the NEP as a "transition strategy" or "transition period" of a long-term character spread among many of the Bolshevik leaders, who came to believe that they had finally discovered the most appropriate way to overcome the isolation from the masses and to strike deeper roots in the social milieu. The key idea here now became "organic change," reformism, gradualism. War communism collapsed, it was argued, because it believed stages could be skipped. But the fallacy begot disaster and could not but be coercive. Moving more slowly, Lenin's new strategy proclaimed, would mean delaying ambitious aims, slowing down the restructuring, but gaining in social support and avoiding overall statism, with its unpalatable implications.

The alternation in actual historical development of two models—war communism and NEP—suggested that two main alternatives were available to the party. The NEP variety, as its main spokesman, Bukharin, expressed it, was based on a revision of a set of assumptions inherent in the isolationist syndrome and challenging it.[4] The peasantry was for him more amenable to cooperation with the party than the more alarmist versions supposed; the peasantry, as reinterpreted by him, ceased to be seen as an automatic begetter of capitalism, and the party therefore could be seen as stronger and socially less vulnerable than the isolationist would suggest. There was therefore no need to hurry with imposing on this society the movement's long-term aims.

As this approach was discarded and replaced, finally, by a revised version of the civil war model, some concluded that things were in any case predetermined and alternatives were not in fact available. The seeds of the new stage and the new extreme model have been seen by some scholars either in Leninism itself, or in the incompatability of socialist aims with the backward Russian environment, or else as an inevitable outcome in harmony with Russian historical destinies. All these assumptions can be disputed. The factors operating in Lenin's period which are sometimes presented as simple prerequisites and seeds of a further Stalinist stage (i.e., just much more of the same) could also be interpreted rather as pre-requisites for one or another variety of an authoritarian, oligarchic system, of which Lenin's regime itself was already one example. Under him, the strategy was to maintain a strong state but not to engage in "statism." It was a strategy that kept the powder dry but looked seriously for a maximum of social support, not only for the purpose of staying in power but also for the purposes of peaceful transformation and development. The leader-ship wanted police but did not engage in building a police state; they felt themselves isolated but did not transform this feeling into "isolationism," etc. Still more traits of the political version of Lenin's days can be listed that warrant viewing it as a species of its own, still open to changes in several directions. Had this not been the case, NEP would not have been possible at all, nor Lenin's conversion to it, nor its wholehearted adoption by quite a squad of (though not all) party leaders. Thus "Leninism" had, as it were, even in the harsh Russian conditions, several "potentials."[5] Why was the NEP, or any modifications thereof, discarded? The answer does not necessarily lie in its unfeasibility. Nor is it at all obvious that the stamping out of social autonomies of any kind, refusal to compromise with social groups, total cultural controls, and other delights of the next version of statism, as well as the glorification of the state, or the nationalist-isolationist bent of its ideology, were the only alternative; the idea that the outcome was a result of a set of circumstantial interactions of different factors is equally plausible. If it could be argued that Russia was too backward to move up quickly without massive terror and all that followed, the same premise makes it difficult to dismiss Bukharin's thinking as unrealistic. How unrealistic was it to assume that Russia was not ready for socialist objectives there and then and needed cautious transitional strategies?

There is sometimes a tendency to mistake the very availability of an alternative (or alternatives) in the NEP situation with the political condi-tions or power relations inside the decision-making structure. These were characterized, broadly speaking, by a constant narrowing of the apex where the decisions were taken, making the party dependent on the vagaries of kitchen political maneuvering, uncontrollable even by the higher- and middle-rank echelons, and hence vulnerable to a significant element of chance in the outcome of political struggles. Moreover, during the pre-Stalinist period, two important trends inside the party contributed to such a "narrowing." The first was the disruption (leading to suppression) of whatever political play there was in the party's upper layers, as a result of which the ruling group lost its unity, its capacity for action, and its ability to counteract moves detrimental to its own freedom. As the leaders elimi-nated each other by denying each other the right to opposition or other institutionalized forms for argument, they ensnared themselves in an ever narrowing political circle. The second was a parallel phenomenon—the appearance and development of the party apparatus—which worked in the same direction. It became ever less important, as it still was in the earlier stages, to win over the party in order to conduct a policy, and ever more important to win over the machinery. As the 1920s unfolded and this trend asserted itself, the question of why one group won is not very complex in itself: one has to study the existing competing perceptions of the situation and the unfolding of events whereby one group eliminates the other and imposes its own blueprint. But there seems no need at this stage to resort to factors of predetermination, although they can be useful at some other stages.

Later events in Eastern Europe help clarify this proposition. There was no internal reason, e.g., in postwar Poland, to stop the "nepien" policies. They could have continued but were interrupted in 1949 by the imposition of re-Stalinization by external intervention. The switch to a fully fledged Stalinist model in postwar Poland rather than the continuation of a more relaxed experimentation resulted from this intervention of a powerful external factor, which also ensured the feasibility of the imposed model. NEP Russia was a relatively underdeveloped country in which an outstanding part was played by a strongly centralized state. It was open to the continuation of the existing model or to the imposition of something different. There was enough in the historical environment, tradition, and social relations to sustain different roads. There is no need to be astonished that a police state could develop in Russia and undertake revolutions from above—this was not a very new thing. But neither is it difficult to imagine a continuation of a NEP situation. In fact, NEP was already there and was quite in line with the character of the country. But, as we have said, the political machinery fell into hands that saw the grain crisis as a bad omen for the model, and it played the same role in regard to the Russian social structure in those years as it played twenty years later, acting as an external force, in Poland and Czechoslovakia.

▪ THE "SUPERSTRUCTURE" RUSHING AHEAD

In the social context, already inherited from NEP and characterized first, as we have said, by a relatively modern state facing a basically rural, hence "local" social structure, and, second, by a party as the ruling linchpin inside the state, with its own machinery ready to be taken over by a resolute small group, the stage was set, we argue, for tilting the scales and engaging the whole country in a very new direction. The initial moves were almost as easy as the act of tilting would be; but soon, in the absence of any countervailing factors, the process turned out to be both irreversible and extremely costly. Haste, the tendency to telescope stages of development and condense them, was both the result of the sense of power of the rulers at the apex of the unchallenged machinery and the cause of a specific "disjointed" pattern of development, with the state rushing ahead, presiding over and preceding social and economic development. The whole process thus became, above all, one of hectic state building and expansion of the state administration.

Engels, in a letter from London to C. Schmidt, written on October 2, 1890, had already argued persuasively that the state enjoyed a high degree of autonomy from social and economic factors, and in deploying its potential it might do one of three things: favor development, block it, or engage indecisively in either.[6] In the Soviet case, at its Stalinist stage, the state in many ways did alternately all three; but it also did much more than Engels anticipated. In terms of the ideological metaphor state action was expected to lift the "basis" to the level of the "superstructure," after which the former would impose its influence on the latter. In fact the reverse occurred: the state engaged in a hectic, hasty, and compulsive shaping of the social structure, forcing its groups and classes into a mold where the administrative-and-coercive machinery retained its superiority and autonomy. Instead of "serving" its basis, the state, using the powerful means at its disposal (central planning, modern communications and controlling mechanisms, monopoly of information, freedom to use coercion at will), was able to press the social body into service under its own *diktat*.

Two phenomena, both resulting from the powerful push of the industrialization drive in its first stages, particularly favored such an outcome. One was the general state of flux into which Russia was propelled by the "big drive"; the other phenomenon, related to the first, was a gigantic turnover of positions, a peculiar social mobility which collectivization and industrialization created. Elsewhere I have used the terms "quicksand society" and "musical chairs" to describe these two processes. In a matter of only a few years the bulk of the population changed their social positions and roles, switched into a new class, a new job, or a new way of doing the same (workers went to offices, peasants became workers or officials, many of them found themselves in schools and universities, millions of peasants suddenly experienced the shocks of the kolkhoz system), and everyone was faced in their new environment with unexpected, harsh realities. For a while, before the dust settled, the whole nation became as if déclassé, some déclassé down, some déclassé . . . up.

The state organization that faced the flux, and was itself quite strained and contaminated by it, engaged in strenuous efforts to master the chaos by different devices. To strengthen the administrative and controlling machineries, with a particular stress on the "organs"—the synonym for security police—seemed the obvious way out of chaos.*

This was, then, one aspect of the situation which pushed the state into

* See Chapter 9, "Society, State, and Ideology During the First Five-Year Plan."

displaying its particular dynamism and inherent tendencies and encouraged it to go all the way through to a full blossoming of a new model. But yet another aspect had to be mentioned. The coercive acceleration and stage skipping, by imposing large-scale, supposedly progressive, forms on an unprepared nation of small-scale producers, without allowing for the very concept of "maturing," brought about a state of social warfare against almost the whole nation, but especially against the peasants. This momentous development contributed to the renewal among the leaders of the old sense of isolation from the social base and the tendency and need to lean ever more strongly on the apparently safest social support: the state bureaucracy. In a later, more morbid, evidently pathological stage, if not the rulers, then certainly *the* ruler would feel the support narrowed down even further to the only really "secure" part of the machinery: the security services. . . .

▪ THE RULING SERFS

It was already mentioned that the civil war, the ravages it caused, in particular the weakening of the urban middle classes, constituted a setback from the point of view of social development and a painful gap to fill. This can be seen from the acute sense of dependence on those bearers of the previous bourgeois culture (and system) whom Lenin tried hard to enlist in the service of the new system. The managerial and professional classes, however depleted and often hostile, were indispensable, and, indeed, turned out to be crucial in building the new state. The acute sense of dependence on those factors is epitomized by the objective of having "our own" intelligentsia, "our own" cadres, etc. The anti-NEP development in the big drive, although characterized by a hectic—one would say furious—activity of raising its cadres, curiously began with a drive against those very forces Lenin thought were indispensable, thus accentuating further, for a time, the loss of some of the vehicles of development inherited from the capitalist period. As the wholesale statization now on the agenda unfolded, and no expert group or social agents—even when considered "allies"—were allowed any autonomy, the developmental drive had to be organized, supervised, and carried out by the only social force available for the task—the party and state administration. The social composition, values, and aspirations of the bureaucrcy would therefore unavoidably, sooner or later, exercise a deep influence on the character of the system. But for the time being the bureaucratic machineries were still quite new, quickly growing, heterogeneous bodies. Their social components have been little studied as yet, and only a tentative sketch can be attempted here.

The lower ladders of the now swelling administrations, in the economic, political, and other spheres, were swamped by newcomers from the popular classes, badly prepared for their new positions, in fact, for the most part poorly educated, if not semiliterate. Such people, finding themselves in positions which however menial were nevertheless endowed with some kind of power over others, very quickly learned to make the most out of it, not always necessarily in palatable ways. "Petit bourgeois mentality," to use the language of official disapproval, soon permeated officialdom and all too often combined greed with incompetence. To visualize the problem, one should only imagine what happens when, say, a service as sensitive as criminal investigation is composed of people who not only have no juridical preparation but cannot even write properly. But such was the situation in the prewar period, and the same was going on all over the administrative spectrum, probably also in the middle ranks, not just the lowest; and it is not forbidden to speculate on the social and spiritual climate which such a milieu generated. *Obyvatel'shchina* ("Philistinism"), another term of official disapproval, became a widespread phenomenon, even among the top brass in the sensitive sectors.[7] Furthermore, the atmosphere of terror, of constant and ever more bloody purges, and the general climate of witch hunt and search for enemies all over the place could not be propitious for a serious job of reeducation and raising standards. Improvements would occur in the long run, but in the short run—and so much in Stalinism depended on events and trends triggered off in the short initial period of industrialization—it is possible to suggest that the mass of culturally low-key lower officialdom was certainly a proper milieu—or even a social basis, to some extent—for the flourishing of the "personality cult" and other irrational trends in those years. The party official Rusanov, a product of precisely such a social background as well as of the *apparat* depicted by Solzhenitsyn in his novel *Cancer Ward*, is an evocative figure and can serve as an illustration of our proposition.

Not less momentous and interesting a factor were the upper layers of the different *apparaty*, now being constituted into a powerful class of bosses (*nachal'stvo*) endowed with power, privileges, and status, but suffering also from considerable handicaps. In the situation of flux in the 1930s, such a stratum was an essential scaffolding for running the system and for its stabilization. The top policy makers were ready to pay them a price, including a system of covert privileges, special supplies, and power over the fate of men, but it was characteristic specifically of Stalin's policy that, although elevated and apparently pampered, they were submitted to a regime of insecurity, controls, and, finally, terror, undertaken against them from above, which allowed them neither security of personal position nor crystallization into a self-confident and competent ruling class. Once more, in a pattern not unfamiliar in Russian history, a ruling layer was created by the state, trained, indoctrinated, and paid by it—exactly as the early tsars, some centuries earlier, created the gentry (*dvoryanstvo*) and enserfed the peasantry for them as a prize for their service to the state. The parallel here is not complete, but similarities remain. In a situation of absolutist rule, the dependence of the servants of the state on the arbitrary rule from above finds its indispensable counterpart in the absolutist and arbitrary rule of officials over people below them, or people *tout court*.

Under Stalin, to sum up this point, the network of bosses (*nachal'stvo*), allowed and asked to be authoritarian and rude toward subordinates and the masses in order to discipline them, acquired a dual character, a Janus-like double face: the one looking down, of a despot; the other looking up, of a serf. One is therefore tempted to ask what would be the ethos, values, mentality, interests of such a bureaucracy, and such a *nachal'stvo*? Wouldn't it support, at least for a time, its own version of "autocracy, nationality, and orthodoxy"? In any case, what actually happened was something amazingly similar to just this. We will have to return to this point later.

■ THE *MUZHIK* AND HIS RELIGION

The peasantry, still the bulk of the nation in 1929, and the relations between them and the state—or rather, the violent clash and prolonged hostilities between the two—played a key role in the shaping of the Stalinist phase of the Soviet system, its outlook, and its ideology.

The rural milieu in Russia during the course of Russian history, and still so during the NEP, had all the traits of a distinct social system, set quite apart from the rest of society. The NEP and its policies probably gave many peasants a sense of social promotion as millions of them became *khozyaeva*, i.e., independent, respected, and self-respecting producers in their communities, even if many if not most of them were still very poor. But this only strengthened for a time the specific traits of the rural world as a system on its own, with deeply inbuilt mechanisms for self-perpetuation and a high degree of conservatism. The essence of this system consisted of (1) the family farm as basic socioeconomic unit; (2) the small scale of the farm's operations; (3) village life as the basic environment, with its still viable, more or less developed, communal institutions.

Such basic traits were further strengthened by a widely shared culture, mostly preliterate in character, with a popular religion as its basic spiritual common denominator, even if local differences in beliefs, folklore, ceremonies, and superstitions presented infinite, often picturesque, varieties over the huge territory. Though the peasants' *Weltanschauung* comprised, of course, many perfectly lay assumptions and assertions concerning the reality of rural life or its relations to other classes, it is safe to say that the hard core of their moral outlook and life philosophy were best expressed by the widely shared religious beliefs. Peasant religion, according notably to Pierre Pascal, from whose ideas I borrow liberally in this section,[8] could not but be very different from the apparently identical denomination common to city dwellers. Traditionally, in fact, the rural world dissented from official versions of Orthodoxy, even if the state approved of them. In fact, it was precisely state approval that encouraged such dissent.

Some of the specifics of the popular religious beliefs are of consequence for the events we are studying. The peasantry, mostly illiterate, were little interested in dogma and were not at all "clerical," which meant that they were relatively little dependent on the clergy and even on churches. Well in tune with the basic pattern of family-centered life in villages scattered over an immense territory, their religion was a homestead cult. The priest had to come to the homestead (*dvor*) to perform different rites, and even without him simple liturgy could be performed by the head of the family, about the house or before the icon inside it. In fact, as Pascal says, "The icon plays an immense role,"[9] as well as the cult of images of saints, relics, processions, and pilgrimages.

The ethical world of the peasantry, as expressed in their religion, was influenced by their communal life, which produced social values that emphasized pity and humility, rejected imposed dogmas, and, in particular, tended to reject any hierarchy, clerical or secular—hence any bureaucracy. Traditionally the popular masses in Russia were excluded from participation in government, and even when certain formal rights were granted, peasants remained beyond the pale of politics, retaining a nonpolitical but nevertheless suspicious, even hostile, attitude toward state officialdom and state coercion. From this point of view, among others, the peasant was particularly "anarchistic." It is worth pondering Pascal's interesting statement, "One should not forget that the revolution in 1917 was, for those soldiers and peasants who made it, a movement of Christian indignation against the state."[10] There certainly is more than a grain of truth in it. Lenin's *State and Revolution*, in which he expressed the hope, in the most anarchistic vein, that the state would wither away as soon as the power was safely lodged in proletarian hands (and this statement was flanked by the acceptance of the peasant's aspiration to his own piece of land), would probably appeal to the sense of social justice and the spontaneous anti-statism felt by the rural masses. The trouble was, as we are well aware, that from the very first steps, especially as the civil war unfolded, the victorious revolutionaries themselves engaged in state building, with plenty of officialdom, coercion, and all the other trappings of statehood. The NEP interlude contained a promise of some compromise, but with Stalin's drive from above this state building took a particularly dynamic turn. It was accomplished precisely in a clash, or warfare against the peasants and this particular anti-*muzhik* slant of Stalin's policies deeply influenced—or rather, vitiated—the character of the state. In more than one way it contributed significantly, as will be shown, to the peculiarly "Byzantine" spiritual climate of the Stalinist autocracy.

For the state and its ideologists, the recalcitrance of the peasants to join the kolkhozy overnight and go "socialist" at one stroke was basically—as officially explained—an expression of their petit bourgeois essence, with its lust for property, supposedly intrinsic indiscipline and incapacity for co-operation in large-scale organizations, trading mentality, and inherent potential for recreating capitalism.

Such assumptions were based on an analysis which was, to say the least, quite imperfect. Its more important role was to provide an ideology to justify the coercive methods against the 'socially alien" essence of the peasantry, or any other social class which did not conform to party policies. Bolsheviks were an urban party *par excellence*, ignorant of rural realities and showing little patience with this mass, so backward and conservative. Had they understood the peasants better, they might have discovered—as some among them came, in fact, to believe, and as other peasant-based revolutionary movements later proved—that, ignorance and conservatism notwithstanding, peasants are not automatically bearers of capitalism and can be interested in participating in important cooperative social experiments and change.

But as things stood in Russia, with the state poised to impose a new way of life and production and the peasant ocean trying to stick to its familiar mode, the clash that occurred was one between what were almost two nations or two civilizations, profoundly different in modes of production and modalities of organization, in *Weltanschauungen*, and in religion (the one stubbornly religious, the other as stubbornly antireligious).

The installing of kolkhozy was supposed to lift the peasantry into a higher, more progressive way of production and life, and this would help close the gap and smooth the basic differences between town and country. The results of the whole operation were quite different.

■ *KOLKHOZY*: THE PEASANTS "ON RATION CARDS"*

The kolkhozy, a supposedly higher form of production and social organization, brought to the peasant, first of all, the thing he dreaded most: a wholesale bureaucratization, or, more precisely, a statization painfully perceived by the peasant as a setback and a fall in status, from the position of an independent master in his home (*khozyain*) to the one of an unwilling servant of state interests. The whole power of the dictatorship was displayed—less than that would not do—to teach the peasants the severe lesson that his first "commandment" should be the delivery of huge amounts of his produce to the state—without adequate remuneration. At the same time, the distrust of the state toward the new "higher" form was such that the main production means were taken away from the kolkhozy and entrusted to special state organizations. Detailed instructions and

---

* In Russian, *na paike*, "submitted to rationing." There was an outcry among the peasants against such a prospect, a real mass lament—and this is well documented. We can therefore safely take it as the most genuine expression of peasant feelings.

plans from above, perpetual intereference by numerous agencies, the dominance of administrations—all contributed to this peculiar socialism without the peasant, a deeply anti-*muzhik* system transforming the whole peasantry into a legally and factually discriminated class, the lowest on the social ladder—the place they traditionally occupied in Russia. Feeling gagged, exploited, and cheated, peasants responded with an age-old weapon: "The lords' abuse of force no longer had any counterweight except the amazing capacity for inertia of the rural masses—often to be sure very effective—and the disorder of the lords' own administration."[11] This statement of the great historian Marc Bloch was intended for the medieval manor, but it fits marvelously our twentieth-century situation. The peasants' passive resistance exacerbated the relation and incensed the leadership even more—and they responded with ever more of the same: controls, pressures, and terror. Quarter was not going to be given in this fight for the strategic good: grain. But stagnation, to say the least, of agricultural production was to be a heavy price for the whole operation. Peasants developed subterfuges of different types, looked for ways of making the best out of their tiny private plot, and shirked, if they could, in the social sector of the kolkhoz. After all, the plot did provide a predictable minimum of food for the family, whereas the work in the kolkhoz, unlike the worker's salary, was a residual, a nonguaranteed quantity, and hence not too much of an incentive.

The statization without a guaranteed income, a higher form without higher yields or standards of living, a collective system which could not feed the peasantry without their tiny private plots—all these were results of the imposition of theoretically advanced forms on people who were not ready for them. The huge agricultural sector, with its kolkhozy, sovkhozy, and machinery and tractor stations (MTSs), with its numerous but unreliable peasantry, became a heavy liability for the system, a shaky segment within its foundations, socially unstable and economically indolent. The function of the state, to squeeze without being able to encourage growth, led to the creation of an array of repressive administrative machinery poised against the bulk of Russia's society. As post-Stalinist writings would show, the systems rural policies were a source of misery, as well as a fertile soil not so much for good crops as for perpetuating the harshest and most self-defeating traits of decaying Stalinism.*

This was why, as we just stated, instead of the promised incorporation into the system in an organic way, the peasants found themselves in a position of discrimination and social inferiority: they continued to exist as a separate class and civilization, nursing, as ever, their distaste for officials and for the state, their feelings being amply reciprocated. No

---

* The writings of numerous novelists interested in the Russian peasantry, such as Ovechkin, Yashin, Abramov, Stadnyuk, and Dorosh paint a picture of desolation and bureaucratic oppression which Soviet social scientists have not yet been able to match.

wonder, for the time being, the so-called collectivization broadened instead of bridging the gulf between the traditional "two nations," the official one comprising the rulers and some of the educated, and the other composed mainly of peasants.

The peasant, nevertheless, would defend his country in times of great national danger, as he always did, even when he was a serf, unless he was beaten by a superior enemy or badly served by his own indolent rulers. But Stalin was probably not too sure about this loyalty. According to the state's pet theories, it should not have been expected.

▪ THE TSAR, THE EMPEROR, THE MARSHAL

The discussion of the peasantry's role offers the appropriate moment to ponder over another significant phenomenon in Stalinism: the return of the modernizing Soviet state under Stalin to the models and trappings of earlier tsardom. The popularity of the tsar builders, impetuous and despotic industrializers and state promoters; the growing rehabilitation of traditions from the imperial past; the epaulettes of generals and marshals; Stalin's own bemedaled chest and lofty titles during and after the war; the recostuming of the state bureaucracy, notably the juridical and the foreign services, into a uniformed officialdom complete with titles almost directly borrowed from the "table of ranks"[12]—all these are well-known events. But the more striking is the deeper affinity and sincerity implied in the changeover of historical antecedents from Stepan Razin and Pugachev, leaders of peasant rebellions, to Ivan the Terrible and Peter the Great, respectively the most absolutist of the tsars and the first emperor.

This spiritual conversion was rooted in a set of striking parallels in the social setting and political situation created in the early 1930s.

The first phenomenon already referred to, the gulf between rulers and the basic mass of the ruled, including not only peasants but many of the educated, took on in Stalin's days the form of a forced collectivization and persecution of many of the educated and recreated for a time a situation already known as "classic" in Russian history. The traits of "dual Russia" and its interpretations have been succinctly and cogently shown in an article by Robert Tucker: its traditional "state–society" dichotomy and the seesaw of "revolutions from above," interspersed with recurrent "thaws," were reproduced in Stalin's times with enhanced sharpness.[13] But the parallel goes further: Peter the Great was engaged not only in an effort of modernization but in a more complex set of social and political strategies. He was creating "*de toutes pièces*"[14] a ruling class, preferably composed of foreigners who could be more trusted because of their detachment from local society and dependence on the benefactor; he was building a regular bureaucracy and a modernized governmental machinery;

and at the same time he made the dependent status of the peasantry and the regime in which they lived harsher than ever. In very different circumstances and with notable differences in many aspects, Stalin was engaged in a similar project: industrializing forcefully and impetuously, speedily building and expanding a fully bureaucratic rule, producing his *nachal'stvo* "*de toutes pièces*" (although not necessarily from foreign nationals, rather from the lower classes themselves)—and at the same time changing the status of the peasantry into a new, harsher regime of dependence upon the state and its officials.

The taming of the peasantry, which was thought of as the citadel of backwardness and unruliness, a menace to the state, was thus a repetition of an old theme, duplicated also, and characteristically, on several other planes: the figure of an absolutist ruler, the police state, the dependence of the ruling elite on a capricious rule from above, the no less capricious and deeply resented rule below, the upper layers yielding meekly to the autocrat, the masses to the petty bureaucrat. The reproduction in a new garb of this latter feature—the dominance of local potentates—had a particularly old smell to it.

The building of a mighty state facing a weak society, successfully statized and controlled, is also a remake of an old feature, but on a large scale. The state was here once more engaged in making and unmaking ruling groups, making them into an appendage to itself, imposing forms of social and economic activity, deeply influencing class relations, running the whole of the economy, transforming rulers and ruled alike into cogs of the state. The state thereby reproduced patterns of the past, although, characteristically, not of the near but rather of the earlier, eighteenth-century, versions. Tsardom, after all, began to mellow from the mid-nineteenth century on; it engaged, however halfheartedly, in important social and juridicial reforms; some groups and classes—entrepreneurs, workers, peasants, intellectuals—emerged and began to evolve autonomous, often antitsarist, attitudes and activities. The political structure proved inadequate to reform itself so as to make room for such development and for the further emancipation of social forces, and this is why it was finally rejected, with the hope that more room for social initiative and greater freedoms would be achieved.

Stalinist development brought about a different outcome: as the country was surging ahead in economic and military terms, it was moving backward, compared to the later period in tsarism and even the NEP, in terms of social and political freedoms. This was not only a specific and blatant case of development without emancipation; it was, in fact, a retreat into a tighter than ever harnessing of society to the state bureaucracy, which became the main social vehicle of the state's policies and ethos. Hence the tendency to borrow so much from the earlier, more despotic antecedents, which were so resolutely rejected and repudiated by the new regime in its earlier, more youthful age.

▪ "THE CONTAMINATION EFFECT"

Three factors seem to be crucial in favoring the phenomenon of Stalinism, with its personal rule, extreme dogmatism with strong pseudoreligious undertones, and renewed nationalism—a remodeled "autocracy, nationality, orthodoxy" (*samoderzhavie, narodnost', pravoslavie*) version: (1) the un-hinging of social structures and the flux created by the industrialization effort and its methods; (2) the characteristics of the growing, although as yet far from stabilized and not fully self-conscious bureaucracy; (3) the historical-cultural traditions of the country, in particular those represented by the peasantry. All three factors, in conditions of a strenuous and hasty industrial development, favored a development in the same direction: a reliance on the might of the state, ending up with idolatory of the state— a particularly important trait in the system. The widespread sense of in-security throughout the *apparaty*, including the top layers, prompted many of them to hang on to and support the alleged symbols of security and stability in the system—the general secretary and his "cult." Finally, different layers in the leadership, either as deliberate strategy or as a result of a genuine urge to bridge the gap with the masses and to strengthen the system's links with them, encouraged adoption, diffusion, and concessions to nationalist and other spiritual traditions of the urban, but especially of the rural, masses.

Incidentally, the peculiar factor of haste should be underlined and its influence explored. Its role in shaping events in the sphere of economic planning and management has been studied by economists. It is worth venturing, quite tentatively, on the basis of the Soviet experience, the fol-lowing maxim: The quicker you break and change, the more of the old you recreate. Institutions and methods which seemed to be entirely new, after deeper insight show the often quite astonishing reemergence of many old traits and forms. This does not apply only to the obvious example of the army, but certainly to many or most ministries and other institutions; probably also (why not?) to the secret police. The *sancta sanctorum* of security, inaccessible by definition to unproletarian elements, certainly employed, as the army did, some (if not many) of the specialists of the tsarist police. And they could not but help restore many of the features of the predecessor in the making and functioning of institutions. In any case, whatever the value of this kind of hunch, it is no hunch but hard fact that the more the Stalinist system rushed ahead with its economic development and socialist transformations, the deeper it sank into the quite traditional values of authority, hierarchy, and conservatism.

The spiritual climate, one would expect, must also have been influenced by the basic social fact of those years: the remolding of a rural environment or reshaping of recently ruralized cities. The whole system, society and state, rulers and ruled alike, could not but become deeply transformed— each often in quite unexpected ways—during this prolonged clash of initially opposed principles and forces operating in such a social mileu. In the process of remolding and combatting the "petit bourgeois mentality and spirit" and the religious mind of the masses, a "principle of contamination" (a mock law but with some real content behind it) began to operate and display its astonishing results. In the effort to eradicate the peasant mentality, its religion in particular, the not too successful educators or crusaders often reached the obvious conclusion that ceremonies, festivities, and other deeply seated traditional family and village mores should be combatted by proposing the same but in a secular form. Actually, the failure of the antireligious campaign was to some extent a result of a lack of understanding of this so often berated mentality. The attack on churches and clergy, for example, was a wrong choice of target: the popular religion was homestead-based and could easily adapt itself to the absence of clergymen and liturgy.

But the proposed tactic, which was to offer secular icons instead of religious ones, turned out to be a double-edged sword. In the course of the supposedly Marxist crusade against the "opiate of the people," the whole spiritual climate of the system showed signs of succumbing to some of the age-old currents of the Russian Orthodox civilization, absorbing some of its not necessarily most inspiring values. The traditional devotion to and worship of icons, relics of saints, and processions was apparently being replaced by a shallow imitation of iconlike imagery, official mass liturgy, effigies, and, especially, processions and pilgrimages to a mausoleum sheltering an embalmed atheist.

One telling example of extolling some of the more primitive trends of rural society when state interests seemed to have warranted it, and offering it as a value for the whole nation, is the policy in regard to the family undertaken in the later 1930s. This policy deserves a deeper study, but for our purpose here one point is worth mentioning: it was clearly the large, archaic rural family, with its high demands on the reproductive faculties of women, authoritarian structure, and apparently solid moral stability, that was presented as a model. It is enough to read *Pravda* of 1936, during the campaign for family, fertility, and authority, to discover where the "model" was taken from. The "crusaders" themselves got trapped in some of the least modern, most orthodox, and most nationalistic elements of their tradition, now put to use as ingredients of a renewed worship of the state and of its interests. Somebody might have tried eventually to rationalize these currents as a premeditated strategy indispensable in a country whose people need to worship. Prostrating themselves in awe and adoration before the splendors and trappings of statehood and its head, as it used to be under the old tsardom, might have looked like a display of a good knowledge of mass psychology. In any case, from the idea of emancipating the masses from the mental structures inherited from an unglorious past, the system moved into a stage of recreating replicas, if not better versions of the same. The cult of Stalin could not help begetting demons, agents and saboteurs, sinful criminals, abject and pitiful apostates eager to desecrate all that was sacred. The features of the Russian soul, supposedly balanced between the extremes of downfall and absolute repentance, descent into deepest sin and relief of the fullest confession, were fully catered to in Stalin's "ritual of liquidation."

That many people in Russia took the bait and responded to these out-pourings of demonology is beyond doubt. But was this development really a result of Russian mystical-Orthodox leanings or of popular religious beliefs and a *muzhik* mentality? Or was it, as previously suggested, a re-sponse to what was *believed* to constitute popular irrational needs? The distortion and misrepresentation by city spokesmen of the popular needs of peasants, the camouflage of one's own idiosyncracies as a response to somebody else's needs, are not uncommon in civilizations where the gulf between the popular masses and the political and educated establishment is deep, especially in times of stress and crisis. It is therefore worth consider-ing also the thesis that the cultural trends of the Stalinist era were not necessarily responses to what the peasants wanted to get but rather an expression of the psychic and mental tensions and values of the officials and leaders of a state machinery that was rapidly growing within and in conflict with a still age-old rural civilization. There is no way of explaining what was clearly a deep cultural retreat and the demeaning of culture, to say the least, in terms of some direct influence of the peasantry. But the indirect influence of the rural milieu on the peculiar backward way of moving forward, fraught with tensions and distortions inside the ruling *apparaty* engaged in shaping this milieu, is worth exploring. In other words, then, one is tempted to ask whether Stalin projected his personality over the nation because of politico-strategic considerations, on the basis of his understanding of Russian mentalities, or whether this was an expression of his own psychic drives and needs.

Considering the many traits of his system which went as soon as he disappeared, the latter assumption is a quite tempting one, in the last analysis.

▪ "THE PERSONAL EQUATION"

"Where the legal tradition is weak, the personality of the ruler becomes of crucial importance," maintained a knowledgeable scholar. One could add, where the legal tradition is weak and when whatever there is of it is shattered, propitious conditions are created for the very appearance of such a ruler. Obviously, more than the personal factor should be intro-duced to understand Stalin and his "ism." The broad social background has already been sketched and should be kept in mind when considering a narrower but essential factor: the processes working inside the ruling party, shaping or unsettling it. Two phenomena are crucial on this score. First, the change of "social substance," in other words, the continuous changes in the social composition in the party, from a bare 20,000 in March 1917 to the 250,000 or more at the end of the same year, getting halved and then once more doubled around 1919 alone, with the curve sharply fluctuating till the first million or more at the end of 1928 was reached. At this point there was a pause for a while, but the process then went on unabatedly. This implies a speedy turnover and influx of entrants, and the initial group of founders could not but get immersed in large layers of newcomers, constantly pushed by other newcomers from the depths of Russian society. The newcomers entered a party which was not engaged anymore in fighting tsarism, as the founders were. They did not share the values and motivation, the culture and sophistication of the old guard. Now, facing the country and the new party layers, this old guard, as a group of leading politicians, were unable to unite and to create for themselves conditions indispensable for a stable ruling elite. The failure of the old Bolsheviks to constitute such an elite or oligarchy proved the cause of their demise. As they faltered, the party succumbed to the machinery which emerged and took over—and to those who knew how to build and run such machinery, with one important addition: those at the top of the party *apparat* also had under their control the police and the manipulation of ideology and information.

The stage was thus set for a takeover, on a winner-take-all principle. Today, an enlightened party critic would ask sadly: How did it happen that there were no guranteed or countervailing powers against such a takeover? The fact remains that the pre-1928 history of the party consisted of a set of moves which kept knocking out those countervailing devices that still existed. The last such step was taken by those leaders who preferred Stalin and helped him extinguish the last opposition. They themselves then succumbed to the same mechanism they had used against others. But this is quite well known by now.

Stalin was the man who took what levers of power the previous period offered (he himself had been instrumental in forging some of them earlier), tilted the scale in a new direction, reworked the whole ideological and political framework, and launched the system not only into speedy industrialization but also, unabashedly, into state building of a particular kind: the state as the main tool and as an aim in itself, the highest principle, in fact, of his socialism. He also did more. In the framework of his statism he openly espoused overall terror and even identified himself personally with the police state of his making. He was, in brief, a system founder and its ideologist and did the job of adapting the previous ideological framework to the reality of this new system. But this reality was complex—and so was Stalin's role in it.

Some historians of tsarist Russia point out that in the course of its development the despotic rulers tended to change their roles and the character of their powers, and adapt them to the system they were presiding over, without changing the formal image of the tsar as autocrat (*samoderzhets*). Ivan the Terrible and Peter the Great belonged to those who managed to get rid of pretending social groups and build new subservient elites and machineries instead. Thus Ivan battered the boyars and founded his Oprichnina; thus Peter, too, built "from scratch" a new ruling stratum and a governmental machinery. Founders and modernizers of this kind remain at the top and can preserve the notion of "autocracy" and the reality of it. But a process sets in whereby the machinery and the ruling strata assert themselves, stabilize, and finally change, in substance if not in law, the reality of the 'autocracy" itself. Nicholas I was probably the last real autocrat. The later tsars gradually became heads of this bureaucracy, as their despotic power and their freedom of action was reduced and their dependence on the bureaucracy grew. This change from autocrat to top bureaucrat never worked itself out fully, and the tsars still enjoyed enormous power. But the trend was there. Something similar was also happening under Stalin. Under the tsars, however, the trend took two centuries to make itself felt; under Stalin, when historical processes were immensely intensified and compressed, this occurred in one leader's own lifetime.

Unsettled and shaky as the state machinery still was in its speedy growth during the 1930s, pressure for "settling down," for a regularization of their positions and working conditions and for a say in government began to reassert themselves. Such pressures, emerging from the ruling stratum of the state and the party, certainly began to be perceived by Stalin. We stated that the former found themselves in a situation of powerful serfs. One has only to recollect the description of the atmosphere in the leadership around Stalin, as presented by Khrushchev in his memoirs, to see that here was a textbook case of relations bound to exist between a despotic and powerful ruler, in full control of the job and fate of each of his hand-picked helpers, and even the narrow circle of potentates around him, who are denied the security of their lives, not to say their jobs. A *ruling class without tenure*—this was the system Stalin created for them, and it was far from palatable. No able man among them could have believed that this was somehow "historically" or otherwise justified.

Quite early, therefore, trends and pressures should have emerged to "normalize" the situation. This did not necessarily mean a desire in the machinery to get rid of Stalin—although many certainly would have welcomed it—but to change his functions so that the whole model could be ruled in accordiance with its "logic," i.e., the interests of the bureaucracy and its top layers in particular. This was, in fact, to be achieved, but only after Stalin's death.

Stalin was not ready to accept the role of just a cog, however powerful, in his own machine. A top bureaucrat is a chief executive, in the framework of a constraining committee. The system, in my view, was getting ready for it quite early (the Kirov tendency in 1934 eventually expressed precisely this), and those observers who after Stalin's death were predicting that by the very character of the system a new Stalin must emerge were missing the point. But Stalin had had the power and the taste for it—for ever more of it—since he had led the early stage of the shattering breakthrough and gotten full control over the state in this process. At this point, the traits of his gloomy personality, with clear paranoid tendencies, become crucial. Once at the top and in full control, he was not a man to accept changes in the pattern of his personal power. He continued to defend his place in the system and to inflate its dependence on him. He assumed the role of linchpin in the whole structure, "personalized" this pattern to the utmost, and, well in line with his self-image and personal dynamics, identified the whole with himself, and himself with history. He achieved a position when he would have been fully justified if he had stated, "L'état c'est moi"— and with a vengeance, because this "identification" of a man with a position and with history, concealed a potential for losing the indispensable sense of proportion between the personal and the historical, and thus opening the gate to madness, Consequently, changes in the essence of his power and role in the system were out of the question for him. He therefore took the road of shaking up, of destabilizing the machinery and its upper layers, in order to block the process fatally working against his personal predilection for autocracy. This is a suggestion which helps to explain the purges and also some broader aspects of Stalin's role as ruler in Soviet history. By fighting for the continuation of his power, he took the system into a damaging, "pathological" direction, began actually to wreck it: the more the arbitrary rule unfolded, the more it displayed its inadequacy in running a rapidly developing country and its emerging new social forces, both at the base and at the summit of the social hierarchy.

▪ BOLSHEVISM AND CLAUSE 58⁹ OF THE CRIMINAL CODE

The personal dynamics of Stalin which would not allow him to accept the role of the later tsars and made him prefer the role of the earlier ones is a matter, and quite a complicated one, for biographers. Nevertheless, singling out the personal role of Stalin in "Stalinism" from the other factors revealed by sociohistorical analysis, although it has its difficulties, is a crucial task. In response to real pressures, even if often transformed in his mind into misinterpreted mythological phantoms, Stalin used or manipulated three interdependent levers. First, his own "cult" (he certainly was helped by his would-be "priests" in establishing it) as a peculiar method of communicating with the masses, over the heads of the bureaucracy, as well as with the bureaucratic mass itself, over the heads of their bosses in party and state. But this wouldn't have worked without the additional support generated by the reactivation of trends from the past which were still present in the mentality of many Russians, by the industrial dynamism, and by the forces of inertia and conformism, on which some systems thrive better than others.

But an even more important lever, the second in our count, was the "alliance" of the ruler—a powerful institution by now—with the secret police, without or against the party, and then, thirdly, the provision of an appropriate ideological justification for such an alliance. All three are the essential ingredients of the Stalinist trademark. The building up of the secret police as partner in the "alliance" consisted in elevating them above the party and transforming them from a more or less conventional security force into a powerful economic agency with noneconomic methods at its disposal. This was at the root of the enormous *univers concentrationnaire* (to quote the title of a well-known book by David Rousset), which was to become yet another "essential" part of the Stalinist system. Without it, the term would have meant something quite different.

Vyshinsky, Stalin's great inquisitor, was probably the best spokesman and interpreter of Stalin's intentions and ideologies relevant to our theme. He certainly knew not only his master's written word but also his voice and intentions. The key idea which he quotes from Stalin maintains that the disappearance of classes will come about "not by means of a lessening of class conflict but by means of its intensification." the same applies to the thesis about the withering away of the state, which will occur "not through weakening state power but through a maximum strengthening of the state in order to defeat the remnants of the dying classes and to organize a defense against capitalist encirclement."[15] There is no need to polemicize with such statements. Why should one manage with only a weak state to eliminate the bulk of enemy forces but need a mighty, ever mightier machine of oppression in order to suppress just some remnants? The logic is no object here. The essential thing is that this is Stalin's central strategic *motto*, the very heart of Stalinist strategy. Vyshinsky added more than a touch of characteristic clarification to it and crossed the t's in his attack against Bolshevik jurists (whom, incidentally, he helped to their graves). They reiterated all too often the old Leninist adage about this withering away of the state and of law but gave it, not unnaturally, a different twist from Stalin's. Vychinsky's rhetoric against those lawyers is telling: "We have scarcely understood yet what a diversionary character, in the direct sense of this word, i.e., in the direct sense of Clause 58[9] of the Criminal Code of the Russian Republic, this word had."[16] This venom concerned men like Pashukanis and Stuchka, even Krylenko—but, in fact, the passage was more significant than that. This clause, as well as a few others of the same notorious paragraph 58 of the Criminal Code, defined counter-revolutionary sabotage, diversion, etc., and was used against the bulk of the cadres of the Bolshevik party and against one of the important promises in Leninism, without which it wouldn't have existed at all as a revolutionary force: the promise of more freedom and justice and the emancipation of the masses. This is the deeper meaning of the "withering away" thesis, but now it became a directly criminal, counterrevolutionary action, with the sinister Clause 58⁹ attached to it.

The "remnants of the class enemy" could not have become so dangerous if they engaged in an open fight. But they would act, Stalin taught, surreptitiously (*tikhoi sapoi*) as covert agents of foreign intelligence and would use the most devilish means of masking themselves[17]—and the only agency able to cope with this kind of sneaky enemy would be the secret police. Hence, it becomes for the regime its most cherished institution, its symbol. Of course, the diversionist ex-Bolsheviks were so treacherous precisely because their thesis about the "withering away of state and laws" did aim at those very sacred services of the state. Vyshinsky stated this explicitly: the diversionary work of the previous generation of old Bolshevik jurists "was in essence aimed at suggesting the 'thought' that such state levers and means of struggle as the army, navy, counterintelligence, NKVD, courts, prosecution were unnecessary, that they had, so to speak, exhausted their historical role." One couldn't have expressed more clearly this defense of the police state, as a principle, against the old Bolshevik ideas and, specifically, against the "rightists" with their demands to move forward "peacefully and smoothly" (*mirno i plavno*).

This polemic (which, incidentally, may make Vyshinsky's victims more sympathetic to us, if it was true that they paid with their lives for their dislike of repression and police agencies) offers the full formula for unleashing precisely the oppressive functions of the state and extolling its oppressive organs. For Stalin this aspect became not only a matter of politics but, here too, a mark of personal identification. He trusted the secret police and only them: the management of his household, of his numerous identically built and furnished villas, was actually entrusted, after the suicide of his wife in 1932, to Beria's services.[18]

■ "LEGALITY" AND "EXTRALEGALITY": TWO MODELS IN ONE

Under the label "enemies of the people" perished the flower of the Bolshevik party, the old cadres as well as many newer ones of the post-revolutionary period. The baffling thing about this destruction was its wanton character, its utter folly, as it obviously wrecked the very interests of the system Stalin himself was building and presiding over. If it was madness, as it might well have been, there was nevertheless some method behind it. It was political madness of a man with the supersensitive feelers of a paranoiac. He clearly disliked the past of his party and its ethos—and destroyed it. But he also refused, as we have argued, to accept the contours of the pattern emerging under his own post-Bolshevik rule, whereby the new social groups, especially the state and ruling strata, began to take shape and consolidate their positions. Some other ruler might eventually have yielded to the new order, made the best of it, and accepted an honorary presidency or even a quite effective leadership function.[19] But a man like Stalin might have perceived such tendencies as encroachments by despicable creatures of his own making closing in on him and trying to despoil him. He therefore defended with fury his own power and his own system.

What was in fact emerging and closing in on him was a new political order which he himself helped bring into the world by a caesarian operation. On the face of it, those years were the ones of full Stalinism, although not everything that happened was of Stalin's doing. In fact, he was presiding over the creation of two political models simultaneously, which were not perceptible to contemporaries but can be discerned today, and were perceived, as we have said, dimly and gloomily by Stalin himself. Very soon these two models found themselves in an unhappy and tension-generating coexistence.

The problem of an uneasy if not outright impossible symbiosis of "legality" and "arbitrariness" in those years can help highlight the issue. The seesaw of mass transgressions of "socialist legality" and of campaigns to make the "excesses" good is a well-known trait of Soviet history, especially in the Stalinist period. It is also very characteristic that at the very height of police terror, in the years 1935–38, the theme of reinforcing legality, rehabilitating the concept of law, was being voiced and preached. The theme needs some exploration.

The talented Russian scholar N. M. Korkunov, in his study of the Russian state and law—an equivalent in those days of the modern "political science"—defined "autocracy" and "autocrat" (*samoderzhavie* and *samoderzhets*) as the sovereignty of the ruler, the unlimited character of his rule, but at the same time the need to limit this rule by legal principles, basic laws of his own making. The reason for such a tendency, he maintained, was twofold: (1) legality allows the masses to identify with the system—otherwise the lawless system is felt as tyrannical and cannot be stable; and (2) the ruler, in order to control the state machinery directly and efficiently, requires a clear legal framework for the smooth working of state institutions and bureaucracies. Without it they would be acting purely arbitrarily and would help to destroy the unity of the state instead of serving this unity and the interests of the ruler himself.[20] These remarks help to highlight the problems of the 1930s very aptly. The extralegal massive measures taken in the process of collectivization, industrialization, and, later, the search for "enemies of the people" shattered the social fabric, and there certainly was a deep craving among the officials as well as in the population for the security that only a firm legal framework could provide. To regularize, to consolidate, to reinsure, to ensure a ruly and predictable working of the responsible institutions, some kind of "consti-

ve—the cult, the police, the ideological manipulation, and
e mentality. Not unexpectedly, most of those did not survive
ng.

▪ CO   LUSION

The Stalinist model *sensu stricto* was powerful enough, mightily favored
as it was by the state of social flux in its early stage and by the whole
pattern of social development to which we have referred. It was a pattern
in which the social structure evolved under the influence of an already
existing and all-embracing state organization, became subject to a powerful
controlling mechanism, and in which state control was to some extent
accepted as a fact that was already familiar, although to a lesser degree,
from the previous framework.

In the industrialization process, with the superstructure, as it were, rushing ahead of the emerging social basis, all the important social groups
found themselves "bureaucratized" and fully dependent on state administrations. The statism is important, as its many traits were there to stay.
But its development was a complex and contradictory affair.

On the one hand, it evolved forms and structures of an autocratic power
pattern reminiscent in many aspects, even reproducing directly, traits of
the imperial past. But the meeting of hearts and the affinity with the past
statehood was not a replica of the past but a new, original creation, a
hybrid of Marxism and tsarism, a transitory phenomenon that was confined to the Stalinist stage alone.

As the state developed and the initial tensions and flux began to subside,
the statized structure began to evolve into a stable pattern, but this was
not allowed to take definitive shape because of the vigilant counteraction
of the power pattern in control, the strictly Stalinist one. The latter found
propitious conditions for its development and was offered the opportunity
to run out its full course. After the stage of "development without
emancipation" of the earlier period, this ushered in a stage of "development with oppression," which soon evolved into a full social and political
pathology.

The larger model of a more ruly, oligarchically run bureaucratic system,
which emerged after Stalin's death, could already be perceived in the
shadows of Stalinist rule but could not shake off the harness as long as the
initial stage of the state's warfare against the nation of small producers
went on. In order to tame Stalin, it was necessary to stop this warfare and
the warfare mentality and return to social and economic policies of a
"normal" character. Stalin and his entourage, on the contrary, were thriving
on warfare and siege conditions and mentalities and did all they could to
perpetuate this state of affairs—even by using, as a matter of strategy and
ruling method, the hallucinating procedure of inventing hosts of mythical

enemies and destroying masses of people in the process. This was a case not only of the divorce of a "state" from "society" but also of the divorce of a leadership from the interests of the state. For the nation it was an unmitigated catastrophe.

At the same time, it has proved an embarrassing legacy for the leaders of our day. They share quite a set of assumptions with the demonic leader and cannot easily explain how they, the party, etc., can be presented as innocent of past practices or immune to the dangers of a repetition of the same.

Be that as it may, their system offers further scope for development and serious improvements. The ruling stratum is presided over, not raped; the system's *pays politique* is larger than before; communications and contact with the popular classes have considerably improved; and the quality of leadership in many walks of life is much higher. Whatever the improvements, though, as far as the social system at large is concerned, political domination, ideological monopoly, and the tight controls of this modernized "statism" continue to generate problems—in particular in those areas where the inheritance from the 1930s is concerned. And such areas and principles are still very much present in Soviet policy.

—12—

GRAPPLING
WITH STALINISM

Rather than deal with the phenomenon of Stalinism in any exhaustive way, the aim here is to introduce into the study and discussion of the system and period in Soviet history some elements, not necessarily original, that have not been fully "employed" yet in our search for an adequate explanation of what still continues to be, to a large extent, enigmatic. Facts and ideas derived from the study of the social history of Russia prompts one to get more "historical" in thinking about Russia, to incorporate factors from the past which, it may turn out, were still unextinguished and mightily at work in the earlier stages of the regime and not yet fully accounted for as driving forces that shaped events and structures about to follow.

In fact, a statement like that may even sound a bit trite. But it is a fact that most of the thinking about Russia turned to some general concepts and to political and ideological factors that looked more attractive and, somehow, pushed historical insights aside. Some of those attitudes and theses acquired even the dubious status of obsessions and outright fallacies. One widespread approach insisted on Leninism—and on the Leninist conception of party organization—as the root of Stalinism and Stalin. The former seemed to have implied the latter, carrying the next stage in its womb almost by definition. Thus Leninism, a political ideology, is presented as the main "culprit"—the primary cause of a specific unfolding of Russian

286

postrevolutionary history, a demiurge that exhibits its potential, explains itself, and makes history—without much of an input from social and historical factors. It was lost on many observers that powerful factors were at work, before and after the revolution, that shaped events, leadership, and ideology itself, and they could have affected Leninism and Stalinism in different ways, including the ways the two phenomena related to each other. The aura of a successful revolution—or, if one was opposed to it, its opprobrium—contributed to the not uncommon phenomenon of singling out an outstanding event for its intense heat and spectacular quality and seing in it an absolute divide in historical development, which supposedly cut the links with the past radically. Wasn't this the essence of what was aimed at—and held from now on to be solely responsible for all the future chapters? In the eyes of some of the participants, it actually was responsible only for the nicer things that followed, the less palatable being put at the doorsteps of either "deviations" or "vestiges of the past," which were bound to disappear without a trace anyway. Eric Hobsbawm pointed to the fallacies that overconcentration on revolutions or similar shattering events can beget.[1] And one could add more fallacies that stem from abusing the portmanteau device of "vestiges of the past," of which some Soviet writers are still very fond. Religion, greed for predominantly material possessions, criminal behavior—these are some examples of the supposed "vestiges" for which the regime did not wish to carry the blame. Western scholars rarely "bought" this later type of explanation, but they did often accept the impact of revolution as a quasi-absolute breaking point and perpetuated it in their specializations and departmental divisions, thus causing a considerable loss in interpretative power.

Another widespread approach, mostly interested in leaders, resulted in a set of one-sided conclusions which are to be expected whenever personal ambition and power struggles at the top of the social and political ladder are made into the very substance of historical inquiry. Unavoidably, fascination with the mighty and highly visible makes deeply seated matrices of social relations and profound cultural and long-term economic trends less interesting or, at best, relegates them to the background.

Overreliance on certain types of class analysis by Bolsheviks and their heirs, as well as by some scholars abroad, also became a source of considerable political and conceptual difficulties, especially for the actors and leaders of the events in Russia. An all too eager "application" of a class analysis taken from an armory developed in and for a rather advanced capitalist society, when tried in a society still in the early stages of some expected course of history, in transition or in flux, where a mixture of forms coexisted or meshed, could easily misfire. Tsarist Russia was exhibiting precisely such traits, and the new Soviet rulers still used the same analytical tools and desperately tried to discern in their postrevolutionary society either full-blown classes or at least their clearly discernable prefiguration which could lead to the preferred future or drive the system dangerously back into restoration. This was done in order to gain an insight into the historical process and use it as basis for policy making, but it remains a fact that the postrevolutionary Soviet leadership often looked the other way, in the wrong direction, made a long list of blunders, and, at a later stage, especially during the great purges, ended up compromising the analytical tools altogether by monumentally abusing them.

Again, the analysis suffered either because society after the civil war was too undifferentiated, too homogenous, or too archaic or else, as in the early 1930s, too unsettled by a state of flux and upheavals to yield credible results to a scrutiny misguided by inappropriate concepts.

E. H. Carr also thought that Marxian class analysis was inoperative in the Soviet conditions, although for a different reason: It was not this or another ruling class the dominated Soviet society but rather the state that played the dominant role and made or unmade the social structure, without itself yielding to such domination or to a class analysis. Carr's reasoning reflected a reality which became, appropriately, a center of analysis in the study of Eastern European regimes, tsarist and Soviet included. The growing role of the state in the advanced capitalist and democratic systems added justification to this kind of focus for the developing countries.

There is no intention to declare the approaches mentioned here to be irrelevant or not worthy of pursuing. It is rather this or another form of exaggeration or overemphasis that is contested, and what is underlined is the need to refine the tools, or to introduce new, indispensable data and additional factors. In the case of the state, too, it is the overconcentration on it that is deplored, which leads to unilateral interpretations making it into more autonomous a factor than it actually was or is, into a mold that is not shaped by anything but itself, and into a primary cause that develops and changes by its own devices. That a state can be mighty and dominate the social system, especially at some specific breakthrough periods, is beyond doubt. Situations when the state does unleash itself and acts as a powerful and destructive break on social development were observed often enough, as well as being a prime mover and agent of development. But absolutizing such an interpretation would overpoliticize the analysis, obscure what a longer-term view could well disprove or, at least, seriously modify. A temporary, seeming unshackling of constraints is not really a license for full freedom of action. One can claim that state-induced—or accelerated—social and economic changes would end up in imposing adaptations on state institutions and on the whole state system itself; constraints on them not only do exist but actually form a system of which the state is a part and which limit, frustrate, or otherwise circumscribe its operations. Economic, social, and cultural phenomena have to be introduced into the analysis, even if the object of study is a powerful and arbitrary destructive despot. The validity of such historical interpretation does not stop when human rights are curtailed and when oppressive bureaucracies take over the forefront of the stage.

Our treatment cannot offer any full-fledged analysis that would aim at correcting all the aforementioned shortcomings. But the need to do so is worth underlining. Historical studies can help to restore the balance and come up with more satisfactory interpretations by exercising some of the arcana of their métier, telling the story of events but also sorting out trends, dealing with ideologies but without detaching them from institutions and social structures, studying personalities without forgetting the networks of their helpers as well as the broader masses even if some leaders are scornful of them, and dealing with states as important parts of social systems that change in them and with them.

▪ COMPREHENDING TSARIST RUSSIA

Introducing more "history" into the debate will complicate the picture considerably but may also enrich it. It will make us wonder, for example, whether postrevolutionary Russia was still carrying a legacy from the unfinished or aborted 1861 reform. That post-1861 developments led to two revolutions is known, but it may be less well realized that some crisis phenomena that emerged in this period were still at work in Lenin's Russia, if not later, too. Then the complex and powerful jolts of war-revolution-civil-war certainly played havoc with the old structure, but how they really changed it remains to be told in more detail and insight so as to discover what leftovers from this period still went on plaguing the regime at the next turn to further complicate things. And finally, the same kind of questions should be asked about the next stage of Russia's history, the period of Stalin's "big drive," to ponder the interplay of old and new components of the system which now got another tilt in a new direction, not the first of this kind in the history of the country but certainly unusually powerful. When inquiring about the character of this new direction we thus have to keep in mind the social changes and crisis areas that appeared before World War I, the impact of the 1914–21 period, and the combined effects of the 1920s and early 1930s—a kind of three-stage rocket, each providing its durable forces of propulsion but also new imbalances and crises on top of the old ones, a combination of all three being indispensable for the explanation of the Stalinist period—and, partly, of what went on thereafter.

If this is true, we may still find interesting the concepts used by participants or theoreticians of each period as they tried to make sense of what the Russians historical situation was and where it was going. It is the thinking of these participants in events—not really of pure scholars —that is of special interest because it continues to influence the thinking of Soviet students, and to some extent ours, too. Plekhanov, Lenin, and Trotsky in particular grappled with the complexities of Russia's past, present, and future, although for each of them the future seemed to have been the least problematic. It was the present that baffled them. They badly needed to diagnose the present in order to guide their action in the coming revolutions. The problems they faced stemmed in part from the tendency of analysis to rely on neat categories of social formations and its classes, at a time when the object of study, more than ever, exhibited flux, transitional forms, and an intertwining of components difficult to disentangle. The impatience of action-oriented politicians, who needed those concepts and findings urgently to put them to direct service in politics, did not help. It did, on the contrary, "help" them to "see" more than there was, or to look for what was not there. Of course, each man's temperament and capacity to grasp situations intuitively, sometimes despite some of their theories, could allow for success in action at a time when transition, changing context, new imbalances, and symptoms of crises kept producing unanticipated situations and, actually, a totally un-anticipated reality, refractory to neatly ordered theoretical constructs, in fact, more amenable a reality to be tilted by resolute action in some direction or other than theories would allow for.

Plekhanov, all geared, in his postpopulist period, to welcome the antici-pated results of accelerated capitalist development, was still operating often with the concept of "Asian despotism," to characterize the system in the past as well as the milieu which capitalism was now penetrating and ripping apart.[2] The ancient structures were not yielding that easily, but Plekhanov expected and believed firmly that further advances of economic development would transform the social structure so as to produce the driving forces which theory already observed elsewhere: a capitalist class, pressing also for democratization; a proletariat asking for the same, but also challenging capitalists first; capitalism as such next, in pursuit of its historical interests and mission. Hence this two-stage model which Russian social democracy accepted as its historical prognosis and the basis for its political action.

The snag though was that, although the new classes kept appearing as expected, the interplay between the new and the old formations did not conform to theory and kept complicating the picture and baffling the thinker and the politician. The expected, simplified polarity of bourgeoisie versus proletariat failed to become the only or main driving force (although it did play a role), and the anticipated stages became hopelessly blurred. The collapse of Plekhanov's two-stage model pointed either to a flaw in analysis or to a flaw in the translation of the analysis into a correct revolu-tionary prognosis.

Lenin had to cope with the same problems, the same reality, the same concepts, and Plekhanov's influence on his thought was initially quite considerable. He seemed to have shared fully the two-stage prognosis until the 1905 revolution, but then again began to change quite a number of assumptions which brought him finally, more in action than in theoretical terms, to skip a stage and to leap into a new one and land himself in power. But whether this victory was also a victory of a social analyst, whether his own predictions and expectations, except for the fact of the conquest of power, were more successful than Plekhanov's is open to debate.

Whatever the answer to the last question, Lenin's thinking on tsarist society and his different, however shifting, theoretical constructions in this field were a genuine endeavor, more impressive intellectually than is sometimes realized. We do not have an adequate study of this part of his thinking, and it is interesting to ponder why. Is it because of the ever present polemical character of many of his statements? Or because of the decline of the prestige of the October revolution as its full results became apparent? Or is it because of our insufficient knowledge of tsarist and postrevolutionary society?

The fact is that Lenin's influence, especially on Soviet thinking, is not as despotic or dogmatic as it seems. It all depends on the way his texts are used, as there is enough there for many tastes. He did see the facts and effects of developing capitalism, but he also perceived the lingering web of earlier social relations constantly blocking this development, almost choking it. But in trying to make sense of this kind of a symbiosis he kept wavering in attributing predominance either to the aspects of the new or to the old. The impatience of the young revolutionary made him declare capitalism "the prevailing tendency" before it actually prevailed, as he did, rather effectively, in his youthful *Development of Capitalism in Russia*.[3] At this stage, at the turn of the century, Russia appeared to him firmly set on the capitalist road. During and after the revolution of 1905 came a set of corrections and an admission that he saw actually more than there was,[4] especially in the countryside, and some interesting changes in the realm of strategy, especially the emergence of his concept of a "revolutionary-democratic dictatorship of the proletariat and the peasantry." This expressed the fact, proven by revolutionary events, that the peasantry had failed as yet to split, as expected, into sufficiently clear antagonistic classes and acted in unison, in relation to the *pomeshchiki* and the state, in its fight for land. It still was, Lenin thought, "a class" or "a class-estate," capable of common political action, including an alliance with workers, although potentially never without troublesome prospects of clashing with its ally. We will thus see Lenin at different times proposing an alliance with the entire peasant class; later, with the poorer strata only; and again, rather with the middling peasants. This was partly because situations changed, but partly because Lenin's analysis, although often lucid, never produced a satisfactory understanding of what the Russian peasant really was.

The working class was more developed politically than either the peasantry or the bourgeoisie, Lenin thought, yet it seemed somehow vulnerable to the influence of those classes and could be rather easily swayed by petit bourgeois vacillations. It was up to the leadership and the party to straighten out the political consciousness of the workers. Lenin became also firmly convinced that the bourgeoisie would not be able to run its own revolutionary show and its role would have to be played by somebody else again. The picture was thus extremely complex, and finally it looked as if any class could switch sides and do the opposite of what seemed logical, although this was not how Lenin himself put it.

All those conclusions expressed rather faithfully the results of a situation in which capitalist trends and relations were thickly larded with networks of "vestiges," creating transitional fluid and hybrid forms, and those "vestiges" were not some trifles. They included such powerful factors as the tsarist state—not bourgeois, not really "feudal" either; and the land-owning nobility, mostly shunning modernization, though not state subsidies and mortgages, and contributing its share to the persistence of noncapitalist forms of agriculture. The bureaucracy, heavily staffed at the top by nobility, was a socially mixed bag. Finally, the peasantry, refusing to fit into usual categories and begging for some new ones, was the most "premodern" stratum of all.

The big question—What actually was the social system of prerevolutionary Russia?—remained, in fact, unanswered by Lenin. "Capitalism does rule but vestiges are enormous" remained more or less the main and not entirely satisfactory formula. He bequeathed it to his heirs, notably to Soviet scholars of our day who continue the seesawing with Lenin, with some of them choosing to underline the "vestiges" and others "capitalist development." But the findings in either case may land the Soviet scholar in trouble. By overstating the importance of capitalist development the scholar is politically on the safe side, but he will be in difficulty with too many well-known facts, including numerous quotations from Lenin himself deploring the rule of primitive *aziatchina* in the country. If he overstates the "vestiges," he is courting ideological heresy. An example of how dabbling in tsarist sociology can acquire hot political overtones in the contemporary Soviet Union is worth quoting.

In a discussion that took place in 1960 the excellent Soviet scholar A. M. Anfimov accused another scholar, M. A. Rubach, of exaggerating the degree of capitalist development in agriculture, especially the number of kulaks in the countryside, and raised the following question: "If a changeover happens in the country from serfdom to capitalism, and if, even in the Ukraine, capitalist relations do not constitute the dominating system, what are then the relations in the countryside? How do we characterize such a system?"[5]

Referring to the founding father, Anfimov continued: Capitalism does develop in country and city, said Lenin, but purely "capitalist relations are weighted down to an enormous extent by feudal relations," and

Anfimov returned again to his question: "Allow me to ask then, how can *predominant* relations be at the same time weighted down?"

An ideological conservative knows heresy when he smells it. Rubach, not unexpectedly, interjected: "You are talking about a predominance of feudal relations in the imperialist period in Russia. How can one talk, after this, of any premises for a socialist revolution?"

Indeed. Anfimov did not answer on this occasion. He only repeated that if even in the better developed Ukraine capitalism was weak in the countryside, it had to be even weaker in the rest of Russia—and one would suppose he would let Rubach answer his question alone. And it was certainly a pertinent one. What kind of a formation was it that combined a strong, maybe even overripe capitalist sector with those powerful and omnipresent feudal or semifeudal relations, especially in the countryside?[6] How could one speak of conditions for a *socialist* revolution when "normal" market capitalism had thus far the greatest difficulty in emerging and prevailing?

The question keeps reappearing in Soviet writings. Ten years after the discussion we just quoted, V. V. Adamov, an able editor of another collective work, returned to the same kind of questions and confirmed what was unclear earlier, including in another debate held in 1929, remains "unclear" today too.[7]

And we would add: as long as this remains so, the very character of the Soviet regime, conducted in Leninist terms, remains unclear as well. But raising such problems is politics in the Soviet Union, and delving in tsarist political economy and sociology there means playing with the very character of the regime and its key shibboleths.

▪ LENIN'S AND TROTSKY'S INTUITIONS

There is one additional idea in Lenin, descriptive rather than analytical, that still seems extremely useful. Sometime in the Soviet period already he said that his country contained five different social formations, products of consecutive, historical stages, coexisting in an inextricable mosaic. These were the tribal and nonmarket-oriented sector, mainly in East and Central Asia; the petty commercial producers (mostly peasants, but also artisans); the capitalist producers in city and countryside; the state capitalist; finally, the socialist state sector. Applying this "multiformity"* to the prerevolutionary period, the socialist sector would be missing there, but a semifeudal sector (mostly landowners, using peasant labor and tools) was important as well as a much more important capitalist sector than was visible in NEP Russia. This was a fruitful idea which could be best em-

* The abovementioned book edited by Adamov is inspired by this idea of *mnogoukladnost'*—plurality of formations—and explores its effects and interpretative potential in tsarist Russia.

ployed in conjunction with Trotsky's thought and intuitions concerning the results of backwardness. In addition to threads available in his (and Parvus's) ideas on the "permanent revolution," he explored, in a short but brilliant introduction to his *History of the Russian Revolution*, what he called "the law of combined development," a pioneering contribution on the effects of catching up with developed industrial countries on less-developed ones, including Russia. He showed that such efforts imposed on newcomers the exertion of leaping into the most advanced stage of organization and technology from the most backward, often archaic, starting point. This also imposed the need to accelerate the pace, the need to skip stages, to use state power abundantly as a key factor in this catching up—all causing in turn a whole cascade of results in the social structure, notably, the lingering and very afflicting coexistence, not simply of those five sectors listed by Lenin, but particularly the specific trait thereof: the coeixstence and mutual mutilation of the highly advanced and an enormous tail of very backward forms—all in one system and permeating all facets of life.[8]

This is an important idea, valid equally, although in different variations, for tsarist Russia, for Lenin's Soviet Russia, and for Stalin's rule. What is still missing is the unraveling of the specific social mechanisms that caused, in each of those periods, the perpetuation of the transitional, the blockage of the more modern forms, the maintenance of a very unstable equilibrium that could easily be overtaken by crisis due to war, depression, or acceleration of development, producing again a new jolt into a new direction with incalculable and unpredictable effects. Such a "mechanism" could be discerned in tsarist Russia where capitalism and markets pushed the still very primeval peasantry to sell more on the market before they learned to produce more. Hence the phenomenon of a growing commercialization in a stagnating or feebly growing agriculture. The ensuing results in the countryside were, not unexpectedly, a widespread pauperization of a large segments of the peasantry and the appearance of enormous population and labor surpluses there. According to A. A. Anfimov, by 1913 about 30 percent of the rural population (27 percent at the turn of the century) could be seen as constituting "a surplus."[9]

The general phenomenon of pauperization and the concomitant "surplus" of population and labor created a brake on social and economic development of rural society and of agriculture, and it was the pressure downward in the well-being of the peasant, as populist writers often claimed, that blocked or distorted the desirable social and economic differentiation in many regions, pulling down together both the poorer and the better-off.

Such phenomena had a momentous effect on the functioning of the whole system. First, it "corrupted" the landowning gentry, big and small, enticing them to stick to the old-style *métayage* system (*otrabotki*) by peasants instead of modernizing and employing hired labor. In this way the economic development of both the peasants and the landowners was considerably hampered, and the social and economic status quo of post-reform society was perpetuated with all those "vestiges of the Middle Ages" still going strong. The industrial development of the country also paid a heavy price because the enormous population surplus created a downward pressure on wages and hindered the achievement by workers of standards and status befitting a modern industrial system.

Simultaneously, "the main contradiction" that perpetuated a conservative and not too productive landowning class also perpetuated a state system that was backed by—and was backing—this class. A state ready to pour mortgage money into inefficient estates, as well as to oppose its full might to the demand of distributing these estates to the land-hungry peasants, was certainly a factor that prevented rather than promoted a modern market economy in the countryside—and at large.

At this juncture one can turn to some of the formulas inspired by Barrington Moore[10] to help the Soviets, and ourselves, pursue the inquiry into what happens next and why. The preservation of a traditional peasantry is related, according to Moore, to the preservation of a pre-capitalist state system. He calls such systems (as in China and Russia) "agrarian bureaucracies." In such a context, state, peasantry, and nobility are prevented from modernizing, and the capitalist sector that does exist is also heavily blocked. In such a polity democratic development is precluded. Moore goes on to inquire what the conditions might be for a democratic development to occur, but our area is not endowed enough for such an outcome. The peasantry here keeps paying a very heavy price for whatever development does go on and also carries a heavy burden of a network of old-fashioned relations with the state and the landowners, often also with industrial employers. We can now see why the term "vestiges," when applied to such relations, may be inappropriate: they obscure the fact that the sum total of such relations is precisely the mechanism that perpetuated an unstable and crisis-prone situation.

Now another Soviet contribution—from the already quoted Adamov—can be brought in. He has to avoid names like Trotsky or Barrington Moore but can build an interesting methodological proposition, quite new in the context of Soviet historical writings, by using other pedigrees. He proposes:

> In the center of the analysis has to be put not just backwardness, but its unusual conjunction with acceleration; not only the sharpness of social conflicts, but a new type of connections of interchangeability [vzaimoperekhody] of those conflicts; from referring to the broadest antinomies in terms like "medieval" versus "modern" one has to turn to the most active conflict—namely the different forms and means of integration into modernity.[11]

Adamov would probably agree with Barrington Moore that in a system where a basically still precapitalist polity and society face the strains of modernization for which it makes the peasants pay a heavy price—in cash, in misery, and, in the final analysis, in terms of historical irrelevance— the whole edifice would be vulnerable to a peasant revolution, and not infrequently to a so-called communist-style dictatorship.

But then, once a revolution occurred and a new regime—in our case, one with a socialist outlook—comes to power, further and often very new hurdles appear, sometimes an expanded version of the old ones, that hamper further advance and keep the system crisis-prone and unstable.

■ THE CIVIL WAR AND THE GREAT SOCIAL LEVELING

In such a strained and unbalanced social setting the pent-up forces of crisis and strife could hardly be kept under control; especially when waves of accelerated development or other sudden shocks, like wars, that came on top of the already overheated situation. And this is how revolutions are triggered off. Accelerated growth in the 1890s, the industrial boom of the 1910s, both in conjunction with a war, led respectively to the 1905 and the 1917 revolutionary outbursts. Next, October 1917 and the ensuing civil war caused shock waves of a different type, this time phenomena of deceleration and regress; and again, the acceleration of economic growth in the early 1930s, coming on top of the still recent and unabsorbed results of the earlier upheavals, led to the peculiar phenomenon of Stalinism. We should remember that the time span we are concerned with here— not more than about forty years—is very short in the history of a society and that this span alone contained deep restructuring and waves of un- settling events, without at first solving any of the outstanding problems. On the contrary, each added new ones to the preceding tensions. It would therefore be unthinkable not to go for explanations of the phenomena that interest us, to what happened during this period. In fact, going back to 1861 is equally justified and can be convincingly argued for.

The civil war of 1918–20 caused a deep setback in the country's de- velopment. Not only was its economy a shambles at the beginning of the New Economic Policy in 1921, but its cities were depleted, its bour- geoisie destroyed, and with it much of the professional, administrative, scholarly, and intellectual talent. Significantly, as perceived by the regime, the working class was severely weakened, considering that almost half of the skilled industrial labor force vanished through death, mobilizations, promotions, and returning to the village. The results of these changes and setbacks have not yet been fully grasped by scholars and analysts. It was as if most of the fruits of social and economic development Russia experienced since 1861 were wiped out and its culture, spiritual and political, had re- treated to some earlier primitive stage difficult to define or date. But it has to be incorporated into our thinking and examined in its different consequences and ramifications.

It was true that the revolution, having eliminated the privileged of the previous regime, now opened wide the gates to promotion, education, and power to popular layers previously confined to the bottom of the social ladder. Naturally, during the next few decades, this would bring to schools and government institutions a great mass of unskilled, semiliterate people, mostly of rural origin; the party too, despite its claims to the role of avant-garde and to being the rallying point for the best and the brightest, had to be content with what the country had to offer. Thus, an organization that had in its ranks some 24,000 people at the outbreak of the revolution, in February 1917, some 300,000 in and around October 1917, and a million in 1927, could cite such numbers triumphantly, but the underlying social phenomenon was more complex: The party was flooded by a politically illiterate mass, and the experienced, politically and ideologically strong party elite, considerably weakened by the strains of revolution, civil war, and the wear and tear of power, were actually drowning in the crude mass—and often said so. Educational, political, and cultural standards in all the administrations, including inside the party, could not but express the general decline of the country and exhibit results of this dramatic setback into a more primitive stage.

No doubt the loss of social substance, vigor, and ability of elements in the population most crucial for the country's advance into the industrial era, not to mention some form of socialism, was a big blow. Despite official statements to the contrary, one has to add to the list of losses the elimination or dispersal of leaders and cadres of the different political parties that emerged in Russia, mainly in the twentieth century. It may well be that the Bolshevik leaders did not deplore losing a Milyukov—from our point of view it certainly was a loss—but they knew well that a Martov was badly missing. It is known from Lunacharsky's testimony that he and Lenin often deplored the loss of Martov, who might have been an excellent leader of a right wing inside the party.[12]

In our context here these names only exemplify the problem. Dispersing the other parties and their leaders made the establishing of a one-party rule easier, but the political culture of the country certainly took a nosedive and made the ruling party itself pay a heavy price for it.

So much for the setback caused by the civil war in the urban sector. The trends in the countryside should be added in order to understand what Soviet Russia was, socially and politically, at the time when the coming of peace allowed the new regime to start its work of construction. When the urban and industrial sectors of the country declined, agriculture and the peasantry, however backward—in fact, because they were so backward—weathered the storm much better, and their relative role in the country's economy and society was bound to increase. In Russia it easily comes to mind to call this process, quite obvious and noticed at the time by observers, the "ruralization" and "agrarianization" of the country. Agricultural production was now, as in much earlier stages, the country's main—if not only—asset. The peasantry's percentage in the population was now greater than in tsarist Russia. Through its soldier sons, peasants were crucial in the revolutionary developments in the capitals and on the fronts of the civil war, but the peasantry was also crucial as a revolutionary force in some deeper sense too. In fact, they accomplished a revolution of their own and in their own right, although power accrued to the cities anyway, as always happened. Nonetheless, the way the agrarian revolution was operated, the direct and indirect effects of the peasants' action, made a deep impact on the very character of the system and the outlook of the new regime. By taking over lands of the gentry, they eliminated the previous privileged and ruling class and thus put an end to the old official Russia and its political system. Not less important from the point of view of opening or closing avenues for the future, peasants eliminated all the results of the Stolypin reforms: they redistributed the land according to egalitarian principles which expressed their interests and sense of justice and thereby wiped out effects of social differentiation, namely, the bigger and better producers and forms of farming. Moreover, the declining, supposedly moribund rural community was revived and came back strongly, in its pure form, undiluted and unrestrained in the early stages of the regime by any government-imposed functions. The Soviet regime thus inherited—"got saddled with" is a better term—a peasantry that got rid of whatever capitalist development it experienced before. It curtailed much of its internal inequality, massively assumed a middling outlook, improved somewhat its standards of living and—considerably—its social status (especially in its own eyes), and revived its ancient customary system of the family farm, the *dvor* (household).

This was not all. Compared with tsarist Russia, peasants cut seriously the part of produce supplied to the markets. They thus moved back into a more "natural" economy than in tsarist Russia, but this happened also on a larger front than just the economic. Still a world of its own, the *mir* —which in tsarist times symbolized peace as well as a rural commune in action—now turned even more deeply into its own shell and separated itself from educated, urban, and official society by its village and commune, its customary law, and its own form of religion—a ruralized ancient Christianity, complete with devils and witches. In short, the peasantry became now—and continued to be during the NEP—more traditional, even archaic, more *muzhik* than before. For a time it was going to be a throwback not only into a precapitalist stage but even to some prebourgeois, almost precommercial stage. With its small marketable surpluses, wooden plows, and three-field system and especially with its communautary repartitions of land and collective family ownership of their means of production (other than land), one wonders whether even the term "petit bourgeois" could be applied to them as a socioeconomic definition. And yet this term and constant claims, still continuing today, that a part of this peasantry actually constituted a capitalist class marred official and often unofficial thinking and exemplified one of the gross abuses of scholarly analysis, often with incalculable damage to the peasants and the system at large.

To sum up the results of the revolution and the civil war, it can be said that although the revolutionary leaders knew their country was not ripe for socialism (therefore expectations were often entertained that a revolution in the West would bail them out), they did not realize that what would finally fall into their laps would be by far more backward than tsarist Russia had been. Many important achievements on the road to a modern society which occurred in tsarist Russia were annulled by the events, and the new regime was to begin its action on a social foundation which could not, by any stretch of imagination, be shown as ready to move toward socialist goals. As both the urban and the agricultural sectors, each in its own way, regressed and changed their social and political physiognomy, Russian society was not experiencing upward trends but was in the throes of two regressing curves, which narrowed its choices and predetermined some painful trends and limitations. The bulk of the nation—the peasantry—was not a dynamic force and could not be expected to lead the country out of its predicament. The only dynamic force available at this stage was the new state. The old one already was an important factor in Russia, but its collapsed under the pressure of social forces it could not contain. There was in tsarist Russia an insufficient although important development of the "civil society" and a growing ability of social factors to initiate reform and improve the system. As it did not happen, the events we briefly sketched made Russia lose this potential and weakened its "civil society" very dramatically. The new state was now facing a less articulate body social that was also less capable of action, and its role was *ipso facto* immensely enhanced: reliance on organizations— party, bureaucracies, army—was growing, later to become an all-embracing method. Although the state machinery would itself be seriously deficient because of the depletion of the educated and the influx of "socially reliable" but professionally inexperienced elements, it still was, at least at the top where the aims were formulated, a twentieth-century product. It had the ideology, the will, the monopoly on any available expertise, and the tools of control to lead the country to its next stages.

But it was not to be a straight movement up. What we have called a twentieth-century product (not in itself a carrier of just "progress") was facing a nation the bulk of which was an almost homogeneous, poor social class shaped by centuries and—to judge by its methods of farming, way of life, culture, beliefs, and institutions—belonging to some earlier century. Obviously, the metaphor does not have to be precise. But it remains that "two incompatible centuries" were facing each other and, moreover, that there was not enough of the indispensable intermediary cushion to help compromise and soften the possible shock. Many expected that a clash would have to occur, sooner or later, between the two forces and that this would decide the country's future. In fact, despite some hopes to the contrary, and sound advice to this effect from Lenin himself, despite the efforts undertaken during the NEP, a battle between the state and the popular masses did occur. It happened during the next stage, when a new and unprecedented acceleration was attempted, causing a new upheaval, a violent restructuring again, and a volley of results that deeply influenced society and the very character of the polity. Compared with what was coming, the NEP—with its "social contract" with the peasantry, the professional classes, parts of the bourgeoisie, and some of the cultural elites—would soon look like a golden age of freedom and pluralism. What was going to emerge would be a Leviathan state, which many feared but no one really anticipated, emerging in outpourings of terror and paroxisms of irrationality. These were to be the birth pangs and products of a new autocracy, which was not, of course, the objective for which many people had given their lives in revolutions and civil wars. Many more would now pay for having failed to recognize themselves in the outcome, or for simply having accepted blindly whatever was pushed down their throats.

▪ THE *MUZHIK*—A HEADACHE AGAIN

By the end of the 1920s the day of reckoning seemed to be nearing. Debates on strategy of development, unavoidably enmeshed in a contest for power, and ideological battles with the very soul of the regime at stake, turned around three main planks: (1) how to industrialize, (2) without making the peasantry explode and (3) without letting state and party get out of hand. The last point turned around the character of the system and its by now obvious potential to become an oppressive superstate. Left and right, openly or implicitly, had this worry on their mind. The future Stalinist faction and its chief did not show much sign of sharing such worries. They would discover the price of this omission some seven or eight years later. For the time being it was precisely the organized forces of the state, and all the levers at its command, that would be launched into operating and managing the new "big drive."

In all those future plans and strategies, the *muzhik* was again to become, as so often in the past, the pivotal factor. What to do with him? Was he really the main carrier of an eventual capitalist restoration? Would he support the regime that was trying to overcome a crisis which the same *muzhik* had supposedly created? Would he support the new accumulation process for which he was to pay a higher price?

In the events that followed, known as the collectivization drive—the term "collectivization" certainly being a misnomer—a clash of the main forces on the Russian historical arena could not be averted. The state launched an onslaught on the peasantry—a feat of "social engineering" which by far overshadowed Stolypin's "engineering from above" in scale, daring, and violence. The results were momentous for both the peasantry and the regime.

Had this clash been the only or simply the main front the process could have been handled with less damaging results. But the collectivization of the peasants was only a part of a larger, rather unplanned "offensive." Simultaneously with battling the *muzhik*'s mentality and forcing on him new forms of life and labor, the regime launched an accelerated industrialization, developed new cities and expanded the old ones, educated new important layers of professionals indispensable for the whole process—technicians, scientists, skilled workers, administrators—and constantly expanded the state machinery, its bureaucracies and agencies. The Leviathan was now coming of age, exceeding the worst expectations of earlier critics. There had been similar phenomena in Russian history before, but here all records were probably beaten as far as the scope of state action and the pervasiveness of terror were concerned, as well as the durability of the results. In the process of disciplining the masses of new workers, of the unwilling peasants in the kolkhozy, in the process of indoctrinating, training, terrorizing, and coercing, the growing *apparaty* were themselves submitted to such strains that much of the medicine they were applying to others were applied to them too—including a bloodletting soon to be administered in such doses that it pointed to pathology in the whole system. This so-called second October produced such a cascade of crises and disequilibria that, clearly, the capacity of the regime to act rationally and to cope seemed to have reached its limits. The avalanche of tasks, growing in complexity, was poured on the shoulders of *apparaty*, whose numbers grew but whose abilities could not keep pace with such requirements; in fact, its quality had to fall because of the influx of raw recruits. All these factors contributed to the polity veering precipitiously into a frame and system of violence capped by a capricious autocrat.

In the official language of those days the peasantry appeared as the honorable ally of the working class, and now even a more honorable "kolkhoz peasantry," but it also was considered to have been the main cause of all the obstacles the regime found on its way. In this capacity they were presented as "petit bourgeois," and no one could remonstrate that this was one and the same mass of peasants, supposedly carriers of a new socialist essence as well as of the quite opposite spirit that also kept infecting the working class, officialdom, and even the party.

Out of the peasant mass a special stratum of "super-*muzhiki*" was singled out, better known as "kulaks"—yet another of those abuses of class analysis of which a long list could be supplied. (See Chapter 5.) The small apex of better-off peasants, who in Soviet conditions were producers still basically relying on the labor of members of their families, with an average of about ten hectares, two to three cows, two to three horses, one, rarely two or more hired laborers—for an average family of eight to ten people. To construct from them a "capitalist class," or even a "semicapitalist" one, demanded stretching concepts well into the realm of the chimerical (although there was no need to doubt their distaste for the kolkhoz). Yet, as officially decreed, it was with the elimination of these kulaks "as a class," supposedly the last rampart of capitalism, that the country ushered in the era of socialism. So it was not in October when the real thing was eliminated but in Stalin's "big drive," when a placebo was removed, that socialism came true. Was it really socialism that was attained by an ideological manipulation of this kind?

The problem can best be visualized by reminding ourselves that, according to official data, about 400 million rubles' worth of property was confiscated from this "rural capitalism." The figure was later revised upward, but the modesty of these sums tell the story. One big industrial plant cost more, but the damage to the economy caused by the expropriation and elimination of over a million of the best farmers was staggering. A trait that was characteristic of much of what was done is worth pointing to: speed and a rush into large-scale units for which the countryside was not ripe. Nationalization of productive capacity operated prematurely can cause heavy social and political damage; but there is still a difference between nationalizing a big, bureaucratically organized, industrial corporation, where no more than a change of the board of directors might be needed, and nationalizing huts, cows, and plows. In this latter case, as we know, the act of the state did actually destroy a class of producers, leaving the inheritor with nothing but dust.

This remark applies not only to the expropriation of the kulak but to the whole collectivization process. The fallacy of collectivization Soviet style consisted in imposing on small-scale farmers large-scale forms and methods before the appropriate technical means and cadres had become available and without appropriate transitional stages. Most peasants lived and worked in family-run small farms as well as being incorporated, in a particularly Russian way, in a communal landholding system. Over generations they also had acquired a mentality, culture, and ethics stemming from this mode of life and work and a system of religious beliefs, mainly a specific rural Christianity, heavily tinged with magical practices and sorcery. The leap from sorcery to higher mathematics, to put it in terms often used in the 1920s, demanded much more than just the application of state power. Many thought that communal forms, although age-old and geared to the needs of a primitive and overpopulated countryside, could have been used as a steppingstone to something more modern at some later stage. Yet, befitting the impetuosity of the day, this way was discarded. Speeding up by force becoming, for a time, the cure-all, the price tag attached to this approach was constantly the same: a new and considerable regression in the sphere of agriculture, paralleled by other walks of life, especially the spheres of culture, ideology, and politics.

We remember that the resistant mentality of the peasant was not only a problem in running kolkhozy. Thanks to the vast industrial effort—we do not forget this major fact—they came to towns in the millions. The majority of the new industrial working class, many of the officials, the student body, and a considerable proportion of the new professional classes would be recruited from peasants. They were the material from which the classes of the growing industrial society were constituted. Would they shed their traditional cultural-religious outlook after only a short period of schooling? And in the environment of the fast growing cities of those 1920s, as well as the building sites and overcrowded labor camps of the 1930s? A massive feat of social mobility would, in the short run, produce rather an equally massive disorientation, quite inimical to a quick and serious shedding of old habits. And the phenomena of accelerated restructuring we are studying, as well as their effects, are all "short-run"—and so is our central theme itself. The impact of breathtaking social change will be contradictory, and it is only with hindsight that the long-term aspects can be separated from the shorter waves of change. Some superficial new veneer that is easy to acquire should not be mistaken for change in deeper cultural and psychological layers that take much longer to mature.

As some 17 million peasants settled in cities between 1928 and 1935 alone—not to mention many more millions that came and left the towns during those years and later—the population of the urban sector was thereby doubled in this incredibly short time. Obviously, these people were getting or beginning to get "deruralized," but at the same time, as I have described elsewhere (see Chapter 10), they did "ruralize" the towns, especially the factories. Miscalculations in planning, themselves related to the whipping speedup, were responsible for the excessive scope and suddenness of this process. It was therefore not a simple migration to cities, usually seen as acts of progress and social advance. It was to become all very positive, again, "in the long run." For the time being, the cities and other places were flooded by streams of people—many of them desperate because of their dislike of kolkhozy, or because of dekulakization—that outstripped the power of absorption of those cities and strained to the utmost their institutions and material means. The new arrivals had thus to face a rough and unhospitable environment, a deteriorating economic situation, inadequate lodging—not to mention the complexities of the Soviet industrial and urban system for which the rural mind was badly equipped.

It all amounted to a massive uprooting, cultural and psychological shock, causing widespread disorientation, a crisis of values, and the concomitant phenomena of delinquency, hooliganism, cynicism, mass anomie, and the attraction of not too palatable countercultures.

Such phenomena are crucial for the understanding of the 1930s. Although we deal here, to some extent, with a textbook case of rapid industrialization and urbanization anywhere, the scale and concentration in time, as well as the political circumstances, were very different and unique. The strain and tension imposed on people and on the political system nationally were immense. At this juncture it was what happened to people that was crucial for the understanding of the polity. People, mostly, as said, of rural origin, had to adapt and somehow rebuild their ethical and cultural values, to regain control of their lives and their sanity. For this purpose all that was available from the past and present environments would be used in different doses, the problem being that not much from the old luggage was of use, whereas the new environment too had its capabilities to offer good values greatly impaired. The burden of response and solutions was landing in the lap of the state—itself, to say the least, in high fever, strained to the utmost, relying too much on crude coercion and primitive propaganda, and displaying quite a basket of pathological syndromes. In the midst of this schooling and building, training and pushing, the acculturation process was partly blocked, and a temporary phenomenon for which the term "deculturation" could be suitable set in. This term could account for both the phenomena of massive uprooting experienced by peasants losing old values and cultural molds and not acquiring new ones quickly enough as well as for the results of political and cultural terror and crude propaganda: drabness; uniformity; sloganeering; crude language and mores, both below and higher up; foul countercultures; drinking and criminal behavior.

It is worth repeating that the state operating in this kind of cultural "void" (of its own making, to a large extent) experienced effects of those trends all through its own agencies and *apparaty*. It was therefore going to mobilize all it could to master the tides and to go on ruling. This would demand quite a lot of doing—and would amount to and account for the last chapter in the making of the Stalinist state.

▪ ONE IDEOLOGY—OR MORE?

One of the strategies of social control was the creation or the expansion of a strong scaffolding of bosses, all through the system, called *nachal'stvo* by the people as well as by the interested parties themselves. The term came from the political dictionary and practice of tsarist Russia and was going to both prop up as well as actually typify the system. But to counter the effects of "deculturation" in towns and of similar phenomena and the loss of incentives in the countryside, a more subtle policy was needed. The regime had to offer and inculcate values, to extirpate some and instill some other beliefs, and to legitimize its policies and its very character in the eyes of the populace, at a time when it was both socially lifting up and downgrading millions of people. Success would not be easy in this sphere, and it would demand pressures and compromises on the cultural and ideological fronts and further transformations of the character of the polity.

A comparison with the history of the Christian church and of other great religions in the earlier stages of their development can offer a useful illustration to what was involved in Soviet Russia's efforts to combat the effects of "the petit bourgeois tides" and the demoralizing results of mass anomie and value crisis. "Neither the prophet nor the priest," wrote Reinhard Bendix in his book on Max Weber, "can afford to reject all compromise with the traditional beliefs of the masses."[13] The same goes for regimes, however radical, engaged in the process of changing social relations. In its old fight against forms of paganism and, more broadly, against the whole preliterate popular culture, the church finished by adapting many of its ways to folkways and adopting many elements from the popular religion in order to win out on substance by conceding some points tactically. Whether these points were just trifles or much more is beyond our pursuits here, but the church did use its miracles to compete with their magic, its exorcism to outdo their healers, its versions of devils, witches, and sorcerers to eliminate their spirits and deities. The list of those adaptations and adoptions is much longer, but our concern is with some comparable phenomena in the 1930s in the Soviet Union. Obviously, here was the twentieth century, not the tenth, and things did not occur in centuries but were concentrated in a few years. In addition, the acting forces were not heathen peasants versus a Christian church and kingdom but Christian peasants versus an atheistic government which was not going to introduce a religion—just use methods and structures similar to the religious and church experience for its own purposes. Still, the analogy is quite striking.

Another parallel with church history, which we will go into only very briefly, concerns the phenomena of transformation of sects into churches and the emergence of sects inside established churches, a process that was recurrent in all religions. It can throw a searching light on the transformation of the revolutionary Bolshevik party from a network of clandestine committees into a mighty bureaucracy, with a powerful hierarchy on one pole and a rightless "laity" on the other, with privileges at the top and obligatory catechesis handed from above for the use of the lower rungs, and finally with a laicized version of . . . sin, apostates, and inquisition.

The first visible effort undertaken to compete with popular religion (or the existing religions in general) for the minds of the rural and urban dwellers, on lines that justify our analogy, began initially as a semiconscious strategy with actions like the erecting of Lenin's mausoleum and the encouragement of pilgrimages to Lenin's embalmed body. All these despite the protests and sense of outrage against such practices expressed by Lenin's widow and other old Bolsheviks. Despite also the official disdain for the Orthodox church's practice of venerating relics of saints (*moshchi*).

In the 1920s an interesting and lively debate initiated by the writer Veresaev in *Krasnaya nov'*[14] raised the problem of replacing religious ceremonies, above all those related to the life-cycle rituals that played such an important role especially in the countryside, by something secular and modern, specially conceived for this purpose. In the lively debate warnings were sounded against coercive or artificial methods, against the cultural and psychological damage that can be caused when depriving people of the old but deeply felt and needed symbolisms without replacing them by something acceptable to the recipients.

One discussant even cautioned against replacing one authoritarian and dogmatic set of rituals with another equally authoritarian and dogmatic. The whole operation, in order to make good sense to him, should have consisted only in replacing something authoritarian and conservative by a ceremony that expressed and carried human emancipation onto a higher level—not by another ritual of indoctrination.[15]

The warnings expressed in this interesting debate were not heeded. What was emerging in public life, especially in the 1930s, were ceremonies and a style that looked strikingly as if it had been borrowed from the old: processions with "icons" of living and dead leaders, ritualized public ceremonials, pompous displays of a kind of secular liturgy, the growing use of a vocabulary soaked with religious and semireligious overtones. The frontiers of the country became now "sanctified" (*svyashchennye*); government requirements, such as grain procurements, became "commandments" (*zapovedi*)—modest but ever expanding steps into a strategy aimed at replacing the old national and religious belief system and ritual by a quasi-cult of a secular state. This was to be observed in full blossom already during the later 1930s, which also saw the pinnacle of what can now be seen as the centerpiece of Stalinism and its main achievement: the hectic building of a superstate, heavily spiced by its so-called excesses.

Not much effort is needed to relate the "Stalin cult" to this broader strategy of "sanctifying" the state. The Stalin cult became a linchpin in this revamped secular orthodoxy. Sermons, vows, adulation, and panegyrics cotributed a peculiar "Byzantine" flavor to the neo-autocracy. But besides being a very serious dent in the official Marxist-Leninist ideology, which had no place for such developments, the strategy did not seem sufficient or convincing enough in the battle for people's minds and for the legitimization of the regime. Marxism-Leninism could not convincingly explain the new cult, and both were unable or felt unable to make palatable and acceptable the superstate, the rigid bureaucratic hierarchy, the bureaucratic takeover of all vestiges of popular sovereignty, the appearance of privileged strata in society and at the upper echelons of the bureaucratic ladder.

Many saw treason in such trends, which were discernible already since the early postrevolutionary days, and in fact, by standards of the official creed and its erstwhile commitments, such tendencies were shocking. To mend the ideological fences a strategy of ideological diversion was conceived and applied. First came the taming of the critical potential of the official creed itself through its transformation into a strictly controlled catechesis, only as allowed and amendeed by the "supreme authority."

An additional prop was then sought in those chapters of the imperial past which best suited the new situation and the self-image of the new leader: the great tsars, builders and despots, Ivan the Terrible and Peter the Great, seemed to fit the bill. The imperial past was thus tapped for whatever it could offer in the operation of integrating the peasants, building an industry, and erecting a powerful state, with a despot at its helm, not unlike those days of yore which offered a glitter of regalia, an imperial pomp and an Oprichnina,* with its rake applied against critics and foes.

The imperial past was screened not only for the uses of quasi-religious devices to sustain a modern autocracy (*samoderzhavie*), but also for what it could offer in terms of sustaining nationality (*narodnost'*), too,† as well as to mount a brand of great power nationalism complete with the chant of glory to "Great Russia" (*Velikaya Rus'*), as the Soviet anthem still says.

There was an obvious craving at the top—which probably ascribed the same to the masses—for this kind of supportive symbols and ideologies. It was not just a coolly conceived strategy but a deep psychological need felt by the ruler himself, who might have felt a genuine affinity with those great predecessors—and who certainly believed he was much better.

We can see already that more than one ideology was "drafted" to serve the great restructuring of those years, ideologies that actually were incompatible and therefore necessitated additional constructs.

An attentive observer could soon discern the emergence of yet another ideological production that borrowed elements from the Marxist-Leninist and imperial-national (or nationalist) rhetoric, coupled with some original ingredients—to express the interests and outlook of the growing bureaucracy. This was to be expected, especially at the top of the hierarchy, even if it was not immediately made public or even not allowed clear and full expression by the shattering purges that hit those *apparaty* and hindered them from settling to rule and enjoy their privileges unmolested.

Despite the shakiness in its ranks caused by the general flux of the times and the purges, official ideology could not offer a sufficient expression for what the bureaucracy was doing and was standing for or for its interests

---

* The Oprichnina was, among other things, the personal and secret police established by Ivan the Terrible to deal with his enemies, and to administer lands confiscated from the boyars for the benefit of the state.

† "Autocracy, Nationality, Orthodoxy" was the official state motto expressing the ideology of tsardom under Nicholas I. One could use the principle of "partyness" to replace "Orthodoxy," but there is no need to overdraw the parallel. The similarity is there anyway.

as perceived by it. "Statehood" (*gosudarstvennost'*) would become the central theme which would show what the real goal was and how to assure the internal cohesion of the carrier of this statehood. An important element, though, could be borrowed from the theoretical founding fathers, namely, nationalization of the main means of production as a socialist principle *par excellence*. It was not that important that this was not, really, the central tenet of socialism. But it suited the interest of the bureaucracy to use this formula because it did, in fact, express the source of the state's power and the position of its servants as guardians of the national patrimony. This was a good basis for defending their special role and thus special privileges, justifying the growing self-image and self-importance of the new mandarins of the state: the party apparatchik; the *otvetrabotnik*; and the *krupnyi gosudarstvennyi deyatel'*.* This ideology began its career from the defense of the party apparatus against the onslaught of the opposition in the 1920s, continued through the repudiation of egalitarianism in the early 1930s, blossomed in the imposition and glorification of "one-man management" (*edinonachalie*), and finally found the right casuistry in the thesis that the state would whither away sometime in the future, but not before its powers had expanded to the utmost during the ongoing historical stage. The bureaucracy's sovereignty in the system was thinly camouflaged by extolling the importance of leadership and management, which looked like a simple variation on the theme of the party's leading role. The socialist credential of such principles could be questioned, of course, as well as the principle of state ownership of the means of production. Such ownership, mainly of land, had a precedent in earlier stages of historical development; it could become—and actually was—the basis of all kind of regimes, including the early Moscow princedom and tsardom.

There are some internal, less known, and still unresearched parts of the bureaucratic ideology which operated already in the 1930s and are going stronger today. They concern the justification of open and covert material and other privileges, justification for their life and career practices, deference to authority and superiors, ideas concerning their position in the state compared with that of other classes, and other elements that are not treated in official handbooks and histories but constitute a potent ideological reality.

It is one of the mysteries of Stalinism that it turned much of the fury of its bloody purges against this very real mainstay of the regime. There were among the *apparaty*, probably, still too many former members of other parties or of the original Leninist party, too many participants and victors of the civil war who remembered who had done what during those

---

* An *apparatchik* is a paid official of the party, though this is not what they would call themselves officially; probably rather *partrabotnik*. An *otvetrabotnik* is an employee of some rank and responsibility. *Krupnyi gosudarstvennyi deyatel'*—"prominent state leader"—is a term reserved for top government and party officials of ministerial rank and higher.

days of glory. Too many thus could feel the right to be considered founders of the regime and base on it part of the claims to a say in decisions and to security in their positions. Probably, also, letting the new and sprawling administration settle and get encrusted in their chairs and habits could also encourage them to try and curtail the power of the very top and the personalized ruling style of the chief of state—and this was probably a real prospect the paranoid leader did not relish. I have already briefly proposed the idea that a modern bureaucracy needs and enjoys "tenure," which was denied to it in the most cruel ways by the autocrat. In fact, autocracy could not really block for too long a sociological trend which finally prevailed in Russia beginning with Khrushchev (see Chapter 11).

For the time being, in the midst of a difficult contest with the peasantry, the strenuous efforts to discipline labor during the height of the purge of the party and the government apparatus, yet another, a fourth ideology was put to use. This was felt to be necessary to justify the existence not only of the superstate but of the specific means employed in erecting it: terrorism and mass repression. This was a dip into the darker and irrational traditions and urges of individuals and whole polities, used to glue together an unpalatable reality, an impossible mixture of ideologies and a gruesome and counterrevolutionary onslaught on people and principles. The device, this time, was worthy of a great shaman. The show trials epitomized the visible part of this construct. It made the mythology of the "enemies of the people" look real, when real people, mostly Lenin's comrades and leaders of the revolution, actually confessed to the most improbable crimes. The procedure thus seemed to rehabilitate the mythology, when in fact it only proved what it tried to conceal. As there was no basis in reality to all the accusations, only confession could serve as proof when any analytical or juridical content was missing. Bukharin, during his own trial in 1938, called this procedure "the medieval principle." And rightly so, as this "principle" was the basis for the witch trials and the inquisitorial persecutions of schismatics.

The parallel with such trials was perfect. The victims were depicted as sinners who had sold their souls to the devil and committed the basest of treasons. Torture was also used before those trials, but especially massively, with or without any trials, after Stalin personally authorized in 1937 the use of "physical pressure" against all those traitors.

In this context it is worth remembering that not just some action—however innocent—but even a shadow of doubt about the party line and the leader's wisdom was already the beginning of treason—because doubt was bound to end up serving foreign intelligence services and was thus worthy of being cut down prophylactically, even if it was still buried somewhere in the subconscious. Condoning somebody's doubt without reporting it to the authorities was equally reprehensible—and punishable.

All this is fully documented and well known. What is less realized is that the whole activity, including ferreting out the very function of doubt, using scapegoats to whitewash the regime, producing mythical enemies, belonged to a fourth, independent, and fully operative ideology which was offering now to the mass of people, disoriented by the shocks that were showered on them in those years, both poles of a Manichaean equation: the forces of progress with the idolized leader at the helm; and the array of evil forces, spirits or demons, to explain away all that went wrong or caused suffering, thereby to mobilize the nation around the regime's work of construction and destruction.

We know that many responded by offering a stream of denunciations, although we may never know how many did the denouncing or the arresting or how many were arrested or perished. But the effort here on the part of the regime—or was it mainly caused by the pathological mind of the top leader?—was geared to tapping the psychological and cultural predispositions of a disoriented population in the midst of a crisis of values and a cultural no man's land by making them accept a "demonology" offered by the regime. It also shows how the system that engaged in a contest with a superstitious folk still believing in the evil force (*nechistaya sila*) could catch the bug itself and sink in the deepest superstitions and aberrations which could neither be blamed on any scapegoats nor left at the doorsteps of the popular mentality.

■ A SOCIAL STRUCTURE BREEDING AUTHORITARIANISM

In this chapter we have tried to introduce into the inquiry into the Stalinist phenomenon trends that operated in the longer span of Russian history, the mechanism that undid the previous system but also, and this is our contention, continued to affect the new regime. We have also considered the results of the revolution and the civil war, which not only eliminated the previous ruling classes but also brought into the historical arena a new social layer to run the state and a new type of a ruling institution, the party. Also as a result of those two events the whole socioeconomic system, and in many ways the political system as well, reverted to an earlier, precapitalist stage of social development. Therefore this supposedly postcapitalistic system, although recognizing that its predecessor was not that advanced, was in fact departing from a level of development that had inherited only a fraction of the acquisitions of twentieth-century Russia. This state of affairs influenced the respective positions of "state" and "society," the new state being welded onto and facing, mainly, a socially homogeneous, communautary peasantry, and the relations between the two might be considered as defining and constraining much of what was possible and what was actually going to happen in the next stages.

At the next crisis—and the gist of the argument is that the whole context was imbalanced and crisis-prone—a new acceleration created a third complex of factors and trends that closed certain avenues of development and strongly favored others and, in conjunction with many of the props of the previous stages, finally resulted in the combination of development and terror, a bureaucratic state and an autocratic rule that became known as Stalinism. Stalinism, therefore, with its wholesale statization, destruction of cadres, coercive collectivization, concentration camps, and massive slave labor, emerged in a relatively "primitivized" society that had been pushed up by accelerated industrialization, causing the characteristic twin results of the period: an acculturation that was marred by considerable deculturation; an industrial leap forward that was seriously hampered by a stagnating agriculture, a massive upward mobility with a no less massive loss of status for many others, growing literacy, but a general state of immensely downgraded liberties. In fact, it was going to be, for a generation, a cruelly oppressive police state.

Each floor of the historical structure had contributed to this result. Tsarist Russia had a growing and dynamic capitalist sector that was too weak as yet to chew up the peasantry and to transform the system into a full-fledged capitalist market society. As Lenin saw it, a very advanced modern industrial and financial sector was strongly clogged by a web of constraints coming from the state, or from the economic backwardness of the countryside, where the availability of an enormous surplus of cheap peasant labor prevented most of the gentry from modernizing their estates —and contributed to their loss of substance and of importance in the economy of the country.

The revolution destroyed both sides of the equation: the capitalist sector, and those relations that constituted the "semifeudal" building blocks. But what was it that replaced them? For the time being, it was to be the results of "two retreating curves," whereby the new regime inherited from the past, among other things, a peasantry which was liberated from its shackles but had retreated into a mold more "rural" than before and an urban society deprived of many of its experienced and sophisticated layers.

The situation was thus more propitious than before for an enhanced role of the state and more—not less—authoritarian than before the revolution. The whole social matrix was then breeding just this: authoritarianism. It is the context of a "homogenized," illiterate, and semiliterate society and a "simplified" social structure, facing a web of bureaucracies themselves rather heterogeneous socially, with many holdovers from the previous system, with many new arrivals from the lower classes. The whole government machinery, although itself reflecting in many ways the social and economic decline, still was capable of what the bulk of society was not: using the tools of the twentieth century for ruling and conceiving of their situation and aims in modern, often scholarly terms. All this, as already stated, was conducive to authoritarian relations between the sides, almost by spontaneous and natural reflex. Studies of the emerging administrations after October, in all spheres of governmental action, including the party, shows it convincingly: the tone of command (helped by experiences from the civil war) and bureaucratic supremacy came to the officials, whatever their social origins, naturally and easily. If anything, this trend was going to grow, reaching its apogee in "high Stalinism." Paradoxically, although the socialist ideology influenced some to oppose such trends, others could see in this same ideology a justification for firm, even tough and domineering attitudes, befitting those who know what is best for the popular classes, who were not privy to concepts on the intricacies of historical development.

How the initiated analyzed the situation—although we do not forget that initially they differed quite seriously among themselves—is relevant to the study of the regime. The leader felt, as we have noted, that the state was given a broader scope and monopolistic position when facing the enfeebled social basis. But this situation also created in the leadership of the state, not despite but because of their forward-looking and modernizing ideology, a sense of vulnerability and, finally, a paranoid fear of its own masses. Whether this was objectively justified is an interesting topic for debate. But it certainly was exaggerated—or tended to become so—by the habit of using the tools of class analysis conceived in and for a developed capitalist society. In the social structure after the civil war, with its leveled-down peasantry and its cities, from which higher classes disappeared, the practice of looking desperately for a full-fledged class configuration which did not exist enhanced the sense of vulnerability, hindered the appearance of more appropriate analytical tools, and contributed in many ways to the strengthening of factors of stress and disequilibrium in the system. Misuse of tools of analysis, we claim, was one of the causes of the loss of self-control and of accrued irrationality that came to plague the country during a long period, finally driving the system into a state of acute morbidity.

It is difficult to imagine how such social realities, such hard givens of the initial stage, would not deeply influence the further stages. The structural pattern does not predetermine all policies, nor does it deny certain choices. But it certainly limits those choices and, at least, eliminates certain more desirable alternatives. One does not see a possibility of any democratic solutions in those days—even if Lenin wanted one.[16] More pertinently, socialist solutions were not available either. Officially, a transition period was necessary for it, but finally it was the almost wholesale nationalization that was decreed to be the attribute of socialism. What this meant, in reality, was a statization, which is something different, although in itself not so unexpected in Russia. But the ideological veil helped here to accelerate a broad nationalization that was, by any standard, premature in most of the sectors, not only during the civil war but also later, including in the 1930s. And "premature nationalization"—an idea which cannot be developed here—is one of the underlying factors of a specific type of bureaucratization that went with the enhancement of state power and rigid controls of the population.

Under these conditions, one wonders whether the failure of the Bolsheviks consisted in having relinquished their Octobrist ideals—we are aware how many of them fought against and paid dearly for trying to slow down the trend away from original hopes—or whether they perished because they did not know how to handle an authoritarian state and prevent it from veering into something worse, thereby closing avenues for a social democracy in Russia for an era of unknown length.

The full effects of this kind of failure become clear after a furious acceleration of economic growth was launched in a society little prepared for it all—and precisely because it was so little prepared. The effort to operate a leap in a situation we showed to have been "unbalanced" was the source of deep waves of change and crises, which we have tried to describe. The ensuing additional destabilizations, some of which were underlined in our treatment, helped tilt the scale to an ever growing reliance on "administrative methods," which were, of course, more than just coercion. They created an additional temptation to abuse the levers of coercion and prefer them to other tools, a temptation the regime had no incentives anymore to refuse. If we accept this picture of growing strains, contradictions, and imbalances in the whole system, which were foreshadowed already in the pre-1928 period but expanded in the next one under the impact of the "big drive," then further statization, bureaucratization, more coercion, and the making of a quite archaic personal despot, can be seen as a response to conditions quite favorable for these trends. What happens in agriculture should make the emergence and deepening of the state's totalitarian grip and other of its traits clearer, as this branch—and its carrier, the peasantry—is a key mechanism in this process. In another important sphere of life, the cities, the sudden and unplanned influx to towns described as the ruralization of the cities, and its consequences for social cohesion, culture, standard of living, social and individual psychology, values, collective and personal neuroses, and, finally, criminality can be seen as facets of a "deculturation" that characterized many of the cities. During a number of years the countryside was subjected partly to similar, partly to some specific transformations. The aim of the shattering collectivization policy was twofold: to organize the peasants in more productive larger units and forms and thus to help break the country's dependence on the *muzhik. Raskrest'yanit'*—"depeasantizing"—was the name of the game. The breaking in of the peasant was the least successful of the policies of the Soviet state, although polite formulas are misplaced here. What followed was a creation of a system that was more oriented to and more successful in squeezing than in producing. The peasantry denied the kolkhoz fields its zeal, and concentrated it on the tiny family plots. In this way the *muzhik* perpetuated himself as a social class of an archaic character, except that the economic basis for this was only 3.8 percent of the total sowing—and on this 3.8 percent, the peasant's family and the whole nation depended for their food to a ridiculously high degree well into the 1950s. Forceful extraction of unpaid labor, and a residual method of payment (payment only at the end of the year, in unpredictable quantity, and only after the state, creditors, and the kolkhoz took their share) deeply affected the character of the peasants and made them remember the NEP with nostalgia. From their point of view, collectivization brought them a loss of status and a drop in their standard of living. A whole system of social, economic, and legal restrictions annulled all they had achieved in three previous revolutions, and they kept asking themselves, as their interest in land and in agriculture became atrophied, what their position was in this state, what their social identity was. They were not salaried workers (whom the system officially considered its mainstay); they were not cooperators (everything was controlled and prescribed from above, and elections of kolkhoz officials were just a formality); and they were not the independent producers, the patrons (*khozyaeva*), as they had been during the NEP. Some kind of hybrid, some kind of ridiculous mini-*muzhik* suffering from such a deep sense of depersonalization and loss of identity—such was one of the results of this forceful socioengineering. At the same time a situation somewhat parallel to what occurred in the days of Peter the Great emerged and lasted well into Khrushchev's days. Peter tried and had to build his industrial plants on the basis of serf labor. Stalin carried on his industrialization, especially his industrialization of agriculture, on the basis of extracting unpaid sur-pulses, leaving only "residual remuneration" to *kolkhozniki*—which in no way could be a voluntarily accepted deal. Thus labor-oppressive practices emerged in the countryside and to a lesser extent (and in different forms) in industry as well. A labor-oppressive regimen or numerous elements thereof in the system at large also enabled and was supplemented by a wide sector of slave labor in the camps.

This complex of phenomena belongs to the repulsive and regressive elements in the Soviet industrial and social development. Stalinism was the epitome of such traits, and without them it would not have existed. When its main architect passed away and many traits of his system were dismantled, Russia found itself advancing and powerful, but the grip of the initial social backslide of 1917–21, strongly conducive and favorable to the authoritarian, ubiquitous state system of the 1930s, has not yet been broken to this day—far from it—and the result has been periodic slow-downs, decline, and conservative blockages in the country's development and social relations.

NOTES

Introduction

1. Fernand Braudel (*Ecrits sur l'histoire* [Paris: Flammarion, 1969], p. 303), writes: "Civilizations survive political, social, economic, even ideological upheavals, they actually control them insidiously, sometimes powerfully. The French revolution is not a total break in the French civilization, nor for that matter is the revolution of 1917 in the Russian civilization."

2. Basile Kerblay, *Modern Soviet Society* (New York: Pantheon Books, 1983). Kerblay is a professor of Russian civilization at the University of Paris IV.

3. V. I. Lenin, *Polnoe sobranie sochinenii*, 5th ed., 55 vols. (Moscow, 1958–65), 45: 95. There are more thoughts of a similar character, notably Lenin's statement that "the machine"—meaning the regime—does not move at all in the direction the Party tries to guide it to.

4. Geroid Tanquary Robinson (*Rural Russia Under the Old Regime* [Berkeley and Los Angeles: University of California Press, 1967], p. 65), says: "In very much that it preserved, even in much that it created, the emancipation of the sixties contributed powerfully to the making of the revolution of 1917."

5. Cf., for example, Anatole Leroy-Beaulieu, *L'Empire des tsars et les russes* (Paris, 1889), 3: 330.

6. Norman Cohn, *Europe's Inner Demons: An Enquiry Inspired by the Great Witch-Hunt* (New York: Basic Books, 1975), p. 59.

7. David S. Landes, *The Unbound Prometheus* (London: Cambridge University Press, 1969), p. 7.

8. On this debate, see Moshe Lewin, *Political Undercurrents in Soviet Economic Debates* (Princeton, N.J.: Princeton University Press, 1974), pp. 326–33. Two articles published abroad on these problems in Bukharin's thinking are not in-

cluded here, but see the biography by Stephen F. Cohen, *Bukharin and the Bolshevik Revolution* (New York: Alfred A. Knopf, 1974).

9. Aleksandra Kollontai, *Rabochaya oppozitsiya (na pravakh rukopisi)* (Moscow, 1921), p. 43. On page 4, she raises the problem of "a new social layer of rulers which cannot be pushed out of the consciousness of the masses."

10. Particularly important are the minutes of the meetings of the Central Committee between August 1917 and February 1918, in *The Bolsheviks and the October Revolution*, trans. Ann Bone (New York: Urizen Books, 1976).

11. Naum Jasny, *Soviet Industrialization, 1928–1952* (Chicago: University of Chicago Press, 1961), p. 7.

12. The first five-year plan ended officially in 1932. The year 1933 saw barely any growth at all. The second five-year plan was ratified only at the end of 1934. See *ibid.*; and Alec Nove, *Economic History of the U.S.S.R.*, 2nd ed. (New York: Penguin Books, 1972).

13. See Gyorgi Ranki and Ivan T. Berend, *Economic Development in East Central Europe in the Nineteenth and Twentieth Centuries* (New York: Columbia University Press, 1976), prologue, and pp. 218, 241.

14. Anthony Giddens, *The Class Structure of the Advanced Societies* (New York: Harper & Row, 1975), p. 154, and the chapters on state socialist systems.

15. See the introductory essay to Leon Trotsky, *The History of the Russian Revolution*, trans. Max Eastman (Ann Arbor: University of Michigan Press, 1957).

16. Cf. Craig R. Littler, *The Development of the Labour Process in Capitalist Societies: A Comparative Study of the Transformation of Work Organization in Britain, Japan, and the U.S.* (Exeter, N.H.: Heinemann Educational Books, 1982).

17. A good book on these processes is Robert A. Brady, *The Rationalization Movement in German Industry* (Berkeley: University of California Press, 1933).

18. The speech of the engineer-in-chief of the Magnitogorsk Metallurgical Plant is in *Iz istorii magnitogorskogo metallurgicheskogo kombinata i goroda Magnitogorska (1929–1941gg.): Sbornik dokumentov i materialov* (Magnitogorsk, 1965, p. 208).

19. Figures are taken from L. A. Gordon, E. V. Klopov, and L. A. Onikov, *Cherty sotsialisticheskogo obraza zhizni. Byt gorodskikh rabochikh vchera, segodnya, zavtra* (Moscow, 1977), p. 50.

20. *Ibid.*, p. 51.

21. *Ibid.*, p. 49.

22. *Ibid.*, pp. 56–57.

23. Figures on education are from I. M. Bogdanov, *Gramotnost' i obrazovanie v dorevolyutsionnoi Rossii i v SSSR (istoriko-statisticheskie ocherki)* (Moscow, 1964), p. 156.

24. *Ibid.*, pp. 166–69. His source is the 1939 population census.

25. *Ibid.*

26. Gordon, Klopov, and Onikov, *Cherty*, p. 49.

27. V. I. Lenin, "O nashei revolyutsii," in *Polnoe sobranie sochinenii*, 45: 378–82.

Chapter 2   Popular Religion in Twentieth-Century Russia

1. Sergei M. Kravchinsky, *The Russian Peasantry: Their Agrarian Condition, Social Life, and Religion* (1888); reprint ed., (Westport, Conn.: Hyperion Press, 1977).

2. Reinhard Bendix, *Max Weber: An Intellectual Portrait* (London: Methuen, 1966), p. 92.

Chapter 3   Customary Law and Rural Society in the Postreform Era

1. Robert Redfield, *Peasant Society and Culture* (Chicago: University of Chicago Press, 1956), pp. 17–20, 40–45.

2. The elements of tutelage (*opeka*) kept growing, especially during the 1880s and 1890s, at the expense of self-administration. On the development of this tutelage

there is good material in A. A. Rittikh, ed., *Krest'yanskii pravoporyadok* (St. Petersburg, 1904), pp. 293 ff.

3. The village community and the commune, as well as the *nadel* and *tyaglo*, are studied in minute juridical detail in D. A. Khauke, *Krest'yanskoe zemel'noe pravo* (Moscow, 1914).

4. Peter Czap, Jr., "Peasant Class Courts and Peasant Customary Justice in Russia, 1861–1912," *Journal of Social History* 1, no. 2 (1967). An older work that is still one of our main sources is A. A. Leont'ev, *Volostnoi sud i yuridicheskie obychai krest'yan* (St. Petersburg, 1895).

5. See A. A. Rittikh, ed., *Trudy Redaktsionnoi komissii po peresmotru zakonodatel'stva o krest'yanakh* (St. Petersburg, 1903), 1: 53.

6. A very good description is A. Kozmin, "Obychnye sudy v khutorakh Donskoi oblasti," *Etnograficheskoe obozrenie*, no. 3 (1891); see also V. V. Tenishev, *Pravosudie v russkom krest'yanskom bytu* (Bryansk, 1907), pp. 49–63.

7. Aleksandra Efimenko, *Issledovaniya narodnoi zhizni*, vol. 1, *Obychnoe pravo* (Moscow, 1884). See also her *Yuzhaya Rus'*, 2 vols. (St. Petersburg, 1905).

8. Komitety pri Osobom soveshchanii o nuzhdakh sel'sko-khozyaistvennoi promyshlennosti. On the work of these committees, see Rittikh, *Krest'yanskii pravoporyadok*.

9. A. A. Leont'ev, *Krest'yanskoe pravo* (St. Petersburg, 1909), 1: 14.

10. K. Kachorovskii, *Narodnoe pravo* (St. Petersburg, 1906), pp. 44, 64–67, and *passim*.

11. Kistyakovskii is quoted in N. D. Druzhinin, *Pravo i lichnost' krest'yanina* (Yaroslavl', 1912), pp. 238–39. See also B. Kistyakovskii, "V zashchitu prava," *Vekhi*, 2nd ed. (Moscow, 1909), p. 143.

12. Kachorovskii, *Narodnoe pravo*, pp. 134–37, and *passim*.

13. For example, E. Yakushkin, *Obychnoe pravo* (Yaroslavl', 1896), 2: xxviii–xxx.

14. See A. M. Anfimov and P. N. Zyrianov, "Elements of the Evolution of the Russian Commune in the Post-Reform Period (1861–1904)," *Soviet Studies in History* 21, no. 3 (1982–83): 78.

15. Kachorovskii, *Narodnoe pravo*, pp. 151–57.

16. To the critics discussed in Leont'ev's survey we can add such twentieth-century writers as Rittikh, Witte, and Druzhinin. See especially Druzhinin's *Pravo i lichnost'*.

17. S. Y. Witte, *Zapiski po krest'yanskomu delu* (St. Petersburg, 1905), pp. 94–101.

18. Druzhinin, *Pravo i lichnost'*, pp. 88–92. The Soviet historian Klibanov emphasizes the differences of mentality between state peasants and serfs; A. I. Klibanov, *Religioznoe sektantstvo v proshlom i nastoyashchem* (Moscow, 1973), pp. 98–99.

19. Yakushkin, *Obychnoe pravo*, pp. i–ii.

20. Khauke, *Krest'yanskoe zemel'noe pravo*, p. 9.

21. Leont'ev, *Volostnoi sud*, pp. 70–78; see also his *Krest'yanskoe pravo*, chaps. 6 and 7.

22. For a very thorough examination of these categories and the status of the different types of land, see Khauke, *Kres'tyanskoe zemel'noe pravo*, esp. pp. 75–77, and compare Leont'ev, *Volostnye sudy*, pp. 110–17.

23. See Khauke, *Krest'lanskoe zemel'noe pravo*, pp. 131–33; and A. F. Meiendorff, *Krest'yanskii dvor* (St. Petersburg, 1909), pp. 35, 37–38.

24. There are descriptions of assemblies, drawn from numerous local reports, in Rittikh, *Trudy Redaktsionnykh kommissii*, 1: 129 ff., and Druzhinin, *Pravo i lichnost'*, pp. 117–20.

25. The commune is sharply criticized as a fetter in Rittikh, *Krest'yanskii pravoporyadok*, pp. 232–36, and *passim*, although a small group of regional committees were forceful and articulate in its defense. See also V. P. Danilov, "Obshchina i kollektivizatsiya," *Narody Afriki i Azii*, no. 3 (1973), p. 45; and S. P. Dubrovskii, "K voprosu ob obshchine v Rossii v nachale 20go veka," in *Ezhegodnik po agrarnoi istorii vostochnoi Evropy: 1960 god* (Kiev, 1962), p. 523. Both Danilov and

Dubrovskii may have been influenced by A. Lositskii, "Obshchina i Ukaz 8-go noya-brya," in I. Chernyshev, A. Lositskii, and P. Maslov, *Krest'lanskoe pravo i obshchina pered Gosudarstvennoi dumoi* (St. Petersburg, 1907), pp. 52–55.

26. Such figures are still a matter of controversy; the point here is simply that the commune survived, in various stages of vigor or decline, in proportions that are difficult to pin down. For some relevant statistics and assessments, see Dubrovskii, "K voprosu," pp. 29–30, and a careful study by Dorothy Atkinson, "The Statistics on the Russian Land Commune," *Slavic Review* 32, no. 4 (December 1973): 773–87.

27. On the *razdel* and *vydel* and their role in family formation, see E. I. Busygin et al., *Obshchestvennyi i semeinyi byt russkogo naseleniya Srednego povolzh'ia* (Kazan', 1973), pp. 109–21; L. A. Anokhina and M. N. Shmeleva, *Kul'tura i byt kolkhozni-kov Kalininskoi oblasti* (Kalinin, 1964), pp. 169–71. Both works also discuss the transition from an extended to a nuclear family in the village.

28. For a study of the *bol'shak* and family relations, see Anokhina and Shmeleva, *Kul'tura i byt*, pp. 172–76, 196, and *passim*.

29. For useful data on this and related problems, see Busygin, *Obshchestvennyi i semeinyi byt*, esp. pp. 98–100; in *Semya i vozzreniya russkogo naroda* (Voronezh, 1981), pp. 41–47, A. I. Zhelobov assembled popular sayings about the relations between mother-in-law and daughter-in-law (*svekrov'* and *snokha*).

30. On women in peasant families, see Anokhina and Shmeleva, *Kul'tura i byt*, pp. 174–76; P. A. Matveev, *Ocherki yuridicheskogo byta Samarskoi gubernii* (St. Peters-burg, 1877), pp. 15–24; V. A. Alekseeva et al., *Narody evropeiskoi chasti SSSR*, vol. 1 (Moscow, 1964), pp. 462–66. On relations between spouses in the 1870s and 1880s, see Yakushkin, *Obychnoe pravo*, 1, pp. xx–xxii.

31. Khauke, *Krest'yanskoe zemel'noe pravo*, p. 197.

32. Of the literature on the agrarian reform and the action of the peasants that actually annulled the Stolypin measures, we will mention here only V. Keller and I. Ro-manenko, *Pervye itogi agrarnoi reformy* (Voronezh, 1922), and D. I. Rozenblyum, *Zemel'noe pravo RSFSR*, 2nd ed. (Moscow, 1929) (a rich source for the kinds of issues after the revolution that Khauke treated for the prerevolutionary period, plus problems specific to the NEP). On the return to the pre-Stolypin conceptions of household property, see also *Spravochnik krest'yanina*, 2nd ed. (Tula, 1928), and E. Dombrovskii, *Krest'yanskii dvor i semeino-imushchchestvennye razdely* (Moscow, 1926).

33. The figure applies to the RSFSR; V. P. Danilov, *Sovetskaya dokolkhoznaya* (Mos-cow, 1977), p. 170.

34. *Ibid.*, p. 170 and *passim*.

35. On "socialization" of land as opposed to its "nationalization" see P. I. Stuchka, ed., *Entsiklopediya gosudarstva i prava* (Moscow, 1927), 3: 711–14; and Rozen-blyum, *Zemel'noe pravo*, chap. 2. Most Soviet authors claim that what the peasants really meant was always "nationalization" and never the utopian "socialization" so dear to the SRs.

36. For valuable comments on the Land Code, see Rozenblyum, *Zemel'noe pravo*.

37. For the views of Sukhanov on the commune and other agrarian problems, see *Na agrarnom fronte*, no. 11–12 (1926), p. 101.

38. A detailed study by William Shinn tells the story. He observes that the concept "*dvor*" was banned until 1935, but then reemerged, evidently as a consequence of official acceptance of the private plot in the 1935 kolkhoz statute. W. T. Shinn, "The Law of the Russian Peasant Household," *Slavic Review* 20, no. 4 (1961), esp. 614–15.

39. A full theoretical and ideological rehabilitation of the household, with acknowledg-ment of its historic grounding in customary law, found expression in an article by G. Polyanskaya, "Rol' obychaya v imushchestvennykh otnosheniyakh krest'yanskogo

dvora," *Sovetskoe gosudarstvo i pravo*, no. 1 (1940). That the traditional household continued well into the postwar period can be seen, e.g., in V. A. Liskovets, *Imushchestvennye razdely i vydely v kolkhoznom dvore* (Moscow, 1963), pp. 17–19.

Chapter 4 The Immediate Background of Soviet Collectivization

1. These hopes and this conception are found, *inter alia*, in the Central Executive Committee (TsIK) decree of December 15, 1928. See *Kollektivizatsiya sel'skogo khozyaistva* (collection of documents) (Moscow, 1957), doc. 19.
2. 81.6 million tons of grain in 1913, 76.6 m.t. in 1926/27, 73.3 m.t. in 1927/28, 71.7 m.t. in 1928/29 (E. Zaleski, *Planification de la croissance et fluctuations économiques en URSS* [Paris: SEDES, 1962] 1: 350). On the stagnation in cattle from 1927/28, see L. Kritsman, *Na agrarnom fronte*, no. 6 (1930), p. 8; on absolute decline, Kurbatov, *Na agrarnom fronte*, no. 5 (1929). *Na agrarnom fronte* was the journal of the agrarian institute of the Communist Academy.
3. Data of V. S. Nemchinov, cited by Stalin, *Sochineniya*, 13 vols. (Moscow, 1952–55), 11: 82–83, 85; *Istoriya narodnogo khozyaistva SSSR* (Moscow, 1960), p. 527. Moreover, the figure 13 percent is an underestimation. It takes state procurements alone as the index of *tovarnost'*. Soviet researchers now stress that the *tovarnost'* in effect exceeded 20 percent. This certainly reinforces the argument put forward here. See *Istoriya sovetskogo krest'yanstva i kolkhoznogo stroitel'stva* (Moscow, 1963), p. 258.
4. Asserted by P. Lyashchenko in *Istoriya narodnogo khozyaistva SSSR*, vol. 3, *Sotsializm* (Moscow, 1956), pp. 243–44; G. S. Strumilin, *Planovoe khozyaistvo*, no. 3 (1929), p. 35.
5. On these problems see Kritsman, *Na agrarnom fronte*, no. 6 (1929), p. 8; A. Kurbatov, *Na agrarnom fronte*, no. 5 (1929), p. 82; L'vov, *Na agrarnom fronte*, no. 9 (1928), pp. 56–58; V. P. Milyutin (on the procurements), *Na agrarnom fronte*, no. 9 (1928).
6. A. I. Rykov's speech, in *Pravda*, March 11, 1928.
7. V. M. Molotov, *15-tyi s"ezd . . . stenotchet* (Moscow and Leningrad, 1929), p. 1003. He speaks of "colossal stupidities" perpetrated in price policy. G. Kaminskii, *ibid.*, declared: "An enormous influence on the instability of *tovarnost'* was exerted also by the prices policy."
8. Cf. Kritsman, *Na agrarnom fronte*, no. 6 (1930), p. 8.
9. Kalinin complained at the Fifteenth Congress (*15-tyi s"ezd . . . stenotchet*, p. 1102) that work in the village was, in general, neglected (*zabroshennyi*) and was not regarded as socialist work. On the authorities' lack of interest in cooperation, see M. I. Kalinin, *16-tyi s"ezd . . . stenotchet* (Moscow and Leningrad, 1929), p. 134.
10. That the state-cum-collective sector was not only advancing but at times declining is attested to by Kritsman, *Na agrarnom fronte*, no. 6 (1930), p. 13. On the condition of neglect in which the kolkhozy found themselves the materials are abundant, in particular the numerous articles in *Na agrarnom fronte* from 1925 onward. The credits assigned to kolkhozy in 1927—13.7 million rubles in the RSFSR and 18 m.r. for the whole country—speak for themselves (figures from *Pravda*, May 24, 1927).
11. Cf. A. Gaister and V. Levin, *Bol'shevik*, no. 9–10 (1928), p. 84; Kurbatov, *Na agrarnom fronte*, no. 5 (1928), p. 87. Up to the end of 1927 only 8.5 percent of the peasants introduced any "minor ameliorations." In the summer of 1929 only 8.3 percent of the sown area was sown with selected seeds. The peasants bought very few of the more or less modern implements, owing to lack of money, while the government depots were glutted with such implements.
12. Many voices demanded, from 1925, more energetic promotion of the collective

movement and that the planning of it be undertaken, e.g., Lyashchenko in *Na agrarnom fronte*, no. 1 (1925), p. 28; and two other authors in the same issue, pp. 78–80.

13. Recounted by B. P. Sheboldaev in *Bol'shevik*, no. 11–12 (1930), p. 61.
14. Rykov's speech in *Pravda*, July 15, 1928.
15. Rykov said: "Such a *perekachka* is inevitable and admissible, but solely for the present stage of development, since industry has not grown sufficiently" (*15-tyi s"ezd . . . stenotchet*, p. 772).
16. See, e.g., his concluding speech at the Fifteenth Congress in *ibid.*, pp. 1040–41.
17. *Ibid.*, pp. 771, 774–75.
18. Molotov, *ibid.*, p. 1058.
19. For the Kalinin–Bukharin view, see Kalinin, *ibid.*, p. 1098. For the Stalin–Molotov views, see *ibid.*, pp. 60, 1061–62, and *passim*.
20. Cf. N. Valentinov (Volskii), *Sotsialisticheskii vestnik*, April 1961, p. 70.
21. Stalin, *15-tyi s"ezd . . . stenotchet*, p. 56; and Molotov, *ibid.*, p. 1057.
22. Rykov, concluding speech, *ibid.*, p. 1272; Molotov, *ibid.*, 1072, 1079.
23. Said by G. M. Krzhizhanovsky, in *ibid.*, p. 792.
24. Rykov's speech, *Pravda*, March 11, 1928.
25. See Stalin's speech of October 23, 1927, in *Sochineniya*, 10: 196–97.
26. Cf. A. I. Mikoyan, *Pravda*, February 10, 1928.
27. Stalin, *Sochineniya*, 11: 4–6.
28. *Ibid.*, p. 6. Stalin was not interested in the kolkhozy before his "discovery."
29. *Ibid.*
30. *Ibid.*, pp. 88–89, where he declares the necessity to "introduce a system under which the kolkhozy provide all their marketable wheat to the state and cooperative organs *under threat of being deprived of subsidies and credits from the state*" (emphasis added).
31. Stalin, letter to the Politburo of June 20, 1928, in *Sochineniya*, 11: 159.
32. *Ibid.*, pp. 6, 90–92.
33. Stalin, speech at the July plenum, in *ibid.*, p. 159.
34. *Ibid.*; and speech at the April 1929 plenum, in *Bol'shevik*, no. 23–24 (1929), p. 34 (this speech is also in *Sochineniya*, vol. 12).
35. N. I. Bukharin to L. B. Kamenev, in *Sotsialisticheskii vestnik*, no. 9 (1929), p. 10.
36. The amount granted to kolkhozy in 1928 was 60 m.t. (*KPSS v rezolyutsiyakh i resheniyakh s"ezdov*, vol. 2 [Moscow, 1954], p. 496. On the condition of the kolkhozy and the overwhelmed authorities, see V. I. Kuzmin, *Pravda*, April 10, 1928; Gaister, *Na agrarnom fronte*, no. 12 (1928); Kantor, *Pravda*, March 10, 1928; *Na agrarnom fronte*, no. 11 (1928), p. 137; Kubyak, *Pravda*, March 10, 1928.
37. E. F. Kulikov, *Na agrarnom fronte*, no. 12 (1928), p. 29.
38. Kalinin, *16-tyi s"ezd . . . stenotchet*, p. 143.
39. Stalin, *Sochineniya*, 11: 143.
40. The phrase "trade deserts" (*torgovye pustyni*) was current at the time, denoting the effect of persecution of private traders and the liquidation of their businesses. Reported in *Voprosy istorii*, no. 4 (1964), p. 15.
41. See *Pravda*, December 25, 1928; and Kiselev, *Pravda*, March 5, 1929, protesting against the *obednyachivanie* and other anti-*serednyaki* activities. See also A. Angarov, *Klassovaya bor'ba v sovetskoi derevne* (Moscow, 1929), p. 47.
42. *Kollektivizatsiya sel'skogo khozyaistva*, pp. 105–6.
43. L. M. Kaganovich, *Bol'shevik*, no. 19 (1928), pp. 20, 21. He states: "Certain difficulties which we are encountering in our relations with the *serednyaki* are inevitable."
44. Stalin, *Sochineniya*, 11: 248.
45. For Rykov's opposition to a system of coercion, see Robert V. Daniels, *The Con-*

science of the Revolution (Cambridge, Mass.: Harvard University Press, 1960), pp. 329–30.

46. See N. I. Bukharin, speech at the July 1928 plenum, cited by Daniels, *Conscience*, pp. 331, 335; *KPSS v rezolyutsiyakh*, 2: 559.
47. The propositions of the rightists can be reconstructed from official sources (among others): Stalin, *Sochineniya*, 11: 218–325, 12: 92; *Bol'shevik*, nos. 23, 24 (1929), pp. 30–35, 46; *16-tyi s"ezd . . . stenotchet* (1962 ed.), nn. 56, 133, 135, 215, 266.
48. *16-tyi s"ezd . . . stenotchet* (1962 ed.), n. 135.
49. *Ibid.*, n. 56 (material from the party archives); Rykov's speech at the Sovnarkom, *Pravda*, April 6, 1928.
50. Cf. *KPSS v rezolyutsiyakh*, 2: 558; Y. E. Rudzutak, *16-tyi s"ezd . . . stenotchet*, p. 201; Bukharin against unbridled haste (*skoropalitel'nye tempy*) in his "Politicheskoe zaveshchanie Lenina," *Pravda*, January 24, 1929.
51. N. I. Bukharin, "Zametki ekonomista," *Pravda*, September 30, 1928; and "Politicheskoe zaveshchanie," where he says: "We shall conquer due to scientific economic administration or we shall not conquer at all."
52. Bukharin, "Politicheskoe zaveshchanie."
53. On the agricultural plan, see articdes by N. M. Vol'f in *Planovoe khozyaistvo*, no. 2 (1929), and *Na agrarnom fronte*, no. 4 (1929); resolutions of the Sixteenth Congress in *KPSS v rezolyutsiyakh*, 2: 570–73; resolutions of the Fifth Congress of Soviets, in *Kollektivizatsiya sel'skogo khozyaistva*, n. 41.
54. Vol'f, *Planovoe khozyaistvo*, no. 2 (1929), p. 116; R. E. Veisberg, *Planovoe khozyaistvo*, no. 3 (1929), p. 106.
55. Vol'f, *Planovoe khozyaistvo*, no. 2 (1929), pp. 116–17.
56. M. A. Kraev in his critique of the "five-year plan of cooperation," in *Na agrarnom fronte*, no. 6 (1929). TOZ is a Russian acronym for "association for farming in common." Such associations were a kind of producer's co-ops, preferred by peasants over other, more ambitious forms of collectivization and actually the most widespread as long as the peasants themselves were free to choose. Only plowland was put to farming in common; all the rest remained private, and the crop was divided according to the acreage that each peasant had contributed to the common field of the TOZ.
57. On the "stations" of the Shevchenko type, see E. F. Kulikov, *Na agrarnom fronte*, no. 5 (1929); on the model contract between the "station" and the peasants, see appendix to *16-tyi s"ezd . . . stenotchet*; Kalinin's speeches in *ibid.*, pp. 140 ff., and Fifth Congress of Soviets, *Stenotchet*, bull. 19, pp. 3–4.
58. Vol'f, *Na agrarnom fronte*, no. 4 (1929), pp. 6, 8.
59. Karl Bauman, Moscow party secretary and head of the rural department of the Central Committee, said in June (*Pravda*, June 16, 1929) that Moscow Oblast was preparing to collectivize 25 percent of its peasants in five years and that, over all, a period of twenty years was necessary to collectivize it all.
60. Kalinin (Fifth Congress of Soviets, *Stenotchet*, bull. 15, p. 39) declared: "Whoever thinks that these [good agricultural enterprises] can be established in a hole-and-corner way, primitively, without highly qualified mechanics and specialists, whoever thinks this is neither a Marxist nor a communist but a man of petit bourgeois mentality, a man stricken by peasant narrowness" (!). Rykov (*ibid.*, bull. 7, p. 6) spoke against setting up kolkhozy on the basis of the *sokha* (wooden plow); Stalin said the same thing in April 1929 (*Bol'shevik*, no. 23–24 [1929], p. 34).
61. Stalin, *Bol'shevik*, no. 23–24 (1929), p. 32. Recovery of private agriculture comes last among the tasks set by the Sixteenth Conference (*KPSS v rezolyutsiyakh*, 2: 580).
62. Stalin, *Bol'shevik*, no. 23–24 (1929), pp. 16, 27.
63. *KPSS v rezolyutsiyakh*, 2: 576–77.

64. Stalin, *Bol'shevik*, no. 23–24 (1929), p. 28.
65. *Ibid.*
66. A. I. Mikoyan, *Pravda*, June 13, 1929; see also A. Mendel'son, *Planovoe khozyaistvo*, no. 5 (1929), p. 55.
67. A. I. Mikoyan, *Bol'shevik*, no. 15 (1929), p. 20; A. Mendel'son, *Planovoe khozyaistvo*, no. 8 (1929), p. 14.
68. *Pravda*, February 21, 1929.
69. Mendel'son, *Planovoe khozyaistvo*, no. 8 (1929), p. 65.
70. Lyashchenko (*Istoriya*, p. 244) says that private traders procured 23 percent of the marketed wheat from peasants in 1928/29, whereas in the previous year their share had been only 14 percent.
71. On the progress of the plans, see two studies by Mendel'son in *Planovoe khozyaistvo*, nos. 5 and 8 (1929).
72. E. Zaleski, *La Planification*, pp. 85–87; M. S. Golendo, *Na agrarnom fronte*, no. 10 (1929), p. 11.
73. Cf. Golendo, *Na agrarnom fronte*, no. 10 (1929), pp. 14–15.
74. The five-year plan spoke of 5 million households collectivized toward the end of the quinquennium, covering an area of 21–22 million hectares. In June 1929 Kolkhoztsentr announced an aim of 8 million households with 7–8 million souls for the single year 1930, and half the rural population (and three times the area envisaged in the initial plan) by 1933. In August Mikoyan spoke (for 1930) of 10 million households. In September Gosplan fixed, still for 1929/30, a target of 13 million households with 10 percent of the total population in kolkhozy. In October and November the "control figures" for 1929/30 were altered to 15.2 million households with 12 percent of the population. In December Sovnarkom wanted to collectivize 30 million households—and this was not the end. (These figures are from many sources cited in my study *La Paysannerie et le pouvoir sovietique, 1929–1930* [The Hague: Mouton, 1966]; an English translation appeared from Allen & Unwin in 1968.)
75. On the reform of cooperation, see the Central Committee decision of June 27, 1929, in *Kollektivizatsiya sel'skogo khozyaistva*, doc. 46. The Central Committee admitted in its letter published in May 1928 that agricultural cooperation "is still very weak" (doc. 6, p. 53). Kaminskii, head of Kolkhoztsentr and member of the Central Committee, ascribed the weakness of agricultural production to the weakness of agricultural cooperation. On this occasion he gave to understand that part of the cooperative network was more formal than real (*Pravda*, January 11, 1929). On the destruction of the agricultural cooperative network, see the articles by F. A. Tsilko in *Na agrarnom fronte*, no. 6 (1930), and L'vov in *Pravda*, June 13, 1930 (supplement of discussion material for the Sixteenth Congress).
76. Decision of the Central Committee on contracts in *Kollektivizatsiya sel'skogo khozyaistva*, doc. 52, and of Sovnarkom in *ibid.*, doc. 57. On the weaknesses and deceptions of this enterprise, see L'vov, *Na agrarnom fronte*, no. 7 (1929); Kalinin, Fifth Congress of Soviets, *Stenotchet*, bull. 15, pp. 25–26. On the check to contract making during the sowing in the spring of 1920, see Mendel'son, *Planovoe khozyaistvo*, no. 5 (1930), p. 216.
77. The November 1929 plenum authorized these *agrarnoindustriyal'nye kombinaty* (*KPSS v rezolyutsiyakh*, 2: 651); in February 1929 the Central Committee called for experiments in *sovkhoznokolkhoznye ob"edineniya* (*Pravda*, February 19, 1929). The giant kolkhozy were set up from the end of 1928.
78. See *Pravda*, editorial, August 7, 1929, and the Central Committee decision concerning the Ukraine in *KPSS v rezolyutsiyakh*, 2: 662. But decisions at the local levels, obliging members of rural party cells to join the kolkhozy, had been taken before the intervention of the Central Committee; see I. Vareikis, *Na agrarnom fronte*, no. 8 (1929), pp. 67–70.

79. Decree of the TsIK and Sovnarkom on the "kolkhoz system" in *Kollektivizatsiya sel'skogo khozyaistva*, doc. 45; on the creation of Traktortsentr in *ibid.*, docs. 21 and 44.
80. See *ibid.*, doc. 42, pp. 173–74.
81. On the decision to double the area of "giant kolkhozy" see G. Kaminskii, *16-tyi s"ezd . . . stenotchet*, p. 187. On the general percentage of collectivization, see V P. Danilov, ed., *Ocherki istorii kollektivizatsii sel'skogo khozyaistva v soyuznykh respublikakh* (Moscow, 1963), pp. 32–33.
82. See B. A. Abramov in Danilov, *Ocherki*, pp. 96–97; N. A. Ivnitskii, *Voprosy istorii KPSS*, no. 4 (1962), p. 71.
83. See Abramov in Danilov, *Ocherki*; cf. also *Materialy po istorii SSSR*, vol. 7 (Moscow, 1959), p. 234 (the report submitted by Kolkhoztsentr to the Politburo). The report says, concerning the Khopersk *okrug*, which was declared the first *okrug sploshnoi kollektivizatsii*: "It is essential to note that Khopersk *okrug* is not particularly outstanding in tempo of collectivization or in its economic importance. The value of its manifestation lies in its being the first to pose the problem of planning the total [*sploshnaya*] collectivization of the *okrug* in the course of the quinquennium."
84. Cf. *Pravda*, October 8, 1929; *Bol'shevik*, no. 21 (1929), pp. 64–65; *Na agrarnom fronte*, no. 10 (1929), p. 19.
85. *Pravda*, editorial, October 31, 1929.
86. Cf. A. G. Shlikhter, "Kak perestroit' pyatiletku," *Pravda*, November 1, 1929.
87. See Danilov, *Ocherki*, pp. 95–97; and B. A. Abramov, *Voprosy istorii KPSS*, no. 1 (1964), pp. 32–33.
88. On these reservations, see Abramov, *Voprosy istorii KPSS*, no. 1 (1964), p. 33.
89. The decisions of the November 1929 plenum are in *KPSS v rezolyutsiyakh*, 2: 642–44, 645, 651.
90. Molotov's speech (abridged) is in *Bol'shevik*, no. 22 (1929), pp. 10–23. See especially pp. 13 and 14 and the passages of his speech cited from the party archives in Danilov, *Ocherki*, p. 97.
91. For the most detailed account of this commission, see B. A. Abramov, "O rabote komissii Politbyuro TsK-a VKP(b)," *Voprosy istorii KPSS*, no. 1 (1964). On the changes made by Stalin, see *ibid.*, pp. 40–41; on the dissolution of the subcommission, see Ivnitskii, *ibid.*, no. 4 (1962), pp. 68–69.
92. See Bukharin, "Zametki ekonomista."
93. See Sheboldaev, *Bol'shevik*, no. 11–12 (1930), p. 61.
94. Molotov affirmed at the Fifteenth Congress (*15-tyi s"ezd . . . stenotchet*, p. 1074) that these "simple associations" contained 1 million householders (the figure is probably exaggerated) but that only 6 percent of this number were embraced by cooperation, the rest being "wild."
95. See Abramov in Danilov, *Ocherki*, pp. 96–97; Ivnitskii, *Voprosy istorii KPSS*, no. 4 (1962), p. 71.
96. See R. Schlesinger, "Notes on the Context of Early Soviet Planning," *Soviet Studies* (July 1964).
97. *Ibid.*, pp. 29, 30.
98. *Ibid.*, p. 29.

Chapter 5 Who Was the Soviet Kulak?

1. V. I. Lenin, *Sochineniya*, 4th ed., 36 vols. (Moscow, 1941), 3: 333–34. But he knows that the countryside is precapitalist and says so.
2. *Ibid.*, 28: 39; Larin, *Sovetskaya derevnya* (Moscow and Leningrad, 1928), p. 173.
3. Table quoted by V. Yakovtsevsky, *Agrarnye otnosheniya v SSSR v period stroitel'stva sotsializma* (Moscow, 1954), p. 156.
4. Leon Trotsky, *Histoire de la révolution russe* (Paris: Seuil, 1950), 2: 355.

5. *Postroenie fundamenta sotsialisticheskoi ekonomiki v SSSR 1926–1932* (Moscow, 1960) estimates that in 1927 95.5 percent of the land was in communal ownership, 2.6 percent in *otruba*, 0.9 percent in *khutora*.
6. In 1926 30.5 percent of peasants in the RSFSR had no draft animal. In grain-producing regions—Lower and Middle Volga, North Caucasus—this percentage was 40 or over (V. P. Danilov, ed., *Ocherki istorii kollektivizatsii v soyuznykh respublikakh* [Moscow, 1963], pp. 75–76). Many households had no plow.
7. A. P. Smirnov's pamphlet is quoted in *Na agrarnom fronte*, no. 9 (1930), pp. 20–21.
8. N. I. Bukharin, *Put' k sotsializmu i raboche-krest'yanskii blok* (Moscow and Leningrad, 1926), p. 13.
9. Article by V. Bazarov in *Planovoe khozyaistvo*, no. 2 (1928), p. 42; N. N. Sukhanov's opinion is implicit in his statement to the Communist Academy (*Na agrarnom fronte*, no. 6–7 [1928], p. 184).
10. Quoted by E. H. Carr, *Socialism in One Country, 1924–1926*, vol. 1 (New York: Macmillan, 1958), pp. 236–37.
11. Decree of TsIK-SNK, in *Kollektivizatsiya sel'skogo khozyaistva* (Moscow, 1957), doc. 59.
12. Y. Trifonov, *Ocherki klassovoi bor'by SSSR v gody Nepa* (Moscow, 1960), p. 189.
13. Speech by V. P. Danilov, in *Istoriya sovetskogo krest'yanstva i kolkhoznogo stroitel'stva v SSSR* (Moscow, 1965), p. 63.
14. See S. G. Strumilin, *Planovoe khozyaistvo*, no. 8 (1929), pp. 49 ff.
15. *Ibid.*, p. 49.
16. V. P. Milyutin, in *55-tyi s"ezd . . . stenotchet* (1929), p. 1191.
17. Danilov, *Istoriya*, p. 51.
18. K. Naumov, *Na agrarnom fronte*, no. 6–7 (1928), p. 184.
19. Moshe Lewin, *Cahiers du monde russe et sovietique* (Paris), January–March 1965.
20. N. N. Sukhanov, *Na agrarnom fronte*, no. 6–7 (1928), pp. 178 ff.; S. M. Dubrovsky, *Pravda*, February 10, 1928.
21. See Lyashchenko, *Istoriya narodnogo khozyaistva SSSR*, vol. 3 (1956), p. 238; Danilov, *Istoriya*, p. 58. Up to 200 rubles' worth of the means of production was the criterion of semiproletarian (*bednyak*); 200–800 rubles, *serednyak*; 800–1,600 rubles, well-to-do *serednyak (zazhitochnyi)*.
22. Details about the commission and its work will be found in Larin, *Agrarnaya struktura SSSR i sud'by agrarnogo perenaseleniya* (Moscow and Leningrad, 1928), esp. p. 23.
23. *Ibid.*
24. Summary in N. Lifshits, *Bol'shevik*, no. 2 (1929), p. 63.
25. *Sobranie zakonov i rasporyazhenii*, no. 12 (March 1929), art. 103.
26. *Kollektivizatsiya sel'skogo khozyaistva*, doc. 38, pp. 163–64; and *Sobranie zakonov i rasporyazhenii*, no. 34 (June 1929), art. 301.
27. See, for example, Lifshits, *Bol'shevik*, no. 2 (1929).
28. Carr, *Socialism in One Country*, p. 99.
29. For Narkomzem evaluation, see *Bol'shevik*, no. 2 (1929), p. 7; Stalin, at November 1929 plenum, in *Sochineniya*, 11: 265.
30. *Planovoe khozyaistvo*, no. 2 (1929), pp. 100–1; and Danilov, *Istoriya*, p. 61.
31. The commission's figure is given by Larin, *Agrarnaya struktura*, p. 45; the commission's figure in 1929 is in *Voprosy istorii KPSS*, no. 4 (1962), p. 68.
32. I take it upon myself here to omit the precise sources for all these figures.
33. Lyashchenko, *Istoriya*, p. 238.
34. Nemchinov's famous table is quoted in Yakovtsevsky, *Agrarnye otnosheniya*, p. 156.
35. For Molotov's speech, see *15-tyi s"ezd . . . stenotchet*, p. 1091; Strumilin, *Planovoe khozyaistvo*, no. 8 (1929), p. 57.
36. L. Kritsman, *Na agrarnom fronte*, no. 4 (1928), p. 120.

37. Trifonov, *Ocherki*, p. 37.
38. For Sokol'nikov's speech, see *15-tyi s"ezd . . . stenotchet*, p. 1011; the figure of 900 million poods is in *Na agrarnom fronte*, no. 2 (1928), p. 6.
39. See A. Gaister, *Na agrarnom fronte*, no. 11–12 (1927), for a detailed study of the social strata; for the reserves, see *ibid.*, no. 1 (1930), p. 96, where he says "the kulaks' reserve fell by 10 percent in 1927–28, by 20 percent in the following year, and by 22.5 percent in 1929–30," but he does not give a figure for the total of these reserves.
40. Yakovtsevsky, *Agrarnye otnosheniya*, p. 247; for Danilov's use of all three indices, see Danilov, *Ocherki*, p. 62, but he does put the hiring out of the means of production in the first place there. The preponderance of the hiring out of the means of production as the principal factor belongs to the school of Kritsman, who defended it at the Communist Academy. See *Na agrarnom fronte*, no. 4 (1928), pp. 114–40, and the discussion.
41. Yakovtsevsky, *Agrarnye otnosheniya*, p. 245.
42. Danilov, *Ocherki*, p. 61.
43. Yakovtsevsky, *Agrarnye otnosheniya*, p. 247; and Danilov, *Ocherki*, p. 61.
44. *Postroenie fundamenta*, p. 272; Lyashchenko, *Istoriya*, p. 238. According to the former it is 41.6 percent of all kulaks; according to Lyashchenko, 39.2 percent.
45. Kas'yan, in *Istoriya sovetskogo krest'yanstva*, p. 148.
46. Danilov, *Ocherki*, p. 61.
47. *Ibid.*, p. 59; and Yakovtsevsky, *Istoriya*, p. 252. Their figures are often taken from the archives.
48. Yakovtsevsky, *Istoriya*, p. 259.
49. Lyashchenko, *Istoriya*, pp. 238–39, says 37.4 percent only.
50. Yakovtsevsky, *Istoriya*, p. 252.
51. *Ibid.*, p. 256.
52. Danilov, *Ocherki*, p. 51.
53. Kas'yan, in *Istoriya sovetskogo krest'yanstva*, p. 148.
54. See the statements by M. L. Bogdenko and I. E. Zelenin in *ibid.*, p. 219.
55. More exactly 51.1 percent, according to Lyashchenko, *Istoriya*, p. 238.
56. It was Kritsman who asserted to the Communist Academy that only 1 percent of households had more than one paid worker. See *Na agrarnom fronte*, no. 4 (1929), p. 117.
57. *Ibid.*, p. 111.
58. Quoted by A. I. Rykov, *Bol'shevik*, no. 2 (1929), p. 74.
59. Larin, *Na agrarnom fronte*, no. 4 (1927). The phenomenon is also mentioned in Trifonov, *Ocherki*, p. 183, and is implicit in the article by Koshelev, "Krest'yanskie zabastovki," *Na agrarnom fronte*, no. 10 (1929), pp. 84–86 and *passim*.
60. *Pravda*, December 14, 1928.
61. A. Angarov, *Klassovaya bor'ba v sovetskoi derevne* (Moscow, 1929), pp. 30–41.
62. *Ibid.*, p. 31, notes; the same statement is in Karpinsky, *Bol'shevik*, no. 11 (1929), p. 31.
63. *Dokumenty po istorii sovetskogo obshchestva*, vol. 7 (Moscow, 1959), shows the recrudescence of the defensive activity of the kulaks from the moment that they learn of the existence of the decision to remove them to the outskirts of the villages. This occurred at the end of summer 1929, and it is not yet an expropriation so much as a "setting apart."
64. Angarov, *Klassovaya bor'ba*, p. 31.
65. S. I. Syrtsov, speech at the 16th conference in April 1929, *Stenograficheskii otchet* (Moscow, 1962), p. 322.
66. *Ibid.*
67. *Dokumenty po istorii*, 7: 240 ff.; article by Karavaev, *Na agrarnom fronte*, no. 10 (1929); *Bol'shevik*, no. 19 (1929), esp. p. 60.

68. *Bol'shevik*, no. 10 (1929), p. 60.
69. Cf. Karpinsky, "O kolkhozakh i kulake," *Bol'shevik*, no. 11 (1929), p. 34.
70. M. I. Kalinin, *Pravda*, December 14, 1928.
71. See *Bol'shevik*, no. 20 (1929), pp. 66–67.
72. Details in V*oprosy istorii KPSS*, no. 4 (1958), p. 77.
73. For details, see M. L. Bogdenko, V*oprosy istorii*, no. 5 (1965), p. 31.
74. S. G. Strumilin, *Planovoe khozyaistvo*, no. 3 (1929), p. 34.
75. See, for example, *Dokumenty po istorii*, pp. 241–43.
76. N. M. Antselovich, *16-taya konferentsiya VKP(b) . . . stenotchet* (Moscow, 1962), p. 428.
77. Particularly in *Bol'shevik*, no. 12 (1929), pp. 41, 49.
78. Data on the weakening of the kulaks are to be found in, among others: Gaister, *Na agrarnom fronte*, no. 1 (1930), pp. 96–97; G. Konyukhov, *KPSS v bor'be s khlebnymi zatrudneniyami v strane, 1928–9* (Moscow, 1960), p. 201; Danilov, *Ocherki*, pp. 88–89, 172; *Postroenie fundamenta*, p. 272.
79. Bogdenko, V*oprosy istorii*, no. 5 (1965), pp. 147–48.

Chapter 6   "Taking Grain": Soviet Policies of Agricultural Procurements Before the War

1. This is Oscar Lange's term: see his "The Role of Planning in Socialist Economics," in Morris Bornstein, ed., *Comparative Economic Systems* (Homewood, Ill.: Irwin, 1965), p. 200.
2. The figures are in A. A. Barsov, in *Istoriya SSSR*, no. 6 (1968), p. 71.
3. Whether peasants did actually engage in any deliberate sabotage at that time is more than doubtful. Many top leaders believed then that the "crisis" had nothing definitive to it and could have been averted or mitigated by appropriate policies. This opinion was held not only by the leaders of the "right" (Bukharin, Rykov, Tomskii) but also by such supporters of Stalin as Mikoyan. According to archival sources, he believed in 1928 that the difficulties of the "grain crisis" resulted to a considerable degree from policy errors and that such errors could have been avoided. Quoted in E. I. Turchaninova, *Podgotovka i provedenie sploshoi kollektivizatsii sel'skogo khozynaistva v Stavropolskom krae* (Dushanbe, 1963), pp. 106–7.
4. The events of the "grain crisis" are described in E. H. Carr and R. W. Davies, *Foundations of a Planned Economy, 1926–1929*, vol. 1 (London: Macmillan, 1969), chaps. 2 and 3; and in my own *Russian Peasants and Soviet Power* (Evanston, Ill.: Northwestern University Press, 1968), chap. 9.
5. S. Kossior, the Ukrainian party secretary, admitted in *Pravda*, April 26, 1930, that the "worst side of the grain *zagotovki*—the method of pressure—was applied automatically to collectivization"—exactly as the critics were saying earlier. But what Kossior stated here with regret very soon became common practice, including on the part of Kossior himself.
6. Organizing the campaign, launching and supervising it, became the task of the party secretaries at the administrative levels. The technical apparatus for actually doing the job of collecting was provided by the agricultural cooperative organization Khlebotsentr and its local branches, but the grain had to be turned over to the state agency Soyuzkhleb, created in 1928 under the auspices of the Commissariat for Foreign and Internal Trade (from 1931, under the Commissariat of Supplies, which became separated from the Commissariat for Foreign Trade); Soyuzkhleb would also collect grain from sovkhozy directly through its own local branches, and the same was true for the milling tax (*garnets*). The central planner of the campaign was Mikoyan, the head of the commissariat, acting in coordination with other bodies, especially with the Commissariat for Agriculture (headed by Yakovlev). A body called the Special Council for *Zagotovki* of Grain was created inside

Narkomtorg, including representatives of all the other commissariats and agencies concerned. The appropriate decrees can be found in *Sobranie zakonov i rasporyazhenii raboche-krest'yanskogo pravitelstva* (1928–29); a good detailed description of the functioning of the whole system is in M. A. Chernov, ed., *Spravochnik po khlebnomu delu* (Moscow, 1932).

7. The norms are in *Kollektivizatsiya sel'skogo khozyaistva: Vazhneishie postanovleniya* (Moscow, 1957), pp. 534–44. On depriving peasants of reserves, see Y. A. Moshkov, *Zernovaya problema v gody sploshnoi kollektivizatsii* (Moscow, 1966), pp. 72–73. This is an excellent book which we shall be using very often.
8. On the faulty distribution of quotas, see the article by Vinogradsky, in *Ekonomicheskaya gazeta*, June 16, 1930. This type of target planning was applied to other agricultural activities too, not only to *zagotovki*.
9. Cf. *ibid*. The author urges the drawing up of such balances and basing the imposition on them in order to avoid undermining the production capabilities of the countryside. Soon such demands would come under attack as "antistate," and sometimes the very drawing up of balances would be forbidden.
10. See *ibid*., and Moshkov, *Zernovaya problema*, p. 163. The reader will find data on the "intervillage" grain circulation in R. W. Davies, "A Note on Grain Statistics," *Soviet Studies* 21, no. 3 (January 1971), commenting on Jerzy Karcz's article, in *Soviet Studies* 18, no. 4 (April 1967). Both articles will introduce the reader to the problems of "commercial grain."
11. Another step is worth mentioning here which further contributed to weakening the resources of the countryside: from 1928, the milling tax (*garnets*) was to be paid exclusively to the government. In order to make it work, all private mills were nationalized. This tax added some 2 million tons of grain to the government's income. See Chernov, *Spravochnik po khlebnomu delu*, p. 25.
12. Cf. A. I. Mikoyan, in *Bol'shevik*, no. 1 (1931), pp. 12–14, 16.
13. Chernov, *Spravochnik po khlebnomu delu*, pp. 27–28.
14. For details, see *ibid*. There were private peasants who had to sign and some who did not have to, but the latter had to engage in so-called self-impositions, which were, in fact, prescribed by the authorities. To avoid unnecessary complexities, we do not enter into such details in this chapter. In any case, the government made opposition to delivering grain liable to prosecution under paragraph 61 of the Criminal Code, with penalties ranging from a fine up to five times the value of the arrears (in market prices) to two years' imprisonment, with or without deportation. According to explanations of the Supreme Court, penal clauses had to be avoided with regard to nonkulaks, who were to be punished by fines and deprivation of different services and allowances—but not so anymore if they persisted; in such cases the full sting of this law was to be applied. See *Code pénal de l'R.S.F.S.R.* (Paris, 1935) pp. 53, 288–89; and *Sbornik raz'yasnenii verkhovnogo suda RSFSR* (Moscow, 1932), pp. 293–94.
15. Moshkov, *Zernovaya problema*, p. 152.
16. N. I. Nemakov, *Kompartiya—organizator massovogo kolkhoznogo dvizheniya* (Moscow, 1966), p. 258.
17. The sources on ways of evading *zagotovki* are numerous, especially in the journal of Komzag (Committee for Procurements), *Na fronte sel'sko-khozyaistvennykh zagotovok*; see, e.g., no. 14 (1933), pp. 3–6, dealing, among other phenomena, with the "hairdressers."
18. Moshkov, *Zernovaya problema*, pp. 155–56 and *passim*; also *Sovetskaya yustitsiya*, no. 11 (1931), p. 18, for sample figures on court cases.
19. Further material on repression can be found in M. A. Chernov, in *Bol'shevik*, no. 21 (1931), p. 49, and in an article by I. F. Ganzha, in V. P. Danilov, ed., *Ocherki po istorii kollektivizatsii sel'skogo khozyaistva v soyuznykh respublikakh* (Moscow, 1963), pp. 199–200.

20. Chernov, in *Bol'shevik*, no. 21 (1931), pp. 50, 52.
21. *Na agrarnom fronte*, no. 1 (1932), pp. 23, 27; *Sotsialisticheskoe zemledelie*, November 14, 1931; *ibid*., no. 1–2, January 28, 1932, p. 14.
22. For the political difficulties, see Danilov, *Ocherki*, *passim*; Moshkov, *Zernovaya problema*, p. 194; I. E. Zelenin, *Istoricheskie zapiski*, no. 76 (1965), p. 44.
23. *Kompartiya Ukrainy v rezolyutsiakh i resheniyakh s"ezdov i konferentsii, 1918–1957* (Kiev, 1958), p. 569.
24. *Ibid*., pp. 569–70.
25. Moshkov, *Zernovaya problema*, p. 202.
26. For the appeals of the Ukrainian CC on its session on July 9, 1932, see *Kompartiya Ukrainy v rezolyutsiyakh*, p. 576.
27. For details, see V. N. Kleiner, in *Planovoe khozyaistvo*, no. 4 (1933), pp. 17, 19, 27. The 1931 Circular of the Commissariat of Justice is in *Code pénal*, p. 227.
28. Kleiner, in *Planovoe khozyaistvo*, no. 4 (1933): 29. Kleiner was deputy chairman of Komzag. The chairman himself, Chernov, stated the same in *Na fronte sel'skokhozyaistvennykh zagotovok*, no. 11 (1933), pp. 1–2. He blamed the leniency of the previous period, which had made the repressions indispensable later.
29. Moshkov, *Zernovaya problema*, p. 211.
30. *Ibid*., p. 214.
31. Stalin, in *Bol'shevik*, no. 1–2 (1933), p. 19.
32. For events in the North Caucasus, see speech by N. S. Khrushchev, in *Pravda*, March 10, 1963, quoting the exchange of letters between Sholokhov and Stalin; Moshkov, *Zernovaya problema*, p. 217; Zelenin, in *Istoricheskie zapiski*, no. 76 (1965), pp. 43–44.
33. On the famine, see Dana G. Dalrymple, in *Soviet Studies*, no. 3 (1964); Zelenin, in *Istoricheskie zapiski*, no. 76 (1965); p. 47; Roy Medvedev, *Let History Judge* (London: Macmillan, 1972), pp. 94–96, quotes several sources; W. H. Chamberlain, in his *Russian Iron Age*, published in 1935, gave a detailed account based on personal observation. (Reprint ed., Salem, N.Y.: Ayer, 1970)
34. Moshkov, *Zernovaya problema*, p. 186.
35. For figures on exports of grain, see *Istoriya SSSR*, no. 5 (1964); on imports of grain in the spring of 1932, see *ibid*., no. 4 (1962), p. 104, which added that even the modest food rations of city dwellers had to be curtailed, and in some regions supplementary *zagotovki* of grain had to be conducted.
36. For the main decrees concerning the creation of Komzag, see *Sobranie zakonov*, no. 10 (1932), para. 53; and *ibid*., no. 11 (1933), para. 58.
37. The political departments (*politotdely*) were established by the decision of the January 1933 plenum of the Central Committee. See *KPSS v rezolyutsiyakh i resheniyakh s"ezdov*, 7th ed., vol. 2 (Moscow, 1957), pp. 187–98. For a good book on the MTSs and a chapter on *politotdely*, see Robert F. Miller, *One Hundred Thousand Tractors* (Cambridge, Mass.: Harvard University Press, 1970).
38. The basic decree is in *Sobranie zakonov*, no. 4 (1933), para. 25; detailed instructions on how to prepare and operate the campaign in all its stages are in *ibid*., no. 16 (1933), para. 95, and the instruction which follows this paragraph.
39. A. Y. Yakovlev, *Voprosy organizatsii sotsialisticheskogo sel'skogo khozyaistva* (Moscow, 1933), p. 119.
40. Decree of June 25, 1933, in *Sobranie zakonov*, no. 39 (1933), para. 234.
41. By 1937, payment-in-kind to the MTSs supplied almost 50 percent of the state's income in grain (as against 15.7 percent in 1933). The share of the tax-in-kind, i.e., the basic *zagotovki* lot (*khlebopostavki*), fell to about 35 percent. The rest was collected in the form of so-called purchases (*zakupki*), which we describe later. It goes without saying that for both the government and the peasants all these categories were just *zagotovki*, and the official statistics subsumed all the

categories (often including also the income from the milling tax) under the rubric of *khlebozagotovki*.

42. For this hint, see *Planovoe khozyaistvo*, no. 4 (1933), p. 25.
43. The Central Commission for Assessing Yields and Crops (TsGK) was constituted in December 1932 under V. V. Osinskii, and attached to Sovnarkom. The instructions for its composition and organization are in *Sobranie zakonov*, no. 3 (1933), para. 46; no. 44, para. 279; no. 17, para. 97a. There were more decrees and quite hectic activity around these commissions, with Stalin and Molotov signing the most important enactments. But *Istoriya SSSR*, no. 5 (1964), p. 13, derided the whole thing as a waste of time and contended that the objective of the TsGK was to inflate artificially the "commercial surpluses" of the kolkhozy by producing exaggerated crop assessments.
44. M. A. Chernov, in *Na fronte sel'sko-khozyaistvennykh zagotovok*, no. 11 (1933), p. 4; *Sel'skoe khozyaistvo RSFSR*, no. 22, August 1, 1931, pp. 10–11.
45. *Planovoe khozyaistvo*, no. 4 (1933), p. 25.
46. The latest account about Kirov, his role, and his assassination is in Medvedev, *Let History Judge*, chap. 5. For earlier sources which Medvedev probably did not know, see B. I. Nicolaevsky, *Power and the Soviet Elite* (New York: Praeger, 1965).
47. S. M. Kirov, in *Pravda*, July 19, 1934.
48. Leading article in *Na fronte sel'sko-khozyaistvennykh zagotovok*, no. 19 (1934).
49. *Ibid.*, no. 27–28 (1934), pp. 2–3, for example. Such sources are numerous. We should remember that this review is an organ of Komzag, which was attached to Molotov's office and therefore obviously voiced his opinions.
50. Zelenin, in *Istoricheskie zapiski*, no. 76 (1965), pp. 77–78.
51. *Na fronte sel'sko-khozyaistvennykh zagotovok*, no. 17–18 (1934), has much correspondence from districts reporting on this kind of repression of officials.
52. Zelenin, in *Istoricheskie zapiski*, no. 76 (1965), pp. 76–77; see also *Na fronte sel'sko-khozyaistvennykh zagotovok*, no. 17–18 (1934).
53. Zelenin, in *Istoricheskie zapiski*, no. 76 (1965), p. 57.
54. The political departments in the MTSs were dissolved in November 1934 (see *KPSS v rezolyutsiyakh*, pp. 260–65), but they continued to function in sovkhozy until 1940.
55. Decree signed by Molotov and Stalin, *Pravda*, February 28, 1934.
56. Decree of April 3, 1934, in *Sobranie zakonov*, no. 18 (1934), para. 139. This, as were many others that we quote, was signed by Molotov and Stalin, which meant that this was a government and party enactment—a common practice in those years. At that time fewer than half of the kolkhozy (but more than half of the sown area) were served by the MTSs. The kolkhozy which could escape signing up with the MTSs were relieved because the MTS did its job badly and cost a lot of grain. To reward kolkhozy which were serviced by the stations, the delivery norms for such kolkhozy were quite substantially lower than for the others.
57. This decree is in *Sobranie zakonov*, no. 46 (1934), para. 362.
58. Molotov, in *Pravda*, July 8, 1934.
59. P. P. Lyubchenko, in *Bol'shevik*, no. 11 (1934), pp. 21–22.
60. A decree on the levy is in *Sobranie zakonov*, no. 49 (1934), para. 380. Stalin is quoted from archives in *Istoriya SSSR*, no. 5 (1964), p. 24.
61. *Sobranie zakonov*, no. 48 (1934), para. 370, and no. 49 (1934), para. 380.
62. S. M. Kirov, in *Stat'i i rechi* (Moscow, 1934), pp. 130–32.
63. *Narodnoe khozyaistvo SSSR v 1958 godu* (Moscow, 1959), pp. 350, 352; M. A. Vyltsan, *Ukreplenie material'no-tekhnicheskoi bazy kolkhoznogo stroya* (Moscow, 1959).
64. Vyltsan, *Ukreplenie*, p. 125.
65. Kirov, in *Stat'i i rechi*, pp. 106–7. His probable source is the estimate of the Com-

mission of Yields and Crops, presented by Bryukhanov in *Pravda*, July 20, 1934. Samples taken in different grain-producing regions invariably showed a discrepancy of 30–40 percent between the estimates of the yields *na kornyu* (standing crop) and the crops actually harvested.

66. The figures for the three years 1925–27 show an average of 73.3 million tons of grain per year. For the five precollectivization years, 1925–29, the estimates vary between 73 and 74 million tons per year, substantially the same as during the subsequent quinquennia, but with higher yields per hectare, as sown area was considerably expanded during the first five-year plan. Cf. V. P. Danilov, ed., *Sozdanie kolkhoznogo stroya i material'no-tekhnicheskikh predposylok kollektivizatsii sel'skogo khozyaistva v SSSR* (Moscow, 1957), pp. 94–95.

67. The catastrophic drop in numbers of cattle stopped in 1934 (for cows, in 1935), and henceforward a slow improvement in numbers of heads began, but toward the beginning of 1941 the figures were still far below the 1916 level.

68. *Narodnoe khozyaistvo SSSR v 1958 godu*, p. 355, shows increasing crops of the main technical plants, but substantially dwindling yields; as to the population, it remained stationary in the country between 1913 and 1940, but grew in the cities from 28,420,000 to 63,112,000.

69. For data on prices and the value of the ruble, see A. A. Barsov, in *Istoriya SSSR*, no. 6 (1968), p. 72; Lazar Volin, *A Century of Russian Agriculture* (Cambridge, Mass.: Harvard University Press, 1970), p. 251. Producers' prices were even lowered in 1931, but later rose by some 28 percent for grain and 20 percent for animal foodstuffs; but rises of this scope did not change very much.

70. *Istoriya SSSR*, no. 5 (1964), p. 19.

71. I. E. Zelenin, *Zernovye sovkhozy SSSR, 1933–1941* (Moscow, 1966), pp. 181–87 and *passim*.

72. V. G. Lopatkin, *Tovarnye otnosheniya i zakon stoimosti pri sotsializme* (Moscow, 1963), pp. 366, 243; Volin, *A Century of Russian Agriculture*, quoting a study by Holtzman, estimated that procurement rose by about 25 percent, but prices of consumer goods in shops rose seven times, and on kolkhoz markets seventeen times.

73. Cf. Zelenin, in *Istoricheskie zapiski*, no. 76 (1965), p. 58.

74. Cf. Kirov, in *Stat'i i rechi*, p. 155; *Na fronte sel'sko-khozyaistvennykh zagotovok*, no. 19 (1934), p. 31.

75. Numerous data can be found in *Na fronte sel'sko-khozyaistvennykh zagotovok* during 1933 and 1934, notably no. 3 (1934), p. 18.

76. On prices paid for *zakupki*, see Vyltsan, *Ukreplenie*, p. 132; also data in *Na fronte sel'sko-khozyaistvennykh zagotovok*, no. 19 (1934).

77. Barsov, in *Istoriya SSSR*, no. 6 (1968), p. 19.

78. See Lopatkin, *Tovarnye otnosheniya*, pp. 46, 236; for angry criticisms by other authors of the destructive effects of the *zagotovki* policies on the rural economy for a whole generation, see, e.g., G. S. Lisichkin, in *Novyi mir*, no. 9 (1965), p. 221; Moshkov, *Zernovaya problema*, p. 220, and *passim*; Nemakov, *Kompartiya-organizator*, p. 261.

79. For this type of statement, see Kirov, in *Pravda*, July 19, 1934; Chernov, in *Na fronte sel'sko-khozyaistvennykh zagotovok*, no. 11 (1933), p. 1; M. I. Kalinin, in *Stat'i i rechi* (1935), p. 81; S. Leikin, in *Na agrarnom fronte*, no. 2–3 (1935), p. 61; Vareikis, in *XVII-aya konferentsiya VKP(B)* (Moscow, 1932), p. 190.

Chapter 7   The Kolkhoz and the Russian Muzhik

1. Soviet researchers published in the 1960s material from the archives showing that although a special high-ranking body appointed by the Central Committee in November 1929 to decide about how to collectivize and what to do with the richer peasants recommended the preservation of private plots and especially letting every family keep a cow in private possession, such provisions were simply deleted from

the proposed decree by Stalin and Molotov, causing havoc to Soviet agriculture. See V. P. Danilov, ed., *Ocherki po istorii sel'skogo khozyaistva v soyuznykh respublikakh* (Moscow, 1963), p. 19; and B. A. Abramov, in *Voprosy istorii KPSS*, no. 1 (1964), p. 40.

2. Stalin spoke about this "minor misunderstanding about the cow" at the first Congress of Kolkhoz Shockworkers in 1933. See *Na agrarnom fronte*, no. 2–3 (1935), n. 9.

3. The statute of the kolkhozy became law in February 1935. It allowed the family a plot of one-fourth to half an hectare, at least one cow, calves, specified numbers of sheep and pigs, and unlimited numbers of fowl.

4. The law "Concerning measures to safeguard socialized land from embezzlement" is in *Sobranie uzakonenii*, no. 34 (1939), § 235. For an assessment showing that peasants did not actually fully use the norms for land and cattle ownership, see I. V. Arutyunyan's article in *Voprosy filosofii*, no. 5 (1966), pp. 51–61.

5. V. B. Ostrovskii, *Kolkhoznoe krest-yanstvo SSSR* (Saratov, 1966), p. 69; and *Kolkhozy vo vtoroi stalinskoi piatiletke* (statistical handbook) (Moscow, 1939), pp. 11–12.

6. See Karl-Eugen Wädekin, *The Private Sector in Soviet Agriculture* (Berkeley: University of California Press, 1973), p. 57; M. A. Vyltsan, using material from the archives, in *Voprosy istorii*, no. 9 (1963), p. 27.

7. These figures for 1937 are in Vyltsan, *Voprosy istorii*, no. 9 (1963), pp. 17, 19.

8. Ostrovskii, *Kolkhoznoe krest'yanstvo*, p. 91.

9. G. I. Shmelev, *Lichnoe podsobnoe khozyaistvo i ego svyazi s obshchestvennym proizvodstvom* (Moscow, 1971), pp. 110–11.

10. Ostrovskii, *Kolkhoznoe krest'yanstvo*, p. 131, for the year 1940; but we should add that youngsters and the elderly also worked.

11. This was admitted already by D. Lurye, in *Bol'shevik*, no. 22 (1934), pp. 36–37.

12. Wädekin, *The Private Sector*, p. 197—but not after 1964 any more. A Soviet author, V. A. Morozov, in *Trudoden', den'gi i torgovlya na sele* (Moscow, 1965), assessed for the year 1964 that one hour's work on the plot produced 2–3 times more income than one hour in the kolkhoz.

13. Some of the relevant figures from Soviet sources are used in Chapter 6 in this volume. It also contains the relevant information on procurements and prices paid to producers—referred to later in the essay.

14. Morozov, *Trudoden'*, p. 9.

15. Cf. V. V. Gusev, *Kolkhoz kak samoupravlyayushchayasya sistema* (Moscow, 1971), p. 31.

16. Wädekin, *The Private Sector*, p. 18.

17. This meant that the *kolkhoznik* was paid only from what remained after the kolkhoz paid its debt to the state and deducted material and financial means to its own production funds. Sometimes not much remained. The *kolkhoznik* did not know what he could expect till the end of the year, and he had not much influence on this "residual." Morozov, in *Trudoden'*, p. 113, calling this *ostatochnyi rezhim*, exclaimed bitterly, "In truth, how could one speak of cost accounting and profitability in the kolkhoz if any mismanagement in it can be covered up by the expense of just curtailing the pay for the *kolkhoznik*'s labor."

18. Shmelev complained about these taxes as exactions, in *Lichnoe podsobnoe*, pp. 111, 112, and lists them as: direct procurements, market tax, milling tax, compulsory insurance of cattle and crops, voluntary contribution to culture-cum-lodging fund, which became a normal obligatory tax. All are abolished today. But let us note that these were, except the last, levied from peasants only.

19. Morozov, *Trudoden'*, p. 176.

20. *Ibid.*, pp. 172–73.

21. N. Aristov, in *Planovoe khozyaistvo*, no. 11 (1939), p. 94, explains the reasons for

those minimums and other disciplinary measures by the fact that millions of *kolkhozniki* tended to do nothing in the kolkhoz.

22. *Problemy ekonomiki*, no. 3 (1940), devoted an article to the problem of time spent by *kolkhozniki* in reaching markets and trading on them. The article somewhat embellished the situation, but the fact remains that millions of working days went into it.

23. L. S. Blyakhman and O. I. Shkaratan, NTR, *rabochii klass i intelligentsiya* (Moscow, 1973), p. 210.

24. Yu. Arutyunyan, in *Voprosy filosofii*, no. 6 (1966), p. 57.

25. By 1940 about one-third of the kolkhoz family had no cows. There were 18.5 million homesteads in kolkhozy, and only 12.5 million had cows. Some of them might not have wanted cows, but on the whole cowlessness was a traditional Russian syndrome of poor peasants.

26. Michael T. Florinsky, *The End of the Russian Empire* (New York: Macmillan, 1961), p. 180.

Chapter 9 Society, State, and Ideology During the First Five-Year Plan

1. Frank Lorimer, *The Population of the Soviet Union: History and Prospects* (1946; reprint ed., New York: AMS Press, 1976), pp. 38–39, 40.

2. *Ibid.*, p. 22.

3. L. M. Spirin, *Klassy i partii v grazhdanskoi voine v Rossii, 1917–1921* (Moscow, 1968), p. 301.

4. *Ibid.*, p. 386.

5. *Ibid.*, pp. 386–87. His material is from the Central Party Archives.

6. O. I. Shkaratan, *Problemy sotsial'noi struktury rabochego klassa SSSR* (Moscow, 1970), pp. 351–54.

7. *Ibid.*, p. 256. He explains these phenomena as well as the oppositions inside the party at that time—notably the Workers' Opposition—as results of vacillations under the pressure of "spontaneous forces" (*stikhiya*).

8. A. A. Matyugin and D. A. Baevskii, eds., *Izmeneniya v chislennosti i sostave sovetskogo rabochego klassa* (Moscow, 1961), p. 83.

9. Computed by Sovnarkom's Committee for the Assessment of the Tax Burden, published in *Statisticheskii spravochnik SSSR za 1928 god* (Moscow, 1929), pp. 42–43, where we took our figures on the social groups. The figures deal with "employed" (without their families). The figures are rounded off throughout this chapter, since we are interested only in the order of magnitude.

10. I. Magidovich, in *Statisticheskoe obozrenie*, no. 11 (1928), p. 80.

11. *Statisticheskii spravochnik SSSR za 1928 god*, pp. 796–97.

12. A. Y. Levin, *Sotsial'no-ekonomicheskie uklady v SSSR v period perekhoda ot kapitalizma k sotsializmu: Goskapitalizm i chastnyi kapital* (Moscow, 1967), p. 23, for the year 1925/26.

13. I. Magidovich, in *Statisticheskoe obozrenie*, no. 11 (1928), p. 87. All such figures have to be treated with considerable caution. People were prudent and left undeclared everything they could. But the scope of the capitalist sector is certainly reflected here realistically.

14. The chairman of the agriculture department in Ivanovo-Voznesensk *guberniya*, himself of peasant stock, stated quite clearly: "The peasant is used to seeing in the government an alien force." Quoted in M. P. Kim, ed., *Sovetskaya intelligentsiya: Istoriya formirovaniya i rosta* (Moscow, 1968), p. 140.

15. See the excellent paper by V. P. Danilov, "The Rural Population of the USSR on the Eve of Collectivization," *Istoricheskie zapiski*, no. 74 (1963), p. 96.

16. Y. V. Arutyunyan, *Sotsial'naya struktura sel'skogo naseleniya SSSR* (Moscow, 1971), p. 26.

17. *Statisticheskii spravochnik SSSR za 1928 god*, p. 42.
18. V. P. Danilov, in *Istoricheskie zapiski*, no. 779 (1966), p. 37; N. A. Ivnitskii, *Klassovaya bor'ba v derevne i likvidatsiya kulachestva kak klassa* (Moscow, 1972), pp. 71, 74.
19. Ivnitskii, *Klassovaya bor'ba*, p. 65.
20. In 1928 there were only 233,000 specialists with higher education, and among them only about 48,000 engineers. A further 288,000 people had secondary specialized education. See *Trud v SSSR: Statisticheskii sbornik* (Moscow, 1968), pp. 251, 262.
21. Roger Pethybridge, *The Social Prelude to Stalinism* (New York: St. Martin's Press, 1974), p. 196. The quotation is taken from the title of a chapter in this book.
22. See table in Kim, *Sovetskaya intelligentsiya*, p. 134.
23. S. G. Strumilin's computation, quoted in L. Averbakh, *Na putyakh kul'turnoi revolyutsii*, 3rd ed. (Moscow, 1929), p. 72.
24. A. I. Rykov and A. V. Lunacharsky quoted in Averbakh, *Na putyakh*, pp. 64 and 68, respectively.
25. Arutyunyan, *Sotsial'naya struktura*, p. 38. In 1924 a peasant would have, on the average, two to three years' schooling; children in cities, 3.1 years per child. Such data give a fair picture of the low starting point, in terms of popular education, the regime had to build on.
26. Averbakh, *Na putyakh*, p. 166.
27. *Ibid.*, pp. 186–87, quoting Trotsky's "anti-Leninist" opinion from *Literatura i revolyutsiya*.
28. According to Kim (*Sovetskaya intelligentsiya*, p. 174), workers and peasants occupied half the places in higher educational institutions (*vuzy*, rendered as "universities" in text). The other half—and after 1926 even more—went to "employees" and "others" (i.e., children of the propertied classes, past and present).
29. Quoted in M. P. Kim, ed., *Kul'turnaya revolyutsiya v SSSR, 1917–1965* (Moscow, 1967), p. 95.
30. Quoted in Averbakh, *Na putyakh*, p. 121.
31. *Ibid.*, p. 176.
32. Pethybridge, *Social Prelude*, p. 350; and see his chapter on "Illiteracy."
33. M. A. Vyltsan, *Sovetskaya derevnya nakanune Velikoi otechestvennoi voiny* (Moscow, 1970), p. 142; Lorimer, *Population*, p. 112, states that the overall growth rate for the years 1926–39 was 1.23 percent a year. This was very high when compared with other countries, but it was much higher in the USSR itself in 1926 and 1927, as well as, probably, in 1938. Tsarist Russia saw its population grow by 1.74 percent a year during the period 1897–1914.
34. *Sotsialisticheskoe stroitel'stvo v SSSR* (Moscow, 1935), p. xlviii, claims a population of 165,748,400 at the end of 1932, but the 1939 census found only about 5 million inhabitants more. Something must have been very wrong. The 1937 census was disavowed by the government; many statisticians were purged as "wreckers."
35. For information on *otkhod* in those years, see A. M. Panfilova, *Formirovanie rabochego klassa SSSR v gody pervoi pyatiletki* (Moscow, 1964).
36. *Narodnoe khozyaistvo SSSR v 1956 g.* (Moscow, 1957), p. 656; Arutyunyan, in A. P. Dadykin, ed., *Formirovanie i razvitie sovetskogo rabochego klassa 1917–1961* (Moscow, 1964), pp. 113–15; M. I. Pisarev, *Naselenie i trud v SSSR* (Moscow, 1966), p. 68 and *passim*.
37. M. I. Sonin, *Vosproizvodstvo rabochei sily v SSSR i balans truda* (Moscow, 1959), p. 143; *Statisticheskii spravochnik SSSR za 1960 g.* (Moscow, 1961), p. 110. It is quite revealing to read Stalin saying in June 1931: "There is no longer any 'flight of the peasant to the city' or 'spontaneous movement [*samotek*] of the labor force' "

(Stalin, *Sochineniya*, 13 vols. [Moscow, 1952–55], 13: 53). Soviet scholars had to repeat this outrageous misrepresentation for years. What was really happening was pandemonium—both "flight" and "spontaneous movement" as never before.

38. A. V. Kornilov, *Na reshayushchem etape* (Moscow, 1968), pp. 158–59; Panfilova, *Formirovanie*, p. 80.

39. G. R. Ordzhonikidze, *Stat'i i rechi*, vol. 2 (Moscow, 1957), pp. 411–12.

40. For some data on this, see *ibid.*; *Pravda*, November 15, 1931; *Spravochnik partiinogo rabotnika*, 8th ed. (Moscow, 1934), pp. 846–49; *Bol'shevik*, no. 7 (1934), p. 16.

41. Nicholas S. Timasheff, *The Great Retreat: The Growth and Decline of Communism in Russia* (New York: E. P. Dutton, 1946).

42. Ivnitskii, *Klassovaya bor'ba*, p. 242.

43. N. I. Nemakov, *Kommunisticheskaya partiya—organizator massovogo kolkhoznogo dvizheniya (1929–32)* (Moscow, 1966), pp. 159, 168. The category of *lishentsy* was abolished in 1935 (*Pravda*, December 30, 1935).

44. *Sobranie zakonov i raporyazhenii raboche-krest'yanskogo pravitel'stva SSSR*, no. 50 (1930), art. 524. This is an interesting document in which the sociologist and historian may study the condemned capitalist elements, most of whom never saw much of any "capital" in their lives.

45. *Ibid.*, no. 19 (1930), art. 212, lists such actions as "abuses" and forbids them, but this could not have had any effect since the same people could easily be persecuted under other headings.

46. S. Bulatov, in *Sovetskoe gosudarstvo*, no. 4 (1933), p. 71.

47. Data in *Statisticheskoe obozrenie*, no. 2 (1928), p. 80; on capital value per average shop or commercial enterprise, see Levin, *Sotsial'no-ekonomicheskie uklady*, p. 125.

48. A full list of offenses that either increased considerably or became the object of a special campaign, and therefore looked particularly ominous, is given in *Sovetskaya yustitsiya*, no. 34 (1932), p. 13.

49. Shkaratan, *Problemy*, p. 264.

50. A. Stepanyan, in Semenov, *Klassy, sotsial'nye sloi i gruppy v SSSR* (Moscow, 1968), pp. 20–21.

51. *Sovetskaya yustitsiya*, no. 2 (1932), p. 15.

52. *Sobranie zakonov*, no. 78 (1932), art. 475, and no. 45 (1932), art. 244.

53. Quoted in Jeremy R. Azrael, *Managerial Power and Soviet Politics* (Cambridge, Mass.: Harvard University Press, 1966), pp. 247–48.

54. L. M. Kaganovich, in *Bol'shevik*, no. 13 (1936), p. 54.

55. S. M. Kirov, *Izbrannye stat'i i rechi* (Moscow, 1957), pp. 700–7.

56. Arutyunyan, *Sotsial'naya struktura*, p. 158.

57. *Ibid.* One quarter of the peasants still could not read in 1939.

58. Yaroslavskii, quoted in Kim, *Kul'turnaya revolyutsiya*, p. 248.

59. S. I. Syrtsov, in *Bol'shevik*, no. 5 (1930), pp. 47–49, which is the source of the summary that follows.

60. *Okazenivanie krest'yan* is the term used by the peasant delegate in *6-toi s"ezd sovetov* (bulletin), no. 20 (1931), p. 3. He explained that this meant depriving them of the results of their labor and said that kulaks laughed at the *kolkhozniki* because they were now "on rations" (*na paike*).

61. A. Y. Yakovlev, *Voprosy organizatsii sotsialisticheskogo sel'skogo khozyaistva* (Moscow, 1933), p. 184. Sheboldaev is quoted from *16-taya konferentsiya VKP(b): Stenograficheskii otchet* (Moscow, 1932), p. 208.

62. L. M. Kaganovich, in *Na agrarnom fronte*, no. 1 (1933), p. 40.

63. The Central Committee decision is in *Partiinoe stroitel'stvo*, no. 5 (1933), p. 62. The document illustrates the kind of menacing language the Central Committee was then using.

64. *Sovetskaya yustitsiya*, no. 5–6 (1932), p. 16. The same periodical (no. 15 [1933])

adds more categories of typical transgressions of the "crude administrative" variety: forcing the kolkhoz to feed all kinds of parasites favored by the *raion* bosses; imposing illegal corvées; preempting money from the bank accounts o fthe kolkhozy; taking cattle away from them, and so on.

65. S. Krasikov, *Sergei Mironovich Kirov* (Moscow, 1964), p. 176.
66. Summarized from *Sputnik kommunista v derevne*, no. 2 (1933), p. 48.
67. Kirov is quoted from Krasikov, *Kirov*, p. 176; Stalin from *Partiinoe stroitel'stvo*, no. 5 (1933), p. 3.
68. There was even a formal prohibition against creating mutal aid funds from kolkhoz resources: it could be done only on the basis of private contributions from the *kolkhozniki*. See *Sputnik kommunista v derevne*, no. 1 (1933), p. 48.
69. *Sotsialisticheskoe zemledelie*, no. 16–17 (1933), p. 9.
70. Arutyunyan, *Sotsial'naya struktura*, p. 57.
71. Ordzhonikidze speaking at the Seventeenth Party Congress 1932, in *Stat'i i rechi*, 2: 340.
72. Quoted in Kim, *Sovetskaya intelligentsiya*, pp. 48, 56.
73. V. I. Lenin, *Polnoe sobranie sochinenii*, 5th ed., 55 vols. (Moscow, 1958–65), 40: 199, 218.
74. Kim, *Sovetskaya intelligentsiya*, pp. 126–27; S. A. Fedyukin, *Velikii oktyabr' i intelligentsiya* (Moscow, 1972), p. 377.
75. Kim, *Sovetskaya intelligentsiya*, p. 127, admits that such fears were well founded, but he puts the blame on "Makhaevite tendencies" among workers and exempts policy makers from any share in it.
76. *Pravda*, August 17, 1931.
77. Suicides were committed even in such inconspicuous places as Rzhev, where intellectuals could not have been too numerous. The party leadership was disturbed by the phenomenon. See *Smolensk Archives WKP 55* (document dated July 1930).
78. Kim, *Sovetskaya intelligentsiya*, pp. 324–25.
79. Pisarev, *Naselenie*, p. 41.
80. Figures from the 1930 survey are in M. P. Kim, ed., *Industrializatsiya SSSR 1929–1932* (Moscow, 1970), p. 571; data on the 1933 survey are in *Sotsialisticheskoe stroitel'stvo SSSR* (Moscow, 1935), p. 522.
81. This is an assessment for the year 1937 made in S. I. Senyavskii, *Izmeneniya v sotsial'noi strukture sovetskogo obshchestva 1938–1970* (Moscow, 1973), p. 299. According to him, by 1940 the intelligentsia (in which he includes only specialists with higher or secondary professional education) constituted only 3.3 percent of the employed population, whereas the "nonspecialized officials" constituted 13.2 percent of the total employed work force.
82. *Sobranie zakonov*, no. 44 (1931), art. 322.
83. B. Borisov, in Kim, *Kul'turnaya revolyutsiya*, p. 138. Such figures can be used only as indications of trends; their precision is very questionable.
84. V. I. Kuzmin, *Istoricheskii opyt sovetskoi industrializatsii* (Moscow, 1963), p. 149.
85. G. Shklovskii, in *Revolyutsiya prava*, no. 7 (1930), p. 89.
86. *Ibid.*
87. *Ibid.*, pp. 59–61.
88. P. I. Stuchka, in *ibid.*, no. 10 (1930), p. 19.
89. Ordzhonikidze, *Stat'i i rechi*, 1: 228–29.
90. "You can dig there as much as you like, they won't give you exact data" (*ibid.*, p. 228).
91. These are quotations from Pavel Postyshev's speech in Kharkov, in *Partiinoe stroitel'stvo*, no. 5 (1933). He was expressing the generally accepted tenets of what was then the "Bolshevik art of leadership."
92. S. I. Syrtsov, *O nedostatkakh i zadachakh* (Moscow and Leningrad, 1930), p. 15 (speech of February 1930).

93. *Bol'shevik*, no. 21 (1934), p. 12.
94. *KPSS v rezolyutsiyakh s"ezdov i konferentsii*, vol. 2 (Moscow, 1957), pp. 541, 546.
95. L. F. Morozov and V. P. Portnov, *Organy partiino-gosudarstvennogo kontrolya 1923–1934* (Moscow, 1964), pp. 139–42.
96. S. Ikonnikov, *Sozdanie i deyatel'nost' obedinennykh organov TsKK-RKI v 1923–1934 godakh* (Moscow, 1971), p. 212.

Chapter 10 Social Relations Inside Industry During the Prewar Five-Year Plans

1. Periodization borrowed from Basile Kerblay, *Modern Soviet Society* (New York: Pantheon Books, 1983), p. 207–8.
2. For example, V. F. Maier, *Dokhody Naseleniya i rost blagosostoyaniya naroda* (Moscow, 1968), pp. 96–97; L. A. Gordon, E. V. Klopov, *Sotsial'noe razvitie rabochego klassa SSSR* (Moscow, 1974), p. 143.
3. TsGANKh, *Industrializatsiya SSSR, 1938–1941: Dokumenty i materialy* (Moscow, 1973), p. 277 (TsGANKh is the Central State Archive of the National Economy.
4. M. P. Tomskii, *8-oi s"ezd profsoiuzov, sten. otchet* (Moscow, 1928), p. 30.
5. S. I. Senyavskii, *Izmenenie sotsyal'noi struktury sovetskogo obshchestva, 1938–39* (Moscow, 1970), pp. 299, 302.
6. M. P. Kim, ed., *Sovetskaya intelligentsia* (Moscow, 1968), pp. 206–9.
7. TsGANKh, *Industrializatsiya SSSR*, p. 252.
8. John Scott, *Behind the Urals: An American Worker in Russia's City of Steel* (1942; reprint ed., Salem, N. H.: Ayer, 1971), p. 75.
9. M. S. Zeltyn', *Raxvitie sostialisticheskoi organizatsii truda v gody sovetski vlasti* (Moscow, 1968), p. 105.
10. Jeremy R. Azrael, *Managerial Power and Soviet Politics* (Cambridge, Mass.: Harvard University Press, 1966) is a pioneering work on the "Red Directors."
11. Kerblay, *Modern Soviet Society*, pp. 189, 191.
12. The word *rabochii* means, of course, worker; *rabotnik*, sometimes erroneously translated as "worker," means an employee of some rank; an *otvetrabotnik* is an official of still higher rank but not yet at the very top; the designation *gosudarstvennyi deiatel'*, meaning a leading politician, is reserved for those at the top of the ladder.

Chapter 11 The Social Background of Stalinism

1. Material on the physical and mental stress which caused accelerated wear and tear on the old Bolshevik cadres is found in, among others, S. G. Strumilin, *Rabochii byt v tsifrakh* (Moscow and Leningrad, 1926), pp. 61–62.
2. A good example of such reasoning is in V. I. Lenin, "O nashei revolyutsii," in *Polnoe sobranie sochinenii*, 5th ed., 55 vols. (Moscow, 1958–65), 45: 378–89.
3. Interesting new material from archives about the *posevkomy* and the concomitant statist ideology for running the rural economy can be found in Y. A. Polyakov, *Perekhod k Nepu i sovetskoe krest'yanstvo* (Moscow, 1967), pp. 213–30.
4. On two basic models and their alternation, see Moshe Lewin, *Political Undercurrents in Soviet Economic Debates* (Princeton, N.J.: Princeton University Press, 1974), chaps. 4 and 5.
5. Stephen F. Cohen proposed a similar point in his *Bukharin and the Bolshevik Revolution: A Political Biography, 1888–1938* (New York: Alfred A. Knopf, 1973), pp. xvi–xvii, 3–5.
6. The letter is in Karl Marx and Friedrich Engels, *Polnoe sobranie sochinenii*, 2nd ed., vol. 37(Moscow, 1965). The relevant passage is on page 417.
7. M. Strogovich gives data on the unbelievably low literacy, if not outright illiteracy,

of the criminal investigators in *Za sotsialisticheskuyu zakonnost'* 7 (1934): 21. Vyshinsky's bitter complaint against both the low educational and professional level as well as the spirit of Philistinism among the investigators and prosecutors is in the same review, vol. 7 (1936): 74–76.

8. Pierre Pascal, *La Religion du peuple russe* (Lausanne: I'Age d'Homme, 1973).
9. *Ibid.,* p. 23.
10. *Ibid.,* p. 48.
11. Marc Bloch, *La Société féodale* (Paris, 1968), p. 347.
12. *Vedomosti verkhovnogo Soveta SSSR,* vol. 39 (1943), carries the decree of September 16, 1943, introducing the following ranks *(chiny)* for the juridical profession: *deistvitel'nyi gosudarstvennyi sovetnik yustitsii,* equivalent to an army general; next, *gosudarstvennyi sovetnik yustitsii,* first-, second-, third-class equivalent, respectively, of the military ranks of colonel-general, lieutenant-general, major-general, etc., etc. His Marxist Excellency Vyshinsky became therefore *deistvitel'nyi gosudartsvennyi sovetnik yustitsii* and thus eligible to be Gogol's hero in *Revizor.*
13. Robert C. Tucker, "The Image of Dual Russia," in *The Soviet Political Mind,* rev. ed. (New York: W. W. Norton, 1971), pp. 121–42.
14. See Pascal, *La Religion du peuple russe,* p. 10.
15. A. Y. Vyshinsky, *Voprosy teorii gosudarstva i prava,* 2nd ed. (Moscow, 1949) quotes this passage on p. 62, from Stalin, *Voprosy Leninizma,* 10th ed. (19), p. 509.
16. Vyshinsky, *Voprosy,* p. 64.
17. The role of "masks" in Stalin's perception of human behavior is shown in Tucker, *Stalin as Revolutionary,* p. 453.
18. Svetlana Alliluyeva, *Twenty Letters to a Friend* (London: Hutchinson, 1967), pp. 138–43, shows this function and role of the secret police in running Stalin's household.
19. This is Adam Ulam's interpretation (which he calls "a plot by adulation") of the efforts in 1934 to get rid of Stalin by making him even more of a god by pushing him up and out of interference with politics. See Ulam, *Stalin: The Man and His Era* (New York: Viking Press, 1973), pp. 372–73.
20. N. M. Korkunov, *Russkoe gosudarstvennoe pravo,* vol. 1 (St. Petersburg, 1901), pp. 204–7.

Chapter 12 Grappling with Stalinism

1. Eric Hobsbawm, in M. W. Flinn and T. C. Smout, ed., *Essays in Social History* (New York: Oxford University Press, 1974).
2. For a good presentation of Plekhanov's historical and political interpretations of Russia, see Samuel H. Baron, *Plekhanov, the Father of Russian Marxism* (Stanford, Calif.: Stanford University Press, 1963), pp. 295–307.
3. Lenin's "Razvitie kapitalizma v Rossii" is in volume 3 of his *Polnoe sobranie sochinenii,* 5th ed., 55 vols. (Moscow, 1958–65). The fourth edition is available in English, and this text is to be found there in volume 3.
4. Lenin's change of position about the degree of penetration of capitalism in the countryside is in a text of 1907, in *Polnoe sobranie sochinenii,* 16: 268.
5. A. M. Anfimov, in *Osobennosti agrarnogo stroya Rossii v period imperializma* (Moscow, 1960), pp. 327–28.
6. Anfimov is quoting from Lenin, *Polnoe sobranie sochinenii,* 21: 306. This article (pp. 310–16) and another (pp. 380–86) in the same volume are good and popular presentations of his opinions on the subject on the eve of World War I.
7. V. V. Adamov, ed., *Voprosy istorii kapitalizma v Rossii: Problema mnogoukladnosti* (Sverdlovsk, 1970), pp. 98–99.
8. Trotsky's *History of the Russian Revolution,* volumes 1 and 2, has different editions and translations. He began reflecting on these problems, under the impact of

studying Klyuchevskii and other historians, in his *Results and Prospects*, published in 1906. For a recent U.S. edition, see *The Permanent Revolution* [originally published 1930] *and Results and Prospects* (New York: Pathfinder Press, 1969).

9. A. N. Anfimov, *Krupnoe pomeshchichee khozyaistvo v evropeiswoi Rossii* (Moscow, 1969), p. 371.

10. Barrington Moore, *Social Origins of Dictatorship and Democracy* (Boston: Beacon Press, 1966), pp. 420, 422, 477, and *passim*.

11. Adamov, *Voprosy*, p. 98.

12. A. V. Lunacharsky, *Revolyutsionnye siluety* (Kiev, 1924).

13. Reinhard Bendix, *Max Weber: An Intellectual Portrait* (1960; reprint ed., Berkeley: University of California Press, 1978), p. 92.

14. V. Veresaev, "Ob obryadakh," *Krasnaia nov'*, no. 11 (1926).

15. Letter to Veresaev, in *ibid*.

16. See Stephen F. Cohen and Robert C. Tucker, eds., *The Great Purge Trial* (New York: Grosset & Dunlap, 1965), pp. 653–67. This remark does not aim to explain events and results in the polity by claiming that consequences flow predictably and unavoidably from the described social setting in a rigidly predetermined manner. The broad outlines of the emerging type of polity are, of course, deeply influenced by this setting, which presents obvious limiting factors. But inside such a general framework choices and alternatives exist, and much depends on the quality of decisions and on the abilities of the battling factions.

INDEX

grain procurement (*cont.*)
  excesses in, 152–55
  famine and, 153–56
  first five-year plan and, 144–45
  GPU in, 152, 157
  grain and fodder balance in, 147
  as incentive, 164–66
  Komzag and, 156–57
  local officials in, 161–63, 165
  in NEP era, 143–44
  overtaxing in, 152–53
  as percentage of crop, 166–69
  private dealers and, 143–44
  quotas in, 146–50, 161–64
  "reductionist tendencies" and, 161–62, 165
  sabotage of, 150, 161–62
  sowing acreage and, 159
  state agency competition in, 144
  supplies promised for, 149, 152, 172
  surpluses in, 146, 149
  as tax, 152–53, 157–58, 164
  threshing process and, 160
  timing of, 143*n*
  as *vykolachivanie*, 161–62
  yearly totals for, 166–69
  zakupki in, 170–71
Great Reform, 11
"Great Turn," 113

"hairdressers" (*parikmakhery*), 150
history, Russian, 10–11
  periods of, 10–11
  rural nexus in, 11
History of the Russian Revolution (Trotsky), 294
Hobsbawn, Eric, 287
horse stealing, 55
household
  family and, 82–83
  head of, 82–83
  in popular religion, 62–64, 269
  property of, 82–83, 85–86
  Stolypin reforms and, 85

icons, 61, 68, 269
idealism, 258
Ilf, Il'ya, 214
imperialism, 192, 194

industrial goods, as rewards, 149, 152, 172
industrialization, 12, 18–21, 25, 207, 218–22, 301–4
  agriculture and, 28, 115–16
  Bolshevik party and, 25–26, 31–32
  Central Committee and, 109
  choices in, 118–19
  compulsion in, 103–5
  démesure and, 27–30
  excessive rate of, 115
  first five-year plan and, 108–9
  grain crisis and, 108–9
  growth of cities during, 219–20
  market rejection and, 30–31
  party and, 26, 31–32
  peasants in, 219–20, 303–4
  resources wasted in, 115
  right-wing position on, 103–5
  social disorientation from, 303–4, 313
  social mobility from, 265
  in tsarist Russia, 210
industry
  apparaty in, 246
  bonuses in, 254
  "bourgeois specialists" in, 245, 248
  bureaucracy in, 246
  civil war and, 212
  complaints in, 247–48, 255–56
  director's power in, 251–53
  education level in, 244–45
  inconsistent policies of, 256
  intelligentsia attacked by, 242
  ITR in, 244–45
  labor discipline in, 242
  labor force growth in, 241–47
  modernization of, 249
  nachal'stvo in, 243–44
  one-man rule in, 203, 226, 251–52, 308
  otryv in, 256
  party cells in, 251–52
  peasants in, 219–20, 303–4
  postrevolutionary control of, 195–96
  praktiki in, 234
  purges and, 244–45
  sluzhashchie in, 245–47

ABOUT THE AUTHOR

Moshe Lewin was born in Wilno, Poland, in 1921. During the Second World War he worked on a collective farm and in a metallurgic plant in the USSR and served in the Russian army.

After the war he returned to Poland. He then lived in France, in Israel for eleven years, and in France again, where he earned a Ph.D. in history at the Sorbonne. He was the director of studies at the École Pratique des Hautes Études, in Paris, and a reader and professor in Russian and Eastern European studies at the University of Birmingham, England. He is currently a professor of history at the University of Pennsylvania, in Philadelphia.

Lewin has been a senior fellow at the Russian Institute, Columbia University (1967–1968); the Institute for Advanced Study, Princeton (1972–1973); and the Kennan Institute at the Woodrow Wilson Center, Washington, D.C. (1976–1977). He is the author of *Lenin's Last Struggle, Russian Peasant and Soviet Power,* and *Political Undercurrents in Soviet Economic Debates.*